# Table of Contents

# Getting Started

Congratulations on working with a Heinle book. *iLrn: Heinle Learning Center* gives you access to a wealth of data about your performance, thereby allowing you to learn more effectively. Moreover, you'll enjoy *iLrn: Heinle Learning Center* because it is fun to use and gives you instant feedback when you complete an exercise. *iLrn: Heinle Learning Center* simply requires you to set up your account with your book key and then to log in each time you use it.

# Registration

### Creating an Account

## To set up your account, follow these steps:

Step 1: Go to *http://ilrn.heinle.com*

Step 2: Click the *Login* button.

Step 3: Click *Create account*.

Step 4: Enter your user information and click *Submit*.

Step 5: You will be prompted to enter your book key printed inside the sleeve that came bundled with your book. Click *Go.* (You can also purchase an access code online from cengagebrain.com )

Step 6: Your book also requires an instructor's course code. You must get the course code from your instructor to gain access to your course. If you already have it, enter it when prompted. Otherwise, you can enter it the next time you login.

Figure 1: Student Workstation: Before entering course code

## Login Instructions

To access your book after you have added it to your account, follow these steps:

Step 1: Go to *http://ilrn.heinle.com*

Step 2: Click the *Login* button.

Step 3: Enter your username and password. You are taken to the Student Workstation.

Step 4: Click on the book cover to open the *iLrn: Heinle Learning Center*.

If you experience any problems with setting up your account, ask Quia for help. You can submit a request at http://hlc.quia.com/support.html, email Quia at bookhelp@quia.com or call them at 1-877-282-4400.

## Updating Your Profile

When you create your iLrn: *Heinle Learning Center* account, the information you enter, such as your name and email address, is saved in your profile.

### To update your profile:

1. Login to the *Student Workstation*.

2. Click *Profile* in the upper right corner of your screen.

3. Update the information and press *Save changes*.

Make sure your email address is current in your profile, as Quia uses this email address to respond to technical support questions and provide forgotten username/password information.

# Student Workstation

Once you have entered your book and course keys, the Student Workstation will appear like the screen below each time you login.

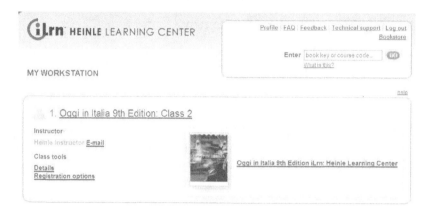

Figure 2: Student Workstation: After entering course code

In this view, you can choose one of the five options:

## 1) Click on book cover to access resources

Click on the book title or cover. This brings you to the *Welcome page* for *iLrn: Heinle Learning Center*, where you have access to all the resources available for your course.

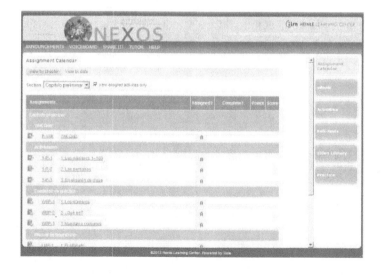

Figure 3: Student Workstation: Assignment Calendar Welcome Screen

## From the Welcome page, you have access to these tabs:

▸ *Assignment calendar*— Provides one place for you to go to access all of your assigments (Text and SAM Activities).  Here you can locate all assignments by due date or by chapter.

▸ *eBook*—This page-for-page reproduction of the printed book features embedded audio, video, as well as note-taking and text highlighting capabilities. You can complete textbook activities directly from the eBook interface. You can also see whether it is assigned, completed or graded. Just look for the ◯ icon to see what is assigned and when it is due. Hover the mouse over the ◯ icon to see your grade for a completed assignment. The page view can be magnified and the content searched via the index, table of contents, or search functions. Within the ebook, your instructor can also write and post notes for the whole class to view. Beginning with 2013 copyright titles and going forward, all ebooks with be iPad compatible.

▸ *Activities*— Textbook and Student Activity Manual activity tabs have been consolidated into one tab where you can locate all assignments. You can select a chapter and view all of the Textbook and SAM exercises for each chapter. Click on the title to open an activity.  Links to the exercises are available here, the Assignment Calendar and directly from the eBook.

▸ *Self-Tests*— You may take an online self-test before or after working through a textbook chapter to get an initial assessment of what you know and what you still need to master. Your results are graded automatically and displayed according to learning outcomes.

A Personalized Study Plan, based on the automatically graded test, directs you to additional study aids that focus your efforts and study time on the areas where you need the most help. Please see the *Selft-Tests and Personalized Learning* section for more information.

▸ *Video Library*— For every chapter, you can access accompanying video segments. You can can also turn closed captioning on and off as an aid to understanding. Video segments may be accompanied by pre and post-viewing exercises.

▸ *Practice*—Depending on the title, practice activities might include any or all of the following additional activities: vocabulary flashcards; grammar and pronunciation tutorials; additional self-graded quizzing; access to Heinle iRadio's MP3-ready cultural exploration activities; and access to Student Multimedia CD-ROM activities.

▸ *Online exams* - Your instructor may choose to make exams available online. If you are in a distance course, this may be the sole method of taking exams in your course. To access your exam, click the book cover from your Student Workstation. On the left-hand navigation bar, click on the ⊞ to expand a chapter. Click on the *Exam* for that chapter. Your instructor can assign times when the exams are available. If the exam is not yet available, you will not be able to access it. If it is available, just click *Start* to begin.

## 2) Class details

In your Student Workstation you will find the details related to your course including:

> ▸ Course Information: Name (the title and section), Instructor (with a button to click for easy contact, Code (course number), School, Duration (dates of course)

> ▸ Book Information: Book title, Publisher, Book duration.

## 3) My results

Here you will see information about your performance, with a clear presentation of several categories viewable by book and chapter. The Book drop-down menu allows you to view your results for Student Activities Manual and Textbook activities or both.

Figure 4: My Results Screen

> ▸ My scores (for Graded Activities)
> ▸ Statistics (broken down by chapter)
> ▸ Performance Summary (Exercise #, Due Date, Submitted, Time Completed, Time Elapsed, Points, Score)

You can also see your scores in the Assignment Calendar tab, under the full list of assignments or the calendar.

Please see the **Calendar** section for another way to view results by week.

## Grading Status Indicators

Many of the exercises in your *iLrn: Heinle Learning Center* book are completely computer graded. As soon as you complete an exercise, *iLrn: Heinle Learning Center's* software immediately corrects your work, reports a score, and stores your results. Open-ended questions, like those requiring written paragraphs or essays, still require instructor review.

*Please note that for yellow and red activities, your results will display 0% until your instructor grades the assignment.

## 4) Announcements

You can consult this to see if the instructor has created any announcements.

## 5) Registration options

You can drop a course, transfer to a different class, or transfer to a different course or instructor.

To drop a course:

1. Login to the Student Workstation.

2. Click the *Registration options* button in the course you wish to drop.

3. Click *Drop course* to drop your enrollment in this course. Your instructor will be notified. After dropping this course, you will still be able to view your scores; however, you will no longer be able to access the books in this course.

To transfer to a different course or instructor:

1. Login to the Student Workstation.

2. Click the *Registration options* button in the course you wish to transfer from.

3. Click *Change course/instructor*.

4. Enter the new course code and click *Submit*.

To transfer to a different class:

1. Login to the Student Workstation.

2. Click the *Registration options* button in the course you wish to transfer from.

3. Click *Change class*.

4. Select the class you want to enroll in and click *Submit*.

# Assignment Calendar

To access all of your assignments by date:

1. Login to the Student Workstation. Click on the book title or cover.

2. Click on the *Assignment Calendar* tab on the right-hand side. Then click on "View by Date" in the blue toolbar.

Figure 5: Calendar

3. You will see all Textbook and Student Activities Manual assignments that are due. This icon [img] indicates a Textbook Activity and this icon [img] indicates a SAM Activity.
Click an activity to complete it.

4. You can also check your grades on completed assignments. If you see the ⬤ icon, your assignment needs to be graded by your instructor.

5. To see assignments for previous or future weeks, select a date from the calendar during the week you wish to view.

To access all of your assignments by chapter:

Alternatively, you can view the assignments for each chapter.

1. From the Welcome page, click *Assignment Calendar* tab on the right-hand side.

Then click on "View by Chapter" in the blue toolbar.

2. Select a chapter from list to see all assignments for that chapter. A due date will appear under the Due Date column for all assigned activities. If an assignment has been completed, the date will be indicated.

3. Select an activity from the list to open and complete.

Figure 6: Assignment List

# Review & Practice Activities

With enhanced feedback, student are given additional support. At the end of each chapter students will find additional auto-grade grammar activities with specific explanations to their answers. This way students are given direct support and guidance while practicing.

**Your response:**
mochilas
**Points earned:** 1 out of 1

Feedback: To form the plural of a noun that ends in a vowel, add -s.

Figure 7: Enhanced Feedback

The new **Review It!** button appears with grammar and vocabulary activities and links to relevant resources in the Textbook and Student Activities Manual. Located in the accent toolbar, when a you click the button for an accompanying activity you'll see links to ebook pages covering relevant lessons, flashcards for vocab terms in the activity, podcasts and tutorials that review grammar lessons in the activity, and other resources found in the iLrn for that topic all in one place. This gives will help you learn how to self-correct.

Figure 8: Review it! Button links

# Voice-enabled Activities

Voice-enabled activities can be completed alone, with a partner, or with a group. You can talk to your partner or team and write instant messages to work together on the activity, then record a conversation that your instructor will grade.

## Tips for setting up your computer

It is important that your computer is configured correctly to capture the voice-enabled activities. Here are some tips for ensuring you have the proper setup:

▸ *Microphone* — The latest browser versions and Adobe Flash works best with USB (Universal Serial Bus) connected microphones. Internal microphones, WebCam microphones and the older stereo-jack (male connection) microphones can be problematic.

▸ **Adobe Flash** — You should have the latest version of Adobe Flash installed. Also make sure your Flash settings are configured on your web browser for the program to recognize the microphone being used for Voiceboard. To this follow this steps:

   1. Open a voiceboard exercise and right-click on the *Record* button. Select *Settings*.

   2. At the bottom of the menu, click the second tab from the left (it looks like a monitor with an eye on it).Make sure the *Allow* option and the *Remember* check box are selected.

   3. Click the fourth tab (the one with a microphone on it). Make sure the record volume is up all the way and the correct microphone is selected from the drop-down list.

▸ *"Lab" environment*— In a "Lab" environment, your IT department needs to make sure that the network port "1935" is enabled for voice. If this port is disabled from the school's network voice will not transmit.

## Find a partner/team

   1. Click on *Voiceboard* at the top of your student Welcome page screen.

   2. From the *Voice activities*, select the activity you want to complete.

   3. If you need a partner, click the *Find a partner* link at the top of the *Partner Record and Chat box*. This will take you to the partner switchboard where you can invite someone online to partner with you.

Figure 9: Partner Switchboard

4. If you are working with one partner, his or her name will appear at the top of the *Partner Record and Chat box*.

5. If the assignment requires you to work in teams, you will either need to join an existing team, or invite others to join you. To join an existing team, check the Partnership/Team column and find the name of a person whose team you would like to join. Click his/her name and send him/her a private chat to request an invitation.

6. To form your own team, find an available partner from the Partnership/Team column, click his/her name and the *Invite to partner* link. To add more team members, click their names and the *Invite to team* link. Note that if you have four teammates, you cannot invite more – teams are restricted to five members.

## Complete a voice-enabled activity

1. To send text messages to your partner or team, type in the text box and press Send or press the *Enter* key.

2. To talk to your partner or team before recording, press the *Talk to your partner* button. Make sure that you and your partner have microphones and a headset or speakers, and that the volume is turned on. Note: Your partner cannot speak to you or hear what you say until he or she presses *Talk to your partner* as well. Your conversation will not be recorded unless you click the *Record* button.

3. Coordinate with your partner or team on what you'd like to say. When you're ready to record the conversation, press the *Record* your conversation button. The computer will start to record your conversation ONLY after all partners or teammates have clicked the *Record* button. You will know it is recording because a message in red appears saying "recording..." until either one of the partners presses *Stop recording*.

Figure 10: Activity in recording mode

4. Press *Stop* when you want to stop recording. You can still talk with your partner or team when the recording stops.

5. To listen to your recording, press *Play*. You can pause the recording at any time by pressing *Pause*. If you are not satisfied with your recording, you may record again. Each recording is saved and you can choose which recording (from a drop-down list) you want to submit.

6. When you are satisfied with your recording, press *Submit answers* to send your recording to your instructor. Note: All partners and teammates must press *Submit* in order for the recording to be counted in all of your grades.

7. If you can't find a partner or team, you can record answers on your own; just press *Record* to record your voice, then stop the recording and submit it when you're done. Check with your instructor to see if an individual recording is acceptable, since these activities are designed to be done with a partner.

## Share it!

The new Share it! feature allows you to upload a file, image or video to the Share it! tab where your classmates can comment and rate your file. You can make comments on your classmates files as well.

Your instructor may assign Share it! activities. These will be prompts asking you to upload a file to complete the assignment. When you submit the activity, it will go to the gradebook for your instructor to assign a grade. It will also publish directly the the Share it! tab.

# Self-Tests and Personalized Learning

You may take an online self-test before or after working through a text chapter to get an initial assessment of what you know and what you still need to master. Your results are graded automatically and displayed according to learning outcomes. A Personalized Study Plan, based on the automatically graded test, directs you to additional study aids available in *iLrn: Heinle Learning Center*, including Student Activities Manual activities and pages in the eBook, that focus your efforts and study time on the areas where you need the most help.

▸ Step 1 ...Pre-Test (or What Do I Know?) provides an evaluation of what you already know.

▸ Step 2 ... Personalized Study Plan (or What Do I Need to Learn?) provides a focus for your work. Chapter sections and additional study materials are chosen to cover concepts that you had problems with in the pre-test.

▸ Step 3 ... Post-Test (or What Have I Learned?) provides an evaluation of what you have learned after working through the personalized study plan.

Figure 11: Personalized Study Plan

# Using Personal Tutor

## What is Personal Tutor?

▸ Personal Tutor provides tutors exclusively from among experienced and qualified instructors. Tutors have achieved high grades in their degrees (many have a Master's degree and higher) and have real classroom teaching experience. All of Personal Tutor's tutors are located in Tampa, FL, and are monitored on-site by a director, who also holds a Ph.D.

## How does Personal Tutor work?

▸ Personal Tutor provides whiteboard technology for synchronous tutoring (Q&A sessions) that also includes video and audio capabilities (for those students who want these extra features).

## How many hours of tutoring do students get on Personal Tutor?

▸ Personal Tutor provides students with 5 hours of tutoring time.

▸ Students have 3-semesters to use the 5 hours of tutoring

▸ Students have the option of purchasing additional tutoring directly from Personal Tutor if their hours/paper submissions are used up before the end of a semester. The cost is significantly less at $29.99 for an entire month of tutoring versus paying $35 per hour from other services.

## When will tutoring be available?

▸ Tutors are available for online tutoring seven days a week, and offline questions and papers can be submitted at any time, 24 hours a day. Online tutoring is available for languages at the times below. Responses to offline questions can take 24 to 48 hours to be returned, however, they are usually returned within one day.

|  | Spanish | French | Italian | German |
|---|---|---|---|---|
| MONDAY | 9AM-1PM 9PM-12AM |  |  |  |
| TUESDAY | 9AM-1PM | 4-8PM |  | 8PM-Midnight |
| WEDNESDAY | 9AM-1PM 9PM-12AM |  | 6PM-10PM |  |
| THURSDAY | 9AM-1PM | 4-8PM | 8PM-12PM |  |
| FRIDAY | 9AM-1PM 5PM-9PM | 4-8PM |  |  |
| SATURDAY | 12PM-4PM | 4-8PM |  |  |
| SUNDAY |  |  | 3PM-7PM | 7PM-11PM |

# Technical Support

▸ Visit *http://hlc.quia.com/support.html*

▸ View FAQs at *http://hlc.quia.com/help/books/faq.html* for immediate answers to common problems.

▸ Send an e-mail to *bookhelp@quia.com*

▸ Call Toll-free 1-877-282-4400


# System Requirements

## Microsoft® Windows 98, NT, 2000, ME, XP, VISTA, 7
Browsers: Internet Explorer 7.x or higher, or Firefox version 3.x or higher

## Macintosh OS X
Browsers: Firefox version 3.x or higher, or Safari 3.x or higher.

## Additional Requirements
▸ A high-speed connection with throughput of 256 Kbps or more is recommended to use audio and video components.

▸ Screen resolution: 1024 x 768 or higher

▸ CPU: 233MHz

▸ RAM: 128MB

▸ Flash Player 10 or higher

▸ You will need speakers or a headset to listen to audio and video components, and a microphone is necessary for recording activities.

# What is VAK?

YOU CAN APPROACH the topic of learning styles with a simple and powerful system—one that focuses on just three ways of perceiving through your senses:

- Seeing, or *visual learning*
- Hearing, or *auditory learning*
- Movement, or *kinesthetic learning*

To recall this system, remember the letters VAK, which stand for **v**isual, **a**uditory, and **k**inesthetic. The theory is that each of us prefers to learn through one of these sense channels. To reflect on your VAK preferences, answer the following questions. Circle the answer that best describes how you would respond. This is not a formal inventory—just a way to prompt some self-discovery.

**When you have problems spelling a word, you prefer to**

1. Look it up in the dictionary.
2. Say the word out loud several times before you write it down.
3. Write out the word with several different spellings and then choose one.

**You enjoy courses the most when you get to**

1. View slides, videos, and readings with plenty of charts, tables, and illustrations.
2. Ask questions, engage in small-group discussions, and listen to guest speakers.
3. Take field trips, participate in lab sessions, or apply the course content while working as a volunteer or intern.

**When giving someone directions on how to drive to a destination, you prefer to**

1. Pull out a piece of paper and sketch a map.
2. Give verbal instructions.
3. Say, "I'm driving to a place near there, so just follow me."

**When planning an extended vacation to a new destination, you prefer to**

1. Read colorful, illustrated brochures or articles about that place.
2. Talk directly to someone who's been there.
3. Spend time at that destination on a work-related trip before vacationing there.

**You've made a commitment to learn to play the guitar. The first thing you do is**

1. Go to a library or music store and find an instruction book with plenty of diagrams and chord charts.

2. Listen closely to some recorded guitar solos and see whether you can sing along with them.
3. Buy a guitar, pluck the strings, and ask someone to show you a few chords.

**You've saved up enough money to lease a car. When choosing from among several new models, the most important factor in your decision is**

1. The car's appearance.
2. The information you get by talking to people who own the cars you're considering.
3. The overall impression you get by taking each car on a test drive.

**You've just bought a new computer system. When setting up the system, the first thing you do is**

1. Skim through the printed instructions that come with the equipment.
2. Call up someone with a similar system and ask her for directions.
3. Assemble the components as best as you can, see if everything works, and consult the instructions only as a last resort.

**You get a scholarship to study abroad next semester in a Spanish-speaking country. To learn as much Spanish as you can before you depart, you**

1. Buy a video-based language course on DVD.
2. Download audio podcasts that guarantee basic fluency in just 30 days.
3. Sign up for a short immersion course in which you speak only Spanish.

Name _____ Date _____

Now take a few minutes to reflect on the meaning of your responses. The number of each answer corresponds to a learning style preference.

**1 = visual          2 = auditory          3 = kinesthetic**

|  | Visual | Auditory | Kinesthetic |
|---|---|---|---|
| My totals |  |  |  |

My dominant Learning Style(s): _____

_____

Do you see a pattern in your own answers? A pattern indicates that you prefer learning through one sense channel over the others. Or you might find that your preferences are fairly balanced.

Whether you have a defined preference or not, you can increase your options for success by learning through *all* your sense channels. For example, you can enhance visual learning by leaving room in your class notes to add your own charts, diagrams, tables, and other visuals later. You can also key your handwritten notes into a computer file and use software that allows you to add colorful fonts and illustrations.

To enhance auditory learning, reinforce your memory of key ideas by talking about them. When studying, stop often to summarize key points and add examples in your own words. After doing this several times, dictate your summaries into a voice recorder and transfer the files to an iPod or similar device. Listen to these files while walking to class or standing in line at the store.

For kinesthetic learning, you've got plenty of options as well. Look for ways to translate course content into three-dimensional models that you can build. While studying grammar, for example, create a model of a sentence using different colors of clay to represent different parts of speech. Whenever possible, supplement lectures with real-world audio and video input and experiences, field trips to Spanish-speaking neighborhoods, and other opportunities for hands-on activity. Also recite key concepts from your courses while you walk or exercise.

These are just a few examples. In your path to mastery of learning styles, you can create many more of your own.

# Cuadros

SPAN 1100 – Basic Spanish I

William Paterson University

Sheri Spaine Long
Sylvia Madrigal Velasco
Kristin Swanson
María Carreira

CENGAGE
Learning·

Australia • Brazil • Japan • Korea • Mexico • Singapore • Spain • United Kingdom • United States

**Cuadros: SPAN 1100 – Basic Spanish I, William Paterson University**

Source:

Cuadros Student Text, Volume 1 of 4: Introductory Spanish, 1st Edition
Sheri Spaine Long - University of Alabama at Birmingham
Sylvia Madrigal Velasco
Kristin Swanson
María Carreira - California State University at Long Beach

Executive Editors:
 Maureen Staudt
 Michael Stranz

Senior Project Development Manager:
 Linda deStefano

Marketing Specialist:
 Courtney Sheldon

Senior Production/Manufacturing
Manager:
 Donna M. Brown

PreMedia Manager:
 Joel Brennecke

Sr. Rights Acquisition Account Manager:
 Todd Osborne

Cover Image:
Getty Images*

*Unless otherwise noted, all cover images used by
Custom Solutions, a part of Cengage Learning,
have been supplied courtesy of Getty Images with
the exception of the Earthview cover image, which
has been supplied by the National Aeronautics and
Space Administration (NASA).

ALL RIGHTS RESERVED. No part of this work covered by the copyright herein may be reproduced, transmitted, stored or used in any form or by any means graphic, electronic, or mechanical, including but not limited to photocopying, recording, scanning, digitizing, taping, Web distribution, information networks, or information storage and retrieval systems, except as permitted under Section 107 or 108 of the 1976 United States Copyright Act, without the prior written permission of the publisher.

For product information and technology assistance, contact us at
**Cengage Learning Customer & Sales Support, 1-800-354-9706**
For permission to use material from this text or product,
submit all requests online at cengage.com/permissions
Further permissions questions can be emailed to
**permissionrequest@cengage.com**

This book contains select works from existing Cengage Learning resources and was produced by Cengage Learning Custom Solutions for collegiate use. As such, those adopting and/or contributing to this work are responsible for editorial content accuracy, continuity and completeness.

**Compilation © 2012 Cengage Learning**

ISBN-13:  978-1-133-88788-1

ISBN-10:  1-133-88788-0

**Cengage Learning**
5191 Natorp Boulevard
Mason, Ohio 45040
USA

Cengage Learning is a leading provider of customized learning solutions with office locations around the globe, including Singapore, the United Kingdom, Australia, Mexico, Brazil, and Japan. Locate your local office at:
**international.cengage.com/region.**

Cengage Learning products are represented in Canada by Nelson Education, Ltd. For your lifelong learning solutions, visit **www.cengage.com /custom.**
Visit our corporate website at **www.cengage.com.**

Printed in the United States of America

# To the Student

*¡Bienvenidos!* Welcome to the *Cuadros* introductory Spanish program. Spanish is one of the most useful languages you can learn; it is spoken by nearly 500 million people across the globe, including over 50 million Hispanics in the United States alone—one out of every six Americans. It is the most spoken language in the world after Mandarin Chinese and English. As you undertake your study of the Spanish language with *Cuadros*, keep in mind the following:

- We strive to present the Spanish-speaking world in all its diversity, with particular attention to indigenous and African-Hispanic populations, as well as European and Latin American immigrant populations.

- We guide you to make cross-cultural comparisons between the cultures you learn about and your own. Too often, the emphasis has been on the differences among cultures, when what may be surprising is the number of things we have in common with Spanish speakers around the world.

- We encourage you to look at your own community and to meet and interact with the Spanish speakers you encounter in both local and global communities. Spanish is all around you—just keep your eyes and ears open for it!

- *Cuadros* is designed to enrich your language-learning experience—while you are learning another language, you are also gathering information *about* the people who speak it and the countries where it is spoken. At first, you may think that you are unable to read or understand much Spanish, but in *Cuadros*, the focus is on getting the main ideas, and the tasks expected of you are limited to what you have already learned or what you can safely deduce from context. You will be surprised to see that you can comprehend more than you think you can!

- *Cuadros* features a variety of resources to help you achieve your language-learning goals more easily. Media icons at relevant points throughout the print book tell you exactly which component to use for additional practice or support. Or, work right from the eBook for direct access to all of the program's resources, including audio recordings of key vocabulary and grammar terms, instant activity feedback, and online chat and commenting functionality.

- Learning a language is easier if you relax and have fun. Keeping this in mind, we've included humorous and contemporary content with the goal of making language learning enjoyable and interesting.

We hope you enjoy your introduction to the Spanish language and its many peoples and cultures. Learning a language sets you on a course of life-long learning. It is one of the most valuable and exciting things you can do to prepare yourself to be a global citizen of the twenty-first century.

—The Authors

# Student Components

## Student Text

Your **Student Text** contains all the information and activities you need for in-class use. Volumes 1 and 2 each contain a preliminary chapter followed by five regular chapters that contain vocabulary presentations and activities, grammar presentations and activities, video-related practice, cultural information, reading selections, and writing practice. There are also valuable reference sections at the back of each book, including Spanish-English and English-Spanish glossaries and verb charts. In addition, Volume 2 contains an appendix that reviews all of the grammar presented in Volume 1.

## Student Activities Manual (SAM): Workbook / Lab Manual / Video Manual

The **Student Activities Manual (SAM)** includes out-of-class practice of the material presented in the Student Text. Volumes 1 and 2 of the SAM are each divided into a Workbook **(Cuaderno de práctica)**, which focuses on written vocabulary and grammar practice, reading, and writing; a Lab Manual **(Manual de laboratorio)**, which focuses on pronunciation and listening comprehension; and a Video Manual **(Manual de video)**, which offers extra practice of the storyline and **Voces del mundo hispano** segments.

## iLrn Heinle Learning Center

An all-in-one online learning environment, including an audio- and video-enhanced interactive eBook, assignable textbook activities, companion videos, assignable voice-recorded activities, an online workbook and lab manual with audio, interactive enrichment activities, a chapter- and volume-level diagnostic study tool for better exam preparation, and now, media sharing and commenting capability through Share It! The iLrn: Heinle Learning Center is offered separately for Volumes 1 and 2.

## Premium Website

You will find a wealth of resources and practice on the *Cuadros* **Premium Website**, accessible for Volumes 1 and 2 at **www.cengagebrain.com.** The **Premium Website** assets should be used as you work through each chapter and as you review for quizzes and exams.

To get access, visit CengageBrain.com

- It provides access to the text audio program, Web activities and links, Google Earth™ coordinates, and an iTunes™ playlist.
- The premium password-protected resources include the SAM audio program, the video program, grammar and pronunciation podcasts, grammar tutorial videos, auto-graded quizzes, and more!
- The web quizzes focus on vocabulary and grammar and provide automatic feedback, which helps you understand errors and pinpoints areas for review.
- The web activities offer the opportunity to explore authentic Spanish-language websites. Cultural web links relate to the **Voces de la comunidad, ¡Fíjate!**, and **¿Quieres saber más?** activities as well as **Tú en el mundo hispano**, which covers volunteer, study abroad, and internship opportunities throughout the Hispanic world and **Ritmos del mundo hispano**, a section that explores traditional and contemporary Hispanic music through music and video links.

# Acknowledgments

## Reviewers and Contributors

We would like to acknowledge the helpful suggestions and useful ideas of our reviewers, whose commentary was invaluable to us in shaping *Cuadros*.

Many thanks go to the following professors, each of whom offered valuable suggestions through their participation in live and virtual focus groups:

### ACTFL: Introductory Spanish Focus Group
Aleta Anderson, *Grand Rapids Community College*
Yolanda González, *Valencia Community College*
Monica Montalvo, *University of Central Florida*
Renee Wooten, *Vernon College*

### Pasadena Focus Group
Esther Castro, *San Diego State University*
Mercedes Limón, *Chaffey College*
Ofelia McQueen, *Los Angeles City College*
Markus Muller, *California State University, Long Beach*
Rosalinda Nericcio, *San Diego State University*
Yelgy Parada, *Los Angeles City College*
Victoria Tirado, *Chaffey College*

### Philadelphia Focus Group
Norma Corrales-Martin, *Temple University*
Judith R. Downing, *Rutgers University – Camden*
April Jacobs, *Temple University*
Maríadelaluz Matus-Mendoza, *Drexel University*
Patricia Moore-Martinez, *Temple University*
Eva Recio-Gonzalez, *University of Pennsylvania*
Kimberly Ann Vega, *Temple University*

### Development Reviews
Karen Berg, *College of Charleston*
Genevieve Breedon, *Darton College*
Matt Carpenter, *Yuba College, Clear Lake Campus*
John Catlett, *Cabrini College*
Daria Cohen, *Rider University*
Carmen García, *Valencia Community College*
Martha García, *University of Central Florida*
Diego Emilio Gómez
Yolanda González, *Valencia Community College*
Laurie Huffman, *Los Medanos College / Florida State College*
Isabel Killough, *Norfolk State University*
Lori Lammert, *Chattanooga State Community College*

Jill Loney, *Urbana University*
Richard McCallister, *Delaware State University*
Meghan Mehlos, *University of Wisconsin – Eau Claire*
Deanna Mihaly, *Eastern Michigan University*
Dianne Moneypenny
Lisa Nalbone, *University of Central Florida*
Janet Norden, *Baylor University*
Catherine Ortíz, *University of Texas at Arlington*
Sieglinde Poelzler-Kamatali, *Ohio Northern University*
Rosalea Postma-Carttar, *University of Kansas*
Laura Ruiz-Scott, *Scottsdale Community College*
Lester Edgardo Sandres Rapalo, *Valencia Community College*
Erika Sutherland, *Muhlenberg College*
David Tate, *Brevard Community College*
Wendy Westmoreland, *Cleveland Community College*
Sandra Wise, *University of Texas at Arlington*

### Testing Program Consultants
Bárbara Ávila-Shah, *University at Buffalo, The State University of New York*
Patrick Brady, *Tidewater Community College*
Marta Nunn, *Virginia Commonwealth University*
Helga Winkler, *Ventura County Community College District – Moorpark College*

We would like to extend our gratitude to the Graduate Teaching Assistant and Adjunct Faculty Focus Group, which discussed the tools needed to ensure a successful transition to a new edition and successful use over the course of the semester.

### Graduate Teaching Assistant / Adjunct Faculty Focus Group
Alison Atkins, *Boston University*
Alison Carberry, *Boston University*
Alejandra Cornejo, *Boston University*
Daniela Dorfman, *Boston University*
Megan Gibbons, *Boston University*
Rebeca Hey-Colón, *Harvard University*
Magdalena Malinowska, *Boston University*
Glenda Quiñónez, *Harvard University*

Finally, special thanks go to the following professors and writers, who have written the outstanding supplements to accompany this program:

Meghan Allen, *Babson College – Volume-level diagnostics and Web assets*

Flavia Belpoliti, *University of Houston – Bridge chapter teaching suggestions*

María Colina – *Lesson plans*

Juan De Urda, *SUNY Fredonia – Web quizzes*

Karen Haller Beer – *Testing program*

Maribel Lárraga, *Our Lady of the Lake University – Testing program and audio script*

Sarah Link – *PowerPoint presentations*

Jeff Longwell, *New Mexico State University – Volume-level oral assessments*

Nina Patrizio-Quiñones, *Our Lady of the Lake University – Testing program and audioscript*

Joshua Pope, *University of Wisconsin – Madison – Information gap activities*

Nidia Schuhmacher, *Brown University – Web searches*

Sierra Turner, *University of Alabama – Activity worksheets*

A hearty thanks to our fine VAK system, Learning Style worksheet writers: **Carlos Abaunza, Rebeca Hey-Colón** from **Harvard University** and **Magdalena Malinowska** from **Boston University**. Through creativity, hard work, and proactive communication, these writers took full ownership of the project from its incipient stages to create a comprehensive set of intuitive and valuable tools for visual, auditory, and kinesthetic learners.

We would also like to thank the World Languages Group at Heinle Cengage Learning for their ongoing support of this project and for guiding us along the long and sometimes difficult path to its completion! Many thanks especially to Beth Kramer and Heather Bradley for their professional guidance and outstanding support. We would also like to thank Kim Beuttler, our development editor, for her enthusiastic support and dedication to the project, her unflagging energy and enthusiasm, and her unerring eye for detail, Sara Dyer for her creative and focused work on the supplements that support *Cuadros*, and Morgen Murphy for her dedication to the quality of the media package. Thanks also to Aileen Mason, our production editor, for her meticulous care, and for her cheerful and good-humored tenacity in keeping the production side of things moving efficiently, and to Katy Gabel for her excellent project management work. We would like to extend our appreciation to Lindsey Richardson, Marketing Director, and Ben Rivera, Senior Marketing Manager, for their outstanding creative vision and hard work on campus, and to Glenn McGibbon, Senior Marketing Communications Manager, for his phenomenal work on marketing and promotional materials. We would like to acknowledge our copyeditor Janet Gokay, our proofreaders Pilar Acevedo and Jonathan Jucker, our art director, Linda Jurras, for her inspired design work, our illustrators JHS Illustration Studio and Fian Arroyo, Hilary Hudgens for his creative design contributions, and the many other design, art, and production staff and freelancers who contributed to the creation of this program.

**¡Mil gracias a todos!**

To my inspirational students, who helped shape *Cuadros*, and to *mi querida familia*, John, Morgan, and John, who have accompanied me on my life's magical journey as a Hispanist. *Gracias por el apoyo infinito.*
—S. S. L.

I am particularly appreciative of the help and encouragement of my husband, Bartlett Mel, my father, Domingo Carreira, and my colleagues Ana Roca, Najib Redouane, and Irene Marchegiani Jones.
—M. C.

I would like to thank my parents, Dulce and Óscar Madrigal, for bequeathing to me their language, their culture, their heritage, their passion for life, and their *orgullo* in *México, lindo y querido.*
—S. M. V.

A special thanks to Mac Prichard and to Shirley and Bill Swanson for their constant support and encouragement, both personal and professional.
—K. S.

# Scope and Sequence

## Volume 1

## Reference Materials

# ¡Bienvenidos a la clase de español!

The Spanish alphabet has 29 characters—the same as the English alphabet, plus the extra letters **ch, ll,** and **ñ**. When using a Spanish dictionary to look up words that begin with **ch** and **ll**, note that they do not have a separate listing, but are instead listed alphabetically under the letters **c** and **l**.

In 2010, the **Real Academia de la Lengua Española** updated the Spanish names of some letters. **Ve** and **doble ve** are now **uve** and **doble uve**, and **i griega** has been shortened to **ye**, but the adoption of these names is not universal among Spanish speakers. In addition, **ch** and **ll** have not been considered independent letters since 1994.

Go to the **Pronunciación** section of the preliminary chapter in the *Student Activities Manual* or *eSAM* and practice the sounds of the alphabet.

**The purpose of these pages is to introduce you to some of the "nuts and bolts" of Spanish you'll need right away.** Familiarize yourself with these words and expressions and do the activities described. Don't worry about memorizing it all—you'll have many more opportunities to work with these words as you progress through *Cuadros*.

## El alfabeto

| | | | | | | |
|---|---|---|---|---|---|---|
| a | *a* | **A**rgentina | n | *ene* | **N**icaragua |
| b | *be* | **B**olivia | ñ | *eñe* | Espa**ñ**a |
| c | *ce* | **C**osta Rica | o | *o* | **O**taval**o** |
| ch | *che* | **Ch**ichén Itzá | p | *pe* | **P**araguay |
| d | *de* | **D**inamarca | q | *cu* | **Q**uito |
| e | *e* | **E**cuador | r | *erre* | Pe**r**ú |
| f | *efe* | **F**ilipinas | s | *ese* | **S**antiago |
| g | *ge* | **G**uatemala | t | *te* | **T**oledo |
| h | *hache* | **H**onduras | u | *u* | C**u**ba |
| i | *i* | **I**nglaterra | v | *uve* | **V**enezuela |
| j | *jota* | **J**alisco | w | *doble uve* | Bots**w**ana |
| k | *ka* | **K**enya | x | *equis* | Mé**x**ico |
| l | *ele* | **L**os Ángeles | y | *ye* | **Y**ucatán |
| ll | *elle* | Va**ll**adolid | z | *zeta* | **Z**acatecas |
| m | *eme* | **M**arruecos | | | |

## Los números 1–100

| | | | | | |
|---|---|---|---|---|---|
| **0** | *cero* | **20** | *veinte* | **40** | *cuarenta* |
| 1 | *uno* | 21 | *veintiuno* | 41 | *cuarenta y uno* |
| 2 | *dos* | 22 | *veintidós* | 42 | *cuarenta y dos* |
| 3 | *tres* | 23 | *veintitrés* | 43 | *cuarenta y tres* |
| 4 | *cuatro* | 24 | *veinticuatro* | 44 | *cuarenta y cuatro* |
| 5 | *cinco* | 25 | *veinticinco* | 45 | *cuarenta y cinco* |
| 6 | *seis* | 26 | *veintiséis* | 46 | *cuarenta y seis* |
| 7 | *siete* | 27 | *veintisiete* | 47 | *cuarenta y siete* |
| 8 | *ocho* | 28 | *veintiocho* | 48 | *cuarenta y ocho* |
| 9 | *nueve* | 29 | *veintinueve* | 49 | *cuarenta y nueve* |
| | | | | | |
| **10** | *diez* | **30** | *treinta* | **50** | *cincuenta* |
| 11 | *once* | 31 | *treinta y uno* | 51 | *cincuenta y uno* |
| 12 | *doce* | 32 | *treinta y dos* | 52 | *cincuenta y dos* |
| 13 | *trece* | 33 | *treinta y tres* | 53 | *cincuenta y tres* |
| 14 | *catorce* | 34 | *treinta y cuatro* | 54 | *cincuenta y cuatro* |
| 15 | *quince* | 35 | *treinta y cinco* | 55 | *cincuenta y cinco* |
| 16 | *dieciséis* | 36 | *treinta y seis* | 56 | *cincuenta y seis* |
| 17 | *diecisiete* | 37 | *treinta y siete* | 57 | *cincuenta y siete* |
| 18 | *dieciocho* | 38 | *treinta y ocho* | 58 | *cincuenta y ocho* |
| 19 | *diecinueve* | 39 | *treinta y nueve* | 59 | *cincuenta y nueve* |
| | | | | **60** | *sesenta* |
| | | | | **70** | *setenta* |
| | | | | **80** | *ochenta* |
| | | | | **90** | *noventa* |
| | | | | **100** | *cien* |

Memorize the numbers 1–15.

Notice the pattern for the numbers from 16 to 29: **diez** + **seis** = **dieciséis**; **veinte** + **uno** = **veintiuno**. Notice that 11–15 do not follow that pattern.

Notice the pattern for the numbers over 30: **treinta** + **uno** = **treinta y uno**; **cuarenta** + **dos** = **cuarenta y dos**; **cincuenta** + **tres** = **cincuenta y tres**; etc.

Do not confuse sixty and seventy. Notice that **sesenta** is formed from **seiS**, with an **s**, and **setenta** is formed from **sieTe**, with a **t**.

With a partner, practice counting in Spanish by taking turns (Student 1: **uno;** Student 2: **dos,** etc.). Or, practice a sequence; for example, multiples of three (Student 1: **tres, seis, nueve;** Student 2: **doce, quince, dieciocho,** etc.).

## Las personas

With a partner, name ten people you know. Take turns identifying them first by age and gender and then by their relationship to you: **Marcos Martínez—20 años, hombre, amigo.**

| el hombre | la mujer | el muchacho / el chico | la muchacha / la chica | el niño | la niña |

el estudiante    el profesor    la instructora    el instructor

la estudiante

la profesora

el amigo

la compañera de cuarto

la amiga

el compañero de cuarto

## En el salón de clase

**>>** En el libro de texto

**la actividad** *activity*
**el capítulo** *chapter*
**el dibujo** *drawing*
**la foto** *photo*
**la lección** *lesson*
**la página** *page*

**>> La pregunta** *The question*

**¿Cómo se dice... ?**
*How do you say . . . ?*
**¿Qué significa... ?**
*What does . . . mean?*

**>> La respuesta** *The answer*

**Se dice...** *It's said . . .*
**Significa...** *It means . . .*

el cuarto · el salón de clase · el proyector · la puerta · la pizarra · la pared · la pizarra interactiva · la ventana · la silla · la tiza · el escritorio · el marcador · el diccionario · la computadora portátil · el lector de CD-ROM/DVD · la hoja de papel · la mochila · los apuntes · el CD · la nota · el lápiz · el cuaderno · el bolígrafo · la calculadora · el MP3 portátil · la tarea · el libro · la mesa

© Cengage Learning 2013

**>> Mandatos comunes** *Classroom commands*

**Abran los libros / libros electrónicos.** *Open your books / e-books.*
**Adivina. / Adivinen.** *Guess.*
**Cierren los libros / libros electrónicos.** *Close your books / e-books.*
**Contesta. / Contesten.** *Answer.*
**Entreguen la tarea.** *Turn in your homework.*
**Mándenme la tarea por e-mail.** *E-mail me your homework.*
**Escriban en sus cuadernos / sus computadoras.** *Write in your notebooks / computers.*
**Escuchen el audio.** *Listen to the audio.*
**Estudien las páginas... a...** *Study pages . . . to . . .*
**Hagan la tarea para mañana.** *Do the homework for tomorrow.*
**Lean el Capítulo 1.** *Read Chapter 1.*
**Repitan.** *Repeat.*

With a partner, take turns pointing out objects shown in the illustration that you can see in your classroom.

Your instructor will practice the most common classroom commands with the entire class and before you know it, you will know them by heart! Do not worry about memorizing them.

¡Bienvenidos a la clase de español! **5**

# capítulo 1   ¿Cómo te llamas?

## LA IDENTIDAD PERSONAL

As individuals we value our uniqueness while drawing strength from the similarities and experiences we share with others.

How do you define yourself, both as an individual and as a member of different groups?

## Communication

By the end of this chapter you will be able to

- exchange addresses, phone numbers, and e-mail addresses
- introduce yourself and others, greet, and say goodbye
- make a phone call
- tell your and others' ages
- address friends informally and acquaintances politely
- write a personal letter

# Un viaje por el mundo hispanohablante

1.

Gen Productions/Shutterstock

2.

Jozef Sedmak/Shutterstock

3.

Dmitry Rukhlenko/Shutterstock

**¿Qué sabes?** *(What do you know?)*

1. Match the names of these famous locations in the Spanish-speaking world with their photos.
   a. la Pirámide del Sol, Teotihuacán, México
   b. las Cataratas de Iguazú, Puerto Iguazú, Argentina
   c. la Catedral de la Sagrada Familia, Barcelona, España

2. There are 21 official Spanish-speaking countries in the world, not including the United States. Can you place them in the correct areas of the world? Use the information below to make a list of the six areas. Then list the countries that you think belong in each one. Save your work to check in the **¡Explora y exprésate!** section on page 33.

**Áreas:** África, El Caribe, Centroamérica, Europa, Norteamérica, Sudamérica

**Países:** Argentina, Bolivia, Chile, Colombia, Costa Rica, Cuba, Ecuador, El Salvador, España, Guatemala, Guinea Ecuatorial, Honduras, México, Nicaragua, Panamá, Paraguay, Perú, Puerto Rico, República Dominicana, Uruguay, Venezuela

**Lo que sé y lo que quiero aprender**  Complete the chart in **Appendix A**. Write some facts you *already know* about the Spanish-speaking world in the **Lo que sé** column. Then add some things you *want to learn* about in the **Lo que quiero aprender** column. Save the chart to use again in the **¡Explora y exprésate!** section on page 33.

## Cultures

By the end of this chapter you will have explored

- Spanish around the world
- a brief history of the Spanish language
- some statistics about Spanish speakers
- a few comparisons between Spanish and English
- Spanish in the professional world
- Spanish-language telephone conventions

# ¡Imagínate!

▶ >> **Vocabulario útil 1**

JAVIER: **¡Hola!**

ANILÚ: Hola, Beto. **¿Cómo te va?**

JAVIER: **Bastante bien,** pero… ¿Beto? Yo no soy Beto.

Spanish has formal and informal means of address: singular formal (s. form.), singular familiar (s. fam.), and plural (pl.) for more than one person, formal or informal. You will learn more about how to address people on pages 23–24.

>> **Para saludar** *How to greet*

**Hola.** *Hello.*
**¿Qué tal?** *How are things going?*
**¿Cómo estás (tú)?** *How are you? (s. fam.)*
**¿Cómo está (usted)?** *How are you? (s. form.)*
**¿Cómo están (ustedes)?** *How are you? (pl.)*
**¿Cómo te va?** *How's it going with you? (s. fam.)*
**¿Cómo le va?** *How's it going with you? (s. form.)*
**¿Cómo les va?** *How's it going with you? (pl.)*
**¿Qué hay de nuevo?** *What's new?*
**Buenos días.** *Good morning.*
**Buenas tardes.** *Good afternoon.*
**Buenas noches.** *Good night. Good evening.*

>> **Para responder** *How to respond*

**Bien, gracias.** *Fine, thank you.*
**Bastante bien.** *Quite well.*
**(No) Muy bien.** *(Not) Very well.*
**Regular.** *So-so.*
**¡Terrible! / ¡Fatal!** *Terrible! / Awful!*
**No mucho.** *Not much.*
**Nada.** *Nothing.*
**¿Y tú?** *And you? (s. fam.)*
**¿Y usted?** *And you? (s. form.)*

© Cengage Learning 2013

👥 **1** **Conversaciones** With a classmate, take turns greeting each other and responding. Choose an appropriate response from those provided.

1. Hola, ¿qué tal?
   a. Buenos días.   c. ¿Y tú?
   b. Muy bien, gracias.

2. Buenas tardes. ¿Qué hay de nuevo?
   a. No mucho.   c. Terrible.
   b. Bastante bien.

3. Buenas noches. ¿Cómo le va?
   a. Nada.   c. Fatal.
   b. ¿Y usted?

4. Buenos días. ¿Cómo están?
   a. Regular.   c. No mucho.
   b. Buenas noches.

5. Hola, ¿cómo está?
   a. ¿Cómo te va?   c. Nada.
   b. Bien, gracias, ¿y usted?

6. Buenas tardes.
   a. Terrible.   c. No muy bien. ¿Y tú?
   b. Buenas tardes.
      ¿Qué hay de nuevo?

¿Qué tal?

¡Fatal! ¿Y tú?

© Cengage Learning 2013

👥 **2** **Saludos** Exchange greetings with a classmate. Follow the cues.

1. **Greeting:** It is morning, and you want to know how your classmate is doing.

   **Response:** You had a terrible night and don't feel well.

2. **Greeting:** It is evening, and you run into two classmates; you want to know if anything new has come up.

   **Response:** Not much has happened since you last saw your friend.

3. **Greeting:** You run into a professor in the afternoon; you want to know how things are going.

   **Response:** You're doing quite well and want to know how your student is doing.

👥 **3** **¿Qué tal?** Have a conversation with one of your friends when you first see him or her that day.

MODELO   Tú: *¡Hola, Adriana! ¿Cómo te va?*
         Compañero(a): *Bien, gracias, Rosa. Y tú, ¿cómo estás?*
         Tú: *Regular.*

## ⏵ >> Vocabulario útil 2

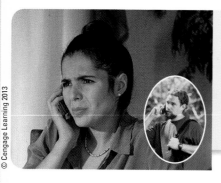

© Cengage Learning 2013

ANILÚ: Pues, ¿cómo te llamas?

JAVIER: ¿Yo? **Soy** Javier de la Cruz. Y yo, ¿con quién hablo?

ANILÚ: **Me llamo** Anilú. Ana Luisa Guzmán. … Pero, **¿cuál es tu número de teléfono?** Yo marqué el 3-39-71-94.

JAVIER: No, ése no es mi número de teléfono. **Mi número es el 3-71-28-12.**

---

Spanish speakers often ask **¿Cuál es tu / su e-mail?**, using the English term rather than **dirección electrónica.**

---

In an e-mail address in Spanish, @ is pronounced **arroba** and **.com** is pronounced **punto com.**

---

>> **Para pedir y dar información personal**
*Exchanging personal information*

**¿Cómo te llamas?** *What's your name? (s. fam.)*
**¿Cómo se llama?** *What's your name? (s. form.)*

**Me llamo…** *My name is. . .*
**(Yo) soy…** *I am. . .*

**¿Cuál es tu número de teléfono?** *What's your phone number? (s. fam.)*
**¿Cuál es su número de teléfono?** *What's your phone number? (s. form.)*

**Mi número de teléfono es el 3-71-28-12.** *My phone number is 371-2812.*
**Es el 3-71-28-12.** *It's 371-2812.*

**¿Dónde vives?** *Where do you live? (s. fam.)*
**¿Dónde vive?** *Where do you live? (s. form.)*

**Vivo en…** *I live in / at / on. . .*
  **la avenida…** *avenue*
  **la calle…** *street*
  **el barrio… / la colonia…** *neighborhood*

**¿Cuál es tu dirección?** *What's your address? (s. fam.)*
**¿Cuál es su dirección?** *What's your address? (s. form.)*
**Mi dirección es…** *My address is. . .*

**¿Cuál es tu dirección electrónica?** *What's your e-mail address? (s. fam.)*
**¿Cuál es su dirección electrónica?** *What's your e-mail address? (s. form.)*
**Aquí tienes mi dirección electrónica.** *Here's my e-mail address. (s. fam.)*
**Aquí tiene mi dirección electrónica.** *Here's my e-mail address. (s. form.)*

## ACTIVIDADES

**4** **Respuestas** Pick from the second column the correct response to the questions in the first column.

1. ¿Dónde vives?
2. ¿Cuál es su dirección electrónica?
3. ¿Cómo se llama?
4. ¿Cuál es tu número de teléfono?

a. Yo soy Rita Rivera.
b. Es el 4-87-26-91.
c. Es Irene29@yahoo.com.mx.
d. En la colonia Villanueva.

**5** **En la reunión** You are at the first meeting of the International Hispanic Student Association at your college. You have been elected secretary and must record in Spanish the name, address, and phone number of every member. With a male and female classmate playing the parts of the members, ask for the information you need. Without looking at the book, listen to their responses and type or write out their personal information. Then ask your partners for their real personal information and record that.

MODELO    Jorge Salinas, avenida B 23, 2-91-66-45
　　　　　　Tú: *¿Cómo te llamas?*
　　　　　　Compañero(a): *Me llamo Jorge Salinas.*
　　　　　　Tú: *¿Dónde vives?*
　　　　　　Compañero(a): *Vivo en la avenida B, veintitrés.*
　　　　　　Tú: *¿Cuál es tu número de teléfono?*
　　　　　　Compañero(a): *Es el dos, noventa y uno, sesenta y seis, cuarenta*
　　　　　　　*y cinco.*

> Notice in the **MODELO** how, except for the first example, all digits of a telephone number in Spanish are given in pairs. Spanish speakers in the United States might not use this convention.

1. Amanda Villarreal, calle Montemayor 10, 8-13-02-55
2. Diego Ruiz, Colonia del Valle, calle Iturbide 89, 7-94-71-30
3. Irma Santiago, avenida Flores Verdes 12, 9-52-35-27
4. Baldemar Huerta, calle Otero 39, 7-62-81-03
5. Ingrid Lehmann, avenida Aguas Blancas 62, 4-56-72-93
6. ¿… ?
7. ¿… ?

> Notice that unlike in English, the street name precedes the number in addresses in Spanish: **Calle Iturbide 12** vs. *12 Iturbide Street.*

**6** **¡Mucho gusto!** With a classmate, role-play a cell phone conversation in which one of you has reached the wrong number. You are curious about the person you have accidentally reached. Try to get as much information from each other as possible.

MODELO    —Hola. ¿Marcos?
　　　　　　—No, yo no soy Marcos.
　　　　　　—Bueno, ¿cómo se llama usted?
　　　　　　—…

© Cengage Learning 2013

In Spain, a cell phone is called **un móvil**. Can you guess what it means?

## ¡Fíjate! Los celulares

Cellular phone technology has revolutionized telecommunications throughout the entire world. Cell phones are as popular in Latin America and Spain as they are in the United States. With the advent of the smartphone, cell phones are now routinely used for e-mail, photos, video, text messaging, games, applications, face-to-face phone conversations, GPS directions, and almost anything else you can do online.

Unas chicas usan su celular para hablar con un amigo.

Although customs for speaking on the phone vary from one Spanish-speaking country to another, here are some useful phrases to get you started.

Remember that most Spanish speakers give their phone number by using pairs after the first digit. For example: **Mi número es el dos, treinta y seis, diez, dieciocho.**

### Familiar Conversation

| | |
|---|---|
| —¡Hola! | *Hello?* |
| —Hola. ¿Qué estás haciendo? | *Hi. What are you doing?* |
| —Nada, ¿y tú? | *Nothing, and you?* |
| —¿Quieres hacer algo? | *Do you want to do something?* |
| —Claro. ¿Nos vemos donde siempre? | *Sure. See you at the usual place?* |
| —Está bien. Hasta luego. | *OK. See you later.* |
| —Chau. | *Bye.* |

### Formal Conversation

| | |
|---|---|
| —¡Hola! / ¿Aló? | *Hello?* |
| —Hola. ¿Puedo hablar con... ? | *Hi, may I speak with . . . ?* |
| —Sí. Aquí está. | *Yes. Here he/she is.* |
| —Lo siento. No está. | *Sorry. He's/she's not here.* |
| —Por favor, dígale que llamó (nombre). Mi número es el... | *Please tell him/her that (name) called. My number is . . .* |
| —Muy bien. | *OK.* |
| —Muchas gracias. | *Thank you very much.* |
| —De nada. Adiós. | *You're welcome. Goodbye.* |
| —Adiós. | *Goodbye.* |

**Práctica**  With a partner, role-play two different phone calls, using the expressions provided. In the first call, you dial a friend's cell phone and speak to him or her. In the second call, you dial a friend's home number and speak to his grandmother. In the second case, the person you are trying to reach is not in and you need to leave a message. Don't forget to use the correct level of address (familiar or formal).

# Vocabulario útil 3

© Cengage Learning 2013

| | |
|---|---|
| **ANILÚ:** | Beto, **quiero presentarte a** Javier de la Cruz. |
| **BETO:** | **Mucho gusto**, Javier. |
| **JAVIER:** | **Encantado**, Beto. |
| **BETO:** | Aquí está tu celular. |
| **JAVIER:** | Gracias, Beto. Y aquí está tu celular. |
| **BETO:** | **Bueno, ¡tengo que irme! Muchas gracias**, Javier. Y gracias a ti también, Anilú. |
| **ANILÚ:** | Pues, Javier, **mucho gusto en conocerte**. |
| **JAVIER:** | **El gusto es mío.** |
| **ANILÚ:** | Pues, entonces, **¡nos vemos!** |
| **JAVIER:** | ¡Hasta luego! Chau. |

## >> Para presentar a alguien *Introducing someone*

**Soy...** *I am . . .*
**Me llamo... / Mi nombre es...** *My name is . . .*
**Quiero presentarte a...** *I'd like to introduce you (s. fam.) to . . .*

**Quiero presentarle a...** *I'd like to introduce you (s. form.) to . . .*
**Quiero presentarles a...** *I'd like to introduce you (pl.) to . . .*

## >> Para responder *How to respond*

**Mucho gusto.** *My pleasure.*
**Mucho gusto en conocerte.** *A pleasure to meet you (s. fam.).*
**Encantado(a).** *Delighted to meet you.*

**Igualmente.** *Likewise.*
**El gusto es mío.** *The pleasure is mine.*
**Un placer.** *My pleasure.*

## >> Para despedirse *Saying goodbye*

**Adiós.** *Goodbye.*
**Hasta luego.** *See you later.*
**Hasta mañana.** *See you tomorrow.*
**Hasta pronto.** *See you soon.*

**Nos vemos.** *See you later.*
**Chau.** *Bye.*
**Bueno, tengo que irme.** *Well / OK, I have to go.*

The word **chau** comes from the Italian word *ciao,* which means both *hello* and *goodbye.* In Spanish, it is only used to say *goodbye.*The spelling has been changed to reflect Spanish pronunciation.

# ACTIVIDADES

**7** **¿Cómo respondes?** Choose the best response to each statement.

1. Me llamo Rubén.
   a. Adiós.
   b. Un placer.
   c. Hasta mañana.

2. Quiero presentarte a Cristina.
   a. Igualmente.
   b. Bueno, tengo que irme.
   c. Mucho gusto.

3. Mucho gusto en conocerte.
   a. Chau.
   b. Igualmente.
   c. Mi nombre es Santiago.

4. Bueno, tengo que irme.
   a. Hasta luego.
   b. Encantado(a).
   c. El gusto es mío.

**8** **Quiero presentarte a…** Introductions are a normal part of everyday life. Study the drawing and, with a partner, create four short conversations in which one person introduces another person to a third party. In each conversation, pick one of the characters in the group and play that role. The labels show the four groups.

Grupo 1

Grupo 2

Grupo 3

Grupo 4

© Cengage Learning 2013

**9** **Fiesta** You're at a party and you meet someone you really like who speaks only Spanish. Write out the conversation you might have with that person. Include the following:

greeting
response
introduction
exchange of phone numbers and e-mail addresses
exchange of addresses
goodbyes

**10** **Un e-mail** Write an e-mail to your Spanish instructor introducing yourself. In it, give your name, address, e-mail address, phone number, and any other information you think your Spanish instructor should know about you. Send it!

> ¡Hola, profesora!
>
> Me llamo Gretchen Murray. Soy estudiante en su clase de español. Mi dirección electrónica es gmurray@xyzmail.com. Vivo en el campus. Mi número de teléfono es el 5-12-49-47. ¡Nos vemos pronto!
>
> Saludos,
> Gretchen

© Cengage Learning 2013

**11** **¡Mucho gusto en conocerte!**
You are at a party with a group of four or five classmates. Greet each other, introduce yourselves, present at least one other member of the group to the others, and then carry on as lively a conversation as you can, exchanging as much personal information as you normally would. Find a natural way to end the conversation and then say goodbye to each other.

Juan Silva/Getty Images

# A ver

You may not understand every word in the activities throughout the chapter, but focus on getting the main idea. You'll be surprised at how much you do understand!

## ESTRATEGIA

### Viewing a segment several times

When you first hear authentic Spanish, it may sound very fast. Stay calm! Remember that you don't have to understand everything and that, with video, you have the opportunity to replay. The first time you view the segment, listen for the general idea. The second time, listen for details.

**Antes de ver 1**  How many of the characters in this video segment do you already know? Go back to pages 8, 10, and 13 and identify the people you see in the photos there.

**Antes de ver 2**  Review some of the key words and phrases used in the video.

These words are to help you understand the video only. You will not be tested on them.

| | |
|---|---|
| **Ha sido un placer.** | *It's been a pleasure.* |
| **Marqué…** | *I dialed . . .* |
| **¡Tengo prisa!** | *I'm in a hurry!* |
| **Voy a marcar…** | *I'm going to dial . . .* |

**Antes de ver 3**  Before you watch the video, read items 1–3. Then, as you watch, listen for this information.

1. Las personas que hablan por celular: ¿Cómo se llaman?
2. Las personas al final: ¿Cómo se llaman?
3. _____ tiene *(has)* el celular de _____.

**Ver**  Now watch the video segment as many times as necessary to answer the questions in **Antes de ver 3**.

**Después de ver**  Are the following statements about the video segment true **(cierto)** or false **(falso)**? Correct the false statements.

1. Javier tiene el celular de Anilú.
2. Anilú es una amiga de Javier.
3. Beto es un amigo de Anilú.
4. El número del teléfono celular que tiene Javier es el 3-39-71-94.
5. El número de teléfono de Beto es el 3-39-71-94.
6. Anilú le presenta Javier a Beto.

© Cengage Learning 2013

# Voces de la comunidad

 **Voces del mundo hispano**

In this video segment, people from around the Spanish-speaking world introduce themselves. First read the statements below. Then watch the video as many times as needed to say whether the statements are true (**cierto**) or false (**falso**).

1. Ela y Sandra son de Puerto Rico.
2. Aura y Dayramir son de Honduras.
3. Claudio tiene 42 años (*is 42 years old*).
4. David tiene 19 años.

5. Ricardo es estudiante universitario.
6. Patricia y Constanza son profesoras de español.

 **Voces de Estados Unidos**

Track 2

## Spanish speakers in North America

In 1787, Thomas Jefferson had this advice for his nephew, Peter Carr: **❝Apply yourself to the study of the Spanish language with all of the assiduity you can. It and the English covering nearly the whole of America, they should be well known to every inhabitant who means to look beyond the limits of his farm.❞**

Today, the U.S. is the fourth-largest Spanish-speaking country in the world. The 44 million Hispanics (or Latinos) who make their home in this country represent the fastest-growing segment of the U.S. population, comprising nearly 16.66% of the total population. For its part, Canada is also home to a thriving community of over 300,000 Hispanics.

U.S. Hispanics are enjoying a period of unprecedented prosperity. Their estimated buying power of $800 billion a year more than doubles the combined buying power of all other Spanish-speaking countries in the world. Through Spanish-language websites, publications, and advertising aimed at the lucrative Hispanic market, U.S. companies are continually striving to better understand, entice, and serve Latino consumers.

The **Voces de la comunidad** section of Chapters 2–20 of *Cuadros* features an outstanding North American Hispanic from these and other areas, people whose contributions have direct relevance to the theme of the chapter.

**¿Y tú?** What are your reasons for studying Spanish? Do you want to use it for personal or professional reasons?

# ¡Prepárate!

### Identifying people and objects: Nouns and articles

## Cómo usarlo

*Nouns* identify people, places, and things: **señora Velasco, calle,** and **teléfono** are all nouns. *Articles* supply additional information about the noun.

1. *Definite* articles refer to a specific person, place, or thing.

   **La** Avenida Central es **la** calle          *Central Avenue is **the** most*
      más importante de **la** universidad.          *important street in **the** university.*
   *(You already know which avenue*
      *and university you are talking about.)*

2. *Indefinite* articles refer to a noun without identifying a specific person, place, or thing.

   **Un** amigo es **una** persona que te gusta.     *A friend is **a** person you like.*
   *(You are making a generalization,*
      *true of any friend.)*

## Cómo formarlo

The idea of gender for non-person nouns and for articles does not exist in English, although it is a feature of Spanish and other languages. When learning new Spanish words, memorize the article with the noun to help remember gender.

## LO BÁSICO

- *Number* indicates whether a word is singular or plural: **la calle** *(sing.)*, **las calles** *(pl.)*, **un escritorio** *(sing.)*, **unos escritorios** *(pl.)*
- *Gender* indicates whether a word is masculine or feminine: **una avenida** *(fem.)*, **el teléfono** *(masc.)*

3. Noun gender and number

   - **Gender:** Often you can tell the gender of a Spanish noun by looking at its ending. Here are some general guidelines.

When nouns ending in -**ión** become plural, they lose the accent on the **o: la corporación**, but **las corporaciones**.

| Masculine | Feminine |
|---|---|
| 1. Nouns ending in -**o**: **el amigo, el muchacho** | Exception to rule #1: **la mano** *(hand)* |
| Exceptions to rule #2: words ending in -**ma**: **el sistema, el problema, el tema, el programa**; also **el día, el mapa** | 2. Nouns ending in -**a**: **la compañera de cuarto, una chica** |
| Exceptions to rule #3: **el avión, el camión** | 3. Nouns ending in -**ión**, -**dad**, -**tad**, and -**umbre** are usually feminine: **la información, una universidad, una costumbre** *(custom)* |

Nouns referring to people often reflect gender by changing a final **o** to an **a** (**chico / chica, amigo / amiga**) or adding an **a** to a final consonant (**profesor / profesora**). For nouns ending in -**e**, -**ista**, or -**a** that refer to people, the article or context indicates gender (**el estudiante / la estudiante, el guitarrista / la guitarrista, Juan / Juanita es atleta**).

- **Number:** Spanish nouns form their plurals in several ways.

| Singular | Plural |
|---|---|
| Ends in vowel: **calle** | Add **s: calles** |
| Ends in consonant: **universidad** | Add **es: universidades** |
| Ends in -**z: lápiz** | Change **z** to **c** and add **es: lápices** |

**Décima Feria de las Mascotas**

sábado, 11 de mayo, 10:00 a 14:00, Plaza Central

¡Ven a ver y a llevarte algunos de los perros, gatos, pájaros, lagartos y serpientes más raros del mundo!

How many plural nouns can you identify in this poster for a pet fair? Can you find the two definite articles?

Photos: Ameng Wu/iStockphoto.com (Boa); Eric Isselee/iStockphoto.com (Dog and Cat; Ameng Wu/iStockphoto.com (Chameleon); Content © Cengage Learning 2013

**4.** Definite and indefinite articles

- Here are the Spanish definite articles, which correspond to the English article *the*.

| | Singular | Plural |
|---|---|---|
| **Masculine** | **el amigo**<br>*the friend (male)* | **los amigos**<br>*the friends (male or mixed group)* |
| **Feminine** | **la amiga**<br>*the friend (female)* | **las amigas**<br>*the friends (female)* |

In the past, **los** and **unos,** rather than **las** and **unas,** were used to refer to groups containing one or more males. The **Real Academia de la Lengua Española** recently ruled that the feminine forms should be used for groups with more females than males, but usage is changing slowly.

- Here are the Spanish indefinite articles, which correspond to the English articles *a*, *an*, and *some*.

|  | Singular | Plural |
|---|---|---|
| **Masculine** | **un amigo** <br> a friend *(male)* | **unos amigos** <br> some friends *(male or mixed group)* |
| **Feminine** | **una amiga** <br> a friend *(female)* | **unas amigas** <br> some friends *(female)* |

- Remember that you use masculine articles with masculine nouns and feminine articles with feminine nouns. When a noun is in the plural, the corresponding plural article (masculine or feminine) is used: **el hombre, los hombres.**

- When referring to a person's *profession*, the article is omitted: **Liana es profesora y Ricardo es dentista.**

- However, when you use a *title* to refer to someone, the article is used: **Es el profesor Gómez.** When you address that person directly, using their title, the article is not used: **Buenos días, profesor Gómez.**

> When the noun is modified, the article is used: **Liana es una profesora excelente.**

The following titles are typically used with the article when referring to a person, and without the article when addressing that person directly.

| | | | |
|---|---|---|---|
| **señor (Sr.)** | *Mr.* | **señorita (Srta.)** | *Miss / Ms.* |
| **señora (Sra.)** | *Mrs. / Ms.* | **profesor / profesora** | *professor* |

## ACTIVIDADES

🔊 **1** ¿Femenino o masculino? Listen to the speaker name a series of items and people. First, write whether the noun mentioned is masculine (**M**) or feminine (**F**), or both (**M/F**). Next, write the singular form of the noun with its correct definite article. Lastly, write the plural noun with its correct definite article.

Track 3

MODELO *M*
*el libro*
*los libros*

👥 **2** ¿Definido o indefinido? Work with a partner. Try to guess from the context whether it makes more sense to use the definite article, the indefinite article, or no article in each of the following pairs of sentences. Then say which article to use if one is required. If no article is required, mark X.

1. Es _____ calle en mi colonia.
   Es _____ calle central de mi colonia.

2. Es _____ profesor en mi universidad.
   Es _____ profesor de español.

3. Es _____ estudiante *( fem.)* más *(most)* inteligente de mi clase.
   Es _____ estudiante.

4. Es _____ avenida más importante de mi colonia.

   Es _____ avenida en mi colonia.

5. Es _____ universidad en mi estado (state).

   Es _____ universidad más importante de mi estado.

**3** **Presentaciones** With a partner, complete the following introductions with the correct definite or indefinite articles where needed. If no article is needed, mark with an X.

1. —Sra. Oliveros, quiero presentarle a _____ Srta. Martínez.

   —Un placer. ¿Dónde vive usted?

   —Vivo en _____ calle Colón, en _____ colonia Robles.

2. —Oye, Ricardo, quiero presentarte a mi amiga Rebeca. Ella es _____ dentista.

   —¡Mucho gusto, Rebeca! Yo soy _____ profesor de matemáticas.

   —¿De veras? Yo tengo (I have) _____ amigo que es profesor también.

3. —Buenas tardes. Yo soy _____ Sr. Bustelo.

   —Sr. Bustelo, ¿cuál es su número de teléfono?

   —Es _____ 8-21-98-32.

4. —¡Hola!

   —Buenos días. ¿Puedo hablar con _____ Sr. Lezama?

   —Lo siento. No está.

   —Por favor, dígale que llamó _____ Sra. Barlovento. Tenemos (We have) clase de administración mañana y necesito darle (I need to give him) _____ apuntes.

**4** **Más presentaciones** Introduce yourself to another classmate. Exchange information about where you live, phone numbers, and e-mail addresses. Then prepare to introduce your classmate to the entire class.

© Cengage Learning 2013

# Gramática útil 2

### Identifying and describing: Subject pronouns and the present indicative of the verb **ser**

**Estar,** which you have already used in the expression **¿Cómo estás?,** also means *to be.* You will learn other ways to use **estar** in **Chapter 4.**

## Cómo usarlo

The Spanish verb **ser** can be used to identify people and objects, to describe them, to make introductions, and to say when something will take place.
It is one of two Spanish verbs that are the equivalents of the English verb *to be.*

| | |
|---|---|
| Mi teléfono **es** el 2-39-71-49. | *My telephone number **is** 2-39-71-49.* |
| Yo **soy** Mariela y ella **es** Elena. | *I **am** Mariela and this **is** Elena.* |
| La fiesta **es** el miércoles. | *The party **is** on Wednesday.* |

## Cómo formarlo

### LO BÁSICO

- *Pronouns* are words used to replace nouns. (Some English pronouns are *it, she, you, him,* etc.)
- Verbs change form to reflect *number* and *person. Number* refers to singular versus plural. *Person* refers to different subjects.
- A verb's *tense* indicates the time frame in which an event takes place (for example, *talk, talked, will talk*). The *present indicative tense* refers to present-time events or conditions (*I talk, I am talking*).

**1.** Subject pronouns

- Subject pronouns are pronouns that are used as the subject of a sentence. Here are the subject pronouns in Spanish.

¿**Tú** eres Javier?

| Singular | | Plural | |
|---|---|---|---|
| **yo** | *I* | **nosotros / nosotras** | *we* |
| **tú** | *you (fam.)* | **vosotros / vosotras** | *you (fam.)* |
| **usted (Ud.)** | *you (form.)* | **ustedes (Uds.)** | *you (fam., form.)* |
| **él, ella** | *he, she* | **ellos, ellas** | *they* |

© Cengage Learning 2013

- The **vosotros / vosotras** forms are primarily used in Spain. They allow speakers to address more than one person informally. In most other places, Spanish speakers use **ustedes** to address several people, regardless of the formality of the relationship. The **vosotros** forms of verbs are provided in *Cuadros* so that you can recognize them, but they are not included for practice in activities.

In Spanish, it is not always necessary to use the subject pronoun with the verb, as long as the subject is understood. For example, it's less common to say **Yo soy Rafael**, because **Soy Rafael** is clear enough on its own.

2. Formal vs. familiar

English has a single word—*you*—to address people directly, regardless of how well you know them. As you have already seen, Spanish has two basic forms of address: the **tú** form and the **usted** form.

- **Tú** is used to address a family member, a close friend, a child, or a pet.
- **Usted** (often abbreviated **Ud.**) is a more formal means of address used with older people, strangers, acquaintances, and sometimes with colleagues.
- Remember that the **ustedes** form is normally used to address more than one person in both *informal* and *formal* contexts (except in Spain, where **vosotros**(as) is used in informal contexts).

Levels of formality vary throughout the Spanish-speaking world, so it's important when traveling to listen to how **tú** and **usted** are used and to follow the local practice.

In some countries, you will hear **vos** forms (Argentina and parts of Uruguay, Chile, and Central America). This is a variation of **tú** that is used only in these regions.

To show respect, you sometimes hear the titles **don** and **doña** used with people you address as **usted**. **Don** and **doña** are used with the person's first name: **don Roberto, doña Carmen**.

3. The present tense of the verb **ser**

The present indicative forms of the verb **ser** are as follows. Note the subject pronouns associated with each form.

| ser *(to be)* | |
|---|---|
| **Singular** | |
| **yo soy** | *I am* |
| **tú eres** | *you (s. fam.) are* |
| **usted es** | *you (s. form.) are* |
| **él es** | *he is* |
| **ella es** | *she is* |
| **Plural** | |
| **nosotros / nosotras somos** | *we are* |
| **vosotros / vosotras sois** | *you (pl. fam.) are* |
| **ustedes son** | *you (pl. form. or pl. fam.) are* |
| **ellos son** | *they (masc. or mixed) are* |
| **ellas son** | *they (fem.) are* |

ACTIVIDADES

**5 Descripciones** With a partner, match each of the following descriptions with the correct group of individuals.

_____ 1. two teens     a. Son compañeras de cuarto.

_____ 2. one professor     b. Es profesor de periodismo (*journalism*).

_____ 3. two roommates     c. Somos profesores en la universidad.

_____ 4. two professors     d. Son estudiantes.

**6 Manuel** Manuel writes an e-mail to a new Facebook friend describing himself and his two best friends. Complete his e-mail with the correct forms of **ser**.

¡Hola! Yo (1) _____ Manuel Ybarra. (2) _____ estudiante en la Universidad Nacional Autónoma de México, que (3) _____ una de las universidades más importantes de las Américas. ¡La población estudiantil (4) _____ de más de 270.000 estudiantes!

Tengo dos amigos íntimos. Mi amiga Susana (5) _____ una persona muy sincera. Ella y yo (6) _____ inseparables. Mi amigo Hernán (7) _____ muy cómico. Hernán y yo (8) _____ compañeros de cuarto. Susana y Hernán (9) _____ buenos amigos también. Y tú, ¿cómo (10) _____?

**7 ¿Quiénes son?** Use **ser** to say who the following people are.

1. [Nombre] _____ mi compañero(a) de clase.
2. [Nombre] _____ el profesor (la profesora) de español.
3. [Nombre] _____ el instructor (la instructora) en la clase de español.
4. Nosotros _____ estudiantes de español.
5. Tú…
6. Usted…
7. Ustedes…
8. Ellos…

**8 Le presento a…** In groups of three or four, act out an introduction in front of the class. Decide beforehand the ages and the social standing of the people you are role-playing, as well as how informal or formal the situation is. The class must guess whether the introduction is formal or informal. Follow the model.

MODELO (formal)
—Buenos días, profesora García.
—Buenos días, Susana.
—Profesora García, le presento a mi amigo Paul.
—Encantada, Paul.

**24** Capítulo 1

# Gramática útil 3

## Expressing quantity: **Hay** + nouns

### Cómo usarlo

1. **Hay** is the Spanish equivalent of *there is* or *there are* in English.

Aquí **hay** un problema.

| | |
|---|---|
| **Hay** una reunión en la cafetería. | ***There is*** *a meeting in the cafeteria.* |
| **Hay** tres estudiantes en la clase. | ***There are*** *three students in the class.* |
| **Hay** unos libros en la mesa. | ***There are*** *some books on the table.* |
| **Hay** una fiesta el viernes. | ***There is*** *a party on Friday.* |

2. **Hay** is used with both singular and plural nouns, and in both affirmative and negative contexts.

   **Hay** un bolígrafo, pero no **hay** lápices en la mesa.

3. **Hay** can be used with numbers or with indefinite articles (**un, una, unos, unas**), but it is never used with definite articles (**el, la, los, las**).

| | |
|---|---|
| ¡**Hay** tres profesores en la clase, pero sólo **hay** una estudiante! | ***There are*** *three professors in the class, but* ***there is*** *only one student!* |

4. With a plural noun or negative, typically no article is used with **hay** unless you are providing extra information.

| | |
|---|---|
| **Hay papeles** en la mesa. | ***There are papers*** *on the table.* |
| **No hay libros** en el escritorio. | ***There aren't (any) books*** *on the desk.* |
| **Hay quince personas** en la clase. | ***There are fifteen people*** *in the class.* |

BUT:

| | |
|---|---|
| **Hay unas personas interesantes** en la clase. | ***There are some interesting people*** *in the class.* |

### Cómo formarlo

**Hay** is an *invariable verb form* because it never changes to reflect number or person. That is why **hay** can be used with both singular and plural nouns.

# ACTIVIDADES

**9** **¿Sí o no?** Look at the form and then answer the questions using **hay** or **no hay.** Follow the model.

**Nombre:** Alicia Monteverde Salinas
**Dirección:** 1742 NE Cleary Street, Portland, OR 97208
**Número de teléfono:**
　　**casa:** _____　　**celular:** 971-555-2951　　**oficina:** 503-555-8820
**Contacto personal:** _____
**Dirección electrónica:** Alims@netista.org
**Referencia:** _____

© Cengage Learning 2013 is a sidebar rotated text
© Cengage Learning 2013

MODELOS　¿Hay... *un nombre?*
　　　　　*Sí, hay.*
　　　　　¿Hay... *un número de teléfono de la casa?*
　　　　　*No, no hay.*

**¿Hay...**

1. ...una dirección?
2. ...un número de teléfono de la oficina?
3. ...un número del celular?
4. ...un contacto personal?
5. ...una dirección electrónica?
6. ...una referencia?

**10** **Hay...** Say how many of the following things are in the places mentioned.

MODELO　ventana (5): salón de clase
　　　　*Hay cinco ventanas en el salón de clase.*

1. computadora (15): laboratorio
2. policía (2): calle
3. libro (5): escritorio
4. profesor (3): reunión
5. estudiante (40): cafetería
6. persona (20): fiesta
7. verbo (35): pizarra
8. celular (1): mochila

**11** **¿Cuántos (How many) hay?** In groups of four or five, find out how many of the following objects there are in your group.

MODELO　*Hay tres teléfonos celulares en el grupo.*

1. teléfonos celulares
2. cuadernos
3. diccionarios
4. computadoras portátiles
5. MP3 portátiles
6. ¿... ?

**12** **¿Hay o no hay...?** With a classmate, take turns asking and answering whether the items indicated are in the classroom.

**Objetos posibles:** una computadora, un escritorio, un libro, un mapa, una mesa, una mochila, una pizarra digital interactivo, una ventana, ¿... ?

# Sonrisas

© Cengage Learning 2013

**Comprensión** Answer the following questions about the cartoon.

1. Según (*According to*) Dieguito, ¿qué hay en su cuarto?
2. En realidad, ¿qué hay en el cuarto de Dieguito?
3. Según el papá de Dieguito, ¿qué hay en el jardín (*garden*)?
4. En realidad, ¿hay un elefante en el jardín?

**Gramática útil 4**

**Expressing possession, obligation, and age: Tener, tener que, tener + años**

**Tienes** el cellular de mi amigo Beto.

© Cengage Learning 2013

### Cómo usarlo

1. The verb **tener** means *to have*. It is used in Spanish to express possession and to give someone's age. You can also use it with **que** and another verb to say what you have to do: **Tengo que irme.** *(I have to go.)*

| | |
|---|---|
| **Tengo** dos teléfonos en casa. | *I **have** two telephones in my house.* |
| Elena **tiene** veinte años. ¿Cuántos años **tienen** Sergio y Dulce? | *Elena **is** twenty years old. How old **are** Sergio and Dulce?* |
| **Tengo que** irme porque **tengo** clase. | *I **have to** go because I **have** class.* |

2. When **tener** is used to express possession, the article is usually omitted, unless number is emphasized or you are referring to a specific object.

3. Note that where Spanish uses **tener... años** to express age, the English equivalent is *to be . . . years old.*

### Cómo formarlo

Remember, it's better to use the verb without a subject pronoun unless the subject is unclear or you want to emphasize it.

1. Here are the forms of the verb **tener** in the present indicative tense.

| tener *(to have)* | | | |
|---|---|---|---|
| yo | **tengo** | nosotros / nosotras | **tenemos** |
| tú | **tienes** | vosotros / vosotras | **tenéis** |
| Ud., él, ella | **tiene** | Uds., ellos, ellas | **tienen** |

In Spanish the word for birthday is **cumpleaños**, which literally means "completes (**cumple**) years (**años**)." Many Spanish speakers celebrate their saint's day (**el día de su santo**), which is the birthday of the saint whose name is the same as or similar to their own. For example: **El 19 de marzo es el día de San José.**

2. When talking about age, it's helpful to know the months of the year so that you can say when people's birthdays are celebrated.

**¿Cuándo es tu cumpleaños?** *When is your birthday?*

| | |
|---|---|
| enero | julio |
| febrero | agosto |
| marzo | septiembre |
| abril | octubre |
| mayo | noviembre |
| junio | diciembre |

3. When giving dates in Spanish, the day of the month comes first: **el quince de abril** = *April 15th*. When writing the date with numbers, the day always comes before the month: 15/4/10 = **el quince de abril de 2010**.

## ACTIVIDADES

**13** **¿Qué tienen?** Say what each person has or has to do.

MODELO  Yo *tengo* un cuaderno en el escritorio.

1. Yo _____ un celular en la mochila.
2. Nosotros _____ que leer el libro.
3. Ellos _____ unos apuntes en el cuaderno.
4. Tú _____ dos libros en la mochila.
5. El profesor _____ cinco lápices en el escritorio.
6. Ustedes _____ que escuchar el audio.

**14** **¿Cuántos años tienen?** Tell a friend the birthdays and ages of the following people.

MODELO  Arturo (28/3; 25 años)
   *El cumpleaños de Arturo es el veintiocho de marzo.*
      *Tiene veinticinco años.*

1. Martín (12/4; 21 años)
2. Sandra y Susana (14/7; 24 años)
3. mamá (16/6; 45 años)
4. papá (22/2; 47 años)
5. Gustavo (7/9; 17 años)
6. Irma y Daniel (19/1; 19 años)

> The number **veintiuno** shortens to **veintiún** when it's used with a noun: **veintiún años**.

**15** **La fiesta** Listen to the conversation between Marta and Juan. They are talking about the birthdays and ages of various friends. Write down the age and the birthday of each person.

Track 4

| | Edad | Cumpleaños |
|---|---|---|
| 1. Miguel | | |
| 2. Arturo | | |
| 3. Enrique | | |
| 4. Isabel | | |

**16** **Yo tengo...** With a classmate, take turns asking and telling which of the following objects you have and don't have with you today. Follow the model.

MODELO  Tú: *¿Tienes un libro?*
   Compañero(a): *Sí. Tengo tres libros.*

**Objetos posibles:** bolígrafo, celular, computadora portátil, cuaderno, diccionario, lápiz, marcador, mochila, ¿...?

# El español: ¡una lengua global!

## Información general ▶

- Spanish is the official language of 21 countries.
- With almost 500 million native and second-language speakers internationally, Spanish is one of the most widely spoken languages in the world.
- Spanish ranks second worldwide for number of native speakers, with 329 million. (Chinese is first, with 1.2 billion native speakers, and English is a close third, with 328 million speakers.)
- Spanish is spoken by 34.5 million people in the United States and by approximately 480,000 people in Canada. It is one of the most widely studied and fastest-growing languages in both countries.

| Top 5 languages on the Internet | Internet users by language | Internet users as percentage of total |
|---|---|---|
| English | 536,564,837 | 27.3% |
| Chinese | 444,948,013 | 22.6% |
| Spanish | 153,308,074 | 7.8% |
| Japanese | 99,143,700 | 5.0% |
| Portuguese | 82,548,200 | 4.2% |

Adapted from Top Ten Languages Used in the Web chart at http://www.internetworldstats.com/stats7.htm, Copyright © 2010, Miniwatts Marketing Group. All rights reserved worldwide.

Ryan McVay/Getty Images

# Vale saber...

- Spanish originated on the Iberian Peninsula as a descendant of Latin.
- King Alfonso X tried to standardize the language for official use in the 13th century in the Castile region of Spain.
- By 1492, when Christopher Columbus headed for the Western Hemisphere, Spanish had already become the spoken and written language that we would recognize today.
- Spanish was brought to the New World by explorers who colonized the new territories under the Spanish flag for the Spanish Empire. At its peak, *el Imperio español* was one of the largest empires in world history.
- Today, there are far more Spanish speakers in Latin America than there are in Spain.

Prisma Archivo/Alamy

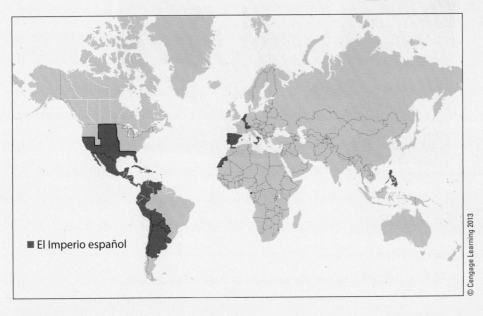

■ El Imperio español

© Cengage Learning 2013

# Idioma

- Spanish is referred to as either **español** or **castellano**.
- Like all languages, Spanish exhibits some regional variations, limited mainly to vocabulary and pronunciation. In spite of these variations, Spanish speakers from all over the world communicate without difficulty.
- Spanish and English share many cognates, due to the fact that many of their words have the same linguistic roots in Latin and Arabic.

| family | *familia* | computer | *computadora* |

## Profesiones

- Here are just a few of the professions where Spanish is in high demand in the United States:

| | |
|---|---|
| law | investment banking |
| medicine | sales and marketing |
| tourism | government |
| social sciences | human resources |
| education | interactive media |

Marty Lederhandler/AP Images

## >> En resumen

### La información general

1. In how many countries is Spanish the official language?
2. In what place does Spanish rank in terms of numbers of native speakers?
3. Where did Spanish originate?
4. Who tried to standardize Spanish in the 13th century?
5. What do English and Spanish have in common?

**Los países de habla hispana**  Did you place the countries in the correct areas? With a partner, check your list from **¿Qué sabes?** on page 7 against the list below to see how many you got right.

| África | Guinea Ecuatorial |
|---|---|
| El Caribe | Cuba, Puerto Rico*, República Dominicana |
| Centroamérica | Costa Rica, El Salvador, Guatemala, Honduras, Nicaragua, Panamá |
| Europa | España |
| Norteamérica | Canadá, Estados Unidos**, México |
| Sudamérica | Argentina, Bolivia, Chile, Colombia, Ecuador, Paraguay, Perú, Uruguay, Venezuela |

*Es un Estado Libre Asociado (Commonwealth), no un país independiente.
**Se habla español, pero el español no es la lengua oficial.

**Los beneficios de hablar el español**  With a partner, discuss your reasons for studying Spanish. What professional or personal benefits do you expect to get out of your study of this language? Do a search for key words such as "medical careers in Spanish" to find out why knowing Spanish will be useful to you in your career.

### ⊕ ¿QUIERES SABER MÁS?

Return to the chart that you started at the beginning of the chapter. Add all the information that you already know in the column **Lo que aprendí**. Then look at the column labeled **Lo que quiero aprender**. Are there some things that you still don't know? Pick one or two of these, or choose from the topics listed below, to investigate further online. You can also find more key words for different topics at **www.cengagebrain .com**. Be prepared to share this information with the class.

**Palabras clave: (Historia)** la Península Ibérica, la influencia árabe, el Nuevo Mundo, Cristóbal Colón **(Profesiones)** derecho, medicina, finanzas, tecnología, turismo, traducción **(Hispanos históricos célebres)** Alfonso X de Castilla y León, los Reyes Católicos.

⊕ **Tú en el mundo hispano**  To explore opportunities to use your Spanish to study, volunteer, or hold internships in any part of the Spanish-speaking world, follow the links at **www.cengagebrain.com**.

🎞 **Ritmos del mundo hispano**  Follow the links at **www.cengagebrain.com** to hear music from across the Spanish-speaking world.

# A leer

## ESTRATEGIA

### Identifying cognates to aid comprehension

You have already learned a number of *cognates*—words that look similar in both Spanish and English but are pronounced differently. Some cognates you have already learned are **regular, terrible,** and **teléfono**. Cognates help you get a general idea of content, even if you don't know a lot of words and grammar.

**¡OJO!** *False cognates* are words that look similar in English and Spanish but mean different things. For example, **dirección** usually means *address,* not *direction,* in English. If a word that looks like a cognate doesn't make sense, you may need to look it up in a dictionary to discover its true meaning.

**¡OJO!** (literally, "Eye!") is used in Spanish to direct a person's attention to something. It is similar to saying "Watch out!" or "Be careful!" in English.

---

**1** Look at the headline and the four sections of the following article. See if you can get the main idea of the article by relying on cognates and words you already know.

1. Put a check mark by the words that you already know in the title and the four bulleted sections.
2. Underline the cognates that appear in these sections. Can you guess their general meaning, based on context and where they appear in the sentence?

**2** Now read the article, concentrating on the cognates and words you already know. Then answer the following questions, based on what you have read.

1. Según (*According to*) el artículo, las personas que tienen una dirección electrónica con su nombre son…
   a. misteriosas     c. emocionales
   b. honestas     d. introvertidas

2. Las personas que son lógicas y poco emocionales tienen una dirección electrónica…
   a. con números     c. de fantasía
   b. con su nombre     d. descriptiva

3. Las personas que se describen (*describe themselves*) con su dirección electrónica son…
   a. un poco inocentes     c. agresivas
   b. aventureras     d. introvertidas

4. ¿Cuál es el nombre de fantasía que usan en el artículo?

5. En tu opinión, ¿es correcta o falsa la información sobre tu personalidad?

## LECTURA

# ¡Tu dirección electrónica revela tu personalidad!

¿Es simbólica la dirección electrónica que usas? Muchas personas creen[1] que no, pero en realidad, los "nombres de computadora" que usamos revelan información importante sobre nuestras características más secretas. ¿Revela todo[2] tu dirección electrónica? ¡Vamos a ver!

Escoge[3] el tipo de dirección electrónica más similar a la tuya[4]…

### Nombre

**ejemplo: lucidíaz@woohoo.net**
En este caso, la dirección electrónica puede[5] representar a una persona directa y honesta. Prefiere la realidad y es práctica y realista. No le interesa el misterio o la fantasía. Estas personas son muy aptas para los negocios[6] a causa de su estilo directo.

### Números

**ejemplo: 1078892@compluservicio.com**
Las personas con los números en las direcciones electrónicas no tienen mucho interés en las cortesías diarias o las interacciones sociales. ¡Prefieren el mundo[7] súper racional de los números y las matemáticas puras! Otra explicación es que prefieren ser anónimos —quieren[8] mantener su misterio con un nombre que revela muy poco[9]!

### Autodescripción

**ejemplo: románticoloco29@universidad.edu**
Las personas que se describen con la dirección electrónica necesitan comprensión y cariño[10]. Pueden ser amables, afectuosas y un poco ingenuas o inocentes. Pero, ¡cuidado[11]! ¡Estos nombres pueden ser totalmente falsos! Los nombres que indican que una persona es honesta o responsable pueden distorsionar la realidad completamente…

### Fantasía

**ejemplo: frodo4ever@ciberífico.net**
Por lo general, estas personas consideran el ciberespacio como una oportunidad para la reinvención personal. Prefieren identificarse como un personaje imaginario para participar en lo que es, para ellos, ¡un drama cibernético! Pueden ser aventureras, emocionales y extrovertidas. Estos nombres también pueden atraer a las personas introvertidas que tienen la fantasía de presentarse completamente diferente de su realidad diaria.

[1]think [2]everything [3]Choose [4]yours [5]can [6]business [7]world [8]they want to [9]very little [10]affection [11]careful

## >> Después de leer

**3** With a partner, try to invent as many names in each of the last two categories (**autodescripción** and **fantasía**) as you can. Use cognates from the reading when possible and be as creative as you can!

**4** Now take the list of e-mail names you created in **Activity 3** and add your own e-mail name to the list. (Or, if your e-mail name is simply your name or number, create a name that you would like to use.) Then, with your partner from **Activity 3,** form a group with two other pairs. Share your lists and see if you can guess each other's e-mail addresses.

All of the reading passages in *Cuadros* include translations of key (but not all) unknown words. Try to get the gist of the passage before you look for the definitions. Saving them as a last resort allows you to read the passage more quickly and to concentrate on getting the main idea.

# A escribir

As you use *Cuadros,* you will learn to write by using a *process* that moves from prewriting (identifying ideas and organizing them) through writing (creating a rough draft) and ends with revising (editing and commenting on writing). In each **A escribir** section, you will learn strategies that help you improve your techniques in each of the three phases of the writing process.

## ESTRATEGIA

### Prewriting—Identifying your target audience

Before you write, consider who will read your work. Your intended reader's identity is the crucial element that helps you establish the format, tone, and content of your written piece. Imagine you are writing two descriptions of the same event. How would your description vary if you were writing it for a close friend or for someone you have never met? Remembering your audience is the first step toward creating an effective written piece.

**1** You are going to write an e-mail to your new Spanish-speaking roommate whom you have not yet met. With a partner, create a list of the information you should include in your message and identify its tone.

**2** Taking your list of information from **Activity 1**, study the following partial model and see if you have included everything you need.

Para:                               Enviar
Sujeto:                          Adjuntar

B  *I*  U  T  ≡ ≡ ≡ ■

<nombre>,

Me llamo… . Soy tu nuevo(a) compañero(a) de cuarto. Vivo en… . (*Ask about him/her.*)

Aquí tienes mi dirección…, mi teléfono… y mi dirección electrónica…. (*Ask for his/her personal information.*)

Tengo un estéreo, un refrigerador y un televisor para el cuarto. ¿Qué tienes tú?

Bueno, es todo por ahora.

Tu nuevo(a) compañero(a) de cuarto,
<tu nombre>

© Cengage Learning 2013

# Composición

**3** Using the previous model, write a rough draft of your e-mail. Try to write freely without worrying too much about mistakes or misspellings. You will have an opportunity to revise your work later. Here are some additional words and phrases.

| | |
|---|---|
| **una cafetera** | *coffee maker* |
| **Es todo por ahora.** | *That's all for now.* |
| **un estéreo** | *stereo* |
| **una impresora** | *printer* |
| **una lámpara** | *lamp* |
| **un microondas** | *microwave oven* |
| **para el cuarto** | *for the room* |
| **un refrigerador** | *refrigerator* |
| **un televisor** | *television set* |

Yellow Dog Productions/Getty Images

# Después de escribir

**4** Exchange your rough draft with a partner. Read each other's work and comment on its content and structure. For example, put a check mark next to places where you would like more information. Put a star by the sentence you like best. Put a question mark where the meaning is not clear. Underline any places where you are not certain the spelling and grammar are correct.

**5** Now go back over your letter and revise it. Incorporate your partner's comments. Use the following checklist to check your final copy. Did you . . .

- make sure you included all the necessary information?
- match the tone of your writing to your audience?
- follow the model provided in **Activity 2**?
- check to make sure you used the correct forms of **ser** and **tener**?
- watch to make sure articles and nouns agree?
- look for misspellings?

# Vocabulario

## Para saludar  *How to greet*

**Hola.**  *Hello.*

**¿Qué tal?**  *How are things going?*

**¿Cómo estás (tú)?**  *How are you? (s. fam.)*

**¿Cómo está (usted)?**  *How are you? (s. form.)*

**¿Cómo están (ustedes)?**  *How are you? (pl.)*

**¿Cómo te va?**  *How's it going with you? (s. fam.)*

**¿Cómo le va?**  *How's it going with you? (s. form.)*

**¿Cómo les va?**  *How's it going with you? (pl.)*

**¿Qué hay de nuevo?**  *What's new?*

**Buenos días.**  *Good morning.*

**Buenas tardes.**  *Good afternoon.*

**Buenas noches.**  *Good night. Good evening.*

## Para responder  *How to respond*

**Bien, gracias.**  *Fine, thank you.*

**Bastante bien.**  *Quite well.*

**(No) Muy bien.**  *(Not) Very well.*

**Regular.**  *So-so.*

**¡Terrible! / ¡Fatal!**  *Terrible! / Awful!*

**No mucho.**  *Not much.*

**Nada.**  *Nothing.*

**¿Y tú?**  *And you? (s. fam.)*

**¿Y usted?**  *And you? (s. form.)*

## Para pedir y dar información personal  *Exchanging personal information*

**¿Cómo te llamas?**  *What's your name? (s. fam.)*

**¿Cómo se llama?**  *What's your name? (s. form.)*

**Me llamo...**  *My name is . . .*

**(Yo) soy...**  *I am . . .*

**¿Cuál es tu número de teléfono?**  *What's your phone number? (s. fam.)*

**¿Cuál es su número de teléfono?**  *What's your phone number? (s. form.)*

**Mi número de teléfono es el 3-71-28-12.**  *My phone number is 371-2812.*

**Es el 3-71-28-12.**  *It's 371-2812.*

**¿Dónde vives?**  *Where do you live? (s. fam.)*

**¿Dónde vive?**  *Where do you live? (s. form.)*

**Vivo en...**  *I live at . . .*

  **la avenida...**  *avenue . . .*

  **la calle...**  *street . . .*

  **el barrio... / la colonia...**  *neighborhood . . .*

**¿Cuál es tu dirección?**  *What's your address? (s. fam.)*

**¿Cuál es su dirección?**  *What's your address? (s. form.)*

**Mi dirección es...**  *My address is . . .*

**¿Cuál es tu dirección electrónica?**  *What's your e-mail address? (s. fam.)*

**¿Cuál es su dirección electrónica?**  *What's your e-mail address? (s. form.)*

**Aquí tienes mi dirección electrónica.**  *Here's my e-mail address. (s. form.)*

**Aquí tiene mi dirección electrónica.**  *Here's my e-mail address. (pl.) (s. form.)*

**arroba**  @

**punto com**  *.com*

## Para presentar a alguien  *Introducing someone*

**Soy...**  *I am . . .*

**Me llamo... / Mi nombre es...**  *My name is . . .*

**Quiero presentarte a...**  *I'd like to introduce you (s. fam.) to . . .*

**Quiero presentarle a...**  *I'd like to introduce you (s. form.) to . . .*

**Quiero presentarles a...**  *I'd like to introduce you (pl.) to . . .*

## Para responder  *How to respond*

**Mucho gusto.**  *My pleasure.*

**Mucho gusto en conocerte.**  *A pleasure to meet you.*

**Encantado(a).**  *Delighted to meet you.*

**Igualmente.**  *Likewise.*

**El gusto es mío.**  *The pleasure is mine.*

**Un placer.**  *My pleasure.*

## Para despedirse   *Saying goodbye*

**Adiós.** *Goodbye.*
**Hasta luego.** *See you later.*
**Hasta mañana.** *See you tomorrow.*
**Hasta pronto.** *See you soon.*

**Nos vemos.** *See you later.*
**Chau.** *Bye.*
**Bueno, tengo que irme.** *Well / OK, I have to go.*

## Para hablar por teléfono   *Talking on the telephone*

**Familiar**

—**¡Hola!** *Hello?*
—**Hola. ¿Qué estás haciendo?** *Hi. What are you doing?*
—**Nada, ¿y tú?** *Nothing, and you?*
—**¿Quieres hacer algo?** *Do you want to do something?*
—**Claro. ¿Nos vemos donde siempre?** *Sure. See you at the usual place?*
—**Está bien. Hasta luego.** *OK. See you later.*
—**Chau.** *Bye.*

**Formal**

—**¡Hola! / ¿Aló?** *Hello?*
—**Hola. ¿Puedo hablar con...?** *Hi, may I speak with . . . ?*
—**Sí. Aquí está.** *Yes. Here he/she is..*
—**Lo siento. No está.** *Sorry. He's/she's not here.*
—**Por favor, dígale que llamó (nombre).** *Please tell him/her that (name) called.*
  **Mi número es el...** *My number is . . .*
—**Muy bien.** *OK.*
—**Muchas gracias.** *Thank you very much.*
—**De nada. Adiós.** *You're welcome. Goodbye.*
—**Adiós.** *Goodbye.*

## ¿Cuándo es tu cumpleaños?   *When is your birthday?*

**enero** *January*
**febrero** *February*
**marzo** *March*
**abril** *April*
**mayo** *May*
**junio** *June*

**julio** *July*
**agosto** *August*
**septiembre** *September*
**octubre** *October*
**noviembre** *November*
**diciembre** *December*

## Palabras útiles   *Useful words*

**Títulos**
**don** *title of respect used with male first name*
**doña** *title of respect used with female first name*
**señor / Sr.** *Mr.*
**señora / Sra.** *Mrs., Ms.*
**señorita / Srta.** *Miss, Ms.*

**Los artículos definidos**
**el, la, los, las** *the*

**Los artículos indefinidos**
**un, una** *a*
**unos, unas** *some*

**Los pronombres personales**
**yo** *I*
**tú** *you (fam.)*
**usted (Ud.)** *you (form.)*

**él** *he*
**ella** *she*
**nosotros / nosotras** *we*
**vosotros / vosotras** *you (fam. pl.)*
**ustedes (Uds.)** *you (fam. or form. pl.)*
**ellos / ellas** *they*

**Los verbos**
**estar** *to be*
**hay** *there is, there are*
**ser** *to be*
**tener** *to have*
**tener... años** *to be . . . years old*
**tener que** *to have to (+ verb)*

**Expresiones**
**Tengo prisa.** *I'm in a hurry.*

# Repaso y preparación

Complete these activities to check your understanding of the new grammar points in **Chapter 1** before you move on to **Chapter 2**.

The answers to the activities in this section can be found in **Appendix B.**

## Nouns and articles (p. 18)

**1** For each blank, decide whether an article is needed. If it is, write the correct definite or indefinite article. If no article is needed, write X.

1. ¡Bienvenida a _____ Doctora Silvina Madrones! Ella es
2. _____ profesora de estadísticas y tiene su doctorado de
3. _____ Universidad Autónoma de México. Además (*Besides*) de ser
4. _____ profesora, es 5. _____ escritora y 6. _____ autora de
7. _____ libros de texto muy populares. Ella es 8. _____ adición
agradable a 9. _____ Departamentos de Matemáticas y Ciencias Sociales.

*Rudyanto Wijaya/iStockphoto*

## Subject pronouns and the present indicative of the verb **ser** (p. 22)

**2** For sentences 1–3, write in the missing subject pronouns. For sentences 4–6, write in the missing forms of the verb **ser** in the present indicative.

1. _____ eres dentista.
2. _____ somos profesores.
3. _____ soy veterinario.
4. Ella _____ taxista.
5. Uds. _____ arquitectos.
6. Nosotras _____ actrices.

## Hay + nouns (p. 25)

Remember to leave out the indefinite article with **no hay: Hay una silla, pero no hay escritorio.**

**3** Say whether the drawing shows the following items. If you see more than one of an item, say how many there are.

© Cengage Learning 2013

1. ¿una chica?
2. ¿un hombre?
3. ¿una mujer?
4. ¿un niño?
5. ¿una computadora?
6. ¿una mochila?
7. ¿una serpiente?
8. ¿un elefante?

**Tener, tener que, tener + años** (p. 28)

**4**   Complete each sentence with the correct present indicative form of **tener**.

1. Marcos, ¿_____ un bolígrafo?
2. Profesor Martín, ¿_____ la tarea?
3. Yo _____ tu dirección.
4. Nosotras _____ muchos amigos.
5. Ellos no _____ el libro.
6. Tú _____ las fotos.

**5**   Write forms of **tener que** to tell what the following people have to do.

1. Yo _____ presentarte a mis amigos.
2. ¡Ellos _____ conocerte!
3. Nosotros _____ entregar la tarea.
4. Él _____ contestar la pregunta.
5. Tú _____ escuchar el audio.
6. Ustedes _____ leer el capítulo.

**6**   Say how old each person is, based on the year he or she was born.

1. tú (1957)
2. ellos (2005)
3. usted (1962)
4. ella (1975)
5. yo (1992)
6. nosotros (1990)
7. ustedes (1983)
8. tú y yo (1995)

LWA/Dann Tardif/Getty Images

¿Cuántos años tiene?

## Preparación para el Capítulo 2

Starting in **Chapter 2,** the **Preparación** section provides review and practice of grammar topics presented in *previous* chapters. The objective of this section is to help you remember previously learned structures that will be useful when you learn new grammar topics in the next chapter. Because this is the first chapter, however, there is no previous grammar to review.

To prepare for **Chapter 2,** reread **Chapter 1: Gramática útil 1.**

## capítulo 2 | ¿Qué te gusta hacer?

# GUSTOS Y PREFERENCIAS

We express aspects of our personalities through our likes and dislikes. In this chapter, we explore the relationship between personalities and preferences.

**How do you think that the activities you like and dislike define who you are?**

## Communication

By the end of this chapter you will be able to

- express likes and dislikes
- compare yourself to other people and describe personality traits
- ask and answer questions
- talk about leisure-time activities
- indicate nationality

# Un viaje por las áreas hispanohablantes de Estados Unidos

Estos diez estados *(states)* tienen las poblaciones más grandes *(biggest)* de hispanohablantes de Estados Unidos. ¿Puedes *(Can you)* identificar los cinco estados con las poblaciones más grandes?

| Orden | Estado |
|---|---|
|  | Arizona |
|  | California |
|  | Colorado |
|  | Florida |
|  | Georgia |
|  | Illinois |
|  | Nueva Jersey |
|  | Nuevo México |
|  | Nueva York |
|  | Texas |

Some U.S. states have Spanish equivalents that are fairly common in speech, while others do not. *Cuadros* provides the Spanish state name only if it is frequently used by native speakers, e.g., Nueva York, Nuevo México. Otherwise, the English name is provided, e.g., Rhode Island, Massachusetts.

**¿Qué sabes?** Di si las siguientes oraciones son **C (ciertas)** o **F (falsas)**.

1. No hay ningún *(none)* estado del Medio Oeste *(Midwest)* en la tabla.
2. La mayoría *(Most)* de los estados con muchos hispanohablantes están en el Sur *(South)*, el Suroeste *(Southwest)* o el Oeste.
3. Los nombres de algunos *(some)* de los estados son de origen español.

**Lo que sé y lo que quiero aprender** Completa la tabla del **Apéndice A**. Escribe algunos datos que **ya sabes** sobre los hispanohablantes de Estados Unidos en la columna **Lo que sé** *(What I already know)*. Después, añade *(add)* algunos temas que **quieres aprender** a la columna **Lo que quiero aprender** *(What I want to learn)*. Guarda *(Save)* la tabla para usarla otra vez en la sección **¡Explora y exprésate!** en la página 71.

## Cultures

By the end of this chapter you will have explored

- world nationalities
- bilingual culture in the U.S. and Canada
- some statistics about Hispanics in the U.S.
- Hispanic groups in the U.S.: brief overview of their history and culture
- some famous U.S. Hispanics talking about themselves and their heritage

Globe Art: Adapted from Shutterstock/rtguest

## ¡Imagínate!

**▶ >>** ## Vocabulario útil 1

| | |
|---|---|
| **BETO:** | Autora14, **¿qué te gusta hacer** los domingos? |
| **DULCE:** | Los domingos generalmente **estudio** en la biblioteca. |
| **ANILÚ:** | ¡Qué aburrida! |
| **BETO:** | **¡Estudias!** |
| **ANILÚ:** | Dile que **bailas** y **cantas** y **escuchas** música. |
| **BETO:** | ¿No te gusta hacer otras cosas? |
| **DULCE:** | Pues sí. A veces mis amigos y yo **tomamos un refresco** en el Jazz Café o **alquilamos un video**. |

**>>** ### Las actividades *Activities*

**A ti, ¿qué te gusta hacer los fines de semana (los viernes, los sábados y los domingos)?**

*What do you like to do on the weekends (Fridays, Saturdays, and Sundays)?*

## ACTIVIDADES

**1** **Los verbos** What Spanish verbs do you associate with the following? Choose from the list. (Some items can have more than one answer.)

1. _____ los murales
2. _____ la música
3. _____ los deportes
4. _____ una presentación oral
5. _____ un instrumento musical
6. _____ la familia

a. preparar
b. pintar
c. tocar
d. visitar
e. escuchar
f. practicar
g. conversar
h. estudiar
i. mirar

**2** **Le gusta…** Your friends like to participate in certain activities. Say what they like to do, based on the information provided.

MODELOS   Ernestina: murales
*Le gusta pintar.*
Leo: orquesta de música clásica
*Le gusta tocar un instrumento musical.*

1. Neti: ballet
2. Antonio: himnos y ópera
3. Javier: paella y enchiladas
4. Clara: cámara
5. Ernesto: estéreo
6. Beti: programas de comedia, noticias
7. Susana: celular
8. Luis: páginas web

**3** **Mis actividades favoritas**

1. Make a list of five activities you like to do.

MODELO   *Me gusta patinar en el parque.*

2. Now ask three other students what their favorite activities are and record their responses.

MODELO   —*¿Qué te gusta hacer?*
—*Me gusta caminar.*
You write: *A Heather le gusta caminar.*

3. Compare responses to see who, if anyone, has similar favorite activities, and share this list with the class.

MODELO   *A Marta y a Juan les gusta sacar fotos.*

4. Make a list of the most frequent activities mentioned by your classmates. Write a short paragraph about what students like to do and what activities they don't like to do.

## ¡Fíjate!    "Spanglish": la mezcla de dos idiomas

With permission of Perseus Books

When two cultures are in close proximity, eventually their languages will influence each other. Because native speakers of Spanish and native speakers of English have lived side by side for hundreds of years in the United States, a new hybrid form of the two languages has begun to spring up in conversation on the street, in poetry and fiction, and even in the articles of academic linguistic journals.

Strict language purists, including parents who want their children to be fluent and literate in both languages, and intellectuals who view the mixing of languages as a degradation of the original languages, do not approve of the casual use of Spanglish among the newer generations of Latino Americans. Ilan Stavans, a Mexican native, award-winning essayist, and the Lewis-Sebring professor in Latin American and Latino Culture at Amherst College, illustrates this point in his book *Spanglish: The Making of a New American Language*:

> Asked by a reporter in 1985 for his opinion on el espanglés, . . . Octavio Paz, the Mexican author of *The Labyrinth of Solitude* (1950) and a recipient of the Nobel Prize for Literature, is said to have responded with a paradox: "ni es bueno ni es malo, sino abominable"—it is neither good nor bad but abominable. This wasn't an exceptional view: Paz was one of scores of intellectuals with a distaste for the bastard jargon, which, in his eyes, didn't have gravitas.

"Cover of Ballantine edition", copyright © 1993 by Ballantine, from DREAM IN CUBAN by Cristina Garcia. Used by permission of Ballantine, a division of Random House, Inc.

Spanglish is not easy to master. It takes a profound understanding of the nuances of both English and Spanish in order to syncopate the linguistic components of each and produce a comprehensible and communicative statement. Bilingual puns, bilingual wordplay, and bilingual sentence fusion can be found in the works of many Latino American writers such as Francisco Alarcón, Julia Álvarez, Sandra Cisneros, Cristina García, Tato Laviera, and Junot Díaz.

Even Stavans admits, "Over the years my admiration for Spanglish has grown exponentially. . . ," and he continues:

> And, atención, Spanglish isn't only a phenomenon that takes place en los Unaited Esteits: in some shape or form, with English as a merciless global force, it is spoken—and broken: no es solamente hablado sino quebrado—all across the Hispanic world, from Buenos Aires to Bogotá, from Barcelona to Santo Domingo.
> Beware: Se habla el espanglés everywhere these days!

### Práctica

1. How do you feel about the mixing of two languages? Can you find any other instances in the history of the world where this has occurred?
2. Do you know any bilingual speakers? Do you know of any books that use the fusion of Spanish and English in some form? Do some research in your community or on the web and try to find two or three examples of a bilingual statement that amuses you.

# Vocabulario útil 2

| | |
|---|---|
| SERGIO: | ¿Con quién hablas? |
| BETO: | No sé. Es una estudiante de la Universidad. Su nombre electrónico es Autora14. |
| SERGIO: | Dile que tienes un amigo muy **guapo**. |

## >> Características físicas *Physical traits*

Notice that you say **Tiene el pelo negro / rubio / castaño**, etc., but when someone is a redhead, you say **Es pelirrojo(a)**. You can also say **Es rubio(a)** to indicate that someone is a blond. **Es moreno(a)** may indicate that someone is either a brunette or has dark skin.

## ACTIVIDADES

**4** **Sergio, Beto, Anilú y Dulce** Complete the following descriptions of the video characters.

1. Sergio…
   a. es rubio.
   b. es muy, muy pequeño.
   c. es guapo.

2. Anilú…
   a. es pelirroja.
   b. tiene el pelo castaño.
   c. es gorda.

3. Beto…
   a. es viejo.
   b. es gordo.
   c. es delgado.

4. Dulce…
   a. tiene el pelo negro.
   b. tiene el pelo rubio.
   c. es baja.

**5** **Descripciones** Describe the people in the illustrations below. Use as many physical descriptions as you can.

1. Eduardo

2. el señor Bernal

3. Sofía

4. Roque

© Cengage Learning 2013

**6** **¿Cómo soy yo?** Describe yourself in a paragraph for your Internet blog. You can also include activities that you like to do. Read your description to your partner. Then have him or her read their description to you.

MODELO   *Soy alta y tengo el pelo negro. Me gusta tomar el sol y escuchar música.*

# ○ >> Vocabulario útil 3

ANILÚ: Y tú, Experto10, ¿qué te gusta hacer los domingos?

SERGIO: Autora14, soy un hombre **activo.** Bailo, canto, toco la guitarra, cocino…

BETO: ¡Sergio! **¡Mentiroso!** ¡No me gusta bailar, no me gusta cantar, no toco la guitarra y no cocino!

SERGIO: ¡Qué **aburrido** eres, hombre!

## >> Características de la personalidad *Personality traits*

| | | |
|---|---|---|
| aburrido(a) | divertido(a); interesante | *boring / fun; interesting* |
| activo(a) | perezoso(a) | *active / lazy* |
| antipático(a) | simpático(a) | *unpleasant / pleasant* |
| extrovertido(a) | introvertido(a); tímido(a) | *extroverted / introverted; timid, shy* |
| generoso(a) | egoísta | *generous / selfish, egotistic* |
| impaciente | paciente | *impatient / patient* |
| impulsivo(a) | cuidadoso(a) | *impulsive / cautious* |
| inteligente | tonto(a) | *intelligent / silly, stupid* |
| mentiroso(a) | sincero(a) | *liar / sincere* |
| responsable | irresponsable | *responsible / irresponsible* |
| serio(a) | cómico(a) | *serious / funny* |
| trabajador(a) | perezoso(a) | *hard-working / lazy* |

## ACTIVIDADES

**7** **Diferentes** You and a partner have differing opinions of the same person. Your partner will say that this imaginary person is a certain way, and you will counter by saying they are just the opposite. Take turns describing several imaginary people this way. Follow the model.

MODELO Tú: *Arturo es activo.*

Compañero(a): *¡No! Arturo es perezoso.*

Compañero(a): *Carmela es impulsiva.*

Tú: *¡No! Carmela es cuidadosa.*

© Cengage Learning 2013

**8** **¿Cómo son?** Benjamín describes himself and several of his friends and relatives. Which adjective best describes each person?

1. No me gusta mirar televisión. Prefiero practicar deportes o levantar pesas.
   a. serio  b. activo  c. impulsivo

2. A mi amiga Marta le gusta ayudar *(to help)* a sus amigos.
   a. antipática  b. mentirosa  c. generosa

3. Mi profesora es una maestra muy buena. Explica la lección y repite todas las instrucciones.
   a. paciente  b. impaciente  c. interesante

4. Mi amigo Joaquín tiene una imaginación muy buena. Le gusta inventar historias falsas.
   a. tímido  b. tonto  c. mentiroso

5. Mi amigo Alberto habla y habla y habla… ¡pero no es muy interesante!
   a. aburrido  b. serio  c. divertido

6. Mi amiga Linda tiene muchas ideas buenas sobre qué hacer los fines de semana. Además es una persona muy cómica.
   a. inteligente  b. tonta  c. divertida

**9** **La clase de psicología** What personality traits does it take to succeed in various professions? Choose characteristics on the right that you think best fit the professions on the left. Follow the model.

MODELO  *Los políticos tienen que ser honestos,…*

| Profesiones | Características | |
| --- | --- | --- |
| los políticos | sistemáticos | serios |
| los artistas | deshonestos | estudiosos |
| los criminales | honestos | sinceros |
| los actores | inteligentes | pacientes |
| los científicos | creativos | talentosos |
| los doctores | simpáticos | impulsivos |
| los policías | extrovertidos | egoístas |
| los estudiantes | trabajadores | mentirosos |
| | curiosos | cuidadosos |
| | temperamentales | ¿…? |
| | responsables | |

Notice that you use the **-a** form of all the adjectives in this activity because the adjectives modify the feminine noun **persona**. You will learn more about adjective endings later in this chapter.

**10** **Mis amigos** Describe two people from your family to your partner. Provide both physical and personality traits in your descriptions. Then have your partner describe two people from his or her family.

MODELO  —*Es una persona alta y delgada. Tiene el pelo castaño. También (Also) es una persona cómica y divertida…*

# A ver

**Antes de ver** Review these key words and phrases used in the video.

| | |
|---|---|
| **apagar** | *to turn off* |
| **Dile que...** | *Tell him/her that . . .* |
| **No sé.** | *I don't know.* |

## ESTRATEGIA

### Using questions as an advance organizer

One way to prepare yourself to watch a video segment is to familiarize yourself with the questions you will answer after viewing. Look at the questions in **Después de ver 1**. Before you watch the video, use these questions to create a short list of the information you need to find. Example: **la dirección electrónica de Beto, la dirección electrónica de Dulce, el nombre del amigo de Beto**, etc.

© Cengage Learning 2013

**Ver** Now watch the video segment as many times as needed to find the information in your list.

**Después de ver 1** Answer (in Spanish) the following questions about the video.

1. ¿Cuál es la dirección electrónica de Beto? ¿Y la de Dulce?
2. ¿Cómo se llama el amigo de Beto? ¿Y la amiga de Dulce?
3. ¿Cuáles son las actividades preferidas de Dulce?
4. Según *(According to)* Sergio, ¿cuáles son las actividades preferidas de Experto10?

**Después de ver 2** Now say whether the following statements about the video segment are true **(cierto)** or false **(falso)**.

1. Según Anilú, Dulce es una persona muy aburrida.
2. Sergio es una persona muy sincero.
3. Dulce generalmente estudia en casa los domingos.
4. A Beto le gusta bailar, cantar y tocar la guitarra.
5. Según Anilú, un hombre que cocina y canta y baila es el hombre ideal.
6. Sergio apaga la computadora porque Anilú quiere *(wants)* su número de teléfono.

## ● >> Voces del mundo hispano

© Cengage Learning 2013

In this video segment, the speakers say where their families are from and talk about their personalities and pastimes. First read the statements below. Then watch the video as many times as needed to say whether the statements are true **(cierto)** or false **(falso)**.

1. La mamá de Nicole es de Guatemala.
2. El papá de Liana es de la República Dominicana.
3. Según Inés, ella es activa, extrovertida y feliz *(happy)*.
4. Según los amigos y familiares de Inés, ella es alegre, cuidadosa y tímida.
5. A Constanza le gusta caminar.
6. A Jessica y Ana María les gusta leer.

## ◀)) >> Voces de Estados Unidos

Track 5

### Isabel Valdés, ejecutiva y autora

Courtesy of Isabel Valdéz

❝ **Hispanics are becoming more and more entrenched in American society. Their participation is reflected in the growing number of Hispanic associations, libraries, research centers, and businesses throughout the United States. Furthermore, Hispanics are increasingly active in government at the federal, state, county, and city levels. They have also made significant contributions to American art, theater, literature, film, music, and sports.** ❞

Isabel Valdés es responsable de muchas campañas publicitarias en español en Estados Unidos y Latinoamérica. Sus clientes incluyen firmas tales como PepsiCO y Frito-Lay. Esta chilena-estadounidense es autora de cuatro libros sobre el mercado *(market)* hispano en Estados Unidos. Es además la directora de IVC, una empresa *(business)* consultora que ofrece servicios estratégicos a compañías para alcanzar *(to reach)* a consumidores multiculturales en EEUU y los mercados globales. Valdés dedica mucho tiempo al trabajo voluntario para ayudar a *(help)* varias organizaciones, entre ellas *The Nacional Council of La Raza* y *The Latino Community Foundation.*

**¿Y tú?** What are your interests? Do you identify yourself as part of a market segment? If so, which one(s)?

# ¡Prepárate!

## >> Gramática útil 1

### Describing what you do or are doing:
### The present indicative of regular -ar verbs

© Cengage Learning 2013

**Bailo, canto, toco** la guitarra, **cocino**...

The use of the present tense to talk about future plans is used more in some regions of the Spanish-speaking world than others.

### Cómo usarlo

In English we use a variety of structures to express different present-tense concepts. In Spanish many of these are communicated with the same grammatical form. The present indicative tense in Spanish can be used. . .

- to describe routine actions:

    **¡Estudias** mucho!                          *You study a lot!*

- to say what you are doing now:

    **Estudias** matemáticas hoy.          *You are studying mathematics today.*

- to ask questions about present events:

    ¿**Estudias** con Enrique todas          *Do you study with Enrique las semanas?                                    every week?*

- to indicate plans in the immediate future:

    **Estudias** con Enrique el viernes, ¿no?  *You're going to study with Enrique on Friday, right?*

Notice how the same form in Spanish, **estudias**, can be translated four different ways in English.

### Cómo formarlo

## LO BÁSICO

- An *infinitive* is a verb before it has been conjugated to reflect person and tense. **Bailar** *(To dance)* is an infinitive.
- A *verb stem* is what is left after you remove the **-ar, -er,** or **-ir** ending from the infinitive. **Bail-** is the verb stem of **bailar**.
- A conjugated verb is a verb whose endings reflect person *(I, you, he/she, we, you, they)* and tense *(present, past, future, etc.)*. **Bailas** *(You dance)* is a conjugated verb (person: *you familiar singular;* tense: *present*).

1. Spanish infinitives end in **-ar**, **-er**, or **-ir**. For now, you will learn to form the present indicative tense of verbs ending in **-ar**. To form the present indicative tense of a regular **-ar** verb, simply remove the **-ar** and add the following endings.

| **bailar** *(to dance)* | | | |
|---|---|---|---|
| yo | bail**o** | nosotros / nosotras | bail**amos** |
| tú | bail**as** | vosotros / vosotras | bail**áis** |
| Ud., él, ella | bail**a** | Uds., ellos, ellas | bail**an** |

2. Remember, as you learned in **Chapter 1**, you do not need to use the subject pronouns (**yo, tú, él, ella**, etc.) unless the meaning is not clear from the context of the sentence, or you wish to clarify, add emphasis, or make a contrast.

**Camino** en el parque todos los días.     *I **walk** in the park every day.*
But:
**Yo camino** en el parque, pero Lidia     *I **walk** in the park, but Lidia*
   camina en el gimnasio.     *walks in the gymnasium.*

3. You may use certain conjugated present-tense verbs with infinitives. However, do not use two conjugated verbs together unless they are separated by a comma or the words **y** *(and)*, **pero** *(but)*, or **o** *(or)*.

**Necesitamos trabajar** el viernes.     *We **have to work** on Friday.*
Los sábados, **trabajo, practico**     *On Saturdays **I work, play***
   deportes y **visito** a amigos.     *sports, and **visit** friends.*
Los domingos, **dejo de trabajar**.     *On Sundays **I stop working**.*
   ¡**Bailo, canto** o **escucho** música!     *I **dance, sing**, or **listen** to music!*

> Notice that in this usage, Spanish infinitives are often translated into English as *-ing* forms: *I stop working.*

4. To say what you don't do or aren't planning to do, use **no** before the conjugated verb.

¡**No estudio** los fines de semana!     *I **don't study** on the weekends!*

5. Add question marks to turn a present-tense sentence into a *yes/no* question.

¿**No estudias** los fines de semana?     ***Don't you study** on the weekends?*
¿**Tienes que estudiar** este fin     ***Do you have to study** this*
   de semana?     *weekend?*

6. Other regular **-ar** verbs:

| | | | |
|---|---|---|---|
| **apagar** | *to turn off* | **llegar** | *to arrive* |
| **acabar de** (+ infinitive) | *to have just done something* | **necesitar** (+ infinitive) | *to need (to do something)* |
| **buscar** | *to look for* | **pasar** | *to pass (by); to happen* |
| **cenar** | *to eat dinner* | **preparar** | *to prepare* |
| **comprar** | *to buy* | **regresar** | *to return* |
| **dejar de** (+ infinitive) | *to leave; to stop (doing something)* | **usar** | *to use* |
| **descansar** | *to rest* | **viajar** | *to travel* |
| **llamar** | *to call* | | |

> The expression **acabar de** can be used with any infinitive to say what activity you and others have just completed: **Acabo de llegar.** *(I just arrived.)* **Acabamos de cenar.** *(We just ate dinner.)*

**1  Beto**  Beto describes his day in an e-mail to a friend. Complete his description with the correct form of the verb in parentheses.

A las siete de la mañana, (1. caminar) a la universidad. (2. Llegar) a las siete y media. Si tengo tiempo, (3. estudiar) un poco antes de las clases.

A veces (4. necesitar) comprar unos libros. (5. Comprar) los libros en la librería. Generalmente (6. cenar) en la cafetería. Después (7. pasar) por un café y (8. tomar) un café o un té. (9. Regresar) al dormitorio a las siete de la noche. (10. Hablar) con mis amigos por teléfono o (11. navegar) por Internet.

**2  Anilú y Sergio**  Anilú and Sergio do different things. Say what each of them does. Use **pero** *(but)* to contrast what they do. Follow the model.

MODELO    Anilú: cenar en un restaurante; Sergio: cocinar en casa
                *Anilú cena en un restaurante, pero Sergio cocina en casa.*

1.  Anilú: bailar; Sergio: levantar pesas
2.  Anilú: trabajar; Sergio: descansar
3.  Anilú: tomar un refresco; Sergio: tomar café
4.  Anilú: estudiar; Sergio: navegar por Internet
5.  Anilú: alquilar un video; Sergio: mirar televisión
6.  Anilú: escuchar música rap; Sergio: tocar la guitarra

**3  Tú**  Interview a partner about his or her activities.

MODELO    estudiar en la biblioteca
                Tú: *¿Estudias en la biblioteca?*
                Compañero(a): *Estudio en la biblioteca.*

1.  caminar a la universidad
2.  tocar la guitarra
3.  visitar mucho a la familia
4.  trabajar los fines de semana
5.  cenar en la cafetería
6.  necesitar una computadora

**4  Ellos y nosotros**  Work in pairs to compare the activities of you and your friends (**nosotros**) and someone else's friends (**ellos**).

MODELO    estudiar
                *Nosotros estudiamos en la biblioteca. Ellos estudian en casa.*

1.  estudiar
2.  cenar
3.  trabajar
4.  visitar a la familia
5.  necesitar
6.  llegar a la universidad
7.  navegar por Internet
8.  ¿…?

**5** **Los fines de semana** What do you generally do on the weekends? First, make a chart like the one below and fill in the **Yo** column. Compare your list with those of two classmates. Then write a paragraph comparing your typical weekend to theirs. (**¡OJO!: por la mañana / tarde / noche** = *in the morning / afternoon / night*)

| ¿Cuándo? | Yo | Amigo(a) #1 | Amigo(a) #2 |
|---|---|---|---|
| viernes por la noche: | Descanso en casa. | | |
| sábado por la mañana: | | | |
| sábado por la tarde: | | | |
| sábado por la noche: | | | |
| domingo por la mañana: | | | |
| domingo por la tarde: | | | |
| domingo por la noche: | | | |

MODELO  *Los viernes por la noche generalmente descanso en casa.*
*Mi amigo Eduardo generalmente…*

**6** **¿Quién?** You work at a dating service and you have to decide who to introduce to whom. You have some descriptions in writing and some on audio. First read the following profiles. Then listen to the audio descriptions. For each description you hear, write the person's name next to the profile below that is most compatible with that person.

Track 6

**Perfiles:** Andrés, Marta, Jorge, Ángela, Rudy, Sara

**Rosa:** Me gusta escuchar música de todo tipo. ¡Soy muy divertida!
Sugerencia para Rosa: ———

**Isidro:** Levanto pesas tres veces por semana. Soy muy atlético.
Sugerencia para Isidro: ———

**Roberta:** Me gusta mirar películas. No practico deportes.
Sugerencia para Roberta: ———

**Carmen:** Uso Internet mucho en mis estudios. Soy introvertida.
Sugerencia para Carmen: ———

**José Luis:** Estudio mucho. Soy un poco serio.
Sugerencia para José Luis: ———

**Antonio:** Todos los días hablo por teléfono con mis amigos. Mis amigos son muy divertidos.
Sugerencia para Antonio: ———

Now use the information above to find the best match for you and your classmates, based on the information you provided in **Activity 5.**

MODELO  *Antonio es la persona más compatible con* (with) *Katie.*

### Saying what you and others like to do: **Gustar** + infinitive

**Cómo usarlo**

Un hombre que cocina...
y también ¡**le gusta bailar**
y **cantar**!

The Spanish verb **gustar** can be used with an infinitive to say what you and your friends like to do. Note that **gustar**, although often translated as *to like*, is really more similar to the English *to please*. **Gustar** is always used with pronouns that indicate *who is pleased* by the activity mentioned.

—**Me gusta bailar** salsa.

> *I like to dance salsa.*
> *(Dancing salsa pleases me.)*

—¿**Te gusta bailar** también?

> *Do you like to dance, too?*
> *(Does dancing please you, too?)*

—No, pero a **Luis le gusta** mucho.

> *No, but **Luis likes it** a lot. (No, but it pleases Luis a lot.)*

**Cómo formarlo**

## LO BÁSICO

The pronouns used with **gustar** are indirect object pronouns. They show the person who is being pleased or who likes something. You will learn more about them in **Chapter 8**.

1. When **gustar** is used with one or more infinitives, it is always used in its third-person singular form **gusta**. Sentences with **gusta** + *infinitive* can take the form of statements or questions without a change in word order.

   —**Nos gusta cocinar** y **cenar** en restaurantes.

   > *We like to cook and to eat dinner in restaurants.*

   —¿**Te gusta cocinar** también?

   > *Do you like to cook also?*

¡**OJO**! Do not confuse **me, te, le, nos, os**, and **les** with the subject pronouns **yo, tú, él, ella, Ud., nosotros, vosotros, ellos, ellas**, and **Uds.** that you have already learned.

2. **Gusta** + *infinitive* is used with the following pronouns.

| gusta + *infinitive* | |
|---|---|
| **Me** gusta cantar. *I like to sing.* | **Nos** gusta cantar. *We like to sing.* |
| **Te** gusta cantar. *You like to sing.* | **Os** gusta cantar. *You (fam. pl.) like to sing.* |
| **Le** gusta cantar. *You (form.) / He / She like (s) to sing.* | **Les** gusta cantar. *You (pl.) / They like to sing.* |

3. When you use **gusta**, you can also use **a** + *person* to emphasize or clarify *who* it is who likes the activity mentioned. Clarification is particularly important with **le** and **les,** because they can refer to several people.

| | |
|---|---|
| **Le gusta** navegar por Internet. | *He/She likes to browse the Internet. (Who does?)* |
| **A Beto / A él le gusta** navegar por Internet. | *Beto / He likes to browse the Internet.* |
| **A ellos les gusta** cantar. | *They like to sing.* |
| **A nosotros nos gusta** conversar. | *We like to talk.* |
| **A Sergio y a Anilú les gusta** bailar. | *Sergio and Anilú like to dance.* |

4. If you want to emphasize or clarify what you or a close friend like, use **a mí** (with **me gusta**) and **a ti** (with **te gusta**).

| | |
|---|---|
| **A mí me gusta** alquilar películas, pero **a ti te gusta** mirar televisión. | *I like to rent movies, but **you like** to watch television.* |

> Notice that **mí** has an accent, but **ti** does not.

5. To create negative sentences with **gusta** + *infinitive*, place **no** before the *pronoun* + **gusta**.

| | |
|---|---|
| **No nos gusta trabajar.** | *We don't like to work.* |
| A Roberto **no le gusta cocinar**. | *Roberto **doesn't like to cook**.* |

6. To express agreement with someone's opinion, use **también**. If you want to disagree, use **no** or **tampoco**. If you want to ask a friend if they like an activity you've already mentioned, ask **¿Y a ti?**

| | |
|---|---|
| —¿Te gusta cocinar? | *Do you like to cook?* |
| —**A mí, no.** No me gusta. Me gusta comer en restaurantes. **¿Y a ti?** | *No, not me. I don't like it. I like to eat in restaurants. **And you?*** |
| —**A mí también.** Pero no me gusta comer en restaurantes elegantes. | *Me too. But I don't like to eat in fancy restaurants.* |
| —**¡A mí tampoco!** | *Me neither!* |

A mí me gusta sacar fotos.

Konstantin Sutyagin/Shutterstock

**7** **Atleta 23** Can you tell what the following people like to do, based on their online names? Pick their preferred activities from the column to the right.

MODELO   Cantante29
   *A Cantante29 le gusta cantar.*

1. Pianista18
2. Atleta23
3. Artista12
4. Estudiante31
5. Fotógrafo11
6. Cocinero13
7. Bailarina39

estudiar
cocinar
cantar
tocar el piano
sacar fotos
bailar
practicar deportes
pintar

**8** **En el parque** With a partner, describe what everyone in the illustration likes to do.

Melinda y Celia

Miguel y Natalia

David

Héctor

Ana

Elena y Francisco

Carlos

© Cengage Learning 2013

◀)) **9** **Les gusta** Susana and Alberto like to participate in certain activities
Track 7 together, but prefer to do other things alone. First listen to what they say and
decide who likes to do the activity mentioned. After you listen, use the verbs
indicated to create a sentence saying who likes to do what. Follow the models.

MODELOS  *(A Susana y a Alberto) Les gusta bailar.*

|  | Susana | Alberto | Susana y Alberto |
|---|---|---|---|
| bailar |  |  | x |

*(A Susana) Le gusta caminar en el parque.*

|  | Susana | Alberto | Susana y Alberto |
|---|---|---|---|
| caminar en el parque | x |  |  |

|  | Susana | Alberto | Susana y Alberto |
|---|---|---|---|
| 1. hablar por teléfono |  |  |  |
| 2. cocinar comida mexicana |  |  |  |
| 3. sacar fotos |  |  |  |
| 4. navegar por Internet |  |  |  |
| 5. tocar la guitarra |  |  |  |

**10** **El estudiante hispanohablante** A new Spanish-speaking student is
arriving at your dorm today. You want to let him know what activities you and
your friends like to do so he can think about which activities he'd like to do
with you. Write a note to post on your door that tells him what you and your
friends typically like to do and where, so that when he arrives, he can decide
what he wants to do with you.

1. First fill out the following chart to help you organize the information. Here
   are some possible locations: **el parque, el gimnasio, el restaurante, la
   cafetería, la residencia estudiantil, la biblioteca, la discoteca, el
   café, la oficina**.

| Me gusta... | Nos gusta... | ¿Dónde? |
|---|---|---|
|  |  |  |
|  |  |  |

2. Once you complete the chart, use the information to write a note to
   welcome the new student, telling what you and your friends like to do and
   where, so that he can make plans to join you or not.

# Gramática útil 3

### Describing yourself and others: Adjective agreement

**Cómo usarlo**

Creative Study Gat®. "Se busca" advertisement for www.bitsandcream.com. Used with permission from Gat Publicidad.

Find at least three adjectives in this advertisement from a Spanish magazine. What nouns do they modify?

As you learned in **Chapter 1,** Spanish nouns must agree with definite and indefinite articles in both gender and number. This agreement is also necessary when using Spanish adjectives. Their endings change to reflect the number and gender of the nouns they modify.

| | |
|---|---|
| Anilú es **delgada**. | *Anilú is **thin**.* |
| Sergio y Beto son **inteligentes**. | *Sergio and Beto are **intelligent**.* |
| Sergio es un hombre **alto**. | *Sergio is a **tall** man.* |
| Dulce y Anilú son mujeres **jóvenes**. | *Dulce and Anilú are **young** women.* |

Notice that in these cases the adjectives go *after* the noun, rather than before, as in English.

**Cómo formarlo**

## LO BÁSICO

A *descriptive adjective* is a word that describes a noun. It answers the question *What is . . . like?*

*To modify* is to limit or qualify the meaning of another word. A descriptive adjective *modifies* a noun by specifying characteristics that apply to that noun: **un estudiante** vs. **un estudiante inteligente**.

1. **Gender**: If an adjective is used to modify a masculine noun, the adjective must have a masculine ending. If it is used to modify a feminine noun, it must have a feminine ending.

   - The masculine ending for adjectives ending in **-o** is the **o** form.
   - The feminine ending for adjectives ending in **-o** is the **a** form.
   - Adjectives ending in **-e** or most consonants don't change to reflect gender.
   - Adjectives ending in **-or** add **a** to the ending for the feminine form.

| Un professor | Una profesora |
|---|---|
| simpátic**o** | simpátic**a** |
| interesant**e** | interesant**e** |
| trabajad**or** | trabajad**ora** |

2. **Number**: If an adjective is used to modify a plural noun or more than one noun, it must be used in its plural form.

   - To create the plural of an adjective ending in a vowel, add **s**.
   - To create the plural of an adjective ending in a consonant, add **es**.
   - To create the plural of an adjective ending in **-or**, add **es** to the masculine form and **as** to the feminine form.
   - To create the plural of an adjective ending in **-z**, change the **z** to **c** and add **es**.

| El profesor | Los profesores | Las profesoras |
|---|---|---|
| simpático | simpático**s** | simpática**s** |
| interesante | interesante**s** | interesante**s** |
| trabajador | trabajador**es** | trabajador**as** |
| feli**z** | feli**ces** | feli**ces** |

3. As with articles and subject pronouns, adjectives that apply to mixed groups of males and females typically use the masculine form.

4. Most descriptive adjectives are used *after* the noun, rather than before.

5. If you want to use more than one adjective, you can use **y** *(and)* or **o** *(or)*.

   El estudiante es simpático **y** trabajador.
   ¿Es el profesor alto **o** bajo?
   Mis amigos son activos, generosos **y** cómicos.
   ¿Son ellas extrovertidas **o** introvertidas?

   - If **y** appears before a word that begins with an **i**, it changes to **e**.
     La instructora es divertida **e** interesante.
   - If **o** appears before a word that begins with an **o**, it changes to **u**.
     Hay siete **u** ocho estudiantes buenos en la clase.

Numbers do not change to match the number or gender of the nouns they describe. They go *before* the noun, rather than after.

Note that Spanish does not use a serial comma, as English does optionally. In the following English sentence, the comma after *generous* can be kept or omitted: *My friends are active, generous, and funny.* In Spanish, you do not use a comma after **generosos**: **Mis amigos son activos, generosos y cómicos.**

Remember that Puerto Ricans are U.S. citizens.

**6.** Adjectives of nationality follow slightly different rules. These adjectives add **a / as** feminine endings for nationalities whose names end in **-l, -s,** and **-n.** See the nationalities in the following group for examples. Adjectives of nationality are always used after the noun.

| Nacionalidades | | |
|---|---|---|
| **África** | | |
| **ecuatoguineano(a)** Guinea Ecuatorial | | |
| **Asia** | | |
| **chino(a)** China | **indio(a)** India | |
| **coreano(a)** Corea | **japonés, japonesa** Japón | |
| **Australia** | | |
| **australiano(a)** Australia | | |
| **Centroamérica y el Caribe** | | |
| **costarricense** Costa Rica | **guatemalteco(a)** Guatemala | **panameño(a)** Panamá |
| **cubano(a)** Cuba | **hondureño(a)** Honduras | **puertorriqueño(a)** Puerto Rico |
| **dominicano(a)** República Dominicana | **nicaragüense** Nicaragua | **salvadoreño(a)** El Salvador |
| **Europa** | | |
| **alemán, alemana** Alemania | **francés, francesa** Francia | **italiano(a)** Italia |
| **español, española** España | **inglés, inglesa** Inglaterra | **portugués, portuguesa** Portugal |
| **Norteamérica** | | |
| **canadiense** Canadá | **estadounidense** Estados Unidos | **mexicano(a)** México |
| **Sudamérica** | | |
| **argentino(a)** Argentina | **colombiano(a)** Colombia | **peruano(a)** Perú |
| **boliviano(a)** Bolivia | **ecuatoriano(a)** Ecuador | **uruguayo(a)** Uruguay |
| **chileno(a)** Chile | **paraguayo(a)** Paraguay | **venezolano(a)** Venezuela |

**Estados Unidos** is often abbreviated as **EEUU** or **EE.UU.** in Spanish. Some native speakers do not use the article **los** with **EEUU: en Estados Unidos** or **en EEUU.**

Notice the umlaut on the **ü** in **nicaragüense.** It is called a **diéresis** in Spanish. The **diéresis** is placed on the **u** in the syllables **gue** and **gui** to indicate that the **u** needs to be pronounced. Compare: **bilingüe, pingüino** and **guerra, Guillermo.**

**7.** Several adjectives in Spanish may be used *before* or *after* the noun they modify. Three common adjectives of this type are **bueno** *(good)*, **malo** *(bad)*, and **grande** *(big, large)*. When **bueno** and **malo** are used before a singular masculine noun, they have a special shortened form. Whenever **grande** is used before any singular masculine or feminine noun, its shortened form **gran** is used. Note that **grande** has different meanings when used *before* the noun *(great, famous)* and *after* the noun *(big, large)*.

| | | |
|---|---|---|
| un estudiante bueno | BUT: | un **buen** estudiante |
| una estudiante buena | | una buena estudiante |
| un día malo | BUT: | un **mal** día |
| una semana mala | | una mala semana |
| un hotel grande | BUT: | un **gran** hotel |
| una universidad grande | BUT: | una **gran** universidad |

**11** **El profesor y la profesora** Say whether the description refers to **la profesora, el profesor**, or if it could refer to both of them.

MODELO   Es trabajadora.
   *la profesora*

1. Es serio.
2. Es activo.
3. Es extrovertida.
4. Es responsable.
5. Es inteligente.

6. Es cuidadosa.
7. Es paciente.
8. Es interesante.
9. Es sincera.
10. Es generoso.

**12** **Marcos y María** Marcos and María are two of your best friends. They are not at all similar. Describe what they are like. Follow the model.

MODELO   Marcos es divertido.
   *María no es divertida. Es aburrida.*

1. Marcos es paciente.
2. María es responsable.
3. Marcos es extrovertido.
4. María es perezosa.

5. Marcos es sincero.
6. María es antipática.
7. Marcos es rubio.
8. María es delgada.

**13** **También** Your partner tells you that a person you both know has a certain personality or physical trait. Say that two of your friends are just like that person.

MODELO   Compañero(a): *Rocío es alta.*
   Tú: *Tomás y Marcelo también son altos.*

Rocío

1. Gerardo

2. Ángela

3. Miguel

4. Carmela

5. Pablo

6. Jimena

© Cengage Learning 2013

**†† 14 Las nacionalidades** With your partner, take turns asking the nationalities of the following people. Then mention another person of the same nationality.

MODELO   Orlando Bloom (Inglaterra)
           Tú: *¿De qué nacionalidad es Orlando Bloom?*
           Compañero(a): *Es inglés.*
           Tú: *¿De veras? Robert Pattinson es inglés también.*

1. Penélope Cruz y Rafael Nadal (España)
2. Manny Ramírez (República Dominicana)
3. Sonia Sotomayor (Puerto Rico)
4. Audrey Tautou (Francia)
5. Diego Luna y Gael García Bernal (México)
6. Gabriel García Márquez (Colombia)
7. Rigoberta Menchú (Guatemala)
8. Venus y Serena Williams (Estados Unidos)
9. Celia Cruz y Fidel Castro (Cuba)

**††† 15 Personas famosas** In groups of four or five, each person takes a turn describing a famous person. The rest of the group tries to guess who is being described.

**Palabras útiles:** actor (actriz), atleta, cantante, músico(a), político(a)

MODELO   Tú: *Es actriz. Es estadounidense. Es alta, delgada y rubia. Es muy*
                *inteligente y simpática. Habla inglés, francés y español. ¿Quién es?*
           Grupo: *Es Gwyneth Paltrow.*

**†† 16 Tus cualidades** You are appearing in a play and the director wants you to write a short bio for the theatre program. First, make a list of the personal and physical qualities you want to include. Then make a list of all of your favorite and least favorite activities. (If you want to use adjectives and activities you haven't learned yet, look for them in a Spanish-English dictionary.) Exchange your lists with a classmate and suggest changes you think would be helpful.

**††† 17 Tu descripción** Now, using the information you listed in **Activity 16,** write your description. Make sure you write at least five complete sentences, using the third person, since that is how these descriptions normally appear in theatre programs. Then, in groups of three or four, exchange your descriptions and see if you can guess whose ad is whose. If possible, as a follow-up, post your description on the class website under a false name and see if others can guess who it is.

MODELOS   *Shannon Silvestre es una actriz buena... También es... Le gusta...*
              *Shaun Perales es un actor cómico... No le gusta..., pero sí le gusta...*

# Sonrisas

**Comprensión** Answer the following questions about the cartoon.

1. Según el gato *(cat)*, ¿cómo es?
2. Según el perro, ¿cómo es?
3. En realidad, ¿cómo es el gato? ¿Y el perro?
4. ¿Tienen consecuencias serias las mentiras del gato? En tu opinión, ¿son sinceras o mentirosas las personas cuando se comunican por Internet?

# ¡Explora y exprésate!

## Doble identidad: Los latinos en EEUU y Canadá ▶

Andresr/Shutterstock

Los cinco grupos de latinos de mayor número en Estados Unidos son los méxicoamericanos (o los chicanos), los puertorriqueños, los cubanoamericanos, los dominicanos y los salvadoreños. Cada grupo tiene una historia larga y distinta. Sin embargo, tienen en común la doble identidad del bilingüe. El censo de 2010 indica que hay más de 50 millones de latinos en Estados Unidos.

En Canadá, viven 480.000 hispanos de varios países. La población va creciendo (*is increasing*), aumentando un 6% cada año.

When expressing numbers with numerals, Spanish uses a period where English uses a comma (480.000 rather than 480,000). It also uses a comma instead of a period to express decimals (6,5 rather than 6.5).

| Latinos en Estados Unidos* | |
|---|---|
| mexicanos | 31.673.700 |
| puertorriqueños | 4.411.604 |
| salvadoreños | 1.736.221 |
| cubanos | 1.677.158 |
| dominicanos | 1.360.476 |
| guatemaltecos | 1.077.412 |
| colombianos | 916.616 |
| hondureños | 624.533 |
| españoles | 613.585 |
| ecuatorianos | 611.457 |
| peruanos | 557.107 |

*Pewhispanic.org, 2009

| Los cinco estados con las poblaciones hispanas más concentradas* | |
|---|---|
| California | 14.014.000 |
| Texas | 9.461.000 |
| Florida | 4.224.000 |
| Nueva York | 3.417.000 |
| Illinois | 2.028.000 |

*http://pewhispanic.org/files/reports/140.pdf

# Los méxicoamericanos o chicanos

## Vale saber...

- After the Mexican-American War in 1848, Mexico ceded California, Texas, and parts of New Mexico, Arizona, Utah, Nevada, Colorado, Kansas, and Wyoming to the U.S. The majority of Mexicans in these areas elected to stay and were granted citizenship.
- The Chicano movement was born in the 1960s as Mexican-Americans attempted to regain a sense of pride in their Mexican heritage and culture.
- The integration of Mexican culture can be seen in vibrant areas such as the Riverwalk in San Antonio, Texas, the Pilsen and La Villita communities in Chicago, and the Mission District in San Francisco.

The term "Chicano" was adopted by Americans of Mexican descent during the American civil rights movement to distinguish themselves from Mexicans native to Mexico. There are many theories about its origin, none of which can be proven. The term was used by Mexican American activists who wanted to claim a unique ethnic and political identity.

## Los grandes muralistas chicanos

Diego Rivera, José Orozco y David Siquieros eran *(were)* grandes muralistas mexicanos que usaban sus murales para expresar su visión política y reclamar sus orígenes indígenas. El arte del mural como expresión cultural ha sido adoptado *(has been adopted)* por los chicanos en EEUU.

Justin Sullivan/AP Images

# Los puertorriqueños

## Vale saber...

- In 1898, after the Spanish American War, Spain ceded Puerto Rico to the U.S. Nine years later, President Woodrow Wilson signed the Jones Act, which granted American citizenship to all Puerto Ricans.
- Many Puerto Ricans settled in New York City or in other parts of New York State, but younger Puerto Ricans have moved to Texas, Florida, Pennsylvania, New Jersey, Massachusetts and other states.
- El Museo del Barrio, La Marqueta, and el Desfile Puertorriqueño de Nueva York are all testimony to the bicultural life of the "Nuyoricans", also known as "nuyorquinos" or "nuevarriqueños."

## Los poetry slams

Miguel Algarín, profesor de Rutgers, empezó *(began)* The Nuyorican Poets Café en su apartamento del East Village en 1973. Hoy día el Café es una organización sin fines de lucro *(non-profit agency)* que se ha transformado en un foro para poesía, música, hip hop, video, artes visuales, comedia y teatro. Los Poetry Slams son eventos muy populares en el Café.

Philip Scalia/Alamy

# Los cubanoamericanos

## Vale saber…

- All of Florida and Louisiana were provinces of Cuba prior to the Louisiana Purchase and the Adams-Onís Treaty of 1819.
- The largest community of Cuban Americans in the United States is in Miami-Dade County in Florida.
- La Pequeña Habana in Miami is the cultural center of Cuban American life.

Jeff Greenberg/PhotoEdit

## La música

El Buena Vista Social Club era un club en La Habana donde se juntaban los músicos en los años 40. La ilustre historia musical de Cuba sigue en los Estados Unidos con los cantantes Jon Secada, Albita, Celia Cruz, Gloria Estefan y el saxofonista Paquito D'Rivera—todos ganadores del premio Grammy.

# Los dominicanos y los centroamericanos

## Vale saber…

- New York City has had a Dominican population since the 1930s. They largely settled in Quisqueya Heights, an area of Washington Heights in Manhattan. Nowadays, Dominicans also reside in New Jersey, Massachusetts, and Miami.
- In the 1980s and 90s, Dominican immigration to the United States was at its height.
- In the 1980s, political conflicts in Guatemala, El Salvador, and Nicaragua led to a big wave of immigration to the U.S. Many Central Americans made their homes in cities like Los Angeles, Houston, Washington, D.C., New York, and Miami.

LatinContent/Getty Images

## La literatura revolucionaria

El conflicto produce la literatura. La tarea del escritor es captar la verdad *(truth)* de la vida diaria. En países que pasan por una revolución, es urgente describir las condiciones del ser humano por escrito *(in writing)*. Testimonio de la necesidad de escribir en tiempos de conflicto es la importante literatura centroamericana de escritores como Gioconda Belli, Rigoberta Menchú Tum, Claribel Alegría, Ernesto Cardenal y Roque Dalton.

**La información general** Say which Hispanic group each statement describes.

1. Los **nuyoricans** son personas de este grupo que viven *(live)* en Nueva York.
2. Este grupo en Estados Unidos adopta esta forma de arte como expresión cultural.
3. Los conflictos en los países de origen de este grupo produce una literatura revolucionaria.
4. **Chicano** es otro nombre para una persona de este grupo.
5. Esta sección de Miami es el centro cultural de este grupo.
6. La inmigración de este grupo a Estados Unidos ocurre principalmente en las décadas de los 80 y los 90.

### ¿QUIERES SABER MÁS?

Return to the chart that you started at the beginning of the chapter. Add all the information that you already know in the column **Lo que aprendí.** Then, look at the column labeled **Lo que quiero aprender.** Are there some things that you still don't know? Pick one or two of these, or from the topics listed below, to further investigate online. You can also find more key words on different topics at **www.cengagebrain.com.** Be prepared to share this information with the class.

**Palabras clave: (méxicoamericanos):** the Mexican-American War, Treaty of Guadalupe Hidalgo, 5 de mayo; **(puertorriqueños):** Treaty of Paris, Jones Act, Luis Muñoz Rivera; **(cubanoamericanos):** calle Ocho, Ybor City, Louisiana Purchase, Adams-Onís Treaty; **(dominicanos y centroamericanos):** *El Norte*, Rafael Trujillo, Anastasio Somoza, Sandinistas, Civil War in El Salvador

**Tú en el mundo hispano** To explore opportunities to use your Spanish to study, volunteer, or do internships in the U. S. and Canada, follow the links at **www.cengagebrain.com.**

**Ritmos del mundo hispano** Follow the links at **www.cengagebrain.com** to hear music in Spanish from the U.S. and Canada.

# A leer

For more on using a bilingual dictionary, see the **A escribir** section on page 76.

## ESTRATEGIA

### Looking up Spanish words in a bilingual dictionary

When reading in Spanish, try to understand the general meaning of what you read and don't spend time looking up every unknown word. But if there are key words you can't understand, using a dictionary can save you time.

Try to look up only one or two words from each page of text. Focus on words that you cannot guess from context and that you must understand to get the reading's general meaning. When you do look up the word, don't settle on the first definition! Look at the different English translations provided. Which one seems to best fit with the overall content of the reading?

When looking up verbs, remember that you must look up the infinitive form (**-ar**, **-er**, or **-ir**) and not the conjugated form. (**Ser** instead of **soy**, **hablar** instead of **hablas**, etc.) When you look up adjectives, look up the masculine form (**bueno** instead of **buena**, etc.).

**1** When celebrities are interviewed, they often describe themselves and talk about their backgrounds. The point of the interview is to share personal information with the viewer and reader.

1. Look at the quotes of the seven U.S. Hispanics featured on pages 73–74. Read the translated words at the bottom of each page, then skim the quotes themselves. What words don't you know that you might need in order to get the main idea? Make a list of 5 to 10 words.
2. Can you guess from context any of the words you identified? For example, Albert Pujols is listed as a **pelotero** and in his photo he is wearing a uniform. Based on that information, can you guess what a **pelotero** is?
3. Of the remaining words, how many do you really need to know in order to understand the basic idea of what the person is saying? With a partner, create a list that contains only the words you think are necessary to get the main idea.

**2** Now that you have narrowed down your list of unknown but key words, work with a partner to look them up in the dictionary. Be sure to read all the English definitions. Which one(s) fit(s) best in the context of the article?

## LECTURA

# ¿Cómo soy yo?

**Carlos Santana**
**músico de ascendencia mexicana**
"Soy un músico serio, como Paco de Lucía. Serio, pero divertido. Nunca invertí[1] energía en ser rico o famoso".

Roberto Pfeil/dapd/AP Images

Charles Sykes/AP Images

**Zoe Saldana**
**actriz de ascendencia puertorriqueña y dominicana**
"Como latina, pienso que[2] tenemos que sentirnos[3] muy orgullosos de nuestra herencia. Tendemos[4] a buscar raíces[5] europeas y a rechazar las indígenas y las africanas, y eso es un asco, una vergüenza[6]. El latino es una composición de todos".

**Isabel Toledo**
**diseñadora de ropa de ascendencia cubana**
"Ser latina es ser quien soy, no cómo me defino... Es una cultura enamorada de la moda".

Kathy Willens/AP Images

**Albert Pujols**
**pelotero de ascendencia dominicana**
"Yo quiero que la gente me recuerde[7], no sólo como Albert Pujols el buen pelotero, sino por la persona que yo soy, bien humilde[8] y que trata de ayudar[9] a los que lo necesitan".

MLB Photos via Getty Images

[1] *I never invested* [2] *I think that* [3] *to feel* [4] *We tend to* [5] *roots* [6] **un...**: *it's disgusting and a shame* [7] **Yo...**: *I want people to remember me* [8] *humble* [9] **trata...**: *that tries to help*

### Eva Longoria
**actriz de ascendencia mexicana**

"Somos mexicanos de quinta[10] generación en Texas y estoy[11] orgullosa de ser latina y de representar a los latinos en todas partes... Ser mexicana es muy importante en quién soy yo".

Helga Esteb/Shutterstock

Henny Garfunkel/Retna Ltd./Corbis

### Wilmer Valderrama
**actor de ascendencia venezolana**

"Yo soy muy agradecido por mis raíces latinas... A mí me da mucha dicha[12] y un orgullo muy grande cuando la gente latina admira cualquier[13] trabajo que he hecho[14]".

### César Millán
**entrenador de perros ("El Encantador de Perros"), de ascendencia mexicana**

"Sólo soy un tipo instintivo que vive en el momento".

Douglas Kirkland/Corbis

[10]*fifth*  [11]***I am***  [12]**me...**: *it gives me a lot of happiness*  [13]*whatever*  [14]**he...**: *I have done*

**3** Now work with a partner to match the descriptions on the right with each person on the left.

_____ 1. Carlos Santana

_____ 2. Zoe Saldana

_____ 3. Albert Pujols

_____ 4. Isabel Toledo

_____ 5. César Millán

_____ 6. Eva Longoria

_____ 7. Wilmer Valderrama

a. Es muy agradecido por su herencia latina.

b. Vive en el presente, no en el futuro.

c. Es mexicana y muy orgullosa de su herencia.

d. Habla de ser una composición de culturas.

e. Es una persona muy humilde.

f. Es serio, pero divertido.

g. Es de una cultura enamorada de la moda.

**4** With a classmate, take turns interviewing each other and writing down your responses. Answer the following questions based on your own personality or that of a famous celebrity.

1. ¿Cuál es tu herencia? (Soy de ascendencia...)

2. ¿Cómo eres? (Soy...)

3. ¿Qué te gusta hacer? (Me gusta...)

**5** Now, choose a famous Spanish speaker and do a search for him or her online. Find enough information to answer the three questions in **Actividad 4** about that person—**¡en español, por favor!** Be prepared to share your information with the class.

Rafael Nadal, España

Paulina Rubio, México

# A escribir

### ESTRATEGIA

**Prewriting—Looking up English words in a bilingual dictionary**

Since no textbook can provide you with all the words you may want to use when you write, you will want to use a bilingual dictionary to supplement the words you already know. Here's how to use the dictionary most effectively.

1. Decide on the English word you want to translate: for example, *lively*.

2. Think of several English synonyms for that word: *vivacious, energetic*.

3. Look up the original English word in the English-Spanish part of the dictionary and write down all the Spanish equivalents given. Note that semicolons are used to separate groups of words that are similar in meaning. Example: *lively:* **vivo, vivaz, vivaracho; rápido, apresurado; gallardo, galán, airoso; vigoroso, brioso, enérgico; animado, bullicioso; eficaz, intensivo.**

4. Take a Spanish equivalent from each group and look it up in the Spanish part of the dictionary. What is given as its English equivalent? As you look up each word, you'll see that often the different Spanish words express very different ideas in English.

   Example: **Rápido** and **apresurado** are words that apply more to actions, since they are translated as *rapid, quick, swift* and *brief, hasty*.

5. Now look up the English synonyms you listed in step #2 and see what Spanish equivalents are given. Are any of them the same as those that turned up for the first word? Example: *vivacious:* **vivaz, animado, vivaracho;** *energetic:* **enérgico, activo, vigoroso.**

6. Focus on the words that came up more than once: **vivaz, vivaracho, animado, enérgico.** If you need to, look these words up a final time. Which best expresses the shade of meaning you want to use?

**1** You are going to write a short description of a sculpture by Fernando Botero, the well-known Colombian painter and sculptor.

Look at the photo of the sculpture on page 77. What words might you need to describe it? Here are some to get you started, but look up any new words you might require in a bilingual dictionary. **¡OJO!** Remember to cross-check the words you choose in order to get the one that best fits what you are trying to say.

**Palabras útiles: escultura** (*sculpture*), **estatua** (*statue*), **montado a caballo** (*on horseback*), **sombrero** (*hat*).

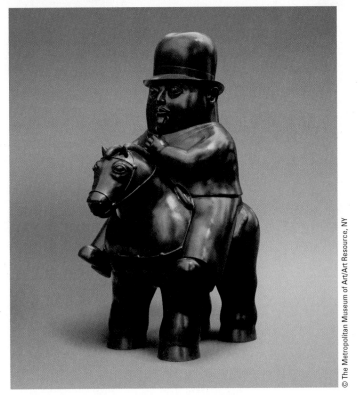

La escultura *Hombre montado a caballo* de Fernando Botero

## Composición

**2** Write three to five sentences that describe the sculpture, using the list of words you generated in **Actividad 1.** Try to write freely without worrying too much about mistakes and misspellings.

## Después de escribir

**3** Now go back over your review and revise it. Use the following checklist to guide you. Did you . . .

- include all the necessary information?
- check to make sure that the adjectives and nouns agree in gender and number?
- make sure that the verbs agree with their subjects?
- look for misspellings?

# Vocabulario

## Para expresar preferencias   *Expressing preferences*

**¿Qué te gusta hacer?** *What do you like to do?*
**A mí me gusta...** *I like . . .*
**A ti te gusta...** *You like . . .*
**A... le gusta...** *You/He/She like(s) . . .*
**A... les gusta...** *You (pl.)/They like . . .*
**¿Y a ti?** *And you?*

**alquilar videos / películas** *to rent videos/movies*
**bailar** *to dance*
**caminar** *to walk*
**cantar** *to sing*
**cocinar** *to cook*
**escuchar música** *to listen to music*
**estudiar en la biblioteca / en casa** *to study at the library/at home*
**hablar por teléfono** *to talk on the phone*
**levantar pesas** *to lift weights*

**mirar televisión** *to watch television*
**navegar por Internet** *to browse the Internet*
**patinar** *to skate*
**pintar** *to paint*
**practicar deportes** *to play sports*
**sacar fotos** *to take photos*
**tocar un instrumento musical** *to play a musical instrument*
   **la guitarra** *the guitar*
   **el piano** *the piano*
   **la trompeta** *the trumpet*
   **el violín** *the violin*
**tomar un refresco** *to have a soft drink*
**tomar el sol** *to sunbathe*
**trabajar** *to work*
**visitar a amigos** *to visit friends*

## Para describir   *Describing*

**¿Cómo es?** *What is he/she/it like?*

**muy** *very*

## Características de la personalidad   *Personality traits*

**aburrido(a)** *boring*
**activo(a)** *active*
**antipático(a)** *unpleasant*
**bueno(a)** *good*
**cómico(a)** *funny*
**cuidadoso(a)** *cautious*
**divertido(a)** *fun, entertaining*
**egoísta** *selfish, egotistic*
**extrovertido(a)** *extroverted*
**generoso(a)** *generous*
**impaciente** *impatient*
**impulsivo(a)** *impulsive*
**inteligente** *intelligent*
**interesante** *interesting*

**introvertido(a)** *introverted*
**irresponsable** *irresponsible*
**malo(a)** *bad*
**mentiroso(a)** *dishonest, lying*
**paciente** *patient*
**perezoso(a)** *lazy*
**responsable** *responsible*
**serio(a)** *serious*
**simpático(a)** *nice*
**sincero(a)** *sincere*
**tímido(a)** *shy*
**tonto(a)** *silly, stupid*
**trabajador(a)** *hard-working*

## Características físicas   *Physical traits*

**alto(a)** *tall*
**bajo(a)** *short*
**delgado(a)** *thin*
**feo(a)** *ugly*
**gordo(a)** *fat*
**grande** *big, great*
**guapo(a)** *handsome, attractive*
**joven** *young*

**lindo(a)** *pretty*
**pequeño(a)** *small*
**viejo(a)** *old*

**Es pelirrojo(a) / rubio(a).** *He/She is redheaded/ blond(e).*
**Tiene el pelo negro / castaño / rubio.** *He/She has black/brown/blond hair.*

## Nacionalidades *Nationalities*

**alemán (alemana)** *German*
**argentino(a)** *Argentinian*
**australiano(a)** *Australian*
**boliviano(a)** *Bolivian*
**canadiense** *Canadian*
**chileno(a)** *Chilean*
**chino(a)** *Chinese*
**colombiano(a)** *Colombian*
**coreano(a)** *Korean*
**costarricense** *Costa Rican*
**cubano(a)** *Cuban*
**dominicano(a)** *Dominican*
**ecuatoguineano(a)** *Equatorial Guinean*
**ecuatoriano(a)** *Ecuadoran*
**español(a)** *Spanish*
**estadounidense** *U. S. citizen*
**francés (francesa)** *French*

**guatemalteco(a)** *Guatemalan*
**hondureño(a)** *Honduran*
**indio(a)** *Indian*
**inglés (inglesa)** *English*
**italiano(a)** *Italian*
**japonés (japonesa)** *Japanese*
**mexicano(a)** *Mexican*
**nicaragüense** *Nicaraguan*
**panameño(a)** *Panamanian*
**paraguayo(a)** *Paraguayan*
**peruano(a)** *Peruvian*
**portugués (portuguesa)** *Portuguese*
**puertorriqueño(a)** *Puerto Rican*
**salvadoreño(a)** *Salvadoran*
**uruguayo(a)** *Uruguayan*
**venezolano(a)** *Venezuelan*

## Los verbos

**acabar de** *(+ inf.) to have just done something*
**apagar** *to turn off*
**buscar** *to look for*
**cenar** *to eat dinner*
**comprar** *to buy*
**dejar** *to leave*
**dejar de** *(+ inf.) to stop (doing something)*
**descansar** *to rest*

**llamar** *to call*
**llegar** *to arrive*
**necesitar** *to need*
**pasar** *to pass (by)*
**preparar** *to prepare*
**regresar** *to return*
**usar** *to use*

## Otras palabras

**los fines de semana** *weekends*
**los viernes** *Fridays*
**los sábados** *Saturdays*
**los domingos** *Sundays*
**el gato** *cat*

**el perro** *dog*
**pero** *but*
**también** *also*
**tampoco** *neither*

# Repaso y preparación

Complete these activities to check your understanding of the new grammar points in **Chapter 2** before you move on to **Chapter 3**.

The answers to the activities in this section can be found in **Appendix B**.

## The present indicative of regular -ar verbs (p. 54)

**1** Look at the illustrations and say what the people indicated are doing.

1.

Esteban y Carolina

2.

usted

3.

Loreta

4.

yo

5.

nosotros

6.

tú

7.

ustedes

8.

tú y yo

## Gustar + infinitive (p. 58)

**2** Read the description of each person. Then say what activity he or she likes to do, choosing from the list. Follow the model.

**Actividades:** estudiar, mirar televisión, pintar, practicar deportes, visitar a amigos, trabajar.

MODELO   Ellos son muy trabajadores.
         *A ellos les gusta trabajar.*

1.  Yo soy muy serio.
2.  Tú eres muy perezosa.
3.  Usted es muy extrovertido.
4.  Nosotras somos muy artísticas.
5.  Ustedes son muy activos.

## Adjective agreement (p. 62)

**3** Use forms of **ser** to describe each person using the cues provided.

1.  Gretchen y Rolf / Alemania / sincero
2.  Brigitte / Francia / divertido
3.  nosotras / España / simpático
4.  yo (feminino) / Estados Unidos / generoso
5.  usted (feminino) / Japón / interesante
6.  tú (masculino) / Italia / activo

# Preparación para el Capítulo 3

## Nouns and articles (Chapter 1)

**4** Complete the description with the definite and indefinite articles that are missing. Make sure the articles agree with the nouns they modify.

A mí me gustan 1. _____ clases que tengo hoy. 2. _____ profesor de historia es muy inteligente y 3. _____ profesora de español es muy interesante. Tengo 4. _____ amigos en 5. _____ clase de ingeniería y por eso es muy divertida. Solamente tengo 6. _____ clase por la tarde. Pero no es 7. _____ día normal. Normalmente tengo clases por 8. _____ mañana y también por 9. _____ tarde. ¡Pero por lo menos, no tengo clases por 10. _____ noches!

Complete these activities to review some previously learned grammatical structures that will be helpful when you learn the new grammar in **Chapter 3**.

Be sure to reread **Chapter 2: Gramática útil 1** and **2** before moving on to the **Chapter 3** grammar sections.

## Subject pronouns and the present indicative of the verb **ser** (Chapter 1)

**5** Match the illustrations on the left with the sentences on the right. Then write in the missing forms of the verb **ser**.

1. _____

2. _____

3. _____

4. _____

5. _____

6. _____

7. _____

© Cengage Learning 2013

a. Ella _____ muy tímida.

b. Nosotros _____ muy perezosos.

c. Yo _____ muy extrovertida.

d. Usted _____ muy impaciente.

e. Tú _____ generoso.

f. Él _____ activo.

g. Ustedes _____ inteligentes.

# ¿Qué clases vas a tomar?

## ¡VIVIR ES APRENDER!

Los estudiantes asisten a clases formales y estudian muchas materias. Pero en un sentido *(sense)* menos formal, todos somos estudiantes. Aprendemos algo nuevo todos los días—de nuestros *(our)* amigos, familiares y experiencias.

Para ti, ¿cuál es la mejor manera *(the best way)* de aprender?

## Communication

By the end of this chapter you will be able to

- talk about courses and schedules and tell time
- talk about present activities and future plans
- talk about possessions
- ask and answer questions

# Un viaje por Cuba, Puerto Rico y la República Dominicana

Estos tres países están situados en el mar Caribe y tienen un clima tropical. Todos también tienen montañas. La República Dominicana comparte *(shares)* una isla con Haití.

| País / Área | Tamaño y fronteras *(Size and Borders)* | Sitios *(Places)* de interés |
|---|---|---|
| **Cuba** 110.860 km² | un poco más pequeño que Pensilvania | las cavernas de Bellamar, la Vieja Habana, la península de Guanahacabibes |
| **Puerto Rico** 8.950 km² | casi tres veces *(almost three times)* el área de Rhode Island | Vieques, El Morro, Viejo San Juan |
| **República Dominicana** 48.380 km² | más de dos veces el área de Nuevo Hampshire; frontera con Haití | Pico Duarte, la sierra *(mountains)* de Samaná, La Universidad Autónoma de Santo Domingo |

**¿Qué sabes?**  Di si las siguientes oraciones son ciertas (**C**) o falsas (**F**).

1. Estos tres países están en el mar Caribe.
2. La República Dominicana es casi dos veces el tamaño de Puerto Rico.
3. No hay una zona vieja en Cuba.

**Lo que sé y lo que quiero aprender**  Completa la tabla del **Apéndice A**. Escribe algunos datos que **ya sabes** sobre estos países caribeños en la columna **Lo que sé**. Después, añade algunos temas que **quieres aprender** a la columna **Lo que quiero aprender**. Guarda la tabla para usarla otra vez en la sección **¡Explora y exprésate!** en la página 111.

## Cultures

By the end of this chapter you will have explored

- facts about Puerto Rico, Cuba, and the Dominican Republic
- Cuba: the campaign for literacy
- Puerto Rico: the bilingual education of the **boricuas**
- República Dominicana: the oldest university in the New World
- the 24-hour clock
- three unusual schools in the Caribbean

Globe Art: Adapted from Shutterstock/rtguest

# ¡Imagínate!

>> **Vocabulario útil 1**

**CHELA:** Para empezar, dime, ¿cuántas clases tienes?

**ANILÚ:** Ay, ¡qué aburrido!, ¿no crees? Si voy a salir por Internet, quiero hacer más que recitar mis clases: **computación, diseño gráfico, psicología**, bla, bla, bla…

**CHELA:** Comprendo que no son las preguntas más interesantes del mundo, pero…

**ANILÚ:** Prefiero hablar de mi tiempo libre, los **sábados**, por ejemplo.

---

Notice that many of the courses of study are cognates of their English equivalents. Be sure to notice the difference in spelling, accentuation, and pronunciation, for example: **geografía**: *geography*.

>> **Campos de estudio**

**Los cursos básicos**
la arquitectura
las ciencias políticas
la economía
la educación
la geografía
la historia
la ingeniería
la psicología

**Las humanidades**
la filosofía
las lenguas / los idiomas
la literatura

**Las lenguas /**
   **Los idiomas**
el alemán
el chino
el español
el francés
el inglés
el japonés

**Las matemáticas**
el cálculo
la computación /
   la informática
la estadística

**Las ciencias**
la biología
la física
la medicina
la química *(chemistry)*
la salud *(health)*

**Los negocios**
la administración de
   empresas
la contabilidad
   *(accounting)*
el mercadeo *(marketing)*

**La comunicación**
   **pública**
el periodismo
   *(journalism)*
la publicidad

**Las artes**
el arte
el baile
el diseño gráfico
la música
la pintura

© Cengage Learning 2013

## >> Lugares en la universidad

¿Dónde tienes la clase de...? | Where does your . . . class meet?
En el centro de computación. | In the computer center.
...el centro de comunicaciones. | . . . the media center.
...el gimnasio. | . . . the gymnasium.

la cafetería | the cafeteria
la librería | the bookstore
la residencia estudiantil | the dorm

> Notice that the week begins on Monday in most Spanish-speaking countries. Also notice that the days of the week are not capitalized in Spanish as they are in English.

## >> Los días de la semana

| lunes | martes | miércoles | jueves | viernes | sábado | domingo |
|-------|--------|-----------|--------|---------|--------|---------|
| 8 | 9 | 10 | 11 | 12 | 13 | 14 |

> To say that something happens *on* a certain day, use the singular article with the day of the week: **La fiesta va a ser *el* sábado.**

> To say that something happens on the same day every week, use the plural article with the day of the week: ***Los* sábados visito a mi madre.** Notice that there is no preposition **en** *(on)* in these cases.

## ACTIVIDADES

**1  Las carreras**  Say what course you would take if you were interested in a certain career.

MODELO  journalist
*el periodismo*

1. psychologist
2. accountant
3. software programmer
4. architect
5. graphic designer
6. teacher

**2  Las clases de Mariana**  With a partner, say on which days Mariana has each of her classes, based on her class schedule.

MODELO  economía
*Mariana tiene economía los lunes, los miércoles y los viernes.*

1. psicología
2. literatura
3. francés
4. contabilidad
5. pintura
6. música

| | lunes | martes | miércoles | jueves | viernes |
|------|-------|--------|-----------|--------|---------|
| 8:00 | economía | | economía | | economía |
| 10:00 | psicología | literatura | psicología | literatura | |
| 11:30 | francés | francés | francés | francés | francés |
| 3:00 | | contabilidad | | contabilidad | |
| 4:00 | pintura | | música | pintura | música |

**3** **Mis clases** Create a chart with your class schedule. Include days, times, and locations. Then, with a partner, ask each other questions about each day of the week. Be sure to save your schedule for later activities.

MODELO Tú: *¿Qué clases tienes los lunes?*
Compañero(a): *Los lunes tengo psicología, arte y computación.*

**4** **¿Dónde?** Ask your partner where he/she does certain activities.

MODELO levantar pesas
Tú: *¿Dónde levantas pesas?*
Compañero(a): *En el gimnasio.*

1. visitar a tus amigos
2. navegar por Internet
3. escuchar los CDs de la clase de español
4. practicar deportes
5. comprar libros
6. vivir
7. tener clase de baile
8. estudiar

**5** **Entrevista** Imagine that you are like Chela in the video and you must approach someone in your class for an interview about their daily schedule. Use as much language as you can from previous chapters. Make a list of questions beforehand. Then record the interview and upload for the class to view or summarize the interview in class. You can use the following questions or make up your own.

**Preguntas:**
Buenos días, ¿qué tal?
¿Cómo te llamas?
¿De dónde eres?
¿Cuántos años tienes?
¿Qué te gusta hacer los domingos?
¿Qué estudias?
¿Cuántas clases tienes?
¿Dónde tienes la clase de…?
¿Cuál es tu clase preferida?
¿Qué día de la semana te gusta más?

**6** **Mi blog** Write a blog post about the interview you did in Activity 5. What were some of the interesting things you learned about your partner?

MODELO *Mi compañero estudia psicología, pero su clase preferida es la clase de baile.*

## ¡Fíjate! El reloj de veinticuatro horas

The 24-hour clock is used globally, and in all Spanish-speaking countries, for schedules and official times. The system is based on counting the hours of the day from zero through twenty-four. The first twelve hours of the day (from midnight until noon) are represented by the numbers 0–12. Any time after noon is represented by that time +12. The **h** after the time stands for **horas**.

Robert Fried/Alamy

For example:

1:00 P.M. = 1:00 + 12 = 13:00h

2:30 P.M. = 2:30 + 12 = 14:30h

5:45 P.M. = 5:45 + 12 = 17:45h

To go from a 24-hour clock time to a 12-hour clock time, you must subtract 12 hours from the 24-hour clock time.

For example:

13:00h − 12 = 1:00 P.M.

14:30h − 12 = 2:30 P.M.

17:45h − 12 = 5:45 P.M.

The 24-hour clock is almost always used in written form. In conversation, Spanish speakers use the 12-hour format, adding **de la mañana** (morning, A.M.), **de la tarde** (afternoon, P.M.), and **de la noche** (evening, P.M.) for clarification.

**Práctica 1** With a partner, look at the schedules below. Convert the times on the 24-hour clock to the 12-hour clock. Follow the model.

MODELO   21:20h = *9:20 P.M.*

1. 23:20h =
2. 14:45h =
3. 18:30h =
4. 16:25h =
5. 15:10h =
6. 19:15h =

**Práctica 2** With a partner, look at the schedules that you used in **Activity 3**. Convert the times on your schedules to hours on the 24-hour clock. Follow the model.

MODELO   Tú: *Mi (My) clase de matemáticas es a las 3:00 de la tarde.*
Compañero(a): *Tu (Your) clase de matemáticas es a las 15:00 horas.*

CHELA: ¿Qué haces los sábados?

ANILÚ: **Por la mañana**, corro por el parque. **A las dos de la tarde**, tengo clase de danza afrocaribeña.

CHELA: ¿Y **por la noche**?

ANILÚ: Por la noche escucho música con mis amigos o vamos al cine o a un restaurante.

CAMARÓGRAFO: Uy, **¿qué hora es?** ¡Tengo que irme!

CHELA: Pero, ¿adónde vas? ¡Necesito otra entrevista!

CAMARÓGRAFO: ¡Tengo clase **a las once**!

CHELA: **Son las once menos cuarto.** Espera un minuto, por favor.

---

Compare the following two questions and responses.

**¿Qué hora es?** *(What time is it?)*

**Es la una.** *(It's one o'clock.)*

**¿A qué hora es la clase de español?** *([At] What time is Spanish class?)*

**Es a la una.** *(It's at one o'clock.)*

>> **Para pedir y dar la hora** *Asking for and giving the time*

**¿Qué hora es?** *What time is it?*

Es la una.

Son las dos.

Son las cinco y cuarto.
Son las cinco y quince.

Son las cinco y media.

Son las cinco y diez.

Son las cinco menos cuarto.
Faltan quince par las cinco.

—**¿Tienes tiempo** para tomar un café?

—**Sí, es temprano.** / —¡Ay, no, **ya es muy tarde**!

**Mañana, tarde o noche**      *Morning, afternoon, or night*
Mira **el reloj** para **decir la hora.**      *Look at the clock to tell the time.*

Son las ocho de la mañana.     Son las tres de la tarde.     Son las nueve de la noche.

© Cengage Learning 2013

| | |
|---|---|
| **Es mediodía.** | *It's noon.* |
| **Es medianoche.** | *It's midnight.* |
| **Es tarde.** | *It's late.* |
| **Es temprano.** | *It's early.* |

**De la mañana** is used for the morning hours between midnight and noon. **De la tarde** is used for daylight hours after noon. **De la noche** is used only for nighttime hours. These hours vary from country to country, given that in some countries it gets dark earlier or stays light later.

Compare the use of **de** and **por** in the following sentences.

> La clase es a las diez **de la mañana**.

> En general estudio **por la mañana**.

Note that you use **de la mañana / tarde / noche** to give a specific time of day. You use **por la mañana / tarde / noche** to give a more general time frame.

## ACTIVIDADES

**7** **¿Qué hora es?** Ask your partner what time it is. He/She will tell you what time it is. Take turns asking the time.

MODELO    1:00 P.M.
       Tú: *¿Qué hora es?*
       Compañero(a): *Es la una de la tarde.*

1. 3:15 P.M.      3. 10:30 A.M.      5. 6:55 A.M.
2. 2:45 P.M.      4. 12:00 noon      6. 9:25 P.M.

**8** **Mi horario** Get out the agenda page that you completed for **Activity 3.** Ask your partner about his/her class schedule. You name a day and a time, and your partner tells you what class he/she has at that time. Talk about all five days of the week.

MODELO    Tú: *Es lunes y son las diez de la mañana.*
       Compañero(a): *Tengo clase de cálculo.*

**9** **Tu horario** Exchange your agenda page with your partner. Your partner names a day and a time, and you tell him/her where he/she is at that time. Take turns with each other's schedules.

MODELO    Compañero(a): *Es viernes y son las dos de la tarde. ¿Dónde estoy?*
       Tú: *Estás en la clase de danza afrocaribeña.*

© Cengage Learning 2013

CHELA: ¿Así que te gustan más los fines de semana que los días de **entresemana**?

ANILÚ: Pues sí, por supuesto. Los fines de semana son mucho más divertidos. Ay, **es tarde**. Yo también tengo clase a las once.

CHELA: Gracias por la entrevista. ...

ANILÚ: Oye, ¿cuándo sale la entrevista en la red?

CHELA: **Mañana.**

>> **Para hablar de la fecha** *Talking about the date*

**¿Qué día es hoy?** *What day is today?*
**Hoy es martes treinta.** *Today is Tuesday the 30th.*

**¿A qué fecha estamos?** *What is today's date?*
**Es el treinta de octubre.** *It's the 30th of October.*
**Es el primero de noviembre.** *It's the first of November.*

**¿Cuándo es el Día de las Madres?** *When is Mother's Day?*
**Es el doce de mayo.** *It's May 12th.*

**el día** *day*
**la semana** *week*
**el fin de semana** *weekend*
**el mes** *month*
**el año** *year*
**todos los días** *every day*
**entresemana** *during the week/on weekdays*

**ayer** *yesterday*
**hoy** *today*
**mañana** *tomorrow*

## ACTIVIDADES

**10** **¿Qué es?** Say what each of the following time periods are.

MODELO   febrero
         *el mes*

1. enero
2. sábado y domingo
3. 2012

4. el 7 de septiembre
5. 7 de noviembre a 14 de noviembre
6. hoy

**11** **Las fechas** Form pairs and look at a current yearly calendar. Your professor will give each team five minutes to answer the following questions. Write out your answers in Spanish. There are some words that you might not know. Try to guess at their meaning, but don't let it hold you up!

1. ¿Qué día de la semana es Navidad (25 de diciembre) este año?
2. ¿Qué día de la semana es el Día de la Independencia (4 de julio) este año?
3. ¿Qué día de la semana es el Día de los Enamorados (14 de febrero) este año?
4. ¿A qué fecha estamos? ¿Cuándo es el próximo *(next)* examen de español?
5. ¿Cuándo son las próximas vacaciones? ¿Qué día regresan los estudiantes de las próximas vacaciones?

**12** **Fechas importantes** Write out in Spanish ten to fifteen dates that are important for you. Then copy them into your calendar. The following are some examples of the dates you might include.

los cumpleaños de los miembros de mi familia
los cumpleaños de mis amigos
el Día de las Madres
el Día del Padre
las fechas de las vacaciones
el aniversario de…
las fechas de mis exámenes finales

© Cengage Learning 2013

# A ver

## ESTRATEGIA

### Using body language to aid in comprehension

When you observe the body language of the person speaking, you can get clues to a person's meaning by watching facial expressions, gestures, hand movements, and so on. For example, if you ask someone a question and the person shrugs and walks away, the meaning is clear, even if no words were uttered!

As a previewing strategy to help guide your comprehension of the video segment, read the items in **Después de ver 1** *before* you view the video.

© Cengage Learning 2013

**Antes de ver**  Review these key words used in the video.

| | |
|---|---|
| **la entrevista** | *the interview* |
| **transmitir** | *to transmit* |
| **la red** | *the Internet* |

▶ **Ver**  Now watch the video segment for **Chapter 3** without sound. Pay special attention to the characters' body language.

**Después de ver 1**  Say whether statements 1-4 are true (**cierto**) or false (**falso**), based on your observation of the characters' body language. Then watch again with sound and complete statements 5–9.

1.  Muchos estudiantes prefieren no participar en la entrevista con Chela.
2.  Chela indica algo *(something)* al estudiante con la cámara.
3.  El estudiante con la cámara no tiene prisa *(is not in a hurry)*.
4.  Anilú observa a Javier (el estudiante que aparece al final del segmento) con mucho interés.
5.  En la opinión del estudiante con la cámara y de Anilú, el tema del programa de Chela es _____.
6.  Anilú tiene clases de computación, diseño gráfico y _____.
7.  Los _____, Anilú corre en el parque.
8.  Los sábados por la noche, Anilú escucha música con amigos o va al _____ o a un restaurante.
9.  El estudiante con la cámara tiene clase a las _____.

**Después de ver 2**  With a partner, dramatize one of the following situations.

- You are the reporter and you are attracted to the interviewee. Try to get the interviewee's phone number.
- You are the interviewee and you are attracted to the cameraman. Try to get the cameraman's phone number.
- You are the interviewee and you don't like the reporter's attitude. Try to evade the reporter's questions.

## ▶ >> Voces del mundo hispano

© Cengage Learning 2013

In this video segment, the speakers talk about their studies and pastimes. First read the statements below. Then watch the video as many times as needed to say whether the statements are true (**cierto**) or false (**falso**).

1. Sandra estudia administración de empresas.
2. Jessica estudia química.
3. A Javier le gusta ver *(to see)* películas.
4. A Dayramir le gusta bailar salsa con sus amigos.
5. Durante los fines de semana, Ela va *(goes)* al parque.
6. Durante los fines de semana, Inés visita a su familia.

## ◀)) >> Voces de Estados Unidos

Track 8

### Sonia Sotomayor, jueza, Corte Suprema de Estados Unidos

Pablo Martinez Monsivais/AP Images

❝ Creo que si las caras de los jueces *(judges' faces)* no reflejan la población a la que sirven, la gente va a tener menos confianza en el sistema de justicia. Es importante que todos los grupos de Estados Unidos estén representados en la función más importante de la sociedad. ❞

Sonia Sotomayor, la primera persona de ascendencia hispana en la Corte Suprema de los Estados Unidos, es la personificación del sueño *(dream)* americano. Nacida *(Born)* en un proyecto público en El Bronx a padres puertorriqueños, la jueza es conocida por su inteligencia, capacidad de trabajo y respeto por sus raíces. Dos tragedias en su niñez forman su carácter: la muerte *(death)* de su padre a los nueve años y la diabetes juvenil. Con la ayuda *(help)* de su madre, Sotomayor triunfa sobre estas adversidades. Asiste a Princeton, y después a la escuela de derecho de Yale. Sin embargo, la jueza nunca olvida sus raíces *(never forgets her roots)*. Sus experiencias como empleada en una dulcería *(candy store)* y una tienda de ropa *(clothing store)* y como camarera *(waitress)* le dan una especial sensibilidad hacia las necesidades de las personas comunes.

¿Y tú?  ¿ Are you interested in working in the public sector? Why or why not?

>> ## Gramática útil 1

### Asking questions: Interrogative words

¿**Cuántas** entrevistas tenemos que hacer?

### Cómo usarlo

You have already seen, learned, and used a number of interrogative words to ask questions. ¿**Cómo te llamas?**, ¿**Cuál es tu dirección electrónica?**, ¿**Dónde vives?**, and ¿**Qué tal?** are all questions that begin with interrogatives: **cómo, cuál, dónde, qué.**

As in English, we use interrogatives in Spanish to ask for specific information. Here are the Spanish interrogatives.

| | | | |
|---|---|---|---|
| ¿**Cuál(es)?** | What? Which one(s)? | ¿**Dónde?** | Where? |
| ¿**Qué?** | What? Which? | ¿**Adónde?** | To where? |
| ¿**A qué hora?** | (At) What time? | ¿**De dónde?** | From where? |
| ¿**De qué?** | About what? Of what? | ¿**Quién(es)?** | Who? |
| ¿**Cuándo?** | When? | ¿**De quién(es)?** | Whose? |
| ¿**Cuánto(a)?** | How much? | ¿**Cómo?** | How? |
| ¿**Cuántos(as)?** | How many? | ¿**Por qué?** | Why? |

1. ¿**Qué?** and ¿**cuál?** may appear interchangeable at first sight, but they are used in very specific ways.

   ¿**Qué?** is . . .

   ■ used to ask for a definition: ¿**Qué es el reloj de veinticuatro horas?**

   ■ used to ask for an explanation or further information: ¿**Qué vas a estudiar este semestre?**

   ■ generally used when the next word is a noun: ¿**Qué libros te gustan más? ¿Qué clase tienes a las ocho?**

   ¿**Cuál?** is . . .

   ■ used to express a choice between specified items: ¿**Cuál de los libros prefieres?**

   ■ used when the next word is a form of **ser** but the question is *not* asking for a definition: ¿**Cuál es tu número de teléfono? ¿Cuáles son tus clases favoritas?**

2. ¿**Dónde?** is used to ask where something is.

   ¿**Dónde** está la biblioteca?               ***Where** is the library?*

© Cengage Learning 2013

3. **¿Adónde?** is used to ask where someone is going.

 **¿Adónde** vas ahora?      *Where are you going now?*

4. **¿De quién es?** and **¿De quiénes son?** are used to ask about possession. You answer using **de**.

 —¿**De quién** es la computadora?   *Whose computer is this?*
 —**Es de** Miguel.        *It's Miguel's.*

 —¿**De quiénes** son los libros?    *Whose books are these?*
 —**Son de** Anita y Manuel.     *They're Anita's and Manuel's.*

5. Questions using **¿por qué?** can be answered using **porque** *(because)*.

 —¿**Por qué** tienes que trabajar?   *Why do you have to work?*
 —¡**Porque** necesito el dinero!    *Because I need the money!*

Notice that **dónde** and **adónde** are both translated the same way into English.

Note that the interrogative is two separate words with an accent on **qué**. **Porque** is one single word with no accent.

## Cómo formarlo

1. Interrogatives are always preceded by an inverted question mark (**¿**). The question requires a regular question mark (**?**) at the end.

2. Notice that in a typical question the subject *follows* the verb.

 ¿Dónde **estudia Marcos**?    *Where does **Marcos study**?*
 ¿Qué instrumento **tocan** ustedes?  *What instrument do **you play**?*

3. **¿Quién?** and **¿cuál?** change to reflect number.

 ¿**Quién** es el hombre alto? / ¿**Quiénes** son los hombres altos?
 ¿**Cuál** de los libros tienes? / ¿**Cuáles** son tus idiomas favoritos?

4. **¿Cuánto?** changes to reflect both number and gender.

 ¿**Cuánto** dinero tienes?    *How much money do you have?*
 ¿**Cuánta** comida compramos?   *How much food should we buy?*
 ¿**Cuántos** años tienes?     *How many years old are you? /*
             *How old are you?*

 ¿**Cuántas** personas hay?    *How many people are there?*

5. When you want to ask *how much* in a general way, use **¿cuánto?**

 **¿Cuánto es?**        **¿Cuánto necesitamos?**

6. Note that interrogatives always require an accent.

7. You have already learned how to form simple *yes/no* questions by adding **no** to a sentence.

 ¿**No escribes** e-mails     *Aren't you writing any*
  hoy?          *e-mails today?*

8. You can also form simple *yes/no* questions by adding a tag question, such as **¿verdad?** *(Isn't that right?)* and **¿no?** to the end of a statement.

 Cantas en el coro con     *You sing in the chorus with*
  Ana, **¿no?**         *Ana, **right?***
 Enrique baila salsa muy    *Enrique dances salsa very*
  bien, **¿verdad?**       *well, **right?***

When a Spanish speaker adds **¿verdad?** or **¿no?** to a question, he or she is expecting an affirmative answer.

ACTIVIDADES

**1** **Las preguntas** What question would you have to ask to produce the response shown? You will hear three questions. Choose the correct one.

Track 9

_____ 1. La clase de informática es a las once de la mañana.

_____ 2. Tengo que ir al centro de computación para la clase de informática.

_____ 3. La computadora portátil es de mi compañero de cuarto.

_____ 4. Hay que comprar tres libros para la clase de informática.

_____ 5. Porque me gustan mucho las computadoras y quiero aprender a programarlas.

_____ 6. La señora Delgado es la profesora de informática.

**2** **En la cafetería** You overhear a conversation between two students in the cafeteria. Fill in the correct form of the question words to complete their conversation.

—¿(1) _____ clases tienes este semestre?
—Tengo arte, literatura, cálculo, química y economía.

—¿(2) _____ son tus clases favoritas?
—El arte y la literatura.

—¿(3) _____ son tus autores favoritos?
—Gabriel García Márquez, Mario Vargas Llosa, Julia Álvarez e Isabel Allende.

—¿(4) _____ es tu profesor de literatura?
—El señor Banderas.

—¿(5) _____ libros necesitas para la clase de literatura?
—Diez, más o menos, pero son libros que puedo sacar de la biblioteca.

—¿A (6) _____ hora tienes la clase de literatura?
—A las diez de la mañana.

—¿(7) _____ vas ahora?
—Al centro de computación.

—¿(8) _____ vas allí?
—Porque necesito usar las computadoras para hacer mi tarea.

—Pero tienes computadora portátil. ¿(9) _____ es la computadora portátil?
—Es de mi compañero de cuarto. ¡Haces demasiadas *(You ask too many)* preguntas!

**3** **Más preguntas** For each activity indicated, take turns asking and answering questions with a partner.

MODELO bailar (cuándo)
Estudiante #1: *¿Cuándo bailas?*
Estudiante #2: *Bailo los viernes.*

1. estudiar (qué)
2. visitar a amigos (cuándo)
3. hablar con la profesora (por qué)
4. caminar (adónde)
5. tener años (cuánto)
6. imprimir los informes (dónde)

**4** **¡Qué curiosidad!** In groups of three or four, take turns coming up with as many questions as you can for each activity listed. (Take turns writing down the questions or keep your own list.) Then compare your group's questions with another group to see who has the most questions for each activity.

1. correr
2. comer
3. tener muchos amigos
4. escuchar música
5. comprar muchos libros
6. tomar clases

**5** **Encuesta #1** In the chapter activities labeled **"Encuesta"** you will gather information from your fellow students in order to write a description of life at your college or university in the **A escribir** section at the end of the chapter.

1. First prepare a questionnaire by creating two questions for each category, using the cues provided or coming up with your own.

   **El horario:** clases por día / semana, lugar preferido para estudiar

   **El trabajo:** lugar de trabajo, horas de trabajo

   **La computadora:** tiempo que pasas en la computadora, sitios interesantes en Internet

   **La universidad:** clases difíciles y fáciles, las horas por semana que estudias, profesores buenos y malos

2. Now work with another group and ask the members to answer your questionnaire. Be sure to answer their questions as well. Keep track of your results. You will need them later in the chapter.

# Gramática útil 2

## Talking about daily activities: The present indicative of regular -er and -ir verbs

### Cómo usarlo

Por la mañana, **corro** en el parque.

In **Chapter 2,** you learned how to use the present indicative of regular **-ar** verbs to talk about daily activities. The present indicative of **-er** and **-ir** verbs are used in the same contexts.

Remember:

1. The present indicative, depending on how it is used, can correspond to the following English usages: *I read* (in general), *I am reading, I am going to read, I do read,* and, if used as a question, *Do you read?*

2. You can often omit the subject pronoun when the subject is clear from the verb ending used or from the context of the sentence.

   **Leo** en la biblioteca todos los días.  *I read in the library every day.*
   **Lees** en la residencia estudiantil, ¿no?  *You read in the dorm, right?*

3. You may use an infinitive after certain conjugated verbs.

   **¿Tienes que imprimir** esto?  *Do you have to print this?*
   **¿Necesitas leer** este libro?  *Do you need to read this book?*
   **¡Dejo de leer** después de medianoche!  *I stop reading after midnight!*

4. However, do not use two verbs conjugated in the present tense together unless they are separated by a comma or the words **y** *(and)* or **o** *(or).*

   **Leo, estudio** y **escribo**  *I read, study, and write*
   composiciones en la biblioteca.  *compositions in the library.*

5. Remember that you can negate sentences in the present indicative tense to say what you don't do or aren't planning to do.

   **No comemos** en la  *We're not eating in the*
   cafetería hoy.  *cafeteria today.*
   **No leo** todos los días.  *I don't read every day.*

### Cómo formarlo

To form the present indicative tense of **-er** and **-ir** verbs, simply remove the **-er** or **-ir** and add the following endings.

| comer *(to eat)* | | | |
|---|---|---|---|
| yo | **como** | nosotros / nosotras | **comemos** |
| tú | **comes** | vosotros / vosotras | **coméis** |
| Ud. / él / ella | **come** | Uds. / ellos / ellas | **comen** |

© Cengage Learning 2013

| vivir (to live) | | | |
|---|---|---|---|
| yo | **vivo** | nosotros / nosotras | **vivimos** |
| tú | **vives** | vosotros / vosotras | **vivís** |
| Ud. / él / ella | **vive** | Uds. / ellos / ellas | **viven** |

Notice that the present indicative endings for -**er** and -**ir** verbs are identical except for the **nosotros** and **vosotros** forms.

Here are some commonly used -**er** and -**ir** verbs.

| -er verbs | | | |
|---|---|---|---|
| **aprender a** (+ infinitive) | to learn to (do something) | **creer (en)** | to believe (in) |
| **beber** | to drink | **deber** (+ infinitive) | should, ought (to do something) |
| **comer** | to eat | **leer** | to read |
| **comprender** | to understand | **vender** | to sell |
| **correr** | to run | | |

| -ir verbs | | | |
|---|---|---|---|
| **abrir** | to open | **escribir** | to write |
| **asistir a** | to attend | **imprimir** | to print |
| **compartir** | to share | **recibir** | to receive |
| **describir** | to describe | **transmitir** | to broadcast |
| **descubrir** | to discover | **vivir** | to live |

## ACTIVIDADES

**6** **¿Qué hacen?** Based on the information provided, what do the people indicated do? Choose verbs from the list. Follow the model.

MODELOS  Carlos ya no necesita esa cámara digital.
_Vende la cámara._

Tú y yo necesitamos hacer ejercicio.
_Corremos en el parque._

**Verbos posibles:** aprender / asistir / comer / compartir / correr / vender

1. ¡Olivia tiene la clase de biología a las tres y ya son las tres y cinco! _____ a la universidad.
2. A Susana no le gusta esa bicicleta. _____ la bicicleta.
3. Raúl y Enrique tienen que viajar a Puerto Rico en dos meses. _____ español.
4. Elena y yo no comprendemos las lecturas del libro. _____ a una clase de estudio.
5. No me gustan los restaurantes aquí. _____ en la cafetería todos los días.
6. Susana vive con una compañera de cuarto. _____ el apartamento con ella.

**7 La vida estudiantil** Say what the people indicated are doing today on campus. The numbers indicate how many actions are going on for each person.

1. Juan Carlos e Isabel (1)
2. Marcos (2)
3. Cecilia y Marta (2)
4. Radio WBRU (1)
5. Y tú, ¿qué haces *(what are you doing)*?

**8 ¿Y tú?** With a partner, take turns asking and answering the following questions.

1. ¿Cuándo asistes a tu primera clase del día?
2. ¿Vives en un apartamento o en una residencia?
3. ¿A qué hora comes la cena *(dinner)*?
4. ¿Recibes muchos e-mails de tu familia?
5. ¿Escribes muchos informes?
6. ¿Dónde lees los libros para tus clases?

**9** **¿Qué hacemos?** Using an element from each of the three columns, create eight sentences describing what you and people you know do in and around campus.

MODELO   *Yo asisto a clases los lunes, los miércoles y los jueves.*

| A | B | C |
|---|---|---|
| yo | aprender a hablar | café por la mañana |
| tú |     español | en el centro de comunicaciones |
| compañero(s) | asistir a | clases *(número)* días de la semana |
|   de cuarto | beber | correspondencia electrónica todos los |
| profesor(es) | comprender |    días |
| estudiante(s) | correr | en el estadio |
| amigo(s) | creer (en) | la importancia de Internet |
| | escribir | clases los *(día de la semana)* |
| | leer | novelas latinoamericanas en el parque |
| | recibir | poemas para la clase de literatura |
| | | las lecturas del libro |
| | | mensajes de texto *(text messages)* |
| | | ¿...? |

**10** **Encuesta #2** Use the cues provided to create a questionnaire. Use the interrogatives you learned earlier in the chapter along with the cues provided. Once your group has completed the questionnaire, ask the questions to members of another group. Remember to save your responses for use later in the chapter.

1. leer libros / por semana
2. compartir cuarto / con compañero(a) de cuarto
3. asistir a clase / todos los días / todas las semanas
4. comer en la cafetería / por semana
5. vender / libros de texto

**11** **La vida universitaria** Write a message to a friend describing your university life. Mention the following things or anything else you might want to talk about. Save your work for use later in the chapter.

- cuántas clases tienes y los días que asistes a clase
- dónde y cuándo comes
- dónde vives
- qué libros lees
- qué actividades te gustan (correr, levantar pesas, mirar televisión, navegar por Internet, leer, escribir, etc.)

## >> Gramática útil 3

### Talking about possessions: Simple possessive adjectives

What two possessive adjectives do you see in this ad for a gym?

Tus horas son nuestras horas

Abierto 24 horas al día para acomodar los horarios
más exigentes... y a los atletas más dedicados

GIMNASIO EL NOCTÁMBULO

www.elnoctambulo.com

1590 Condado Ave., Condado 907 PR

Photos: Chris Fisher/iStockphoto (moon); Libby Chapman/iStockphoto (bar); Soubrette/iStockphoto (background); text: © Cengage Learning 2013

### Cómo usarlo

1. You already have learned to express possession using **de** + a noun or name.

   Es la computadora portátil **de la profesora**.

   It's **the professor's** laptop computer.

2. You can also use possessive adjectives to describe your possessions, other people's possessions, or items that are associated with you. You are already familiar with some possessive adjectives from the phrases **¿Cuál es tu dirección?** and **Aquí tienes mi número de teléfono**.

   —¿Cuándo es **tu** clase de historia?
   —A las dos. Y **mi** clase de español es a las tres.

   When is **your** history class?
   At two. And **my** Spanish class is at three.

3. When you use **su** (which can mean *your, his, her, its,* or *theirs*), the context will usually clarify who is meant. If not, you can follow up with **de** + name.

   Es **su** libro. Es **de la profesora**.

   It's **her** book. It's **the professor's**.

## Cómo formarlo

## LO BÁSICO

*Possessive adjectives* modify nouns in order to express possession. In other words, they tell who owns the item.

**1.** Here are the simple possessive adjectives in Spanish.

| mi<br>mis | *my* | nuestro / nuestra<br>nuestros / nuestras | *our* |
|---|---|---|---|
| tu<br>tus | *your (fam.)* | vuestro / vuestra<br>vuestros / vuestras | *your (fam. pl.)* |
| su<br>sus | *your (form.), his, her, its* | su<br>sus | *your (pl.), their* |

The subject pronoun **tú** *(you)* has an accent on it to differentiate it from the possessive adjective **tu** *(your)*.

**Tú** trabajas los lunes, ¿verdad?

**Tu** libro está en mi casa.

**2.** Notice that . . .

- all possessive adjectives change to reflect number: **mi clase, mis clases; nuestro compañero de cuarto, nuestros compañeros de cuarto.**
- **mi, tu**, and **su** do not change to reflect gender, but **nuestro** and **vuestro** do: **nuestro libro, nuestros amigos, vuestras clases,** but **mi libro, mi clase.**
- unlike other adjectives, which often go after the noun they modify, simple possessive adjectives always go before the noun: **su profesora, nuestras amigas.**

## ACTIVIDADES

**12** **¿De quién es?** Say to whom the following things belong.

MODELO   computadora portátil (yo)
   *Es mi computadora portátil.*

1. apuntes, tarea, CDs, silla (yo)
2. bolígrafos, lápiz, celular, examen (María)
3. calculadoras, cuadernos, dibujo, mochilas (nosotros)
4. diccionario, notas, escritorio, DVDs (tú)
5. libros, tiza, cuarto, papeles (la profesora Roldán)
6. computadora, fotos, salón de clase, apuntes (ustedes)

**13 ¿Es de quién?** Look at the pictures and state what each person has.

MODELO *Marta tiene su guitarra.*

Marta

1.

Martín

2.

Felipe y Eusebio

3.

Sarita y Estela

4.

tú y yo

5.

tú

6.

© Cengage Learning 2013

ustedes

 **14 Conversaciones** You just met someone from Cuba. Write a message to him or her asking for more information. Use the following ideas for your message or make up your own questions.

- dirección
- número de teléfono
- cumpleaños
- clases

- amigos / compañeros de cuarto
- actividades favoritas
- ¿...?

**15 Nuestros amigos** Make two semantic maps like the one below—one each for two of your friends. Put your name at the bottom of each map. In groups of four, give one map to each person. The person whose map it is has to start the conversation. Then, each of the others must say something about the friend using a possessive adjective. Notice whom you're addressing!

Mi amigo(a) se llama _____. ¿Cómo es?

¿nacionalidad? ¿características físicas? ¿características de personalidad? ¿nacionalidad de sus papás?

_____ _____ _____ _____

MODELO
Estudiante #1: *Mi amigo es puertorriqueño.*
Estudiante #2: *Tu amigo puertorriqueño es alto.* (talking to Estudiante #1)
Estudiante #3: *Su amigo puertorriqueño es responsable.* (talking to others)
Estudiante #4: *Su amigo se llama Carlos y sus padres son puertorriqueños también.* (talking to others)

# Sonrisas

© Cengage Learning 2013

**Comprensión** In your opinion, how would you describe the characters in the cartoon?

1. En tu opinión, ¿es generoso y romántico o manipulador el hombre? ¿Por qué?
2. En tu opinión, ¿es inocente y romántica o manipuladora la mujer? ¿Por qué?
3. ¿Crees que los contratos prenupciales son una buena idea o una mala idea?

## >> Gramática útil 4

### Indicating destination and future plans: The verb **ir**

Quiero hacerle una entrevista para un programa que **vamos a transmitir** en la página web de la Universidad.

You have already used similar expressions: **necesitar** + infinitive *(to need to do something)*, **tener que** + infinitive *(to have to do something)*, and **dejar de** + infinitive *(to stop doing something)*.

### Cómo usarlo

You can use the Spanish verb **ir** to say where you and others are going. You can also use it to say what you and others are going to do in the near future.

**Vamos a** la biblioteca mañana.          *We're going to the library tomorrow.*
**Vamos a estudiar.**          *We're going to study.*

### Cómo formarlo

#### LO BÁSICO

An *irregular verb* is one that does not follow the normal rules, such as **tener**, which you learned in **Chapter 1**.

A *preposition* links nouns, pronouns, or noun phrases to the rest of the sentence. Prepositions can express location, time sequence, purpose, or direction. *In, to, after, under,* and *for* are all English prepositions.

1. Here is the verb **ir** in the present indicative tense. **Ir**, like the verbs **ser** and **tener** that you have already learned, is an irregular verb.

| ir *(to go)* | | | |
|---|---|---|---|
| yo | **voy** | nosotros / nosotras | **vamos** |
| tú | **vas** | vosotros / vosotras | **vais** |
| Ud. / él / ella | **va** | Uds. / ellos / ellas | **van** |

2. Use the preposition **a** with the verb **ir** to say where you are going.

**Voy a** la cafetería.          *I'm going to the cafeteria.*

3. When you want to use the verb **ir** to say what you are going to do, use this formula: **ir** + **a** + *infinitive.*

**Vamos a comer** a las cinco hoy. Después, **vamos a ir** al concierto.          *We're going to eat at 5:00 today. Afterward, we're going to go to the concert.*

4. When you use **a** together with **el**, it contracts to **al**. The same holds true for **de** + **el**: **del**.

a + el = **al**          de + el = **del**

Voy **a la** biblioteca y luego **al** gimnasio. Después, **al** mediodía, voy a estudiar en la biblioteca **del** centro de comunicaciones.

© Cengage Learning 2013

## ACTIVIDADES

**16 Vamos a...** Say what the people indicated plan to do and where they are going to do it.

MODELO   yo (estudiar: biblioteca)
         *Voy a estudiar. Voy a la biblioteca.*

1. Pedro y Rafael (levantar pesas: gimnasio)
2. mi compañero de cuarto y yo (correr: parque)
3. Fabiola (escuchar los CDs de español: centro de comunicaciones)
4. Tomás, Andrea y yo (tomar un refresco: cafetería)
5. tú (comprar libros: librería)
6. Lourdes (descansar: residencia estudiantil)
7. tú (leer libros: biblioteca)
8. David y Patricia (comer: restaurante caribeño)

**17 ¡Pobre Miguel!** Listen as Miguel describes his schedule to his best friend Cristina. As you listen, write down where he goes on each day of the week. Then use **ir** + **a** to create seven complete sentences that describe his schedule.

Track 10

1. los lunes:
2. los martes:
3. los miércoles:
4. los jueves:
5. los viernes:
6. los sábados:
7. los domingos:

**18 Encuesta #3** You need to get more information about student life for the description you will be writing later in this chapter. Find out as much as you can about your partner's leisure activities. Ask questions such as the following and take notes. Then, as a class, tally the information you collected.

El tiempo libre

1. ¿Adónde vas los viernes y los sábados por la noche? ¿Con quién vas?
2. ¿Adónde vas entresemana cuando no estudias? ¿Con quién vas?
3. ¿...?

**Vocabulario útil:** un club, una discoteca, el cine *(movie theater)*, un restaurante, un centro comercial *(mall)*, un partido *(game)* de fútbol americano / de básquetbol, pasar tiempo en línea, ir a una fiesta, etc.

# ¡Explora y exprésate!

# Cuba

Christian Kober/Getty Images

## Información general ▶

**Nombre oficial:** República de Cuba

**Población:** 11.477.459

**Capital:** La Habana (f. 1515) (2.200.000 hab.)

**Otras ciudades importantes:** Santiago (450.000 hab.), Camagüey (300.000 hab.)

**Moneda:** peso cubano

**Idiomas:** español (oficial)

**Mapa de Cuba:** Apéndice D

---

Notice that **f.** is the abbreviation for **fundado(a)**, which means *founded*. La Habana, the capital city of Cuba, was founded in 1515.

Notice that **hab.** is the abbreviation for **habitantes**, which means *inhabitants*. This is how population statistics are written in Spanish.

## Vale saber…

- La población de la isla es una mezcla *(mixture)* de los nativos originales (taínos), descendientes de esclavos africanos y europeos, mezcla que produce una cultura única. También hay una población china significante, resultado de la inmigración china a Norteamérica y al Caribe durante los años 1800.

- Raúl Castro (hermano de Fidel) es el actual presidente de Cuba.

## La educación para todos

Cuba se distingue por tener uno de los mejores sistemas de educación del mundo. Desde la revolución cubana en 1959, el sistema de educación ha sido *(has been)* prioridad del gobierno cubano, empezando con la Campaña Nacional de Alfabetización en Cuba en 1960. El objetivo de la campaña fue *(was)* eliminar el anafalbetismo y llevar maestros *(to bring teachers)* y escuelas *(schools)* a todas las áreas del país. La educación, ¡para todos!

Chine Nouvelle/SIPA/Newscom

# Puerto Rico

## Información general

**Nombre oficial:** Estado Libre Asociado de Puerto Rico (Commonwealth of Puerto Rico)

**Población:** 3.997.663

**Capital:** San Juan (f. 1521) (450.000 hab.)

**Otras ciudades importantes:** Ponce (200.000 hab.), Caguas (150.000 hab.)

**Moneda:** dólar estadounidense

**Idiomas:** español, inglés (oficiales)

**Mapa de Puerto Rico:** Apéndice D

Artifan/Shutterstock

## Vale saber…

- A los puertorriqueños también se les conoce como *(are also known as)* "boricuas", ya que antes de la llegada de los europeos en 1493 la isla se llamaba *(was called)* Borinquen.
- Los puertorriqueños son ciudadanos *(citizens)* estadounidenses, pero no votan en elecciones de Estados Unidos.

## La educación bilingüe

La educación en Puerto Rico está garantizada constitucionalmente y es gratuita hasta el nivel secundario *(secondary level)*. El español es el idioma de instrucción, pero los estudiantes toman clases de inglés en todos los grados. Los estudios universitarios son iguales al sistema estadounidense: el bachillerato *(bachelor's degree)*, la maestría *(master's degree)* y finalmente el doctorado *(Ph.D)*. Ser boricua es ser bilingüe.

Suzanne Murphy-Larronde/DDBSTOCK

# República Dominicana

pashapixel/Shutterstock

## Información general

**Nombre oficial:** República Dominicana

**Población:** 9.794.487

**Capital:** Santo Domingo (f. 1492) (2.500.000 hab.)

**Otras ciudades importantes:** Santiago de los Caballeros (2.000.000 hab.), La Romana (300.000 hab.)

**Moneda:** peso dominicano

**Idiomas:** español

**Mapa de República Dominicana:** Apéndice D

## Vale saber…

- La isla que comparten la República Dominicana y Haití se llama La Hispaniola. Estuvo bajo *(It was under)* control español hasta 1697, cuando la parte oeste *(western)* pasó a ser territorio francés.
- Santo Domingo es la primera ciudad del Nuevo Mundo *(New World)*. En esta ciudad capital, se construyeron *(were built)* la primera catedral, el primer hospital y la primera universidad del Nuevo Mundo.

## La universidad más antigua del Nuevo Mundo

Vova Pomortzeff / Alamy

La Universidad Santo Tomás de Aquino, ahora conocida como la Universidad Autónoma de Santo Domingo, se puede considerar *(can be considered)* la universidad más antigua del Nuevo Mundo. Fundada en 1538—unos cien años antes que Harvard en 1636 y Yale en 1701—empezó *(it began)* con cuatro facultades: medicina, derecho *(law)*, teología y artes. ¡Cómo han cambiado los tiempos! *(How times have changed!)* Hoy día la Universidad ofrece muchos más cursos, entre ellos: ingeniería, arquitectura, economía e informática, por supuesto.

**La información general** Answer these questions in English.

1. Look at the maps on page 83. What is the Spanish name of the area in which these three countries are located?
2. Which of the three countries is closest to the United States?
3. Which two countries are islands and which one shares an island with another country?
4. Why are Puerto Ricans called **boricuas**?
5. Which island citizens are also American citizens?
6. Which country boasts the first city in the New World?

**El tema de la educación**

1. What was the objective of Cuba's "Campaña Nacional de Alfabetización"?
2. Why are "boricuas" bilingual?
3. What were the first four academic departments established in the oldest university of the New World?

### ⊕ ¿QUIERES SABER MÁS?

On the chart that you started at the beginning of the chapter, add what you already know under **Lo que aprendí.** For the **Lo que quiero aprender** column, pick one or two of the things you would still like to learn, or one or two of the key words below to investigate online. Be prepared to share this information with the class.

**Palabras clave: (Cuba)** la revolución cubana, José Martí, Celia Cruz; **(Puerto Rico)** Estado Libre Asociado de Puerto Rico, Rosario Ferré, Tito Puente; **(República Dominicana)** Juan Pablo Duarte, las hermanas Mirabal, Sammy Sosa

⊕ **Tú en el mundo hispano** To explore opportunities to use your Spanish to study, volunteer, or do internships in Cuba, Puerto Rico, and the Dominican Republic, follow the links on **www.cengagebrain.com**.

🎧 **Ritmos del mundo hispano** Follow the links at **www.cengagebrain.com** to hear music from Cuba, Puerto Rico, and the Dominican Republic.

### ESTRATEGIA

**Using visuals to aid in comprehension**

When visuals accompany a text, looking at them first can help you determine the subject. When you approach a reading, look first at the visuals and any captions that accompany them to see if they help you understand the content.

**1** Look at the following article about three different schools (**escuelas**) in the Caribbean. Focus on the photos, captions, and headlines, then match the general information on the right with the photos on the left.

1. _____ Foto A
2. _____ Foto B
3. _____ Foto C

a. Aquí los estudiantes estudian técnicas para filmar programas de televisión y cine.
b. Los estudiantes de esta escuela toman clases de música.
c. Esta escuela ofrece cursos de bellas artes, ilustración, diseño gráfico y diseño digital.

**2** The following are some unknown words and phrases you will encounter in the reading passages. Although not all the words are cognates, they are somewhat similar to their English counterparts. See if you can match them up.

1. _____ sin pagar nada
2. _____ se han graduado
3. _____ está afiliada con
4. _____ se admiten
5. _____ construyó
6. _____ villa
7. _____ fue inaugurado
8. _____ se ofrecen
9. _____ edición
10. _____ han recibido

a. *was inaugurated*
b. *village*
c. *without paying anything*
d. *editing*
e. *are admitted*
f. *constructed*
g. *have received*
h. *is affiliated with*
i. *have graduated*
j. *are offered*

**3** Now, using the information you gained from looking at the visuals, read the article, and focus on getting the main idea. Don't forget to use cognates and active vocabulary to help you understand the content. Try not to worry about unknown words and just focus on getting the main information.

## LECTURA

# Tres escuelas interesantes del Caribe

Redferns/Getty Images

**A.** El saxofonista puertorriqueño David Sánchez, uno de los graduados famosos de "La Libre"

### La Escuela Libre[1] de Música Ernesto Ramos Antonini

En Puerto Rico muchos estudiantes de música toman cursos sin pagar nada, gracias a cinco escuelas públicas de educación musical. Establecidas a finales de los años 40 por un político local, estas escuelas han graduado a miles[2] de estudiantes. Entre los graduados famosos están el saxofonista de jazz David Sánchez y el cantante salsero Gilberto Santa Rosa.

La escuela más grande es la de San Juan, que está afiliada con el prestigioso Berklee College of Music en Boston. Los cursos de estudio incluyen la música clásica, rock, jazz, contemporánea y tradicional, y el currículum prepara a los estudiantes para estudiar cursos más avanzados en el Conservatorio de Música de Puerto Rico. En San Juan sólo se admiten 100 estudiantes al año, aunque se reciben solicitudes[3] de más de 600 personas, así que los estudiantes de la escuela son unos de los más talentosos de la isla.

### La Escuela de Diseño Altos de Chavón

Esta escuela data de los años 70 cuando la República Dominicana construyó un centro cultural en la pequeña villa de Altos de Chavón. La Escuela de Diseño, que forma parte del centro, fue inaugurado por Frank Sinatra en 1982 y está afiliada con el famoso Parsons The New School for Design en la ciudad[4] de Nueva York.

Los 110 estudiantes de La Escuela de Diseño se especializan en campos de estudio como bellas artes e ilustración, diseño gráfico, diseño de modas[5], diseño digital y diseño de interiores.

Más de 1.000 estudiantes dominicanos e internacionales se han graduado de la escuela. Los graduados de la escuela son elegibles para transferirse directamente a Parsons en Nueva York o París.

Courtesy of Altos de Chavon/Alex Otero

**B.** Unos estudiantes de arte de La Escuela de Diseño

### La Escuela Internacional de Cine y Televisión

En la Escuela Internacional de Cine y Televisión (EICTV) de San Antonio de los Baños, Cuba, se ofrecen cursos de formación audiovisual para estudiantes cubanos e internacionales. La EICTV fue inaugurada en 1986 y es presidida por el famoso escritor colombiano Gabriel García Márquez. Los profesores, además de ser instructores, son cineastas profesionales que dirigen[6] películas y documentales a nivel mundial[7].

Paul Bennett/Corbis

**C.** Un estudiante de la Escuela Internacional de Cine y Televisión

Los estudiantes de la EICTV estudian siete especialidades en el curso regular: guión[8], producción, dirección, fotografía, sonido[9], edición y documentales. También se presentan unos veinte talleres[10] especializados cada año. Más de 1.500 estudiantes de unos treinta países se han graduado de la EICTV desde su incepción y los graduados de la escuela han recibido más de 100 premios[11] en varios festivales nacionales e internacionales

[1]Free  [2]thousands  [3]**aunque**…: although they receive applications  [4]city  [5]fashion  [6]they direct  [7]**a**…: worldwide  [8]script  [9]sound
[10]workshops  [11]prizes

**4** Answer the following questions about the readings to see how well you understood them.

1. ¿Quiénes son dos graduados famosos de la Escuela Libre de la Música?
2. ¿Con qué institución estadounidense está afiliada la Escuela Libre de la Música?
3. ¿Cuáles son tres tipos de música que los estudiantes estudian en la Escuela Libre?
4. ¿Con qué institución estadounidense está afiliada la Escuela de Diseño Altos de Chavón?
5. ¿Cuáles son cuatro campos de estudio que se ofrecen en la Escuela de Diseño?
6. ¿Cuántos graduados de la Escuela de Diseño hay?
7. ¿Qué autor está afiliado con la EICTV?
8. ¿Cuáles son cuatro campos de estudio que se ofrecen en la EICTV?

**5** With a partner, answer the following questions about the reading and about your own interests.

1. ¿Cuál de las tres escuelas les interesa *(interests you)* más?
2. ¿Cuál de los campos de estudio de esa escuela les interesa más?
3. ¿Conocen *(Are you familiar with)* unas escuelas similares en Estados Unidos? ¿Cómo se llaman?

Esta escuela está en Providence, Rhode Island. ¿Sabes *(Do you know)* cómo se llama y cuál es su especialización?

Andre Jenny / Alamy

## > Antes de escribir

### ESTRATEGIA

**Prewriting—Brainstorming ideas**

When you are planning to write and need ideas, try brainstorming. You can do this verbally with a partner, writing down your ideas, or on your own, writing freely and without restriction. The key thing is to write ideas as they occur, without evaluating them. Then take the list of ideas and decide which work best.

> It is important to try to brainstorm in Spanish. This will get you to start "thinking" in Spanish, which in turn will lead to increased comfort and ease with the language.

**1** Retrieve the information from the three **Encuesta** activities (**Activity 5** on p. 97, **Activity 10** on p. 101, and **Activity 18** on p. 107). With a partner, study the results and brainstorm ideas to describe the life of a typical student at your university.

**2** Look at the following partial diary entry, and organize your information into a similar format. Try to use only words you've already learned.

> viernes, 10 de octubre
>
> ¡Tengo muchas actividades hoy! A las ocho, tengo clase de química. Luego, voy a ir al café para estudiar para el examen de historia a las diez...
> Por la tarde, tengo que... Por la noche, voy a...

© Cengage Learning 2013

## > Composición

**3** Using the previous model, work with your partner on a rough draft of your diary entry. For now, just write freely without worrying about mistakes. Here are some additional words and phrases that may be useful as you write.

| | | | |
|---|---|---|---|
| **primero** | *first* | **finalmente** | *finally* |
| **luego** | *later* | **mucho que hacer** | *a lot to do* |
| **entonces** | *then* | **un día (muy) ocupado** | *a (very) busy day* |
| **después** | *after that* | **con** | *with* |

## > Después de escribir

**4** Now, with your partner, go back over your diary entry and revise it.

Did you . . .

- make sure you included all the necessary information?
- check to make sure the verbs are conjugated correctly?
- make sure articles, nouns, and adjectives agree?
- use possessive adjectives correctly?
- look for misspellings?

# Vocabulario

## Campos de estudio   *Fields of study*

**Los cursos básicos**   *Basic courses*
**la arquitectura**   *architecture*
**las ciencias políticas**   *political science*
**la economía**   *economics*
**la educación**   *education*
**la geografía**   *geography*
**la historia**   *history*
**la ingeniería**   *engineering*
**la psicología**   *psychology*

**Las humanidades**   *Humanities*
**la filosofía**   *philosophy*
**las lenguas / los idiomas**   *languages*
**la literatura**   *literature*

**Las lenguas / Los idiomas**   *Languages*
**el alemán**   *German*
**el chino**   *Chinese*
**el español**   *Spanish*
**el francés**   *French*
**el inglés**   *English*
**el japonés**   *Japanese*

**Las matemáticas**   *Mathematics*
**el cálculo**   *calculus*
**la computación**   *computer science*

**la estadística**   *statistics*
**la informática**   *computer science*

**Las ciencias**   *Sciences*
**la biología**   *biology*
**la física**   *physics*
**la medicina**   *medicine*
**la química**   *chemistry*
**la salud**   *health*

**Los negocios**   *Business*
**la administración de empresas**   *business administration*
**la contabilidad**   *accounting*
**el mercadeo**   *marketing*

**La comunicación pública**   *Public communications*
**el periodismo**   *journalism*
**la publicidad**   *public relations*

**Las artes**   *The arts*
**el arte**   *art*
**el baile**   *dance*
**el diseño gráfico**   *graphic design*
**la música**   *music*
**la pintura**   *painting*

## Lugares en la universidad   *Places in the university*

**¿Dónde tienes la clase de...?**
   *Where does your . . . class meet?*
**En el centro de computación.**
   *In the computer center.*
**...el centro de comunicaciones.**
   *. . . the media center.*
**...el gimnasio.**   *. . . the gymnasium.*

**la cafetería**   *the cafeteria*
**la librería**   *the bookstore*
**la residencia estudiantil**   *the dorm*

## Los días de la semana   *The days of the week*

| | | | |
|---|---|---|---|
| **lunes** *Monday* | **miércoles** *Wednesday* | **viernes** *Friday* | **domingo** *Sunday* |
| **martes** *Tuesday* | **jueves** *Thursday* | **sábado** *Saturday* | |

## Para pedir y dar la hora   *Asking for and giving the time*

**Mira el reloj para decir la hora...**   *Look at the clock to tell the time . . .*
**¿Qué hora es?**   *What time is it?*
**Es la una.**   *It's one o'clock.*
**Son las dos.**   *It's two o'clock.*
**Son las... y cuarto.**   *It's . . . fifteen.*
**Son las... y media.**   *It's . . . thirty.*

**Son las... menos cuarto.**   *It's a quarter to . . .*
**Faltan quince para las...**   *It's a quarter to . . .*

**tarde**   *late*
**temprano**   *early*
**¿A qué hora es la clase de español?**   *(At) What time is Spanish class?*
**Es a la / a las...**   *It's at . . .*

## Mañana, tarde o noche   *Morning, afternoon, or night*

**de la mañana** *in the morning* (with precise time)
**de la tarde** *in the afternoon* (with precise time)
**de la noche** *in the evening* (with precise time)

**por la mañana** *during the morning*
**por la tarde** *during the afternoon*
**por la noche** *during the evening*

**Es mediodía.** *It's noon.*
**Es medianoche.** *It's midnight.*

## Para hablar de la fecha   *Talking about the date*

**¿Qué día es hoy?** *What day is today?*
**Hoy es martes treinta.** *Today is Tuesday the 30th.*

**¿A qué fecha estamos?** *What is today's date?*
**Es el treinta de octubre.** *It's the 30th of October.*
**Es el primero de noviembre.** *It's the first of November.*

**¿Cuándo es el Día de las Madres?** *When is Mother's Day?*
**Es el doce de mayo.** *It's May 12th.*

**el día** *day*
**la semana** *week*
**el fin de semana** *weekend*
**el mes** *month*
**el año** *year*
**todos los días** *every day*
**entresemana** *during the week/on weekdays*

**ayer** *yesterday*
**hoy** *today*
**mañana** *tomorrow*

## Para hacer preguntas   *Asking questions*

**¿Cómo?** *How?*
**¿Cuál(es)?** *What? Which one(s)?*
**¿Cuándo?** *When?*
**¿Cuánto(a)?** *How much?*
**¿Cuántos(as)?** *How many?*
**¿De quién es?** *Whose is this?*

**¿De quiénes son?** *Whose are these?*
**¿Dónde?** *Where?*
**¿Por qué?** *Why?*
**¿Qué?** *What? Which?*
**¿Quién(es)?** *Who?*

## Verbos

**abrir** *to open*
**aprender** *to learn*
**asistir a** *to attend*
**beber** *to drink*
**comer** *to eat*
**compartir** *to share*
**comprender** *to understand*
**correr** *to run*
**creer (en)** *to believe (in)*
**deber** *should, ought*
**dejar de** *to stop (doing something)*

**describir** *to describe*
**descubrir** *to discover*
**escribir** *to write*
**imprimir** *to print*
**ir** *to go*
**ir a** *to be going to (do something)*
**leer** *to read*
**recibir** *to receive*
**transmitir** *to broadcast*
**vender** *to sell*
**vivir** *to live*

## Adjetivos posesivos

**mi(s)** *my*
**tu(s)** *your (fam.)*
**su(s)** *your (sing. form., pl.) his, her, their*

**nuestro(a) / nuestros(as)** *our*
**vuestro(a) / vuestros(as)** *your (pl. fam.)*

## Contracciones

**al (a + el)** *to the*
**del (de + el)** *from the, of the*

## Otras palabras

**porque** *because*
**escuela** *school*

# Repaso y preparación

Complete these activities to check your understanding of the new grammar points in **Chapter 3** before you move on to **Chapter 4**.

The answers to the activities in this section can be found in **Appendix B**.

## Interrogative words (p. 94)

**1** Complete each sentence in the chat with an interrogative word (**cuál, cuándo, cuántas, por qué, qué, quien**), capitalizing as needed.

| | |
|---|---|
| **Finita7:** | Marcos, ¿_____ estudias? |
| **Marcosis:** | Historia. ¿_____? |
| **Finita7:** | ¡Necesito tu ayuda! ¡Por favor! |
| **Marcosis:** | ¿_____ es tu problema? |
| **Finita7:** | ¡Tengo que escribir un informe! |
| **Marcosis:** | ¿Para _____ tienes que entregar la tarea? |
| **Finita7:** | ¡Mañana! |
| **Marcosis:** | ¿_____ páginas? |
| **Finita7:** | ¡Cinco! |
| **Marcosis:** | ¿_____ es el profesor? |
| **Finita7:** | ¡Martínez! |
| **Marcosis** | ¡Noooooooooo! Este problema no tiene solución... |
| **Finita7:** | :-O |

## The present indicative of regular -er and -ir verbs (p. 98)

**2** Complete each sentence with the present-tense form of the verb indicated.

1. Marta _____ (escribir) la tarea para la clase de ciencias políticas.
2. Tú y yo _____ (deber) ir a la biblioteca.
3. Yo _____ (comer) pizza mientras estudio.
4. Uds. _____ (vivir) en la Residencia Central, ¿verdad?
5. La profesora de literatura _____ (leer) muchas novelas.

## Simple possessive adjectives (p. 102)

**3** Complete each sentence with a possessive adjective.

1. No comprendo a _____ padres.
2. ¿Tienes _____ notas?
3. Escribimos _____ tarea.
4. Ella lee _____ papeles.
5. Ellos abren _____ libros.
6. Aquí tienes _____ número.

## The verb ir (p. 106)

**4** Complete the sentences with the present-indicative forms of **ir**.

1. Si yo _____ a la biblioteca, ¿qué _____ a hacer ustedes?
2. Mi amiga _____ a correr, pero nosotros _____ al gimnasio.
3. Tú _____ a la librería, ¿verdad?

# Preparación para el Capítulo 4

### Gustar + infinitive (Chapter 2)

**5** Use the cues to create complete sentences. Follow the model.

**MODELO** (a Marta) / gustar correr
*A Marta le gusta correr.*

1. (a mí) / gustar leer
2. (a nosotros) / gustar comer
3. (a ustedes) / gustar bailar
4. (a ti) / gustar cocinar
5. (a él) / gustar patinar
6. (a mí) / gustar cantar

Complete these activities to review some previously learned grammatical structures that will be helpful when you learn the new grammar in **Chapter 4**.

Be sure to reread **Chapter 3: Gramática útil 2** before moving on to the new **Chapter 4** grammar sections.

### The present indicative of regular -ar verbs (Chapter 2)

**6** Complete the description with present indicative forms.

Tengo dos compañeros de cuarto. Roque es muy serio y 1. _____ (estudiar) mucho. También 2. _____ (cocinar) la cena. ¡Es un chef fantástico! El otro, Raul, 3. _____ (tocar) la guitarra y 4. _____ (cantar). A veces, él y Roque 5. _____ (levantar) pesas y 6. _____ (practicar) deportes, como el tenis y el fútbol. Nosotros 7. _____ (mirar) televisión y 8. _____ (alquilar) videos por las noches. ¿Y yo? Pues, yo 9. _____ (trabajar) mucho y a veces 10. _____ (visitar) a amigos. ¡Yo no 11. _____ (pasar) mucho tiempo allí!

### Present indicative of **ser** (Chapter 1), Adjective agreement (Chapter 2)

**7** Use an adjective from the list to write a sentence with **ser** about each person.

**MODELO** *Neli es muy trabajadora.*

**Adjetivos:** activo(a), divertido(a), egoísta, generoso(a), impaciente, perezoso(a), tímido(a) trabajador(a)

Neli

1.

Rogelio y Mauricio

2.

tú

3.

nosotros

4.

yo

5.

Sandra

6.

Néstor y Nicolás

# ¿Te interesa la tecnología?

## CONEXIONES VIRTUALES Y PERSONALES

Las nuevas tecnologías tienen un impacto tremendo en las áreas de las comunicaciones, los negocios y las relaciones personales, entre otras. ¡Nuestro mundo está cambiando *(is changing)* todos los días!

**¿Cuáles son tus aparatos electrónicos favoritos y para qué los usas?**

### Communication

By the end of this chapter you will be able to

- talk about computers and technology
- identify colors
- talk about likes and dislikes
- describe people, emotions, and conditions
- talk about current activities
- say how something is done

# Un viaje por España

Globe Art: Adapted from Shutterstock/rtguest

España es el único país europeo donde el español es la lengua oficial. España forma la Península Ibérica con Portugal, y por eso tiene costas en el Atlántico, el mar Mediterráneo y el mar Cantábrico. También tiene varias sierras, entre ellas la sierra de Guadarrama en la parte central del país y la sierra Nevada en el sur.

| País / Área | Tamaño y fronteras | Sitios de interés |
|---|---|---|
| **España** 499.542 km$^2$ | un poco más de dos veces el área de Oregón; fronteras con Portugal, Francia y Andorra y con Marruecos (Ceuta y Melilla) | la Alhambra, el Museo del Prado, el Museo Guggenheim, las Islas Canarias, las Islas Baleares |

**¿Qué sabes?**  Di si las siguientes oraciones son ciertas (**C**) o falsas (**F**).

1. España está situada completamente en Europa.
2. Varios grupos de islas también forman parte de España.
3. Hay unos museos importantes en España.
4. España es más pequeña que Oregón.

**Lo que sé y lo que quiero aprender**  Completa la tabla del **Apéndice A**. Escribe algunos datos que **ya sabes** sobre España en la columna **Lo que sé**. Después, añade algunos temas que **quieres aprender** a la columna **Lo que quiero aprender**. Guarda la tabla para usarla otra vez en la sección **¡Explora y exprésate!** en la página 151.

## Cultures

By the end of this chapter you will have explored

- the Spanish empire
- the great artists and writers of Spain
- the Arabic influence on Spanish architecture
- Buika, a Spanish singer who blends many musical styles
- a popular Spanish social networking site
- borrowed words on the Internet

## ⓞ >> Vocabulario útil 1

**BETO:** ¡Estoy furioso!

**CHELA:** Pero, ¿por qué?

**BETO:** Primero llego tarde a la clase de literatura.

**CHELA:** Llegar tarde no es una tragedia.

**BETO:** ¡Tenemos examen! Abro mi **computadora portátil**, pero en la **pantalla** dice que no tengo suficiente **memoria** para abrir la **aplicación**.

>> **La tecnología**
**El hardware**

la computadora
el monitor
el disco duro
la impresora
la computadora portátil
la pantalla
el puerto de USB
el micrófono
el módem interno
el cable
la memoria flash / el pendrive
la tecla
el módem externo
el ratón
el lector de CD-ROM o DVD
el teclado
el altoparlante
los audífonos

> **Notice:** In Spain, **la computadora** is called **el ordenador**. **El computador** is also used, mostly in Latin America. Another term for **hacer clic** is **pulsar**.

## >> La tecnología

**El software**
**la aplicación** *application*
**los archivos** *files*
  **el archivo PDF** *PDF attachment*
**el ícono del programa**
  *program icon*
**el juego interactivo**
  *interactive game*
**el programa antivirus** *antivirus*
  *program*
**el programa de procesamiento de**
  **textos** *word processing program*

**Funciones de la computadora**
**archivar** *to file*
**bajar / descargar** *to download*
**conectar** *to connect*
**enviar** *to send*
**funcionar** *to function*
**grabar** *to record*
**guardar** *to save*
**hacer clic / doble clic** *to click /*
  *double-click*
**instalar** *to install*
**subir / cargar** *to upload*

> PDF stands for **el formato de documento portátil** and is pronounced **pe-de-efe**.

> To describe the hard drive of your computer or its processor, use:
> - **un disco duro con capacidad de 500 GB (gigabytes)**
> - **un procesador a 2.4 o 2.53 GHz (gigahercio)**

## >> Los colores

azul   amarillo   anaranjado   blanco   café, marrón   gris

morado   negro   rojo   rosa, rosado   verde

© Cengage Learning 2013

> When a color is used as an adjective, it comes after the noun it modifies.
> - If it ends in **-o**, it changes to match the gender and number of that noun: **la silla negra**, **los cuadernos rojos**.
> - If the color ends in **-e**, add an **s** to the plural: **las pizarras verdes**.
> - If the color ends in a consonant, add **es** to the plural: **los libros azules**.
> - **Marrón** in the plural changes to **marrones**, with no accent. Can you figure out why, for pronunciation reasons, it loses the accent?
> - Note that **rosa** and **café** change to reflect number, but not gender.
> - If you want to say that a color is dark, use **fuerte** or **oscuro**. For example, **amarillo fuerte** or **amarillo oscuro**. If you want to say that a color is light, use **claro**. For example, **azul claro**.

## ACTIVIDADES

**1** **La computadora** Un amigo necesita hacer *(needs to do)* ciertas cosas en la computadora. ¿Qué parte de la computadora va a necesitar para hacer lo que quiere? Escoge de la segunda columna.

1. _____ Necesito imprimir el correo electrónico.
2. _____ Necesito ver un video de YouTube.
3. _____ Necesito conectar el teclado al monitor.
4. _____ Necesito escuchar música mientras trabajo.
5. _____ Necesito escribir un documento.
6. _____ Necesito archivar un documento.
7. _____ Necesito grabar un mensaje para enviar a mis amigos.
8. _____ Necesito instalar el programa de procesamiento de textos.

a. los audífonos
b. la pantalla
c. el teclado
d. la memoria flash
e. la impresora
f. el cable
g. el micrófono
h. el lector de DVD-ROM

Starting in this chapter, many of the activity direction lines will be presented in Spanish. Here are a few words that will help you understand Spanish direction lines: **di** *(say)*, **haz** *(do)*, **escoge** *(choose)*, **luego** *(then, later)*, **siguiente** *(following)*, **oración** *(sentence)*, **párrafo** *(paragraph)*.

**2** **El sitio web** Tu compañero(a) quiere buscar información sobre ciertos temas en el servicio ¡VIVA! Latino. Tú le dices *(You tell him/her)* en qué ícono debe hacer doble clic. Luego, él o ella te dirige a los íconos que corresponden a tus intereses.

## ¡VIVA! Latino

**Directorio de sitios web**

⭐ **Arte y cultura**
Literatura, Teatro, Museos, Guías

⭐ **Educación**
Primaria, Secundaria, Universidades

⭐ **Deportes y ocio**
Deportes, Fútbol, Juegos, Turismo

⭐ **Espectáculos y diversión**
Cine, Actores, Música, Humor

⭐ **Internet y computadoras**
WWW, Aplicaciones, Chat, Redes

⭐ **Medios de comunicación**
Radio, TV, Revistas, Periódicos

⭐ **Salud**
Medicina, Enfermedades, Ejercicio, Dietas

☆ **Materias de consulta**
Bibliotecas, Diccionarios

**MODELO** el Museo del Prado en Madrid
Tú: *Necesito más información sobre el Museo del Prado en Madrid.*
Compañero(a): *Haz doble clic en el ícono rojo.*

1. una dieta vegetariana
2. mi actor (actriz) favorito(a)
3. un diccionario español / inglés
4. la Copa Mundial de Fútbol
5. un programa de procesamiento de textos
6. la Universidad Complutense de Madrid
7. el periódico *El País* de Madrid
8. ¿…?

**3** **Mi computadora** ¿Puedes describir tu computadora? Incluye en tu descripción todos los componentes de tu computadora y menciona el color de cada uno si es apropiado.

**MODELO** *El monitor de mi computadora es azul y blanco. Los cables son grises. El ratón es blanco. Los altoparlantes son negros. Las teclas en el teclado son blancas…*

---

*Margin notes:*

In some countries, the Internet is referred to as **la Internet**, in others as **el Internet**, and in others still, it is referred to simply as **Internet**, with no article to indicate gender.

If you want to describe the colors of your mousepad, you can say **almohadilla de ratón**, or simply **mousepad**.

**124** Capítulo 4

## ¡Fíjate! El lenguaje de Internet

Pedro Armestre/AFP/Getty Images/Newscom

The Internet is a source of entirely new words in English, a development that has created language issues for translators and Internet users alike. Online word forums in which people from different countries discuss how to translate Internet terms into their own languages are useful in dealing with these issues. In many cases, the universal Internet terms have simply stayed in English. Here are some examples of words that have commonly (or infrequently) used Spanish translations, and others that do not yet (and may never!) have translations.

**Blog:** This is an abbreviated form of Web-log, and is usually referred to simply as *blog*, losing the *We* of Web. In Spanish, it is common to simply say **blog**, but it can also be defined as: **un diario personal en un sitio web que contiene reflexiones, comentarios, fotos, video o enlaces**.

**Forum: Foro** is the common Spanish translation. If you are referring to an announcement board, you would say **un tablón de anuncios**. A message board is **un tablón de mensajes**.

**Podcast: Un podcast** is a radio broadcast that is Portable On Demand. If you want to use only Spanish words, you could say **una emisora radial en Internet. Los podcasts** are downloaded to **un teléfono inteligente** or **un smartphone**, where the user can listen to them at leisure.

**Video conferencing:** Chat with your friends via Internet using **un sistema de video conferencia**.

**Wifi:** Most Spanish speakers simply say **wifi**, with a wide variation in pronunciation from country to country. To be technically correct, you could refer to it as **la red inalámbrica. (Alambre** means *wire,* which is why **inalámbrica** means *wireless.)* Although you would be understood with this mouthful of a phrase, you would probably be considered rather geeky. Stick with **wifi** for now.

**Text messaging:** Everyone texts these days. In Spanish this would be **enviar un mensaje de texto**.

**Instant messaging:** If you instant message someone, this is referred to as **enviar un mensaje instantáneo**.

**Sound files:** Music downloads are **archivos de sonido** or **MP3s** that can be transferred directly to **MP3 portátiles** or **los smartphones**.

**Las redes sociales:** Social networking sites like Facebook and Twitter have become the preferred mode of communication for many people throughout the world.

Without a doubt, the Internet will continue to create new functions and new words as its uses multiply. Don't panic! You can find a site online that will help you find just the Spanish expression you are looking for!

**Práctica** Escribe una lista de términos de Internet en inglés que no sabes decir en español. Con un(a) compañero(a), busca en Internet un sitio con las traducciones y las pronunciaciones, o simplemente verifica que lo más común es usar el término en inglés.

## ◉ >> Vocabulario útil 2

© Cengage Learning 2013

**BETO:** Empiezo a salir del salón de clases. No sé en dónde, pero entre el salón y la biblioteca, pierdo mi **asistente electrónico**.

**CHELA:** Ya me voy. Estoy muy **aburrida** con tu cuento trágico.

### >> Las emociones

**aburrido(a)** *bored*
**cansado(a)** *tired*
**contento(a)** *happy*
**enfermo(a)** *sick*
**enojado(a)** *angry*
**furioso(a)** *furious*
**nervioso(a)** *nervous*
**ocupado(a)** *busy*
**preocupado(a)** *worried*
**seguro(a)** *sure*
**triste** *sad*

### >> Aparatos electrónicos

Products like the iPod®, the iPhone®, Android™, the Blackberry®, Bluetooth®, etc., can all be referred to in English when speaking in Spanish. For example, **¿Tienes un iPhone? ¿De qué color es tu iPod?**

**el asistente electrónico** *electronic notebook*
**la cámara digital** *digital camera*
**la cámara web** *webcam*
**el MP3 portátil** *portable MP3 player*
**el reproductor / grabador de discos compactos** *CD player / burner*
**el reproductor / grabador de DVD** *DVD player / burner*
**la tableta** *tablet computer*
**el teléfono inteligente / smartphone** *smartphone*
**la videocámara** *videocamera*

## ACTIVIDADES

**4  Las emociones**  Las siguientes personas están en ciertas situaciones. ¿Cómo crees que están?

1. A Raúl le gusta navegar por Internet y jugar videojuegos. Hay una tormenta *(thunderstorm)* y por eso no hay electricidad en su casa. No tiene nada *(nothing)* que hacer.
2. Blanca acaba de comprar una computadora portátil pero cuando llega a casa, no funciona.
3. Julio tiene que escribir una composición de diez páginas para su clase de historia mañana y todavía no ha empezado *(hasn't begun)*.
4. Mañana Luis tiene que ir al trabajo por tres horas, estudiar para un examen y hacer una investigación en Internet para la clase de filosofía.
5. Sabrina trabaja diez horas en la biblioteca, va a su clase de aeróbicos y camina a casa del gimnasio.
6. Marcos y Marina toman un refresco, escuchan música y conversan en un café en la Plaza Mayor.

**5  ¿Eres un(a) tecnogeek o un(a) tecnófobo(a)?**  With a partner, come up with a list of items related to technology. Use a point system of 1–5 to rate how tech-savvy someone is (1 = the least advanced and 5 = the most advanced). Then, in groups of four or five, ask each person in the group about each item. Based on your findings, decide who is the most technologically advanced and who is the most technologically inexperienced in the group. Report your findings to the class.

**Sample items**

teléfono inteligente
computadora portátil
tableta
perfil *(profile)* en Facebook
más de una dirección de e-mail

revista *(magazine)* de tecnología
tomar clases virtuales en línea
   *(take classes online)*
bajar videos de YouTube

**6  El Corte Inglés**  El Corte Inglés es el almacén *(department store)* más grande en España. Con un(a) compañero(a), busca el sitio web del Corte Inglés. Entren en el Departamento de Electrónica y contesten las siguientes preguntas.

1. ¿Cuáles son las subcategorías en el Departamento de Electrónica?
2. Entren en la subcategoría DVD & Blu Ray. Nombren tres productos que hay allí y sus precios en euros (€).
3. Quieren comprarle un regalo *(gift)* a un amigo a quien le gusta la música. Busquen un regalo apropiado. ¿Qué es? ¿Cuánto cuesta?
4. Quieren comprarle un regalo a una amiga a quien le gusta grabar videos, pero no tienen mucho dinero *(money)*. Busquen la videocámara con el precio más bajo *(lowest price)*.
5. ¿Qué producto electrónico quieres comprar? ¿Cuánto cuesta?

BETO: ¿Tú? ¿Tú eres Autora14?

DULCE: Sí, yo soy Autora14. ¿Por qué preguntas?

BETO: No, no, nada. ¿Te gustan los **grupos de conversación**?

DULCE: No, en realidad, no. Prefiero el **correo electrónico**.

You are learning two words for e-mail: **correo electrónico** and **e-mail**. **Correo electrónico** refers more to the whole system of e-mail or a group of e-mails, while **el e-mail** refers to a specific e-mail message.

To say you are going to post something on your Facebook page, you can say:

**Voy a publicar un post en mi página de Facebook.**

**Voy a publicar mi estado** (status).

**Voy a publicar mis noticias** (news).

**Voy a publicar algo en el muro** (wall) de mi amigo Javier.

**Voy a subir / bajar fotos / videos a mi página de Facebook.**

>> **Funciones de Internet**

**acceder** *to access*
**el blog** *blog*
**el buscador** *search engine*
**el buzón electrónico** *electronic mailbox*
**chatear** *to chat online*
**el ciberespacio** *cyberspace*
**la conexión** *connection*
**hacer una conexión** *to get online*
**cortar la conexión** *to get offline, disconnect*
**la contraseña** *password*
**el correo electrónico / el e-mail** *e-mail*
**en línea** *online*
**el enlace** *link*
**el foro** *forum*
**el grupo de conversación** *chat room*
**el grupo de noticias** *news group*
**la página web** *web page*
**el proveedor de acceso** *Internet provider*
**la red mundial** *World Wide Web*
**la red social** *social networking site*
**el sitio web** *website*
**el usuario** *user*
**el wifi** *wifi, wireless connection*

© Cengage Learning 2013

**7** **¡Gran sorteo!** Completa el cuestionario para el concurso *(contest)* de la revista *DIGITAL en Español*. Compara tus respuestas con las respuestas de diez compañeros de clase. Haz una gráfica como la de la página 130 que muestre *(shows)* los resultados de tu cuestionario. Llena los espacios en blanco *(Fill in the blanks)* con el número de estudiantes que marcaron *(marked)* esa respuesta.

## Digital en Español — ¡GRAN SORTEO!

Participe en el sorteo de *Digital en Español* y gánate una impresora multifunción que puede colocarse perfectamente sobre cualquier escritorio. Además, resulta fácil de usar y funciona como impresora, escáner, copiadora y fax. Este modelo puede ser conectado fácilmente a tu computadora con conexiones inalámbricas Bluetooth 2.0 o Wi-Fi.

**1.** ¿Usas computadora portátil o una de escritorio?
_____ portátil
_____ de escritorio
_____ ninguna de las dos

**2.** ¿Tienes teléfono inteligente o celular sin capacidades de computadora?
_____ inteligente
_____ celular

**3.** ¿Tienes tableta?
_____ sí
_____ no

**4.** ¿Cuál de tus aparatos electrónicos usas con más frecuencia?
_____ teléfono inteligente
_____ teléfono celular
_____ tableta
_____ computadora portátil
_____ otro aparato

**5.** ¿Cómo usas tu teléfono con más frecuencia?
_____ para hablar por teléfono
_____ para enviar mensajes de texto
_____ para navegar Internet
_____ para publicar en las redes sociales como Facebook y Twitter
_____ otro

**6.** ¿Para qué usas Internet principalmente? Indica sólo tres usos.
_____ compras
_____ servicios de banco
_____ investigaciones
_____ correo electrónico
_____ redes sociales
_____ para mantener mi sitio web
_____ para publicar un blog
_____ ver videos en YouTube
_____ otro

**7.** ¿Cuántas veces por día publicas algo en Facebook?
_____ 0
_____ 1-3
_____ 4-6
_____ más de 7

**8.** ¿Cuál es tu modo preferido de comunicación con tus amigos?
_____ hablar por teléfono
_____ enviar mensajes de texto
_____ enviar e-mails
_____ publicar en Facebook
_____ tuitear
_____ persona a persona
_____ otro

Photo: Courtesy of Canon España; Text: © Cengage Learning 2013

1. _____ portátil
   _____ de escritorio
   _____ ninguna de las dos

5. _____ para hablar por teléfono
   _____ para enviar mensajes de texto
   _____ para navegar Internet
   _____ para publicar en las redes sociales como Facebook y Twitter
   _____ otro

2. _____ inteligente
   _____ celular

6. _____ compras
   _____ servicios de banco
   _____ investigaciones
   _____ correo electrónico
   _____ social media
   _____ para mantener mi sitio web
   _____ para publicar un blog
   _____ ver videos en YouTube
   _____ otro

3. _____ sí
   _____ no

7. _____ 0
   _____ 1–3
   _____ 4–6
   _____ más de 7

4. _____ teléfono inteligente
   _____ teléfono celular
   _____ tableta
   _____ computadora portátil
   _____ otro aparato

8. _____ hablar por teléfono
   _____ enviar mensajes de texto
   _____ enviar e-mails
   _____ publicar en Facebook
   _____ tuitear
   _____ persona a persona
   _____ otro

**8** **¿Cómo usas Internet?** ¿Qué más quieres saber sobre *(do you want to know about)* los hábitos de tus compañeros acerca de Internet? Escribe cinco preguntas más como las del cuestionario en la **Actividad 7**. Luego, hazle las preguntas a tu compañero(a) de clase y que él o ella te haga *(have him or her ask you)* sus preguntas.

MODELO   *¿Te gustan las redes sociales? ¿Cuántas horas al día pasas en las redes sociales?*
*¿Tienes un blog? ¿Cuántas veces por semana escribes en tu blog?*

**9** **Mi blog** Escribe un blog para describir como usas Internet. Ponle todos los detalles que puedas *(that you can)*. Usa las ideas de la **Actividad 8**, de la lista o inventa otras.

Opciones:

- ¿qué te gusta hacer en Internet?
- ¿usas el teléfono inteligente para acceder a Internet?
- ¿cuáles son tus aparatos electrónicos preferidos?
- ¿qué clase de videos te gusta bajar o subir?
- ¿usas la computadora para ver programas de la televisión?
- ¿cuál es tu modo de comunicación preferido?
- ¿…?

**10** **La red social** Escribe tu perfil en español para tu página en la red social. Además de la información básica, escribe un párrafo sobre tu personalidad. Explica un poco sobre tu relación con la tecnología. ¿Eres tecnofóbico o tecnomaestro?

**11** **¿Qué estás pensando?** Ten una conversación con un(a) compañero(a) sobre un post que piensas publicar en la página de tu red social. El post describe cómo vas a usar la tecnología hoy.

MODELO     Tú: *Voy a compartir unas fotos en mi red social.*
           Compañero(a): *¡Qué divertido! ¿Estás tú en las fotos?*

**12** **Los cursos virtuales** Hoy en día es posible tomar cursos virtuales por Internet. Hay muchas universidades de habla española que ofrecen una gran variedad de cursos a distancia.

En grupos de cuatro, escojan *(choose)* un país de la lista de abajo. Visiten los sitios web que corresponden a ese país, usando la lista de enlaces que está en **www.cengagebrain.com**.

**Países:** España, México, Argentina

1. ¿Qué cursos virtuales ofrece la universidad o escuela?
2. ¿En el sitio web es posible hacer una visita virtual? ¿Hay información sobre los profesores de los cursos? ¿Sobre los otros estudiantes?
3. Después de obtener toda la información sobre este sitio web, compárenla con la información de los otros grupos.

© Shutterstock/enigmatico

## ESTRATEGIA

### Watching without sound

Sometimes it helps to watch a segment first without the sound, especially when it contains a lot of action. As you watch, focus on the characters' actions and interactions. What do you think is happening? Once you have gotten some ideas, watch the segment a second time with the sound turned on.

**Antes de ver** Lee la lista de eventos que ocurren en este episodio.

_____ Beto descubre que su computadora no tiene suficiente memoria.

_____ Dulce tiene el asistente electrónico de Beto.

_____ Beto está furioso porque tiene que escribir el examen con bolígrafo y papel.

_____ Beto llega tarde a clase.

_____ Beto ve una hoja de papel con el e-mail de Autora14.

_____ Beto deja su asistente electrónico en el salón de clase.

▶ **Ver** Mira el episodio para el **Capítulo 4** sin sonido _(sound)_.

**Después de ver 1** Ahora vuelve a _(go back to)_ **Antes de ver** y usa números para poner _(to put)_ la lista en el órden correcto.

**Después de ver 2** Mira el episodio otra vez—ahora con sonido—y completa las oraciones siguientes.

1. Beto llega tarde a la clase de _____.
2. Según Chela, ella está muy _____ con la historia trágica de Beto.
3. La dirección electrónica de _____ es Autora14.
4. Dulce prefiere el correo electrónico a _____.

**Después de ver 3** En tu opinión, ¿de qué hablan Dulce y Beto mientras salen juntos al final del episodio? Basándote en lo que ya sabes de sus personalidades, escribe una conversación breve entre ellos mientras se conocen _(they get to know each other)_ un poco mejor.

© Cengage Learning 2013

# Voces de la comunidad

 **>>** ## Voces del mundo hispano

En el video para este capítulo Juan Pedro, Patricia y Sergio hablan de los aparatos tecnológicos y sus hábitos con relación a Internet. Lee las siguientes oraciones. Después mira el video una o más veces para decir si las oraciones son ciertas (**C**) o falsas (**F**).

1. Juan Pedro y Patricia tienen una cámara digital.
2. Sergio tiene un reproductor de MP3.
3. A Juan Pedro le gusta mucho su reproductor de discos compactos.
4. A Patricia le gusta usar su ordenador (computadora) para chatear.
5. Patricia sólo usa Internet durante los días de entresemana.
6. A Sergio no le gusta usar e-mail ni *(nor)* Skype.

© Cengage Learning 2013

 **>>** ## Voces de Estados Unidos

Track 11

### Thaddeus Arroyo, director ejecutivo de información

PRN Images

En la escuela, las matemáticas y la lógica siempre fueron las materias preferidas de Thaddeus Arroyo. Hoy en día, Arroyo, que es Director Ejecutivo de Información *(Chief Information Officer)* en AT&T, es uno de los líderes del campo de la informática y uno de los ejecutivos más importantes del país. Arroyo es conocido mundialmente *(worldwide)* por hacer posible la fusión *(merger)* de Cingular Wireless y AT&T Wireless, creando así la mayor red del país, con unos 60 millones de usuarios. De padre español y madre mexicana, Arroyo explica su éxito *(success)* profesional de esta manera:

**❝Mi mamá y mi papá, los dos, fueron inmigrantes y se concentraron en la educación. Ellos no me permitieron creer que existían barreras insuperables. Creo que más que otra cosa es la fe en el arte de la posibilidad.❞** *("Both my parents were immigrants and focused on education. They would never let me believe there was any barrier I couldn't overcome. I think more than anything else it was believing in the art of the possibility.")*

**¿Y tú?** En tu opinión, ¿qué tipo de preparación escolar y características personales son necesarias para ser un líder en el campo de la tecnología?

# ¡Prepárate!

## >> Gramática útil 1

### Expressing likes and dislikes: **Gustar** with nouns and other verbs like **gustar**

¿**Te gustan** los grupos de conversación?

Remember that when you use **gustar** + infinitive you only use **gusta**: Les gusta comer en la cafetería.

#### Cómo usarlo

As you learned in **Chapter 2,** you can use **gustar** with an infinitive to say what activities you and other people like to do.

**Me gusta estudiar** en la biblioteca, pero **a Vicente le gusta estudiar** en la cafetería.

*I like to study in the library, but Vicente likes to study in the cafeteria.*

You can also use **gustar** with nouns, to say what thing or things you (and others) like or dislike. In this case, you use **gusta** with a single noun and **gustan** with plural nouns or a series of nouns.

—¿**Te gusta** esta **computadora?**
—Sí, ¡pero **me gustan** más estas **portátiles**!

*Do you like this computer?*
*Yes, but I like these laptops more!*

When you make negative sentences with **gusta** and **gustan,** you use **no** before the pronoun + **gusta / gustan.**

**Nos gustan** los programas de diseño gráfico, pero **no nos gustan** los programas de arte.

*We like the graphic design programs, but we don't like the art programs.*

#### Cómo formarlo

### LO BÁSICO

- In Spanish, an *indirect object pronoun* is used with **gustar** to say who likes something. Because **gustar** literally means to *please*, the indirect object answers the question: *Pleases whom?*
- A *prepositional pronoun* is a pronoun that is used after a preposition, such as **a** or **de.**

You will learn more about Spanish indirect object pronouns in **Chapter 8.**

1. As you have already learned, you must use forms of **gustar** with the correct indirect object pronoun.

| Me gusta | el foro. | Nos gusta | el foro. |
|---|---|---|---|
| Me gustan | los foros. | Nos gustan | los foros. |
| Te gusta | el foro. | Os gusta | el foro. |
| Te gustan | los foros. | Os gustan | los foros. |
| Le gusta | el foro. | Les gusta | el foro. |
| Le gustan | los foros. | Les gustan | los foros. |

© Cengage Learning 2013

**2.** As you have learned, if you want to *emphasize* or *clarify* who likes what, you can use **a** + name or noun, or **a** + prepositional pronoun. Note that when **a** + prepositional pronoun is used, there is often no direct translation in English. Notice that except for **mí** and **ti**, the prepositional pronouns are the same as the subject pronouns you already know.

| Prepositional pronoun | Indirect object pronoun | Form of gustar + noun |
|---|---|---|
| A mí | me | gustan los videojuegos. |
| A ti | te | gustan los videojuegos. |
| A Ud. / a él / a ella | le | gustan los videojuegos. |
| A nosotros / a nosotras | nos | gustan los videojuegos. |
| A vosotros / a vosotras | os | gustan los videojuegos. |
| A Uds. / a ellos / a ellas | les | gustan los videojuegos. |

> Notice that while **mí** takes an accent, **ti** does not.

**A mí** me gustan los MP3 portátiles pero **a Elena** no le gustan.
*I like MP3 players, but **Elena** doesn't like them.*

**A ella** le gustan los teléfonos inteligentes que también tocan MP3s.
*She likes smartphones that also play MP3s.*

**3.** A number of other Spanish verbs are used like **gustar.** These verbs are usually just used in two forms, as is **gustar.**

—**Me interesan** mucho estos celulares.
*I'm interested in these cell phones.*

—¿No **te molesta** la recepción mala aquí?
*Doesn't the bad reception here **bother you**?*

| Other verbs like gustar | |
|---|---|
| **encantar** *to like a lot* | ¡Me encanta la tecnología! |
| **fascinar** *to fascinate* | A Ana le fascinan esos sitios web. |
| **importar** *to be important to someone; to mind* | Nos importa tener acceso a Internet. ¿Te importa si usamos la computadora? |
| **interesar** *to interest, to be interesting* | A ellos les interesan las redes sociales. |
| **molestar** *to bother* | Nos molestan las computadoras viejas. |

In Spanish-speaking cultures, courtesy is of utmost importance. It is very common to use phrases like **¿Le importa?** or **¿Le molesta?** to ask someone a question. **¿Le importa si uso la computadora?** would be more likely heard than **Voy a usar la computadora** or **¿Puedo usar la computadora?** It's also common to use **por favor** when asking a question and **gracias** upon receiving the answer. Other common expressions of courtesy are:

**¡Perdón! / ¡Disculpe! / ¡Lo siento!** *Pardon me! / Excuse me! / I'm sorry!*

**No hay de qué. / No se preocupe.**
*No problem. / Not to worry.*

**Con permiso.** *Excuse me. . . / With your permission. . .*

**Cómo no.** *Of course. / Certainly.*

## ACTIVIDADES

**1** **¿Te gusta?** Di si te gustan o no las siguientes cosas.

**MODELO** (Me gustan / No me gustan) las computadoras portátiles.
*Me gustan las computadoras portátiles.*

1. (Me gustan / No me gustan) los juegos interactivos de tenis.
2. (Me gusta / no me gusta) el sitio web de YouTube.
3. (Me gustan / No me gustan) las clases virtuales.
4. (Me gustan / No me gustan) los aparatos electrónicos.
5. (Me gusta / No me gusta) el nuevo CD de Paulina Rubio.
6. (Me gustan / No me gustan) los sitios web y foros sobre España.

**2** **Los gustos** Para cada persona, di si le gustan o no las cosas indicadas.

**MODELO** los teléfonos inteligentes / Marío (no)
*A Mario no le gustan los teléfonos inteligentes.*

1. las computadoras portátiles / tú (sí)
2. las cámaras digitales / Sara y Laura (sí)
3. los juegos interactivos / usted (no)
4. las redes sociales / nosotros (sí)
5. los foros sobre los autos / ustedes (no)
6. los podcasts / tú (no)
7. los grupos de noticias / yo (¿…?)
8. las tabletas / yo (¿…?)

**3** **¿Qué les gusta o gustan?** Mira los dibujos y di qué les gusta (o gustan) a las personas indicadas. Sigue el modelo y usa **gusta** o **gustan** según la(s) cosa(s) o la actividad indicadas.

**MODELOS** Martina / navegar en Internet
*A Martina le gusta navegar en Internet.*

1.

Roque / las computadores portátiles

2.

ustedes / jugar juegos interactivos

3.

nosotros / las tabletas

4.

tú / tu videocámara

5.

yo / mi teléfono inteligente

6.

los niños / ver los videos en la computadora

All art: © Cengage Learning 2013

**4** **¿Y ustedes?** Pregúntales a varios compañeros de clase sobre sus gustos.

MODELO   Facebook (Twitter, Yelp, Foursquare, ¿…?)
　　　　　Tú: *¿Les gusta Facebook?*
　　　　　Compañero(a): *Sí, me gusta Facebook, pero no me gusta Twitter.*

1. el grupo de noticias de profesores de español (de artistas chilenos, de actores de teatro, ¿…?)
2. la página web de Yahoo! en español (de *People en español,* de *Newsweek* o *CNN en español,* ¿…?)
3. el foro de estudiantes de español (de profesores de español, de estudiantes de francés, ¿…?)
4. los juegos interactivos (de mesa, de niños, ¿…?)
5. las computadoras portátiles (PC, Mac, ¿…?)
6. el programa de arte (de diseño gráfico, de contabilidad, ¿…?)

**5** **¿Te interesa?** Pregúntale a un(a) compañero(a) qué opina *(feels)* sobre varios aspectos de la tecnología.

MODELO   interesar: los blogs de personas desconocidas *(strangers)*
　　　　　Tú: *¿Te interesan los blogs de personas desconocidas?*
　　　　　Compañero(a): *No, no me interesan los blogs de personas desconocidas.*

1. molestar: recibir mucha correspondencia electrónica
2. interesar: grupos de noticias
3. gustar: enviar mensajes de texto
4. molestar: buscadores muy lentos *(slow)*
5. interesar: sitios web comerciales
6. gustar: chatear con personas en otros países
7. importar: recibir e-mails de personas desconocidas

**6** **Encuesta** Haz una encuesta con tus compañeros de clase. Pregúntales si les gustan las cosas y actividades indicadas. Después, con la clase entera, comparen los resultados para ver cuáles son los gustos y preferencias de todos los estudiantes.

_____ ¿los juegos interactivos o los juegos tradicionales?
_____ ¿los textos digitales o los libros?
_____ ¿las clases en la universidad o las clases virtuales?
_____ ¿estudiar en la biblioteca o estudiar en un café?
_____ ¿escuchar música cuando estudias o estudiar sin música?
_____ ¿ver películas en la computadora o ver películas en el televisor?

**7** **La tecnología** Pregúntales a seis compañeros qué les gusta de la tecnología y qué les molesta. Escribe un resumen sobre los resultados.

MODELO   *¿Cuáles son tres cosas que te gustan de la tecnología?*
　　　　　*¿Cuáles son tres cosas que te molestan?*

## Gramática útil 2

**Describing yourself and others and expressing conditions and locations: The verb estar and the uses of ser and estar**

**Estoy** muy **aburrida** con tu cuento trágico.

### Cómo usarlo

You already know that the verb **ser** is translated as *to be* in English. You have already used the verb **estar**, which is also translated as *to be*, in expressions such as **¿Cómo estás?** While both these Spanish verbs mean *to be*, they are used in different ways.

1. Use **estar** . . .

   ■ to express location of people, places, or objects.

   | | |
   |---|---|
   | La profesora Suárez **está** en la biblioteca. | *Professor Suárez **is** in the library.* |
   | Los libros **están** en la mesa. | *The books **are** on the table.* |

   ■ to talk about a physical condition.

   | | |
   |---|---|
   | —¿Cómo **está** usted? | *How **are** you?* |
   | —**Estoy** muy bien, gracias. | *I'm well, thank you.* |
   | —Yo **estoy** un poco cansada. | *I'm a little tired.* |

   ■ to talk about emotional conditions.

   | | |
   |---|---|
   | El señor Albrega **está** un poco nervioso hoy. | *Mr. Albrega **is** a little nervous today.* |
   | **Estoy** muy ocupada esta semana. | *I'm very busy this week.* |

2. Use **ser** . . .

   ■ to identify yourself and others.

   | | |
   |---|---|
   | **Soy** Ana y ésta **es** mi hermana Luisa. | *I'm Ana and this **is** my sister Luisa.* |

   ■ to indicate profession.

   | | |
   |---|---|
   | Pablo Picasso **es** un artista famoso. | *Pablo Picasso **is** a famous artist.* |

   ■ to describe personality traits and physical features.

   | | |
   |---|---|
   | **Somos** altos y delgados. | *We **are** tall and thin.* |
   | **Somos** estudiantes buenos. | *We **are** good students.* |

   ■ to give time and date.

   | | |
   |---|---|
   | **Es** la una. Hoy **es** miércoles. | *It **is** one o'clock. Today **is** Wednesday.* |

   ■ to indicate nationality and origin.

   | | |
   |---|---|
   | —**Eres** española, ¿no? | *You **are** Spanish, right?* |
   | —Sí, **soy** de España. | *Yes, I **am** from Spain.* |

   ■ to express possession with **de**.

   | | |
   |---|---|
   | Este celular **es de Anita**. | *This **is Anita's** cell phone.* |

   ■ to give the location of an event.

   | | |
   |---|---|
   | La fiesta **es** en la residencia estudiantil. | *The party **is** in the dorm.* |

> Notice that expressing the location of people, places, and things (other than events) requires the use of **estar**. **Ser** is used only to indicate *where an event will take place*.

## Cómo formarlo

**1.** Here are the forms of the verb **estar** in the present indicative tense.

| estar (to be) | | | |
|---|---|---|---|
| yo | **estoy** | nosotros / nosotras | **estamos** |
| tú | **estás** | vosotros / vosotras | **estáis** |
| Ud. / él / ella | **está** | Uds. / ellos / ellas | **están** |

**2.** In the **¡Imagínate!** section you learned some adjectives that are commonly used with **estar** to describe physical and emotional conditions.

aburrido(a)              nervioso(a)
cansado(a)               ocupado(a)
contento(a)              preocupado(a)
enfermo(a)               seguro(a)
enojado(a)               triste
furioso(a)

Don't forget that when you use adjectives with **estar,** as with any other verb, they need to agree with the person or thing they are describing in both gender and number.

**Los estudiantes están preocupados** por Miguel.

*The students are worried about Miguel.*

**Elena está nerviosa** a causa del examen.

*Elena is nervous because of the exam.*

## ACTIVIDADES

**8**  **¿Dónde están?**  Todos participan en diferentes actividades en diferentes lugares de la universidad. ¿Dónde están?

**MODELO**   Ricardo y Juana estudian. (Está / <u>Están</u>) en la biblioteca.

1. Javier toma un refresco. (Está / Estás) en la cafetería.
2. Mi compañero(a) de cuarto y yo descansamos. (Estoy / Estamos) en la residencia estudiantil.
3. Paula y Pedro navegan por Internet. (Estamos / Están) en el centro de computación.
4. La profesora Martínez lee una novela. (Estás / Está) en el parque.
5. Usted escribe en la pizarra. (Está / Están) en el salón de clase.
6. Nosotros escuchamos el audio de la clase de español. (Estoy / Estamos) en el centro de comunicaciones.
7. Teresa levanta pesas. (Está / Están) en el gimnasio.
8. Tú compras un libro para la clase de filosofía. (Estás / Está) en la librería.

**9** **¿Cómo están?** Tú y varias personas están en las siguientes situaciones. Usa **estar** + adjetivo para describir cómo están. Usa adjetivos de la lista.

**Adjetivos:** aburrido(a), cansado(a), contento(a), enfermo(a), enojado(a), nervioso(a), ocupado(a), preocupado(a), triste

MODELO Sales bien en el examen de francés, tomas el sol por la tarde, cenas con tu mejor amigo(a) y alquilas un video que te gusta mucho.
*Estoy contento(a).*

1. Tienes una entrevista con el director de la universidad para un trabajo que necesitas.
2. Carlos tiene una infección y tiene que ir al hospital.
3. Marta y Mario no tienen nada *(nothing)* que hacer *(to do)* —no hay nada interesante en la tele y su computadora no funciona.
4. Compras una nueva computadora. Llegas a casa y cuando tratas de usarla, no funciona. La tienda de computadoras no abre hasta el lunes.
5. Tú y tu familia tienen mucho que hacer. Entre los estudios, el trabajo, los deportes, la familia y los amigos, no hay suficiente tiempo en el día para hacerlo todo.
6. Elena practica deportes por la mañana, trabaja en la biblioteca por la tarde y estudia por la noche. Cuando llega a casa, descansa.
7. La tarea de matemáticas es muy difícil —Martín no comprende las instrucciones. Es muy tarde para llamar a un amigo. Tiene que entregar la tarea muy temprano por la mañana.
8. El abuelo *(grandfather)* de Pedro y Delia está muy enfermo. Pedro y Delia lo visitan en el hospital.

**10** **Yo soy…** Completa las oraciones con la forma correcta de **ser** o **estar**.

MODELO Yo _____ estudiante. _____ en clase.
*Yo <u>soy</u> estudiante. <u>Estoy</u> en clase.*

1. El señor Ortega _____ muy ocupado.
   _____ en la oficina.
2. Nosotros _____ divertidos.
   _____ contentos ahora.
3. Rogelio _____ profesor.
   _____ alto y delgado.
4. Alejandro y yo _____ de Barcelona.
   _____ aquí en Estados Unidos por un año.
5. Pedro y Arturo _____ enfermos.
   _____ en el hospital.
6. Esta computadora _____ de Lucía.
   Lucía _____ una estudiante muy trabajadora.

**11** *¿Ser o estar?* Trabaja con un(a) compañero(a) de clase para completar las oraciones. Lean las oraciones y juntos decidan si se debe usar **ser** o **estar**. Escriban la forma correcta del verbo. Luego, escriban por qué se usa **ser** o **estar**.

MODELO    <u>*Soy*</u> María Hernández Catina.
           razón *(reason): identidad*

**Razones:** característica física, característica de personalidad, estado físico, estado temporáneo, fecha, hora, identidad, lugar de un evento, nacionalidad, posesión, posición *(location)*, profesión

1. ¿Cómo _____ usted, profesor Taboada? razón:
2. Yo _____ un poco cansado hoy. razón:
3. Isabel _____ de España. razón:
4. ¿Dónde _____ la biblioteca? razón:
5. Mi padre _____ profesor de lenguas. razón:
6. Hoy _____ miércoles, el 22 de octubre. razón:
7. Nati _____ alta, delgada y tiene el pelo castaño. razón:
8. Esta semana Leonardo _____ muy ocupado. razón:
9. Este libro, ¿ _____ de la profesora? razón:
10. ¿Dónde _____ la clase de filosofía? razón:

**12** **¡Pobre Mónica!** Trabaja con un(a) compañero(a) de clase. Miren el dibujo y juntos escriban una descripción de Mónica y de la situación en general. Traten de usar **ser** o **estar** en cada oración y de escribir por lo menos cinco oraciones.

In Spanish-speaking countries, **martes 13**, or Tuesday the 13th, rather than Friday the 13th, is considered an unlucky day.

© Cengage Learning 2013

# Sonrisas

**Comprensión** En tu opinión, ¿cuáles de los siguientes adjetivos describen al hombre rubio? Y al hombre moreno?

- ¿Quién está...?

  aburrido / cansado / contento / enfermo / furioso / nervioso / ocupado / preocupado / seguro / triste

- ¿Quién es...?

  activo / antipático / cómico / cuidadoso / divertido / egoísta / extrovertido / impaciente / introvertido / perezoso / serio / simpático / tonto

# Gramática útil 3

## Talking about everyday events: Stem-changing verbs in the present indicative

### Cómo usarlo

In **Chapters 1** and **2** you learned the present indicative forms of regular **-ar, -er,** and **-ir** verbs in Spanish. There are other Spanish verbs that use the same endings as regular **-ar, -er,** and **-ir** verbs in this tense, but they also have a small change in their stem. (Remember that the stem is the part of the infinitive that is left after you remove the **-ar / -er / -ir** ending.)

—¿Qué **piensas** de este MP3 portátil?
—Me gusta, pero **prefiero** éste.
—¿Verdad? Bueno, ¿por qué no le **pides** el precio al dependiente?

*What **do you think** of this MP3 player?*
*I like it, but I **prefer** this one.*
*Really? Well, why don't **you ask** the sales clerk the price?*

¡Pobre Beto! **Siento** tu frustración.

### Cómo formarlo

1. There are three categories of stem-changing verbs in the present indicative.

| | o → ue: encontrar *(to find)* | e → ie: preferir *(to prefer)* | e → i: pedir *(to ask for)* |
|---|---|---|---|
| yo | enc**ue**ntro | pref**ie**ro | p**i**do |
| tú | enc**ue**ntras | pref**ie**res | p**i**des |
| Ud. / él / ella | enc**ue**ntra | pref**ie**re | p**i**de |
| nosotros / nosotras | encontramos | preferimos | pedimos |
| vosotros / vosotras | encontráis | preferís | pedís |
| Uds. / ellos / ellas | enc**ue**ntran | pref**ie**ren | p**i**den |

2. Note that the stem changes in all forms except the **nosotros / nosotras** and **vosotros / vosotras** forms.

3. Remember, all the endings for the present indicative are the same for these verbs as for the other regular verbs you've learned: **-o, -as, -a, -amos, -áis, -an** for **-ar** verbs; **-o, -es, -e, -emos / -imos, -éis / -ís, -en** for **-er** and **-ir** verbs. The only thing that is different here is the change in the stem.

**4.** Here are some commonly used Spanish verbs that experience a stem change in the present indicative tense.

**e → ie**

| | |
|---|---|
| **cerrar** | *to close* |
| **comenzar (a)** | *to begin (to)* |
| **empezar (a)** | *to begin (to)* |
| **entender** | *to understand* |
| **pensar de** | *to think (of), have an opinion about* |
| **pensar en** | *to think about, to consider* |
| **perder** | *to lose* |
| **preferir** | *to prefer* |
| **querer** | *to want, to love* |
| **sentir** | *to feel* |

**o → ue**

| | |
|---|---|
| **contar** | *to tell, to relate; to count* |
| **dormir** | *to sleep* |
| **encontrar** | *to find* |
| **jugar\*** | *to play* |
| **poder** | *to be able to* |
| **sonar** | *to ring, to go off (phone, alarm clock, etc.)* |
| **soñar (con)** | *to dream (about)* |
| **volver** | *to return* |

**e → i**

| | |
|---|---|
| **pedir** | *to ask for something* |
| **repetir** | *to repeat* |
| **servir** | *to serve* |

*\***Jugar** is the only **u → ue** stem-changing verb in Spanish. It's grouped with the **o → ue** verbs, because its change is most similar to those.

## ACTIVIDADES

**13** **En la clase de computación** Estás en la clase de computación. Escoge la forma correcta del verbo entre paréntesis para describir lo que hacen todos.

1. Yo (pido / pide) el número de teléfono del nuevo estudiante.
2. La profesora (repite / repiten) las instrucciones de la actividad.
3. Nosotros (sirvo / servimos) refrescos después de la clase.
4. Él (prefiere / prefieren) usar los mensajes de texto para comunicarse con su familia.
5. Tú (encontramos / encuentras) la clase muy difícil.
6. Ellos (piden / pedimos) la dirección electrónica de la universidad.
7. Nosotras (preferimos / prefieren) ir a un café con wifi después de clase.
8. Yo (encuentras / encuentro) la clase muy divertida.

👥 **14** **¿Entiendes?** Tú tienes que presentar el nuevo sistema de software a un grupo diverso de asistentes administrativos. Les preguntas si entienden cómo hacer ciertas cosas con los nuevos programas. Tu compañero(a) te contesta.

MODELO  ¿_____ (ustedes) cómo instalar el programa antivirus? (sí)
           Tú: *¿Entienden cómo instalar el programa antivirus?*
           Compañero(a): *Sí, entendemos cómo instalar el programa antivirus.*

1. ¿ _____ (ustedes) cómo abrir la aplicación? (no)
2. ¿ _____ (usted) cómo archivar los documentos al disco duro? (sí)
3. ¿ _____ (tú) cómo funciona el buscador? (no)
4. ¿ _____ (ellos) cómo cortar la conexión a Internet? (sí)
5. ¿ _____ (ustedes) cómo entrar en los foros? (no)
6. ¿ _____ (tú) cómo pedir apoyo técnico (*tech support*)? (sí)

🔊 **15** **¿A qué hora vuelves?** Un amigo te pregunta cuándo vuelven a casa tú, Track 12 tus amigos y varios miembros de tu familia. Escucha la pregunta y escribe la respuesta correcta en una oración completa. Estudia el modelo.

MODELO  Ves: 10:30 A.M.
           Escuchas: *¿A qué hora vuelves de la clase de computación?*
           Escribes: *Vuelvo de la clase de computación a las diez y media de la mañana.*

1. 4:00 P.M.         4. 8:00 P.M.
2. 1:00 A.M.         5. 7:00 P.M.
3. 3:15 P.M.         6. 11:30 A.M.

**16** **En la clase de español** Todos los estudiantes en la clase de español están en medio de alguna actividad. Di lo que hace cada persona.

MODELO  Olga (no entender las instrucciones)
           *Olga no entiende las instrucciones.*

1. Joaquín (cerrar el texto digital)
2. Iris (perder su lugar en el capítulo)
3. Paulo (dormir en su escritorio)
4. Lisa (empezar a hacer la tarea)
5. Arturo (pensar en las vacaciones)
6. Andrés y Marta (jugar en la computadora)
7. Roberto y Humberto (querer ir al gimnasio)
8. Ingrid (preferir hacer la tarea en la computadora)
9. Francisco (no poder abrir la aplicación)
10. la profesora (volver a repetir la tarea)
11. yo (pedir el número de la página de la lectura)
12. yo (repetir la pregunta)

> **Volver a** + *infinitive* means to go back and do something, or to do it over.

**17** **Trucos para tecnófobos** Con un(a) compañero(a) miren el anuncio de un programa de televisión sobre trucos para las personas que no saben mucho de tecnología. Después, contesten las preguntas a continuación.

¿Eres tecnófobo?

¡En este show puedes aprender 50 cosas fáciles para ayudarte con todos tus aparatos! ¿Quieres saber más? Pues, ¡a ver! Canal 22, 19:30

© Cengage Learning 2013

**cosas:** *things*

1. ¿Cuántas cosas fáciles pueden hacer con estos trucos *(tricks)*?
2. ¿Prefieren aprender a usar los trucos o piensan que son una pérdida *(waste)* de tiempo?
3. ¿Pueden usar sus celulares para hacer otras funciones? ¿Cuáles?
4. ¿Tienen todos estos aparatos? ¿Quieren comprar otros aparatos electrónicos? ¿Por qué sí o no?

**18** **¿Quieres ir?** Pregúntale a tu compañero(a) si quiere hacer una actividad contigo. Él o ella te dice que prefiere hacer otra cosa.

**Actividades:** ir a tomar un refresco, ver un video, estudiar en la biblioteca, mirar television, navegar por Internet, tomar el sol, visitar a amigos, bailar, ¿…?

MODELO   Tú: *¿Quieres ver un video?*
             Compañero(a): *No, prefiero jugar un juego interactivo.*

**19** **La vida universitaria** ¿Es la vida del estudiante muy difícil hoy en día? Con tres compañeros de clase, contesten las siguientes preguntas sinceramente. Basándose en las respuestas de sus compañeros, decidan juntos si la vida universitaria produce mucho estrés para el estudiante. Presenten su conclusión a la clase.

1. ¿Sientes mucho estrés? ¿Por qué?
2. ¿A qué hora vuelves a la residencia estudiantil de la universidad?
3. ¿A qué hora duermes? ¿Dónde duermes? ¿Cuántas horas duermes por noche? ¿Duermes lo suficiente?
4. ¿Juegas videojuegos? ¿Juegos interactivos? ¿Juegos en la red? ¿Cuánto tiempo pasas a diario jugando estos juegos?
5. ¿Pierdes tus llaves *(keys)* con frecuencia? ¿Tus gafas *(glasses)*? ¿Tu dinero *(money)*? ¿Tu tarea? ¿Tus libros? ¿Tus cuadernos? ¿Tu mochila?
6. ¿Piensas mucho en el futuro? ¿Puedes imaginar tu futuro?

**20** **Los hábitos del universitario** Haz una gráfica como la de abajo. Usa las frases indicadas para crear preguntas. (Si quieres, puedes escribir tus propias preguntas.) Luego, hazles las preguntas a diez compañeros de clase. Según sus respuestas, apunta el número de estudiantes en la columna apropiada. Luego, escribe una descripción de tus resultados.

| Frases para las preguntas | Número de estudiantes |
|---|---|
| dormir más de seis horas por noche: | 6 |
| no dormir más de seis horas por noche: | 4 |
| preferir hablar por teléfono para comunicarse: | |
| preferir escribir e-mail para comunicarse: | |
| preferir enviar un mensaje de texto para comunicarse: | |
| jugar un deporte: | |
| jugar videojuegos: | |
| sentir mucho estrés: | |
| no sentir mucho estrés: | |
| pensar en su futuro todos los días: | |
| no pensar en su futuro todos los días: | |
| encontrar la vida universitaria difícil: | |
| encontrar la vida universitaria fácil: | |
| ¿...? | |

MODELO    *Seis estudiantes duermen más de seis horas por noche.*
*Cuatro estudiantes no duermen más de seis horas por noche.*

**21** **Mi blog** Escribe un perfil personal para tu blog en Internet. Describe tus características físicas, tu personalidad, tus clases preferidas, tus hábitos en la universidad, tus emociones y lo que te gusta, molesta o interesa, etc. Ponle a tu descripción todo el detalle que puedas.

### Describing how something is done: Adverbs

The magazine *Muy interesante* runs an annual contest to award prizes to top Spanish innovators in a variety of fields. This is a profile of one of them. Can you find the **-mente** adverb and guess its meaning in English?

Personalidades famosas

Carla Royo-Villanova

**Fundadora de Carla Bulgaria Roses Beauty**

"Para mi innovar es una filosofia de vida. Procuro innovar en cada momento profesional y personal y asi no caer nunca en la rutina. Que cada día sea diferente. La idea original de mi empresa fue precisamente gracias a ese espiritu innovador que me caracteriza".

《 **Anterior** 》   《 **Siguiente** 》

Slide of Carla Royo Villanova from *Muy Interestante*, http://premioinnova.muyinteresante.es/index.php. Used with permission from Gruner y Jahr and Carla Royo Villanova.

## Cómo usarlo

When you want to say how an activity is carried out (slowly, thoroughly, generally, etc.), you use an adverb.

**Generalmente**, prefiero usar una contraseña secreta.

*Generally, I prefer to use a secret password.*

Escribo más **rápido / rápidamente** en computadora que con bolígrafo.

*I write more **rapidly** on the computer than I do with a pen.*

Este programa es **muy** lento.

*This program is **very** slow.*

## Cómo formarlo

### LO BÁSICO

An adverb is a word that modifies a verb, an adjective, or another adverb. (Sometimes adjectives can also be used as adverbs—for example, *fast*). *Generally, rapidly,* and *very* are all adverbs. You can identify an adverb by asking the question, *"How?"*

1. To form an adverb from a Spanish adjective, it is often possible to add the ending **-mente** to the adjective: **fácil → fácilmente**. If the adjective ends in an **-o**, change it to **-a** before adding **-mente**: **rápido → rápidamente**.

2. Here are some frequently used Spanish adjectives that can be turned into **-mente** adverbs.

**Lento** and **rápido** can also be used with **muy** for the same effect: **Esta computadora se conecta a Internet muy rápido / muy lento / rápidamente / lentamente.**

| | |
|---|---|
| **fácil** *(easy)* | → **fácilmente** |
| **difícil** *(difficult)* | → **difícilmente** |
| **lento** *(slow)* | → **lentamente** |
| **rápido** *(fast)* | → **rápidamente** |

**3.** The following **-mente** adverbs are also useful to talk about your routine and what you normally do.

| | | | |
|---|---|---|---|
| **frecuentemente** | *frequently* | **normalmente** | *normally* |
| **generalmente** | *generally* | | |

**4.** Here are some other common Spanish adverbs.

| | | |
|---|---|---|
| **bastante** | *somewhat, rather* | Este sistema es **bastante** lento. |
| **bien** | *well* | Tu computadora funciona **bien**. |
| **demasiado** | *too much* | Navego **demasiado** por Internet. |
| **mal** | *badly* | ¡Mi cámara web funciona muy **mal**! |
| **mucho** | *a lot* | Me gustan **mucho** los juegos interactivos. |
| **muy** | *very* | Guardo archivos **muy** frecuentemente. |
| **poco** | *little* | Chateo **poco** por Internet. |

> Remember, adverbs can be used to modify other adverbs, so it's perfectly acceptable to use **muy** with **frecuentemente** or **mal**, for example!

## ACTIVIDADES

**22** ¿**Cómo?** Escucha a Miriam mientras describe su vida a una amiga.
*Track 13* Completa sus oraciones. Escoge el adjetivo más lógico del grupo y conviértelo en un adverbio añadiendo el sufijo **-mente**.

**Adjetivos:** constante, cuidadoso, directo, fácil, frecuente, general, inmediato, lento, normal, paciente, rápido, tranquilo.

1. Puedes instalar el programa antivirus _____.
2. Yo chateo por Internet _____.
3. Hay algunos sitios web que funcionan _____.
4. _____, navego por Internet dos o tres horas por día.
5. Con este módem interno, puedo hacer una conexión _____.
6. Instalo los programas de software en mi computadora _____.
7. Tengo tarea _____.
8. Los domingos prefiero pasar el día _____.

**23** ¿**Cómo te sientes?** Averigua (*Find out*) cómo se sienten tus compañeros de clase en ciertas situaciones. Hazles las siguientes preguntas a varios compañeros y apunta sus respuestas. Luego, dale los resultados de tu encuesta a la clase.

**¿Cómo te sientes cuando...**

1. vas a tener un examen?
2. tu computadora no funciona bien?
3. recibes la cuenta (*bill*) de tu teléfono celular?
4. la batería de tu teléfono no funciona?
5. pierdes los archivos de tu tarea?
6. ¿...?

**Posibles respuestas**

| | |
|---|---|
| bien | bastante nervioso (triste, preocupado, etc.) |
| mal | demasiado nervioso (cansado, furioso, etc.) |
| muy bien | no me afecta |
| muy mal | ¿...? |

# España

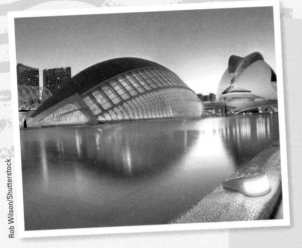

Rob Wilson/Shutterstock

## Información general ▶

**Nombre oficial:** Reino de España

**Población:** 40.548.753

**Capital:** Madrid (f. siglo X) (3.300.000 hab.)

**Otras ciudades importantes:** Barcelona (1.600.000 hab.), Valencia (840.000 hab.), Sevilla (710.000 hab.), Toledo (85.000 hab.)

**Moneda:** euro

**Idiomas:** castellano (oficial), catalán, vasco, gallego

**Mapa de España:** Apéndice D

Spain is often seen as one big culture when, in fact, it is the amalgamation of former kingdoms and separate regions. Many of these are autonomous states and have separate languages and/or dialects, and distinct cultural customs. Spanish is referred to as "castellano" in areas where there is an additional native language. Typically these are bilingual zones.

## Vale saber...

- El Imperio español fue *(was)* el primer imperio global y uno de los más grandes en toda la historia mundial. En su apogeo *(peak)*, España tenía territorios en todos los continentes menos Antártida.

- España ha producido muchos artistas ilustres. En la literatura, se distingue Miguel de Cervantes, escritor de *El ingenioso hidalgo Don Quijote de la Mancha*, que se considera la primera novela moderna. En las artes, los grandes maestros de la pintura española incluyen a El Greco, Diego de Velázquez y Francisco de Goya. En el siglo *(century)* XX, Pablo Picasso, Joan Miró y Salvador Dalí son los innovadores más importantes del arte moderno.

- La influencia árabe en la arquitectura del siglo VIII, construida por los colonizadores musulmanes comúnmente llamados "los moros", es evidente por todo el sur de España, en particular en Granada, Córdoba y Sevilla.

## Buika, artista universal

Paul White/AP Images

Concha Buika, conocida profesionalmente como Buika, es cantante española, hija de ecuatoguineanos y una maravillosa estudiante de todos los estilos musicales del mundo. Boleros, flamenco, jazz, funk, soul y el ritmo africano todos forman parte de su obra musical. Además, le fascinan los ritmos electrónicos y dice que para ella sus 'joyas' *(jewels)* son los aparatos electrónicos que utiliza para hacer música. Con sus ritmos globales y su uso de la tecnología, Buika es una artista universal que rompe *(breaks)* todas las barreras.

### La información general

1. ¿Qué país fue *(was)* el primer imperio global?
2. ¿En qué continentes tenía *(had)* España territorios?
3. ¿Quién es el autor de la primera novela moderna?
4. ¿Quiénes son los grandes maestros de la pintura española?
5. ¿Quiénes son los artistas españoles que se consideran innovadores del arte moderno?
6. ¿Qué tres ciudades españolas tienen una influencia árabe en su arquitectura?

### El tema de la música electrónica

1. ¿De dónde son los padres de Buika?
2. ¿Qué estilos musicales incorpora Buika en su obra musical?
3. ¿Qué considera Buika sus 'joyas'?
4. ¿Qué hace de Buika una artista universal?

🌐 **¿QUIERES SABER MÁS?**

En la tabla que empezaste al principio del capítulo, añade toda la información que ya sabes en la columna **Lo que aprendí.** Escoge uno o dos de los temas que escribiste en la columna **Lo que quiero aprender,** o uno o dos de los temas a continuación para investigar en línea. Prepárate para compartir la información con la clase.

**Palabras clave:** el Imperio español; la Guerra Civil español; la influencia musulmana; Pedro Almodóvar; Penélope Cruz; Rafael Nadal

🌐 **Tú en el mundo hispano** Para explorar oportunidades de usar el español para estudiar o hacer trabajos voluntarios o aprendizajes en España, sigue los enlaces en el sitio web de **www.cengagebrain.com.**

🎬 **Ritmos del mundo hispano** Sigue los enlaces en **www.cengagebrain.com** para escuchar música de España.

# A leer

## ESTRATEGIA

**Using format clues to aid comprehension**

In **Chapter 3**, you looked at the visuals that accompanied an article to get an idea of its content. It is also very helpful to look at an article's format. The headline, a section title, and any kind of highlighted or boxed text (often called sidebars) can give you a general idea of the article's content.

**1** Mira el artículo en la página 153. ¿Cuántas de las siguientes claves *(clues)* de formato puedes identificar en el artículo? Basándote en esas claves, ¿de qué trata el artículo?

- título de sección
- texto del lado *(sidebar)*
- fotos
- título de artículo
- citas *(quotations)*
- ilustraciones o gráficos

**2** Ahora lee el artículo en la página 153 y busca las ideas principales.

>> **Después de leer**

**3** Di si las siguientes oraciones son **ciertas (C)** o **falsas (F)**.

1. _____ Este artículo habla de una plataforma tecnológica de hardware.

2. _____ Tuenti es un sitio exclusivo.

3. _____ Muchas de las personas que trabajan para Tuenti son jóvenes.

4. _____ Para Tuenti, la privacidad no es muy importante.

5. _____ Todas las personas que trabajan para Tuenti son españoles.

**4** Contesta las preguntas con un(a) compañero(a).

1. ¿Puedes usar Tuenti con tu celular?

2. Según Tuenti, ¿cuántas personas usan el sitio web cada día?

3. ¿Cuáles son las nacionalidades de los cofundadores?

4. ¿Cuántas invitaciones recibe cada nuevo usuario?

5. ¿Dónde está la oficina de Tuenti?

6. ¿Qué significa Tuenti?

7. En tu opinión, ¿puede tener éxito *(be successful)* un sitio como Tuenti en Estados Unidos?

# Sólo con invitación

Algunos trabajadores de Tuenti (¡y otro inanimado!).

El País Photos/Newscom

### ¿Qué es Tuenti?

Tuenti es una red social española que es uno de los sitios web más populares del país. Es la creación de dos españoles, Felix Ruiz y Joaquín Ayuso, y dos norteamericanos, Zaryn Dentzel y Kenny Bentley. Y, a diferencia de otras redes sociales como Facebook, es necesario recibir una invitación personal antes de poder juntarse[1] a esta comunidad virtual.

> **"Si no eres tú mismo, no eres nadie[2] en Tuenti"**
> —Zaryn Dentzel, uno de los cofundadores de Tuenti

### ¿Por qué requiere Tuenti una invitación?

Según Dentzel, "Anteponemos[3] la privacidad de nuestro público al crecimiento sin control[4]. De ese modo cuando entras en la red ya tienes, al menos, un amigo".

Esta decisión resulta en una exclusividad bastante inflexible. Cada nuevo usuario recibe sólo tres invitaciones — ¡así que tiene que pensarlo bien antes de usarlas!

| Unos datos sobre Tuenti |
|---|
| ■ El nombre es una abreviatura de "tu entidad". |
| ■ Está basado en Madrid. |
| ■ La edad media de las personas que trabajan para Tuenti es de 24 años. Ellos son de más de quince países diferentes. |

**¿Qué es Tuenti?**
Tuenti es una plataforma social privada, a la que se accede únicamente por invitación. Cada día la usan millones de personas para comunicarse entre ellas y compartir información.

**Social**
Conéctate, comparte y comunícate con tus amigos, compañeros de trabajo y familia.

**Local**
Descubre servicios locales y participa con las marcas que realmente te importan.

**Móvil**
Accede a Tuenti desde tu móvil en tiempo real estés donde estés.

Courtesy of © tuenti 2011

**únicamente:** *only* **marcas:** *brands*

[1]*to join* [2]*no one* [3]*We give preference to* [4]**al…:** *over uncontrolled growth*

# A escribir

## ESTRATEGIA

### Prewriting—Narrowing your topic

After you choose a topic for a piece of writing, but before you begin the writing process, you need to narrow your topic to fit the scope of your written piece. For example, in this section, you will write a note to a friend who is interested in technology. Since most notes are short, you don't want to choose a huge topic to cover.

One way to narrow a topic is to take it and ask yourself questions about it. For example, if your general topic is "computers," ask, "What kind of computer?" You might answer, "A laptop." The next question might be, "Why do you want a laptop?" The answer might be, "Because I like to be able to take it with me." You could then ask, "Where do you want to use your laptop?" with the answer, "At the coffee shop down the corner with free wifi." Once you have progressed through a series of narrowing questions like this, you have narrowed your topic from "computers" to "ways having a laptop can help you save money."

**1** Piensa en dos o tres temas generales que puedes usar para escribir a un(a) amigo(a) que es muy aficionado(a) *(a big fan)* a la tecnología. Un ejemplo de un tema general puede ser **las computadoras**, **el Internet**, etc.

**2** Go back to the list of topics you created in **Actividad 1**. Ahora, elige *(choose)* uno de los temas y practica la técnica de la **Estrategia** para hacer el tema más específico.

**3** Ahora, lee el mensaje modelo a continuación donde Magali habla de sus clases y tarea relacionadas con la tecnología y también de sus planes para el fin de semana. ¿Contiene su mensaje palabras o frases que puedes usar en tu composición? Si hay, apúntalas. Si necesitas otras palabras que no sabes *(you don't know)*, búscalas en un diccionario bilingüe antes de escribir.

© Cengage Learning 2013. Photo: Supri Suharjoto/Shutterstock

**Hola, ¿cómo estás?**

Buscar mensaje 🔍    + Nuevo mensaje

◀ Volver a Mensajes  |  Marcar como no leído  |  Denunciar correo no deseado  |  Eliminar    ▲   ▼

Entre Tú y Magali Fulanita

**Magali Fulanita 19 de enero, 18:00**

Hola, ¿Cómo estás? Todo va bien aquí.☺ Tengo muchos planes para el fin de semana. Primero, voy a trabajar un poco en la computadora.
Tengo que crear la plantilla *(template)* de un sitio web para mi clase de diseño gráfico. ¡Sólo podemos usar los tres colores principales! Muy fácil, ¿verdad? ☺ Bueno, a mí me gustan mucho los colores vivos – el rojo, el amarillo… Entonces, ¡va a ser un programa brillante! Después de trabajar en la computadora, voy a salir el sábado con Laila y Marta. (¿Por qué no vienes?) Y el domingo tengo tarea para la clase de programación.
Así que voy a estar muy ocupada… y un poco cansada! ☺
Bueno, ¡escríbeme pronto para decirme tus noticias!

Un abrazo, Magali

**Respuesta**

Responder

# Composición

**4**   Ahora, escribe un borrador *(rough draft)* de tu mensaje. Incluye información sobre el tema que desarrollaste *(that you developed)* en las **Actividades 1** y **2**. También debes incluir un poco de información personal para tu amigo(a), como en el mensaje modelo. Trata de escribir rápidamente, sin preocuparte *(without worrying)* demasiado por los errores.

# Después de escribir

**5**   Mira tu borrador otra vez. Usa la siguiente lista para revisarlo *(to revise it)*.

- ¿Tiene tu mensaje toda la información necesaria? ¿Está bien organizado?
- ¿Corresponden los sujetos de las oraciones a los verbos?
- ¿Corresponden las formas de los artículos, los sustantivos y los adjetivos?
- ¿Usas correctamente **ser** y **estar**, los verbos con cambio en la raíz *(stem)* y los verbos como **gustar**?
- ¿Hay errores de puntuación o de ortografía *(spelling)*?

# Vocabulario

## La tecnología   *Technology*

**El hardware**   *hardware*

La computadora   *computer*
**el altoparlante**   *speaker*
**el cable**   *cable*
**el disco duro**   *hard drive*
**la memoria flash / el pendrive**   *flash drive*
**el módem externo**   *external modem*
**el micrófono**   *microphone*
**el monitor**   *monitor*
**el puerto de USB**   *USB port*
**el ratón**   *mouse*

La computadora portátil   *Laptop computer*
**los audífonos**   *earphones*
**el módem interno**   *internal modem*
**la impresora**   *printer*
**el lector de CD-ROM o DVD**   *CD-ROM / DVD drive*
**la pantalla**   *screen*
**la tecla**   *key*
**el teclado**   *keyboard*

**El software**   *Software*

**la aplicación**   *application*
**los archivos**   *files*
**el archivo PDF**   *PDF attachment*
**el ícono del programa**   *program icon*
**el juego interactivo**   *interactive game*
**el programa antivirus**   *antivirus program*
**el programa de procesamiento de textos**   *word processing program*

**Funciones de la computadora**   *Computer functions*
**archivar**   *to file*
**bajar / descargar**   *to download*
**conectar**   *to connect*
**enviar**   *to send*
**funcionar**   *to function*
**grabar**   *to record*
**guardar**   *to save*
**hacer clic / doble clic**   *to click / double-click*
**instalar**   *to install*
**subir / cargar**   *to upload*

## Los colores   *Colors*

**amarillo(a)**   *yellow*
**anaranjado(a)**   *orange*
**azul**   *blue*
**blanco(a)**   *white*
**café / marrón**   *brown*
**gris**   *gray*

**morado(a)**   *purple*
**negro(a)**   *black*
**rojo(a)**   *red*
**rosa / rosado(a)**   *pink*
**verde**   *green*

## Las emociones   *Emotions*

**aburrido(a)**   *bored*
**cansado(a)**   *tired*
**contento(a)**   *happy*
**enfermo(a)**   *sick*
**enojado(a)**   *angry*
**furioso(a)**   *furious*

**nervioso(a)**   *nervous*
**ocupado(a)**   *busy*
**preocupado(a)**   *worried*
**seguro(a)**   *sure*
**triste**   *sad*

## Aparatos electrónicos   *Electronic devices*

**el asistente electrónico**   *electronic notebook*
**la cámara digital**   *digital camera*
**la cámara web**   *webcam*
**el MP3 portátil**   *portable MP3 player*
**el reproductor / grabador de discos compactos**   *CD player / burner*

**el reproductor / grabador de DVD**   *DVD player / burner*
**la tableta**   *tablet computer*
**el teléfono inteligente / smartphone**   *smartphone*
**la videocámara**   *videocamera*

## Funciones de Internet  *Internet functions*

**acceder**  *to access*
**el blog**  *blog*
**el buzón electrónico**  *electronic mailbox*
**el buscador**  *search engine*
**chatear**  *to chat online*
**el ciberespacio**  *cyberspace*
**la conexión**  *the connection*
**hacer una conexión**  *to get online*
**cortar la conexión**  *to get offline, disconnect*
**la contraseña**  *password*
**el correo electrónico / e-mail**  *e-mail*
**en línea**  *online*

**el enlace**  *link*
**el foro**  *forum*
**el grupo de conversación**  *chat room*
**el grupo de noticias**  *newsgroup*
**la página web**  *web page*
**el proveedor de acceso**  *Internet provider*
**la red mundial**  *World Wide Web*
**la red social**  *social networking site*
**el sitio web**  *website*
**el (la) usuario(a)**  *user*
**el wifi**  *wifi, wireless connection*

## Verbos como *gustar*

**encantar**  *to like a lot*
**fascinar**  *to fascinate*
**importar**  *to be important to someone; to mind*

**interesar**  *to interest, to be interesting*
**molestar**  *to bother*

## Otros verbos*

**cerrar (ie)**  *to close*
**comenzar (ie)**  *to begin*
**contar (ue)**  *to tell, to relate; to count*
**dormir (ue)**  *to sleep*
**empezar (ie)**  *to begin*
**encontrar (ue)**  *to find*
**entender (ie)**  *to understand*
**jugar (ue)**  *to play*
**pedir (i)**  *to ask for something*
**pensar (ie) de**  *to think, have an opinion about*
**pensar (ie) en**  *to think about, to consider*

**perder (ie)**  *to lose*
**poder (ue)**  *to be able to*
**preferir (ie)**  *to prefer*
**querer (ie)**  *to want; to love*
**repetir (i)**  *to repeat*
**sentir (ie)**  *to feel*
**servir (i)**  *to serve*
**sonar (ue)**  *to ring, to go off (phone, alarm clock, etc.)*
**soñar (ue) con**  *to dream (about)*
**volver (ue)**  *to return*

## Adjetivos

**difícil**  *difficult*
**fácil**  *easy*

**lento**  *slow*
**rápido**  *fast*

## Adverbios

**difícilmente**  *with difficulty*
**fácilmente**  *easily*
**frecuentemente**  *frequently*
**generalmente**  *generally*
**lentamente**  *slowly*
**rápidamente**  *rapidly*

**bastante**  *somewhat, rather*
**bien**  *well*
**demasiado**  *too much*
**mal**  *badly*
**mucho**  *a lot*
**muy**  *very*
**poco**  *little*

*Starting here, stem-changing verbs will be indicated in vocabulary lists with the stem change in parentheses.

# Repaso y preparación

## Repaso del Capítulo 4

Complete these activities to check your understanding of the new grammar points in **Chapter 4** before you move on to **Chapter 5**.

The answers to the activities in this section can be found in **Appendix B**.

### Gustar with nouns and other verbs like gustar (p. 134)

**1** Completa las oraciones con un pronombre de objeto indirecto y escoge la forma correcta del verbo indicado.

1. A ellos _____ (gusta / gustan) los blogs.
2. A mí _____ (encanta / encantan) mi teléfono inteligente.
3. A él _____ (molesta / molestan) perder acceso a Internet.
4. A nosotros _____ (interesa / interesan) los foros sobre la tecnología.
5. A ti no _____ (importa / importan) cambiar tu contraseña frecuentemente.
6. A usted _____ (gusta / gustan) el nuevo programa antivirus.

### The verb estar and the uses of ser and estar (p. 138)

**2** Completa las oraciones con una forma de **ser** o **estar**.

1. Oye, Marcos ¿ _____ enojado?
2. Nosotros _____ en la biblioteca.
3. Yo _____ estudiante.
4. Ellos _____ altos y rubios.
5. ¡Tengo examen! _____ muy nervioso.
6. Ella no puede dormir. _____ cansada.
7. Hoy _____ miércoles.
8. El celular _____ de Marisa.
9. Mi computadora _____ en mi mochila.
10. Mis amigos _____ españoles.
11. La fiesta _____ en el café.
12. Los altoparlantes _____ en la mesa.

### Stem-changing verbs in the present indicative (p. 143)

**3** Haz oraciones completas con los sujetos y verbos indicados.

1. tú / dormir mucho
2. yo / cerrar la computadora portátil
3. ella / entender las instrucciones
4. nosotras / jugar el juego interactivo
5. usted / repetir la contraseña
6. ellos / querer un MP3 portátil
7. yo / poder instalar el programa
8. nosotros / preferir ir a un café con wifi

### Adverbs (p. 148)

**4** Escoge un adjetivo de la lista, cámbialo a un adverbio con **-mente** y úsalo para completar una de las siguientes oraciones.

**Adjetivos:** fácil, general, lento, rápido
1. No me gusta escribir. Escribo muy _____.
2. ¡Está computadora es fantástica! Funciona muy _____.
3. _____ me gusta navegar en Internet, pero no me gusta este sitio web.
4. Ella aprende nuevos programas muy _____. No son difíciles para ella.

## > Preparación para el Capítulo 5

**The present indicative of regular -ar, -er, and -ir verbs (Chapters 2 and 3)**

**5** Completa las oraciones del anuncio (*advertisement*) con la forma correcta del verbo indicado.

Complete these activities to review some previously learned grammatical structures that will be helpful when you learn the new grammar in **Chapter 5**.

Be sure to reread **Chapter 4: Gramática útil 2** and **3** before moving on to the new **Chapter 5** grammar sections.

### ¡Súper rápido, súper ligero!
### Y esta semana, ¡una súper oferta!

**El Incre-Libre 2020 _____ (deber) ser tu nueva computadora si tú...**

- _____ (enviar) o_____ (recibir) archivos grandes por e-mail,
- _____ (grabar) muchos videos o _____ (instalar) programas de software que requieren mucha memoria,
- _____ (llevar) tu portátil siempre contigo y _____ (trabajar) con ella en muchos sitios, ...ésta es la computadora para ti.

**Nuestros clientes _____ (hablar) de su satisfacción con el Incre-Libre:**

"¡Esta computadora _____ (funcionar) muy rápidamente! Yo _____ (bajar) y _____ (subir) archivos a mi sitio web todos los días sin problema."

**–Pilar Torres García, diseñadora de sitios web**

"¡El Incre-Libre no _____ (pesar—*to weigh*) nada! Voy a un café, _____ (sacar) la computadora de mi mochila, _____ (acceder) a Internet y _____ (leer) las noticias del mundo. No importa dónde estoy."

**–Javier Salazar Rojas, profesor**

"Los altoparlantes son increíbles. Cuando mi hermanos y yo _____ (usar) la computadora para mirar videos, ellos siempre _____ (comentar) la calidad del audio."

**–Marcos Villarreal Barrios, estudiante**

**¡Esta semana, nosotros _____ (ofrecer) el Incre-Libre por sólo 1.200 euros!**

**Es nuestra portátil más popular – _____ (vender) casi 100 de ellas cada semana.**

**¡Si quieres una, _____ (deber) actuar AHORA! Nuestros expertos en la computación personal están listos para atenderles.**

© Cengage Learning 2013. Photo: Nata-Lia/Shutterstock

# ¿Qué tal la familia?

## RELACIONES FAMILIARES

En el mundo hispanohablante, las relaciones familiares son un aspecto muy importante de la identidad personal.

¿Es tu familia una parte importante de tu vida diaria? ¿Cuánto tiempo pasas con miembros de tu familia en una semana? ¿En un mes?

## Communication

By the end of this chapter you will be able to

- talk about and describe your family
- talk about professions
- describe daily routines
- indicate ongoing actions

# Un viaje por El Salvador y Honduras

Estos países centroamericanos comparten una frontera y una costa pacífica. Honduras también tiene una costa atlántica. Los dos tienen un clima tropical.

| País / Área | Tamaño y fronteras | Sitios de interés |
| --- | --- | --- |
| **El Salvador** 20.720 km$^2$ | un poco más pequeño que Massachusetts; fronteras con Guatemala y Honduras | el bosque lluvioso *(rain forest)* del Parque Nacional Montecristo; los volcanes de Izalco, Santa Ana y San Vicente; las ruinas mayas de Joya de Cerén; las playas *(beaches)* del Pacífico |
| **Honduras** 111.890 km$^2$ | un poco más grande que Tennessee; fronteras con El Salvador, Guatemala y Nicaragua | las ruinas mayas de Copán, las islas de la Bahía, la arquitectura colonial de Tegucigalpa y San Pedro Sula, el bosque tropical de la región de la Mosquitia |

**¿Qué sabes?** Di si las siguientes oraciones son ciertas (**C**) o falsas (**F**).

1. Estos dos países tienen más o menos el mismo *(same)* tamaño.
2. Hay ruinas mayas en Honduras, pero no en El Salvador.
3. El Salvador tiene muchos volcanes.
4. Hay ejemplos de arquitectura colonial en Honduras.

**Lo que sé y lo que quiero aprender** Completa la tabla del **Apéndice A**. Escribe algunos datos que **ya sabes** sobre estos países en la columna **Lo que sé**. Después, añade algunos temas que **quieres aprender** a la columna **Lo que quiero aprender**. Guarda la tabla para usarla otra vez en la sección **¡Explora y exprésate!** en la página 187.

## Cultures

By the end of this chapter you will have explored

- facts about Honduras and El Salvador
- a unique course of study in Honduras
- a financial cooperative in El Salvador
- careers where knowledge of Spanish is helpful
- the Afro-Hispanic **garífuna** culture of Honduras

Globe Art: Adapted from Shutterstock/rrguest

# ¡Imagínate!

## >> Vocabulario útil 1

ANILÚ: Son fotos de mi **familia**.

DULCE: ¿De veras? ¿En la computadora?

ANILÚ: Sí, mi **hermanito** Roberto tiene una cámara digital.
Saca fotos de la familia y me las manda por Internet.

In Spanish, the masculine plural **hermanos** can mean both *brothers* (all males) and *brothers and sisters / siblings* (both males and females).

### >> La familia nuclear

**la madre (mamá)** *mother*
**el padre (papá)** *father*
**los padres** *parents*
**la esposa** *wife*
**el esposo** *husband*
**la hija** *daughter*
**el hijo** *son*
**la hermana (mayor)** *(older) sister*
**el hermano (menor)** *(younger) brother*

**la tía** *aunt*
**el tío** *uncle*
**la prima** *female cousin*
**el primo** *male cousin*
**la sobrina** *niece*
**el sobrino** *nephew*
**la abuela** *grandmother*
**el abuelo** *grandfather*
**la nieta** *granddaughter*
**el nieto** *grandson*

To refer to a couple, use **la pareja**. For example: **Es una pareja muy elegante.** Also, to ask about someone's partner, you can say: **¿Quién es la pareja de Juan?** Or: **Su pareja es doctor.**

### >> La familia política

**la suegra** *mother-in-law*
**el suegro** *father-in-law*
**la nuera** *daughter-in-law*
**el yerno** *son-in-law*
**la cuñada** *sister-in-law*
**el cuñado** *brother-in-law*

### >> Otros parientes

**la madrastra** *stepmother*
**el padrastro** *stepfather*
**la hermanastra** *stepsister*
**el hermanastro** *stepbrother*
**la media hermana** *half-sister*
**el medio hermano** *half-brother*

Notice that **parientes** is a false cognate: it does *not* mean *parents;* it means *family members.* **Los padres** is the correct term for *parents.*

In Spanish, diminutives are common. You form the diminutive by adding **-ito** or **-ita** to a noun: **hermano → hermanito**. (Other diminutives are formed by adding **-cito / -cita: coche → cochecito**.)

A diminutive is used: 1) to indicate that something or someone is small, or younger. **Una casita** is a small house; **una hermanita** is a younger sister. 2) to express love or fondness. For example, Anilú probably refers to her grandmother as **abuelita** to indicate that she loves her dearly.

To express affection, Spanish speakers also use nicknames. In the video, **Anilú** is a nickname for Ana Luisa, **Beto** for Roberto, and **Chela** for Graciela.

In some countries, the **-astro(a)** ending might be viewed as pejorative, and speakers might refer to **la esposa de mi padre** instead of **mi madrastra**. Be conscious of these nuances.

## ACTIVIDADES

### 1 Los parientes
Completa las oraciones con la respuesta correcta para describir las relaciones entre los parientes de Anilú. Usa el árbol genealógico *(family tree)* de Anilú para identificar las relaciones.

1. Rodrigo es _____ de Adela.
   a. el esposo   b. el suegro   c. el tío
2. Tomás y Rafael son _____.
   a. hermanas   b. primos   c. hermanos
3. Sonia es _____ de Anilú.
   a. la tía   b. la prima   c. la hermanastra
4. Roberto es _____ de Rosa.
   a. el sobrino   b. el nieto   c. el yerno
5. Gloria es _____ de Rodrigo y Adela.
   a. la suegra   b. la hija   c. la nieta
6. Adela es _____ de Amelia.
   a. la madrastra   b. la cuñada   c. la suegra

Arturo Villa González   y   Beatriz Vega Chapa de Villa      Rodrigo Guzmán Corona   y   Adela Flores Romero de Guzmán

Carlos   Irene        Amelia   Pedro        Hernán   Rosa

Tomás   Rafael        Gloria   Anilú   Roberto        Alberto   Sonia

© Cengage Learning 2013

### 2 La familia de Anilú
Con un(a) compañero(a) de clase, háganse preguntas sobre el árbol genealógico *(family tree)* de Anilú de la **Actividad 1.** Túrnense nombrando la persona y diciendo cuál es su relación con Anilú.

**MODELO**   Compañero(a): *¿Quién es Beatriz Vega Chapa?*
Tú: *Es la abuela de Anilú.*

### 3 El árbol genealógico
Dibuja el árbol genealógico de tu familia. Empieza con tus abuelos y sigue con el resto de tu familia. Luego, en grupos de tres, intercambien sus árboles y háganse preguntas sobre sus familias.

**MODELO**   Tú: *¿Tom es tu hermano?*
Compañero(a): *Sí, es mi hermano menor. Tiene quince años y es muy divertido.*
Tú: *¿Quién es Elisa?*
Compañero(a): *Es mi sobrina. Es la hija de mi hermana mayor.*

### 4 Mi familia
Escribe un párrafo corto sobre cada miembro de tu familia nuclear. Para cada individuo, di quién es, cómo se llama y cuántos años tiene. Incluye algunas características físicas y también unas de personalidad. Luego, en grupos de tres, lean sus descripciones al grupo. El grupo te hace preguntas sobre cada miembro de tu familia y tú contestas.

---

Notice that two surnames are given for Anilú's grandparents. In some Spanish-speaking countries, the first surname is the father's, and the second one is the mother's. Anilú's full name is Anilú Guzmán Villa. If she marries someone whose first surname is Rodríguez, Anilú may add it to become Anilú Guzmán Villa de Rodríguez, or Sra. Rodríguez. This tradition is changing, however, and in many Spanish-speaking countries women do not change their names.

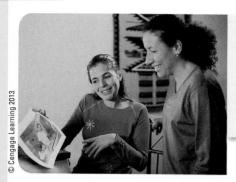

DULCE: ¿Quién es este señor?

ANILÚ: Es mi papá. Se enoja cuando Roberto le saca fotos. No le gusta salir en fotos. Dice que se ve muy gordo.

DULCE: ¿Qué hace tu papá?

ANILÚ: Es **arquitecto**. Diseña edificios para negocios.

When describing someone's profession, don't use an article as we would in English: **Es abogada** translates as *She is a lawyer.*

>> **Las profesiones y las carreras**

la abogada
el periodista
la médica
la artista

**El policía** means a single policeman. **La policía** can mean a single policewoman or the entire police force. You have to extract the correct meaning from context. Other professions whose meaning depends on the context and the article are: **el químico / la química, el físico / la física, el músico / la música, el matemático / la matemática, el guardia / la guardia.**

**La mujer policía** is also used for a single policewoman.

el bombero
la carpintera
la policía
el plomero
el arquitecto

## Más profesiones

| | |
|---|---|
| **el actor / la actriz** *actor / actress* | **el (la) gerente de...** *manager of. . .* |
| **el (la) asistente** *assistant* | **el hombre / la mujer de** |
| **el (la) camarero(a)** *waiter / waitress* | **negocios** *businessman /* |
| **el (la) cocinero(a)** *cook, chef* | *businesswoman* |
| **el (la) contador(a)** *accountant* | **el (la) ingeniero(a)** *engineer* |
| **el (la) dentista** *dentist* | **el (la) maestro(a)** *teacher* |
| **el (la) dependiente** *salesclerk* | **el (la) mecánico(a)** *mechanic* |
| **el (la) director(a) de social** | **el (la) peluquero(a)** *barber /* |
| **media** *director of social media* | *hairdresser* |
| **el (la) diseñador(a) gráfico(a)** | **el (la) programador(a)** *programmer* |
| *graphic designer* | **el (la) secretario(a)** *secretary* |
| **el (la) dueño(a) de...** *owner of. . .* | **el (la) trabajador(a)** *worker* |
| **el (la) enfermero(a)** *nurse* | **el (la) veterinario(a)** *veterinarian* |

As of this printing, no established translation for social media has been agreed upon by Spanish speakers. Most simply use the English "social media."

## ACTIVIDADES

**5** **¿Qué hace?** Escoge la profesión más lógica para cada persona.

1. Alejandro trabaja en un hospital. Es…
2. Catalina trabaja en el teatro. Es…
3. Pedro trabaja en un restaurante. Es…
4. El señor Cortez trabaja en una escuela secundaria *(high school)*. Es…
5. Amelia trabaja en el centro de computación. Es…
6. Irene trabaja en un hospital para animales. Es…

a. cocinero(a)
b. veterinario(a)
c. enfermero(a)
d. actor / actriz
e. maestro(a)
f. programador(a)

**6** **Quiere ser…** Tú y tu compañero(a) hablan de varios amigos. Tú le dices a tu compañero(a) qué es lo que estudia esa persona y tu compañero(a) te dice qué quiere ser esa persona.

MODELO medicina
Tú: *Marcos estudia medicina.*
Compañero(a): *Quiere ser médico.*

1. contabilidad
2. administración de empresas
3. ingeniería
4. informática
5. diseño gráfico
6. arte
7. pedagogía
8. periodismo

**7** **Presentaciones** Estás en la fiesta de un amigo. Él te presenta a varios miembros de su familia. Lee sus presentaciones. Luego, para cada persona, indica cuál es su relación con el narrador y su profesión.

1. Quiero presentarte a Antonio. Él es el hijo de mi tía Rosa. Antonio trabaja en el Hospital Garibaldi. Ayuda a las personas enfermas.

   *Nombre:* Antonio          *Relación:* _____     *Profesión:* _____

2. Te presento a Miranda. Miranda es la hija de mi tío Ricardo. Miranda enseña francés en el Colegio Del Valle.

   *Nombre:* Miranda          *Relación:* _____     *Profesión:* _____

3. Mira, te presento a Olga. Olga trabaja para el periódico *El Universal*. Olga es la esposa de mi hermano.

   *Nombre:* Olga          *Relación:* _____     *Profesión:* _____

4. Quiero presentarte a César. César es el hijo de mi hermano. César trabaja en una pizzería después del colegio.

   *Nombre:* César          *Relación:* _____     *Profesión:* _____

5. Éste es Raúl. Raúl es el hermano de mi padre. Él diseña casas y edificios.

   *Nombre:* Raúl          *Relación:* _____     *Profesión:* _____

6. Te presento al señor Domínguez, el padre de mi esposa. Él escribe software para una compañía multinacional.

   *Nombre:* señor Domínguez     *Relación:* _____     *Profesión:* _____

**8** **¿Qué quieres ser?** En grupos de tres, hablen sobre sus planes para el futuro.

MODELO   Tú: *¿Qué profesión te interesa?*
Compañero(a): *¿A mí? Yo quiero ser director de social media.*
Tú: *¿Dónde quieres trabajar?*
Compañero(a): *Quiero trabajar aquí, en Los Ángeles.*

**9** **El español y las profesiones** En Estados Unidos, hay muchas oportunidades profesionales para personas que hablan español. Aquí hay algunas carreras que utilizan el español.

- abogado(a)
- académico(a)
- enfermero(a)
- intérprete
- médico(a)

- periodista
- policía
- profesor(a) o maestro(a) de español
- secretario(a) bilingüe
- trabajador(a) social

Con un(a) compañero(a) de clase, contesten las siguientes preguntas.

1. ¿Te interesa alguna de estas carreras? ¿Por qué? ¿Crees que poder hablar español es importante para tu futuro?

2. En Europa, los estudiantes de colegio aprenden inglés y muchas veces otro idioma además de su lengua nativa. ¿Crees que es buena idea? ¿Por qué? ¿Crees que los estadounidenses deben aprender otro idioma además del inglés? ¿Por qué?

## ¡Fíjate! Las profesiones y el mundo

Gracias a la tecnología, el mundo va cambiando *(is changing)* muy rápido. Algunas profesiones que no existían ayer, existen hoy. Antes, más profesiones eran locales, es decir, consistían en lo que se podía hacer dentro de *(consisted of what could be done within)* la comunidad: policía, bombero, dentista, doctor, profesor. Ahora es posible elegir una profesión que puede tener un impacto global. ¿En qué campos existen profesiones internacionales?

Marvin Newman/Photolibrary

Science Faction / SuperStock

| | |
|---|---|
| **Asistencia sanitaria internacional** | *International health care* |
| **Banca internacional** | *International banking* |
| **Consultoría de negocios** | *Consulting* |
| **Derecho internacional** | *International law* |
| **Ingeniería multinacional** | *International engineering* |
| **Mercadotecnia internacional** | *International marketing* |
| **Política exterior** | *Foreign policy* |
| **Programas de conservación ambiental** | *Environmental programs* |
| **Servicios financieros** | *Financial services* |
| **Tecnología ambiental** | *"Green" technology* |
| **Telecomunicaciones** | *Telecommunications* |

**Práctica** Ve a Internet y busca tres profesiones internacionales que te interesan. ¿En qué campo están? ¿Qué puedes hacer en tus estudios para empezar a prepararte para cada profesión?

With some professions, there is a lot of confusion about how to specify gender, especially for traditionally male professions like **piloto, bombero, ingeniero, general, mecánico, plomero.** The ambiguity is also due to the number of options for specifying gender. Some professions change the ending, like **el actor** and **la actriz; el maestro** and **la maestra; el alcalde** *(mayor)* and **la alcaldesa.** Other professions simply change the article, with no change to the noun, like **el gerente** and **la gerente, el dentista** and **la dentista.** Sometimes, the word **mujer** or **señora** is used to specify the gender: **la señora juez** *(judge),* **la mujer policía.**

## Vocabulario útil 3

**ANILÚ:** Mamá, ¿está Roberto por allí? Necesito hablar con él.

**MAMÁ:** No puede venir al teléfono. Se está bañando.

**ANILÚ:** ¿Está bañándose? ¿A esta hora?

**MAMÁ:** Acaba de regresar de su partido de fútbol. ¡Ay! ¡No hay ni **toallas** ni **jabón** en el baño! Me tengo que ir. Tengo que llevarle a tu hermano una toalla, el jabón y el **champú**…

>> **En el baño** *In the bathroom*

el desodorante

el champú

el cepillo de dientes

la toalla (de mano)

la máquina de afeitar

el jabón

la pasta de dientes

la rasuradora

el maquillaje

el peine

el cepillo

## ACTIVIDADES

**10** **¿Qué necesitan comprar?** Según la situación, ¿qué necesita comprar cada persona?

MODELO *Él necesita comprar champú.*

1.

2.

3.

4.

5.

6.

**11** **El HiperMercado** Tú y tu hermano(a) ven un anuncio para el HiperMercado en el periódico. Tú le dices qué quieres comprar y él o ella te dice cuánto dinero necesitas para comprar ese artículo.

(**¡OJO!** *Dollars* = **dólares** y *cents* = **centavos**.)

MODELO Tú: *¿Quiero comprar un cepillo y un peine.*
Hermano(a): *Necesitas tres dólares y setenta y nueve centavos para comprar el cepillo y el peine.*

> Unlike grocery stores, which focus mostly on food items, **hipermercados** in Spanish-speaking countries are similar to supermarkets, but tend to sell an even wider range of household products.

### HiperMercado
#### ¡Todo para la familia!
#### ¡Los mejores precios de la ciudad!

Cepillo y peine "La Bella":
 ~~$4,39~~ **$3,79**

Jabón antibacterial "Sanitario":
~~$1,49~~ **$1,19**

Champú "Largo y limpio":
 ~~$3,39~~ **$2,79**

Máquina de afeitar "El Varonil":
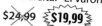 ~~$24,99~~ **$19,99**

Cepillo de dientes y pasta de dientes "Brillante":
~~$4,75~~ **$3,75**

Paquete de seis rasuradoras "Para ella":
 ~~$3,97~~ **$3,47**

Desodorante "Frescura":
 ~~$2,69~~ **$1,99**

Paquete de dos toallas de mano "Elegantes":
 ~~$4,99~~  **$3,99**

All art: © Cengage Learning 2013

¡Imagínate! ▪ ¿Qué tal la familia? **169**

## ESTRATEGIA

### Listening for the main idea

A good way to organize your viewing of authentic video is to focus on getting the main idea of the segment (or of each of its parts). Don't try to understand every word; just try to get the gist of each scene. Later, with the help of the textbook activities, some of the other details of the segment will emerge.

**Antes de ver** Mira las fotos a la izquierda *(on the left)*. Haz correspondencia entre *(Match)* las fotos y los diálogos.

ⓐ

ⓑ

ⓒ

_____ 1. Dulce: ¿Qué hace tu papá?

Anilú: Es arquitecto. Diseña edificios para negocios.

_____ 2. Mamá: Bueno, pero siempre hay que hacer tiempo para llamar a tu mamá.

Anilú: Sí, mamá, está bien. Perdóname.

_____ 3. Anilú: Mira, ven a ver.

Dulce: ¿Qué es?

▶ **Ver** Ahora mira el video para el **Capítulo 5.** Trata de entender la idea principal de cada escena.

**Después de ver** Haz correspondencia entre las escenas y las ideas principales.

1. _____ **Escena 1:** Anilú está mirando *(is looking at)* la computadora.

2. _____ **Escena 2:** Anilú habla con su mama.

3. _____ **Escena 3:** Anilú y Dulce miran una foto en la impresora.

4. _____ **Escena 4:** Roberto llama a Anilú.

5. _____ **Escena 5:** Anilú mira la foto de la fiesta de cumpleaños del abuelo.

a. La mamá de Anilú dice que ella nunca la llama.

b. A Anilú no le gusta la foto pero Roberto cree que es muy cómica.

c. Roberto quiere saber *(to know)* si a Anilú le gustan las fotos.

d. Anilú dice *(says)* que tiene unas fotos digitales.

e. Ven una foto del papá de Anilú.

## ● >> Voces del mundo hispano

En el video para este capítulo Mirna, José y Aura hablan de las profesiones y de sus familias. Lee las siguientes oraciones. Después mira el video una o más veces para decir si las oraciones son ciertas (**C**) o falsas (**F**).

1. Mirna estudia para ser diseñadora gráfica.
2. José ya es paralegal y estudia para ser abogado.
3. Una de las hermanas de Mirna trabaja en administración de empresas.
4. Aura tiene un hermano y dos hermanas.
5. Una hermana de Aura es contadora.
6. José tiene seis miembros de su familia en Estados Unidos.

© Cengage Learning 2013

## ◀)) >> Voces de Estados Unidos

Track 14

### Gloria G. Rodríguez, fundadora de Avance

❝ **Essentially, to be Hispanic is to value children . . . Rarely are children as welcomed and visible with adults as in the Latino culture. Indeed, los hijos son la riqueza de los padres, son nuestro gran tesoro.** ❞

Gloria Rodríguez

L a doctora Gloria G. Rodríguez es fundadora de Avance, una organización nacional que ayuda a familias latinas pobres con niños pequeños. En su libro, *Raising Nuestros Niños: Bringing Up Latino Children in a Bicultural World*, Rodríguez explica la filosofía de Avance así:

Los padres tienen la esperanza y el deseo, hope and desire, that their children succeed, and that they feel un gran orgullo, a great sense of pride, when they do. Esta esperanza y orgullo de los padres, this hope and pride, become tremendous driving forces for Latino parents (p. 3).

Esta méxicoamericana de orígenes muy pobres es ganadora de muchos premios y reconocimientos por su labor con familias hispanas.

**¿Y tú?** ¿Es importante tu familia en tu vida estudiantil? ¿Qué papel juega la familia en la educación de los niños?

# ¡Prepárate!

## >> Gramática útil 1

### Describing daily activities: Irregular-**yo** verbs in the present indicative, **saber** vs. **conocer**, and the personal **a**

**Cómo usarlo**

1. You have already learned the present indicative tense of many verbs. These include regular -**ar**, -**er**, and -**ir** verbs (**hablar, comer, vivir,** etc.), some irregular verbs (**ser, tener, ir**), and some stem-changing verbs (**pensar, poder, dormir,** etc.).

2. Now you will learn some verbs that are regular in all forms of the present indicative except the **yo** form. Like other verbs in the present indicative tense, these verbs can be used to say what you routinely do, what you are doing at the moment, or what you plan to do in the future.

| | |
|---|---|
| Todos los días **salgo** para la universidad a las ocho. | *Every day **I leave** for the university at 8:00.* |
| Ahora mismo, **pongo** mis libros en la mochila y **digo** "hasta luego" a mi compañera de cuarto. | *Right now, **I put / I'm putting** my books in my backpack and **I say / I'm saying**, "See you later" to my roommate.* |
| Esta noche, **traigo** mis libros a casa otra vez y **hago** la tarea. | *Tonight, **I bring / I'll bring** my books home again and **I do / I'll do** my homework.* |

**Cómo formarlo**

Irregular-**yo** verbs

Many irregular-**yo** verbs in the present indicative fall into several recognizable categories. Others have to be learned individually.

1. -**go** endings:

| hacer | to make; to do | **hago**, haces, hace, hacemos, hacéis, hacen |
|---|---|---|
| poner | to put | **pongo**, pones, pone, ponemos, ponéis, ponen |
| salir | to leave, to go out (with) | **salgo**, sales, sale, salimos, salís, salen |
| traer | to bring | **traigo**, traes, trae, traemos, traéis, traen |

2. -**zco** endings:

| conducir | to drive; to conduct | **conduzco**, conduces, conduce, conducimos, conducís, conducen |
|---|---|---|
| conocer | to know a person; to be familiar with | **conozco**, conoces, conoce, conocemos, conocéis, conocen |
| traducir | to translate | **traduzco**, traduces, traduce, traducimos, traducís, traducen |

> **Conducir** is used more frequently in Spain to talk about driving. In most of Latin America, the verbs **manejar** and **guiar** (both regular -**ar** verbs) are used. (**Guiar** uses an accent on the **i** in these forms: **guío, guías, guía, guían**.)

**3.** Other irregular-**yo** verbs:

| dar | to give | **doy**, das, da, damos, dais, dan |
|---|---|---|
| oír | to hear | **oigo,** oyes, oye, oímos, oís, oyen |
| saber | to know a fact; to know how to | **sé**, sabes, sabe, sabemos, sabéis, saben |
| ver | to see | **veo,** ves, ve, vemos, veis, ven |

Note that **oír** requires a **y** in the **tú, él / ella / Ud.,** and **ellos / ellas / Uds.** forms.

**4.** Two irregular-**yo** verbs (-**go** verbs) with a stem change:

| decir | to say, to tell | **digo**, dices, dice, decimos, decís, dicen |
|---|---|---|
| venir | to come, to attend | **vengo**, vienes, viene, venimos, venís, vienen |

**5.** Remember that most of these verbs are irregular only in the **yo** form. Otherwise, they follow the rules for regular **-ar, -er**, and **-ir** verbs that you have already learned. **Oír** uses the regular endings but includes a spelling change: the addition of **y** to all forms except the **yo** form. **Decir** and **venir** also have a stem change in addition to the irregular-**yo** form, but they still use **-ir** present-tense endings.

## Saber vs. conocer

**Saber** and **conocer** both mean *to know*. It's important to know when to use each one.

- Use **saber** to say that you know a fact or information, or that you know how to do something.

    Eduardo **sabe** hablar alemán, jugar tenis y bailar flamenco. Además **sabe** dónde están todos los restaurantes buenos de la ciudad.

    *Eduardo **knows how** to speak German, play tennis, and dance flamenco. He also **knows** where all the good restaurants in the city are.*

Algún día vas a tener hijos y entonces vas a **saber** cómo es.

One way to remember the difference between **saber** and **conocer** is that **saber** is usually followed by either a verb or a phrase, while **conocer** is often followed by a noun and is never followed by an infinitive.

- Use **conocer** to say that you know a person or are familiar with a thing.

    —¿**Conocen** a Sandra?
    —No, pero **conocemos** a su hermana.

    *Do you **know** Sandra?*
    *No, but we **know** her sister.*

    —¿**Conoces** bien Tegucigalpa?
    —Sí, pero no **conozco** las otras ciudades de Honduras.

    *Do you **know** Tegucigalpa well?*
    *Yes, but I don't **know** the other cities in Honduras.*

The personal **a** can also be used with pets: **Adoro a mi perro.**

## The personal **a**

When you use **conocer** to say that you know a person, notice that you use the preposition **a** before the noun referring to the person. This preposition is known as the personal **a** in Spanish and it must be used whenever a person receives the action of any verb (not just **conocer**). It has no equivalent in English.

In **Chapter 3** you learned that a + el = al. The personal **a** is no exception: Veo **al profesor.**

Conocemos **a** Nina y **a** Roberto.
¿Ves **a** tus amigos frecuentemente?

*We know Nina and Roberto.*
*Do you see your friends frequently?*

© Cengage Learning 2013

ACTIVIDADES

**1** **¿Sí o no?** Lee las oraciones y decide si requieren la **a** personal o no. Añade la **a** personal si es necesaria o marca con una **X** si no es necesaria.

1. Veo _____ mis hermanos todos los días.
2. Hago mi tarea con _____ ellos.
3. Les digo las noticias de casa _____ ellos también.
4. Oigo _____ sus comentarios sobre la universidad.
5. Conozco _____ muchos de sus amigos.
6. Conduzco el auto cuando visito _____ mi familia.

**2** **La mamá de Anilú** La mamá de Anilú le describe un día normal a una amiga. Da su descripción desde su punto de vista *(viewpoint)*.

1. salir del trabajo a las cinco
2. generalmente, traer trabajo a casa
3. cuando llego a casa, venir muy cansada
4. hacer la cena *(dinner)* a las siete
5. poner la mesa *(set the table)* antes de hacer la cena
6. cuando la cena está preparada, decir "todo está listo"
7. conocer a mis hijos muy bien
8. saber que tengo que llamarlos varias veces
9. por fin, oír a los niños apagar la tele
10. dar las gracias por otro día más o menos normal

**3** **¿Sabes…?** Con un(a) compañero(a), formen preguntas con las siguientes frases. Túrnense para hacerse las preguntas. Luego, inventen nuevas preguntas usando el verbo en cada frase y háganse esas preguntas.

MODELO conducir para llegar a la universidad
Tú: *¿Conduces para llegar a la universidad?*
Compañero(a): *No, no conduzco para llegar a la universidad.*
Tú: *¿Conduces todos los días?*
Compañero(a): *No, conduzco tres días por semana.*

1. conocer al (a la) presidente de la universidad
2. dar tu contraseña a tus amigos
3. decir siempre la verdad
4. hacer la tarea puntualmente
5. saber escribir programas para los teléfonos inteligentes
6. salir frecuentemente con amigos
7. traducir poemas del inglés al español
8. traer la computadora portátil a la clase
9. venir cansado(a) o aburrido(a) de las clases
10. ver televisión por la mañana, la tarde or la noche

**††** **4** **¿Saber o conocer?** Con un(a) compañero(a), túrnense para hacer las siguientes preguntas. La persona que hace las preguntas tiene que decidir entre los verbos **saber** o **conocer**.

MODELO ¿(Saber / Conocer / Conocer a) hablar español?
Tú: *¿Sabes hablar español?*
Compañero(a): *Sí, sé hablar español.*

1. ¿(Saber / Conocer / Conocer a) el (la) compañero(a) de cuarto de…?
2. ¿( Saber / Conocer / Conocer a) Nueva York, París o Londres?
3. ¿( Saber / Conocer / Conocer a) tocar el violín?
4. ¿( Saber / Conocer / Conocer a) Honduras?
5. ¿( Saber / Conocer / Conocer a) preparar comida hondureña o salvadoreña?

**††** **5** **Sé y conozco** Escribe cinco cosas que **sabes** hacer. Luego escribe el nombre de cinco personas o lugares que **conoces**. Intercambia tu lista con un(a) compañero(a). Tu compañero(a) tiene que informarle a la clase lo que tú **sabes** y **conoces** y tú tienes que hacer lo mismo con la lista de tu compañero(a).

MODELO Tu lista: *Sé jugar tenis.*
*Conozco a muchas personas que juegan tenis.*
Tu compañero(a): *Javier sabe jugar tenis.*
*Conoce a muchas personas que juegan tenis.*

**†††** **6** **Cuestionario** Primero, escribe tus respuestas a las preguntas. Luego, en grupos de tres, háganse las preguntas del siguiente cuestionario. Si quieren, pueden añadir algunas preguntas al cuestionario. Cada uno en el grupo debe contestar cada pregunta.

1. **Tu horario**
   ¿Cuándo haces ejercicio?
   ¿Cuándo haces la tarea?
2. **Tu vida social**
   ¿Sales por la noche? ¿Adónde vas?
   ¿Con quién sales los fines de semana?
3. **Tu medio de transporte preferido**
   ¿Tienes coche? ¿Conduces a la universidad?
   ¿Conduces todos los días o usas otro medio de transporte?
4. **Tu tiempo libre**
   ¿Sabes jugar algún deporte?
   ¿Sabes tocar un instrumento? ¿Cuál?
5. **¿Conoces el mundo?**
   ¿Conoces los países de Latinoamérica? ¿Cuáles?
   ¿Conoces África o Asia?

**Gramática útil 2**

### Describing daily activities: Reflexive verbs

**Cómo usarlo**

Ya es hora de
despertarse
a una nueva
clase de hotel
de negocios.

Hotel Calidad Ejecutiva
www.calidadejecutiva.com  1-800-444-4444
7800 Avenida Norte, San Salvador  2901-8720

This ad for a business hotel in El Salvador uses a reflexive verb. What is it and what does it mean?

1. So far, you have learned to use Spanish verbs to say what actions people are doing or to describe people and things.

| | |
|---|---|
| Elena **habla** por teléfono. | *Elena **talks** on the phone.* |
| Tu hermano **está** cansado. | *Your brother **is** tired.* |

2. Spanish has another category of verbs, called *reflexive* verbs, where the action of the verb *reflects back* on the person who is doing the action. When you use reflexive verbs in Spanish, they are often translated in English as *with* or *to myself, yourself, himself, herself, ourselves, yourselves, themselves.*

| | |
|---|---|
| Lidia **se maquilla**. | *Lidia **puts makeup on (herself)**.* |
| Antes de ir a clase, yo **me ducho, me visto** y **me peino**. | *Before going to class, **I shower, get dressed**, and **comb my hair**.* |

3. Notice how a reflexive verb is always used with a reflexive pronoun. These pronouns always match the subject of the sentence. The action of the verb *reflects back* on the person when the pronoun is used.

The reflexive pronoun and verb must always match the subject of the sentence: **Nosotros nos bañamos, Ellos se afeitan, Mateo se lava,** etc.

| | |
|---|---|
| **Yo me acuesto** a las once. | ***I go to bed (put myself to bed)** at eleven.* |
| **Tú te despiertas** a las diez los fines de semana. | ***You get up (wake yourself up)** at ten on the weekends.* |
| **Nosotros nos bañamos** antes de salir de casa. | ***We bathe (ourselves) before** we leave the house.* |
| **Ellos se afeitan** todos los días. | ***They shave (themselves)** every day.* |

4. Most reflexive verbs can also be used without the reflexive pronoun to express non-reflexive actions, that is, actions that are performed on someone other than oneself.

| | |
|---|---|
| Mateo **se baña** todos los días. | *Mateo **bathes** every day.* |
| Mateo **baña** a su perro. | *Mateo **bathes (washes)** his dog.* |

5. Reflexive pronouns can also be used to indicate *reciprocal actions*.

| | |
|---|---|
| Leo y Ali **se cortan** el pelo. | *Leo and Ali **cut each other's** hair.* |

**Cómo formarlo**

## LO BÁSICO

- A *reflexive verb* is one in which the action described reflects back on the subject.
- A *reflexive pronoun* is a pronoun that refers back to the subject of the sentence. English reflexive pronouns are *myself, herself, ourselves,* etc.

   Hotel ad: (photo) Anton Prado Photo/Shutterstock; (text) © Cengage Learning 2013

1. You conjugate reflexive verbs the same way you would any other verb. The only difference is that you must always include the reflexive pronoun.

2. Here is the reflexive verb **lavarse** conjugated in the present indicative tense.

| lavarse *(to wash oneself)* | |
|---|---|
| yo | **me lavo** |
| tú | **te lavas** |
| Ud. / él / ella | **se lava** |
| nosotros(as) | **nos lavamos** |
| vosotros(as) | **os laváis** |
| Uds. / ellos / ellas | **se lavan** |

3. The only difference in the way that reflexive and non-reflexive verbs are conjugated is the addition of the reflexive pronoun to the verb form. Verbs that are irregular or stem-changing when used non-reflexively have the same irregularities or stem changes when used with a reflexive pronoun.

   **Me despierto** a las seis y media.   *I wake (myself) up at 6: 30.*
   **Despierto a mi esposo** a las siete.   *I wake my husband up at 7: 00.*

4. When you use a reflexive verb in its infinitive form, the reflexive pronoun may attach at the end of the infinitive (most commonly) or go at the beginning of the entire verb phrase.

   **Voy a acostarme** a las once.         OR: **Me voy a acostar** a las once.
   **Necesito acostarme** a las once.      **Me necesito acostar** a las once.
   **Tengo que acostarme** a las once.     **Me tengo que acostar** a las once.

   Notice that with **gustar** (and similar verbs), the reflexive pronoun *must* be attached at the end of the infinitive.

   **Me gusta acostarme** a las once.

   > Remember that when you use a reflexive verb as an infinitive, you still need to change the pronoun to match the subject of the sentence: **Voy a acostarme a las once, pero tú vas a acostarte a medianoche**.

5. Here are some common reflexive verbs, many of which refer to daily routine. Many reflexive verbs have a stem change, which is indicated in parenthesis.

| | |
|---|---|
| **acostarse (ue)** *to go to bed* | **levantarse** *to get up* |
| **afeitarse** *to shave oneself* | **maquillarse** *to put on makeup* |
| **bañarse** *to take a bath* | **peinarse** *to brush / comb one's hair* |
| **cepillarse el pelo** *to brush one's hair* | **ponerse (la ropa)** *to put on (clothing)* |
| **cepillarse los dientes** *to brush one's teeth* | **prepararse** *to get ready* |
| **despertarse (ie)** *to wake up* | **quitarse (la ropa)** *to take off (clothing)* |
| **ducharse** *to take a shower* | **secarse el pelo** *to dry one's hair* |
| **lavarse** *to wash oneself* | **sentarse (ie)** *to sit down* |
| **lavarse el pelo** *to wash one's hair* | **vestirse (i)** *to get dressed* |
| **lavarse los dientes** *to brush one's teeth* | |

Reflexive actions always carry the meaning to *oneself*. Reciprocal actions always carry the meaning *to each other*.

**6.** Some Spanish verbs are used with reflexive pronouns to emphasize a change in state or emotion. Spanish has many more verbs that are used this way than English does. Note that some of these verbs (**casarse, comprometerse,** etc.) are usually used to express reciprocal actions, due to the nature of their meaning.

| | |
|---|---|
| **casarse** *to get married* | **irse** *to leave, to go away* |
| **comprometerse** *to get engaged* | **pelearse** *to have a fight* |
| **despedirse (i)** *to say goodbye* | **preocuparse** *to worry* |
| **divertirse (ie)** *to have fun* | **quejarse** *to complain* |
| **divorciarse** *to get divorced* | **reírse (i)** *to laugh* |
| **dormirse (ue)** *to fall asleep* | **relajarse** *to relax* |
| **enamorarse** *to fall in love* | **reunirse** *to meet, to get together* |
| **enfermarse** *to get sick* | **separarse** *to separate* |

**Reunirse** carries an accent on the **u** when conjugated: **se reúnen**.

**7.** Here are some common words and phrases to use with these verbs.

| | |
|---|---|
| **a veces** *sometimes* | **siempre** *always* |
| **antes** *before* | **todas las semanas** *every week* |
| **después** *after* | **todos los días** *every day* |
| **luego** *later* | **...veces al día /** *. . . times a day /* |
| **nunca** *never* | **por semana** *per week* |

## ACTIVIDADES

MODELO

🔊 **7** **Necesito…** Para vernos y sentirnos bien, todos tenemos que hacer ciertas cosas antes o después de participar en ciertas actividades. Escucha las descripciones y escoge el dibujo que le corresponde a cada descripción.

Track 15

1. _____

2. _____

3. _____

4. _____

5. _____

6. _____

All art: © Cengage Learning 2013

**8** **De visita** Estás de visita en la casa de tu compañero(a) y quieres saber más de la rutina diaria de él o ella y de su familia. Hazle las preguntas de la lista y si quieres, también inventa otras.

MODELO   Tú: *¿A qué hora (acostarse) tus padres?*
Tú: *¿A qué hora se acuestan tus padres?*
Compañero(a): *Mis padres se acuestan a las diez o las once de la noche.*

1. ¿Tú (lavarse) el pelo todos los días?
2. ¿Cuántas veces por semana (afeitarse) tu abuelo?
3. ¿(Despertarse) tarde o temprano tu madre?
4. ¿(Ducharse) por la mañana o por la noche tu hermano?
5. ¿(Maquillarse) tu hermana antes de salir para la universidad?
6. ¿A qué hora (acostar) tu compañero(a) de cuarto?
7. ¿A qué hora (levantarse) tu padre?
8. ¿(Peinarse) antes de salir para el colegio tu primo?
9. ¿Cuántas veces por día (lavarse) los dientes tú y tus hermanos?

**9** **La telenovela** Miguel y Marta son los protagonistas de una telenovela famosa. Tú eres el (la) guionista *(script writer)* y tienes que escribir una descripción del desarrollo de su relación. Sigue el modelo.

MODELO   divertirse en la fiesta de unos amigos
*Miguel y Marta se divierten en la fiesta de unos amigos.*

1. enamorarse después de un mes
2. comprometerse después de un año
3. casarse en la casa de los padres de Marta
4. pelearse frecuentemente
5. quejarse mucho a sus amigos
6. separarse por seis meses
7. divorciarse después de dos años de matrimonio
8. despedirse en el aeropuerto
9. irse a diferentes regiones del país
10. por fin reunirse

**10** **Preguntas personales** Tú y tu compañero(a) quieren saber más sobre sus vidas. Háganse las siguientes preguntas. Luego, inventen cinco preguntas más que usen los verbos de la rutina diaria o los otros verbos reflexivos en las páginas 177–178.

1. ¿A qué hora te acuestas durante la semana? ¿Los fines de semana?
2. ¿A qué hora te levantas durante la semana? ¿Los fines de semana?
3. ¿Te preocupas mucho por tus estudios?
4. ¿Cuántas veces por semana te reúnes con tus amigos?
5.–9. ¿...?

# Gramática útil 3

## Describing actions in progress: The present progressive tense

### Cómo usarlo

Las fotos. ¿**Estás viendo** las fotos?

1. The present progressive tense is used in Spanish to describe actions that are in progress at the moment of speaking. It is equivalent to the *is / are + -ing* structure in English.

| | |
|---|---|
| En este momento **estamos llamando** a los abuelos. | *Right now, **we are calling** the (our) grandparents.* |
| **Están comiendo** ahora. | ***They are eating** right now.* |

2. Note that the present progressive tense is used *much* more frequently in English than it is in Spanish. Whereas in English it is used to describe future plans, in Spanish the present indicative or the **ir + a** + infinitive structure is used instead.

| | |
|---|---|
| **Salimos** con la familia este viernes. | ***We are going out** with the family this Friday.* |
| **Vamos a salir** con la familia este viernes. | ***We are going to go out** with the family this Friday.* |

3. Use the present progressive in Spanish only to describe actions in which people are engaged at the moment. Do not use it to describe routine ongoing activities (use the present indicative), to describe generalized action (use the infinitive), or to describe future actions.

| *Right now:* | No puedo hablar. **Estamos estudiando.** | *I can't talk. **We're studying** (right now).* |
|---|---|---|
| BUT: | | |
| *Routine:* | **Estudio** español, biología, historia e informática. | ***I am studying / I study** Spanish, biology, history, and computer science.* |
| *Generalized action:* | **Estudiar** es importante. | ***Studying** is important.* |
| *Future:* | **Estudio** con Mario el lunes. | ***I will study** with Mario on Monday.* |

### Cómo formarlo

## LO BÁSICO

A *present participle* is the verb form that expresses a continuing or ongoing action. In English, present participles end in *-ing*: *laughing, reading*.

© Cengage Learning 2013

1. Form the present progressive tense by using the present indicative forms of the verb **estar** (which you learned in **Chapter 4**) and the present participle.

> **estoy / estás / está / estamos / estáis / están** + present participle

2. Here's how to form the present participle of regular **-ar, -er**, and **-ir** verbs.

| -ar verbs | -er / -ir verbs |
|---|---|
| Remove the **-ar** from the infinitive and add **-ando**. | Remove the **-er / -ir** from the infinitive and add **-iendo**. |
| caminar → **caminando** | ver → **viendo** |
| | escribir → **escribiendo** |

**Estamos caminando** al centro.    ***We're walking*** *downtown.*
**Estoy viendo** la televisión.    ***I'm watching*** *television.*
Chali **está escribiendo** su trabajo.    *Chali **is writing** her paper.*

3. A few present participles are irregular.

   leer: **leyendo**          oír: **oyendo**

4. All **-ir** stem-changing verbs show a stem change in their present participle as well.

| e → i | | | |
|---|---|---|---|
| despedirse | **despidiéndose** | reírse | **riéndose** |
| divertirse | **divirtiéndose** | repetir | **repitiendo** |
| pedir | **pidiendo** | servir | **sirviendo** |
| o → u | | | |
| dormir | **durmiendo** | morir | **muriendo** |

5. As you may have noticed in the list above, to form the present participle of reflexive verbs, you may attach the reflexive pronoun to the end of the present participle, or place it before the entire verb phrase, the same as when you use reflexive verbs in the infinitive. Note that when the pronoun is attached, the new present participle form requires an accent to maintain the correct pronunciation.

Lina **está levantándose** ahora mismo. /    *Lina **is getting up** right now.*
Lina **se está levantando** ahora mismo.

**Estoy divirtiéndome** mucho. /    ***I'm having*** *a lot of fun.*
**Me estoy divirtiendo** mucho.

◀)) **11** **Preparaciones** La familia González va a una boda *(wedding)* y todos
Track 16 están preparándose. Escucha la conversación telefónica de un miembro
de la familia y escoge la oración que dice qué está haciendo cada persona
mencionada.

**MODELO** _____ La prima está peinándose. / _____ La prima está riéndose.

1. _____ El padre está vistiéndose. / _____ El padre está afeitándose.

2. _____ La madre está duchándose. / _____ La madre está bañándose.

3. _____ El hermano está lavándose los dientes. / _____ El hermano está
lavándose las manos.

4. _____ La hermana está secándose el pelo. / _____ La hermana está
sentándose.

5. _____ Los abuelos están vistiéndose. / _____ Los abuelos están
bañándose.

6. _____ Las tías están cepillándose el pelo. / _____ Las tías están
maquillándose.

👥 **12** **¿Qué están haciendo?** Básandote en los dibujos,
pregúntale a un(a) compañero(a) qué está haciendo la persona
del dibujo. Menciona la profesión de la persona también.

**MODELO** camarero (servir la comida)
Tú: *¿Qué está haciendo el camarero?*
Compañero(a): *Está sirviendo la comida.*

1. la profesora 2. la médica 3. la directora 4. el cocinero 5. la asistente 6. la actriz
de social media

© Cengage Learning 2013

👥 **13** **¡Imagínense!** Trabaja con un(a) compañero(a) de clase. Juntos hagan
una lista de diez personas famosas. Luego, digan qué (en su opinión) están
haciendo en este momento. Escriban por lo menos dos frases para cada
persona. ¡Sean creativos!

👥👥 **14** **¡Chismosos!** Ahora, intercambien sus frases de la **Actividad 13** con
las de otra pareja. Juntos escriban una columna de chismes *(gossip)* para una
revista semanal. Traten de escribir de una manera interesante y descriptiva.
Pueden incluir dibujos de las personas, si quieren.

# Sonrisas

👫 **Expresión** Trabaja con un(a) compañero(a) de clase para imaginar cómo es el día de un(a) presidente de una compañía internacional (o de otra profesión). ¿Cuál es su rutina diaria? Hagan un horario de un día típico.

**MODELO** *Son las ocho de la mañana. Está preparándose para una reunión.*

# Honduras

Robert English/Shutterstock

## Información general ▶

**Nombre oficial:** República de Honduras

**Población:** 7.989.415

**Capital:** Tegucigalpa (f. 1762) (1.200.000 hab.)

**Otras ciudades importantes:** San Pedro Sula (640.000 hab.), El Progreso (90.000 hab.)

**Moneda:** lempira

**Idiomas:** español (oficial), idiomas amerindios

**Mapa de Honduras:** Apéndice D

Christian Wilkinson/Shutterstock

## Vale saber...

- Honduras tiene una gran historia de pueblos indígenas, entre ellos los lencas, los garífunas, los miskitos, los chortis, los pech, los tolupanes, los tawahkas y los mayas.

- En su cuarto y último viaje al Nuevo Mundo, Cristóbal Colón llega a las costas de Honduras en 1502. La conquista española de Honduras empieza dos décadas después, bajo órdenes de Hernán Cortés, y termina en 1537, con la muerte (death) de Lempira, guerrero héroe de orígenes maya-lenca.

- Copán, un centro gubernamental y ceremonial de la antigua civilización maya, se encuentra a orillas (is located on the shores) del río Copán, cerca de la frontera con Guatemala. Se considera uno de los sitios arqueológicos más importantes del Período Clásico.

- Honduras basa su economía en la agricultura, especialmente en las plantaciones de banana, cuya comercialización empezó (began) en 1889 con la fundación de Standard Fruit Company.

# El Salvador

## Información general ▶

**Nombre oficial:** República de El Salvador

**Población:** 6.052.064

**Capital:** San Salvador (f. 1524) (400.000 hab.)

**Otras ciudades importantes:** San Miguel (250.000 hab.), Santa Ana (250.000 hab.)

**Moneda:** dólar estadounidense

**Idiomas:** español (oficial), náhuatl, otras lenguas amerindias

**Mapa de El Salvador:** Apéndice D

Alvaro Calero/iStockphoto

## Vale saber...

- El Salvador es el país más pequeño de Centroamérica pero el más denso en población.

- Durante la época precolombina, El Salvador fue habitado por los pipiles y los lencas.

- Joya de Cerén, un Monumento de la Humanidad de la UNESCO en El Salvador, es un descubrimiento de gran importancia. Es un pueblo *(town)* entero sepultado en el siglo VII por una erupción volcánica. Como una Pompeya americana, Joya de Cerén es de inestimable valor arqueológico e histórico.

- Entre 1980 y 1990, El Salvador vivió en guerra civil. Durante esos años, muchos salvadoreños emigraron a Estados Unidos.

Luis Galdamez/Reuters/Landov

## La mecatrónica

Courtesy of Unitec

En la Universidad Tecnológica Centroamericana (Unitec) de Honduras, puedes hacer la licenciatura en Mecatrónica, un curso de estudio que combina la mecánica, la electrónica y la informática. ¿Qué aprendes si estudias mecatrónica? Cómo diseñar y construir productos mecatrónicos, como los instrumentos médicos, las cámaras fotográficas, los 'chips' que automatizan a las máquinas, aparatos biomédicos y productos innovadores en varios campos como la bioingeniería. ¿Tienes aptitud para la mecatrónica?

## COMEDICA, una cooperativa médica

Hace cuatro décadas *(four decades ago)*, once médicos salvadoreños deciden hacer algo revolucionario para pagar sus costos educativos. Con 100 colones de cada uno, abren una cooperativa para obtener crédito y ahorrar *(save)*. Hoy día, COMEDICA cuenta con $27.12 millones. Entre sus clientes hay médicos, odontólogos, psicólogos, químicos, farmacéuticos y enfermeros. Muchos médicos han adquirido *(have gotten)* sus casas, sus vehículos, equipo para sus clínicas y también sus estudios posgrados con la ayuda de COMEDICA. Los once médicos ilustran el dicho "¡Sí se puede!"

Photo Courtesy of COMEDICA

### La información general

Di a qué país o países se refiere cada oración.

1. Un sitio arqueológico muy importante se encuentra en este país.
2. Las plantaciones de banana son una parte importante de la economía de este país.
3. Es el país más pequeño de Centroamérica.
4. Lempira es un gran héroe de este país.
5. El pueblo indígena de los lencas habita este país.
6. Este país pasó por (*underwent*) una guerra civil que duró (*lasted*) diez años.

### El tema de las profesiones

1. ¿Qué áreas de estudio combina la mecatrónica?
2. ¿Qué productos aprendes a diseñar y construir en la mecatrónica?
3. ¿Quién empezó (*started*) la cooperativa COMEDICA?
4. ¿Qué dicho ilustra las acciones de los once médicos salvadoreños?

---

🌐 **¿QUIERES SABER MÁS?**

Revisa y rellena la tabla que empezaste al principio del capítulo. Luego, escoge un tema para investigar en línea y prepárate para compartir la información con la clase. También puedes escoger de las palabras clave a continuación o en **www.cengagebrain.com**.

**Palabras clave: (Honduras)** los mayas, Lempira, los garífunas, los Miskito, José Antonio Velásques; **(El Salvador)** Tazumal, Acuerdos de Paz de Chapultepec, Óscar Arnulfo Romero, Claribel Alegría

---

🌐 **Tú en el mundo hispano**  Para explorar oportunidades de usar el español para estudiar o hacer trabajos voluntarios o aprendizajes en Honduras y El Salvador, sigue los enlaces en **www.cengagebrain.com**.

🎬 **Ritmos del mundo hispano**  Sigue los enlaces en **www.cengagebrain.com** para escuchar música de Honduras y El Salvador.

# A leer

## ESTRATEGIA

### Skimming for the main idea

When reading authentic materials, it's more important to focus on getting the main idea than to understand every word. Skimming is a reading strategy that helps you get the main idea of each paragraph. When you skim, you read quickly, looking for key words and phrases. Together, these techniques give you the main idea of each paragraph.

**1** Mira la información sobre la cultura garífuna y completa las oraciones a continuación.

Jim Whitmers

Los garífunas son de ascendencia africana, arauaca e indio-caribe. Sus antepasados, exiliados de la isla de San Vicente en 1797, viajaron *(they traveled)* a la costa Atlántica de Belice y Honduras y a las islas de Barlovento de Nicaragua. Viven allí y en otras regiones cercanas *(close)* con la mayor parte de su cultura intacta, incluso su música y arte tradicionales.

1. La cultura garífuna tiene aproximadamente (150 / 220 / 250) años.
2. Los garífunas son de origen (africano / español / inglés).
3. Los garífunas todavía tienen su propia (país / cultura / presidente).

**2** Trabaja con un(a) compañero(a) para hacer correspondencia entre las frases de la lectura a la izquierda y sus equivalentes en inglés a la derecha. Usen los cognados en negrilla *(boldface)* como guía.

1. _____ a las **culturas** que los rodeaban
2. _____ querían que los dejaran en **paz**
3. _____ están **separados** por fronteras **nacionales**
4. _____ se mantienen… **unidos**
5. _____ los **antecesores** han legado
6. _____ han permanecido fieles a su **pasado**

a. *the **ancestors** have left to them*
b. *they maintain themselves **united***
c. *they are **separated** by **national** borders*
d. *have remained faithful to their **past***
e. *to the **cultures** that surround them*
f. *they wanted to be left in **peace***

**3** Ahora lee rápidamente el siguiente artículo sobre la cultura garífuna de Centroamérica. Presta atención en particular a las frases en negrilla. Éstas son importantes para entender la sección. Después de cada sección, vas a tener la oportunidad de ver si entiendes bien las ideas principales.

## LECTURA

# La cultura garífuna

Durante siglos[1] los garífunas, que constituyen un **grupo étnico disperso a lo largo de las costas de cinco países, se han mantenido apartados**[2] de los demás pueblos[3]. Desde el principio, sus antepasados **no buscaron**[4] **conquistar ni asimilarse a las culturas** que los rodeaban. Sólo querían que los dejaran en paz.

    **Aunque están separados por fronteras nacionales, los garífunas se mantienen no obstante unidos** en su determinación por preservar su cultura, rica en influencias africanas y americanas.

Esteban Felix/AP Images

¿Cierto o falso?

1. Los garífunas querían *(wanted to)* asimilarse a otras culturas.

2. La cultura garífuna es rica en influencias europeas.

Las comunidades garífunas **conservan celosamente**[5] **su arte, su música, sus artesanías y sus creencias religiosas**, que en conjunto[6] constituyen una forma de vida muy particular. Los antecesores han legado a los garífunas su **música característica, que incorpora canciones y ritmos africanos y americanos**, y un **expresivo lenguaje** que contiene elementos arauacos y caribes—los idiomas originales de los indios caribes—y yoruba, una lengua proveniente de África Occidental. Los garífunas **han permanecido fieles a su pasado**.

¿Cierto o falso?

3. Mantener las tradiciones del arte, de la música y de las creencias religiosas es muy importante para los garífunas.

4. La música garífuna tiene elementos africanos y europeos.

5. La lengua garífuna tiene elementos de lenguas caribes y de una lengua africana.

A través de[7] los siglos, los garífunas sin duda han mantenido el fuego[8] de su vida cultural. En la actualidad, **la libre práctica de sus antiguas tradiciones asegura el conocimiento de su singular historia** y contribuye a acrecentar[9] la riqueza cultural de los países que los albergan[10], compartiendo las sagradas creencias y las ricas expresiones artísticas de sus orgullosos[11] antepasados.

¿Cierto o falso?

6. En realidad, los garífunas no pueden conservar sus tradiciones antiguas.

7. Los garífunas hacen contribuciones culturales a los países donde viven.

Check yourself: 1. F 2. F 3. C 4. F 5. C 6. F 7. C

[1]*centuries*  [2]**se…:** *they kept themselves separate*  [3]*grupos étnicos*  [4]**no…:** *did not seek to*  [5]*jealously*  [6]**en…:** *como un grupo*  [7]**A…:** *Across, Throughout*  [8]*fire*  [9]*to strengthen, increase*  [10]**los…:** *shelter them*  [11]*proud*

Excerpt from "Los fuertes lazos ancestrales," from *Américas*, Vol. 43, No. 1, 1991. Reprinted from *Américas* magazine, the official publication of the Organization of American States (OAS), published bimonthly in identical English and Spanish editions. Used with permission.

**Después de leer**

👤👤 **4** Ahora que entiendes las ideas principales de las secciones del artículo, trabaja con un(a) compañero(a) de clase. Lean los párrafos otra vez y luego contesten las siguientes preguntas.

1. ¿Dónde viven los garífunas?
2. ¿Cómo es la lengua garífuna?
3. ¿Cómo es la música garífuna?

👤👤 **5** Lee rápidamente la siguiente información sobre los garífunas en Estados Unidos y con un(a) compañero(a), contesten las preguntas a continuación.

Text: © Cengage Learning 2013
Poster: Ivan Moreira

Hay comunidades de garífunas en Estados Unidos también. Una de las más grandes y activas está en y cerca de *(near)* la Ciudad de Nueva York—es la población más grande de garífunas fuera de Centroamérica. La organización Garifuna Coalition USA, Inc. promueve la cultura garífuna de Nueva York y sirve como centro de información sobre sus eventos, noticias y celebraciones.

Todos los años la Coalición organiza el Mes de la Herencia Garífuna y presenta premios *(awards)* a las personas que han promovido *(have promoted)* la cultura garífuna y sus intereses en Estados Unidos. Recientemente organizó una campaña para educar a los garífunas de su comunidad sobre la importancia de identificarse como garífuna en los formularios del Censo 2010.

1. ¿Dónde hay una población grande de garífunas en Estados Unidos?
2. ¿Qué hace la Coalición?
3. ¿De qué trata *(What is it about)* una campaña reciente de la Coalición?

👤👤👤 **6** En grupos de tres o cuatro estudiantes, identifiquen uno o dos grupos culturales de Estados Unidos o de otros países que mantienen sus tradiciones y costumbres diferentes de las de sus países de residencia. En su opinión, ¿es la preservación de tradiciones y costumbres una consecuencia del aislamiento? ¿Hay beneficios de mantenerse aislados? ¿Hay desventajas *(disadvantages)*?

## > Antes de escribir

### ESTRATEGIA

#### Writing—Creating a topic sentence

On page 189, you looked for the main idea, which is usually expressed by the topic sentence. A good paragraph contains a topic sentence and supporting details. When you write, focus on the information you want to convey and write a topic sentence for each paragraph that summarizes its key idea.

**1** Con un(a) compañero(a) de clase, miren el artículo en la página 189. Analicen cada párrafo para identificar la oración que mejor presente la idea principal del párrafo. Ésta es la **oración temática** *(topic sentence).*

MODELO **Párrafo 1:** *Durante siglos los garífunas, que constituyen un grupo étnico disperso a lo largo de las costas de cinco países, se han mantenido apartados de los demás pueblos.*

**2** Vas a escribir unas oraciones temáticas para una composición de tres párrafos sobre tu profesión futura. Piensa en los tres párrafos que vas a usar y escribe una oración temática para cada uno.

> For extra help narrowing your topic, refer to the **A escribir** section in **Chapter 4**.

MODELO **Tema:** *Las profesiones*
**Aspecto específico del tema:** *Mi profesión del futuro*
**Párrafo 1:** (Description of the profession)
**Oración temática:** *Me interesa el diseño gráfico.*
**Párrafo 2:** (Reason you want to have this profession)
**Oración temática:** *Me gusta dibujar y trabajar en la computadora.*
**Párrafo 3:** (What you need to do to prepare yourself for this profession)
**Oración temática:** *Para prepararme, necesito tomar una combinación de cursos de diseño gráfico, de arte y de computación.*

## > Composición

**3** Ahora, usa las tres oraciones temáticas que escribiste para la **Actividad 2** y escribe una composición de tres párrafos sobre tu profesión futura.

## > Después de escribir

**4** Mira tu borrador otra vez. Usa la siguiente lista para revisarlo.

- ¿Tienen tus oraciones temáticas toda la información necesaria?
- ¿Corresponden los sujetos de las oraciones a los verbos correctos?
- ¿Corresponden las formas de los artículos, los sustantivos y los adjetivos?
- ¿Usas correctamente los verbos reflexivos y los verbos irregulares?
- ¿Hay errores de puntuación o de ortografía?

# Vocabulario

## La familia   *The family*

**La familia nuclear**   *The nuclear family*
**la madre (mamá)** *mother*
**el padre (papá)** *father*
**los padres** *parents*
**la esposa** *wife*
**el esposo** *husband*
**la hija** *daughter*
**el hijo** *son*
**la hermana (mayor)** *(older) sister*
**el hermano (menor)** *(younger) brother*
**la tía** *aunt*
**el tío** *uncle*
**la prima** *female cousin*
**el primo** *male cousin*
**la sobrina** *niece*
**el sobrino** *nephew*
**la abuela** *grandmother*
**el abuelo** *grandfather*
**la nieta** *granddaughter*
**el nieto** *grandson*

**La familia política**   *In-laws*
**la suegra** *mother-in-law*
**el suegro** *father-in-law*
**la nuera** *daughter-in-law*
**el yerno** *son-in-law*
**la cuñada** *sister-in-law*
**el cuñado** *brother-in-law*

**Otros parientes**   *Other relatives*
**la madrastra** *stepmother*
**el padrastro** *stepfather*
**la hermanastra** *stepsister*
**el hermanastro** *stepbrother*
**la media hermana** *half-sister*
**el medio hermano** *half-brother*

## Las profesiones y carreras   *Professions and careers*

**el (la) abogado(a)** *lawyer*
**el (la) asistente** *assistant*
**el actor / la actriz** *actor / actress*
**el (la) arquitecto(a)** *architect*
**el (la) artista** *artist*
**el (la) bombero(a)** *firefighter*
**el (la) camarero(a)** *waiter / waitress*
**el (la) carpintero(a)** *carpenter*
**el (la) cocinero(a)** *cook, chef*
**el (la) contador(a)** *accountant*
**el (la) dentista** *dentist*
**el (la) dependiente** *salesclerk*
**el (la) director(a) de social media**
    *director of social media*
**el (la) diseñador(a) gráfico(a)**
    *graphic designer*
**el (la) dueño(a) de...** *owner of . . .*

**el (la) enfermero(a)** *nurse*
**el (la) gerente de...** *manager of . . .*
**el hombre / la mujer de negocios** *businessman / businesswoman*
**el (la) ingeniero(a)** *engineer*
**el (la) maestro(a)** *teacher*
**el (la) mecánico(a)** *mechanic*
**el (la) médico(a)** *doctor*
**el (la) peluquero(a)** *barber / hairdresser*
**el (la) periodista** *journalist*
**el (la) plomero(a)** *plumber*
**el (la) policía** *policeman / policewoman*
**el (la) programador(a)** *programmer*
**el (la) secretario(a)** *secretary*
**el (la) trabajador(a)** *worker*
**el (la) veterinario(a)** *veterinarian*

## En el baño   *In the bathroom*

**el cepillo** *hairbrush*
**el cepillo de dientes** *toothbrush*
**el champú** *shampoo*
**el desodorante** *deodorant*
**el jabón** *soap*
**el maquillaje** *makeup, cosmetics*

**la máquina de afeitar** *electric razor*
**la pasta de dientes** *toothpaste*
**el peine** *comb*
**la rasuradora** *razor*
**la toalla** *towel*
**la toalla de mano** *hand towel*

## Verbos con la forma **yo** irregular

conducir (-zc) *to drive; to conduct*
conocer (-zc) *to know a person; to be familiar with*
dar (doy) *to give*
decir (-g) (i) *to say, to tell*
hacer (-g) *to make; to do*
oír (oigo) *to hear*

poner (-g) *to put*
saber (sé) *to know a fact; to know how to*
salir (-g) *to leave; to go out (with)*
traducir (-zc) *to translate*
traer (-go) *to bring*
venir (-g) (ie) *to come*
ver (veo) *to see*

## Verbos reflexivos

**Acciones físicas** *Physical actions*
acostarse (ue) *to go to bed*
afeitarse *to shave oneself*
bañarse *to take a bath*
cepillarse el pelo *to brush one's hair*
cepillarse los dientes *to brush one's teeth*
despertarse (ie) *to wake up*
dormirse (ue) *to fall asleep*
ducharse *to take a shower*
lavarse *to wash oneself*
lavarse el pelo *to wash one's hair*
lavarse los dientes *to brush one's teeth*
levantarse *to get up*
maquillarse *to put on makeup*
peinarse *to brush / comb one's hair*
ponerse (la ropa) *to put on (clothing)*
prepararse *to get ready*
quitarse (la ropa) *to take off (clothing)*
secarse el pelo *to dry one's hair*
sentarse (ie) *to sit down*
vestirse (i) *to get dressed*

**Estados / emociones** *States / emotions*
casarse *to get married*
comprometerse *to get engaged*
despedirse (i) *to say goodbye*
divertirse (ie) *to have fun*
divorciarse *to get divorced*
enamorarse *to fall in love*
enfermarse *to get sick*
irse *to leave, to go away*
pelearse *to have a fight*
preocuparse *to worry*
quejarse *to complain*
reírse (i) *to laugh*
relajarse *to relax*
reunirse *to meet, to get together*
separarse *to get separated*

## Otros verbos

bañar *to swim; to give someone a bath*
despertar (ie) *to wake someone up*
lavar *to wash*
levantar *to raise, to lift*

manejar *to drive*
quitar *to take off*
secar *to dry something*
vestir (i) *to dress someone*

## Otras palabras y expresiones

a veces *sometimes*
antes *before*
después *after*
luego *later*
nunca *never*

siempre *always*
todas las semanas *every week*
...veces al día / por semana
   *. . . times a day / per week*

Complete these activities to check your understanding of the new grammar points in **Chapter 5** before you move on to **Chapter 6**.

The answers to the activities in this section can be found in **Appendix B**.

## Irregular-yo verbs (p. 172)

**1** Completa la encuesta con las formas correctas de los verbos indicados. Después indica si las oraciones son ciertas (**Sí**) o falsas (**No**) para ti.

| Yo... | Sí | No | Yo... | Sí | No |
|---|---|---|---|---|---|
| 1. ...(saber) hablar francés. | | | 4. ...(hacer) mi tarea todos los días. | | |
| 2. ...(conocer) a una persona famosa. | | | 5. ...(salir) todas las noches. | | |
| 3. ...(conducir) todos los días. | | | 6. ...(ver) a familia todas las semanas. | | |

## Saber vs. conocer (p. 173)

**2** Mira cada cosa o actividad y di si la persona indicada **sabe** o **conoce** cada una. Escribe oraciones completas y no olvides usar la **a** personal cuando sea necesario.

1. tú / Buenos Aires
2. ellos / jugar golf
3. yo / todas las respuestas
4. usted / mis primos
5. nosotras / el chef
6. ella / cocinar bien

## Reflexive verbs (p. 176)

**3** Completa las oraciones con las formas correctas de los verbos indicados.

1. Martina _____ (maquillarse) todos los días.
2. Frecuentemente yo _____ (acostarse) muy tarde.
3. Ustedes _____ (reunirse) todos los miércoles.
4. ¿Tú _____ (levantarse) temprano o tarde?
5. Nosotros nunca _____ (enfermarse).
6. Ellos _____ (pelearse) casi todos los días.

## The present progressive tense (p. 180)

**4** Haz una oración para decir qué está haciendo cada persona en este momento. Usa las actividades de la lista y sigue el modelo.

MODELO  Tú eres actriz.
*Estás maquillándote.*

**Actividades:** escribir un artículo, hablar con un paciente, maquillarse, pintar, preparar la comida, servir la comida, trabajar en la computadora

1. Ella es médica.
2. Yo soy periodista.
3. Ellos son cocineros.
4. Nosotros somos artistas.
5. Usted es camarera.
6. Él es secretario.

# Preparación para el Capítulo 6

### Adjective agreement (Chapter 2)

**5** Tu amigo habla de su familia. Completa sus comentarios con las formas correctas de los adjetivos indicados.

Tengo una familia 1. _____ (grande). Pero todas las personas son muy 2. _____ (extrovertido). Mis hermanas son bastante 3. _____ (simpático) pero mi hermanito es un poco 4. _____ (tonto). Mis primos normalmente están 5. _____ (contento) pero hoy están muy 6. _____ (nervioso). Mis abuelos son 7. _____ (viejo) y muy 8. _____ (divertido). Me gustan mucho mis familiares y estoy 9. _____ (triste) que no puedo ver a mi familia más frecuentemente.

> Complete these activities to review some previously learned grammatical structures that will be helpful when you learn the new grammar in **Chapter 6.**
>
> Be sure to reread **Chapter 5: Gramática útil 1** before moving on to the new **Chapter 6** grammar sections.

### The present indicative of regular **-ar** verbs (Chapter 2), regular **-er** and **-ir** verbs (Chapter 3), and stem-changing verbs (Chapter 4)

**6** Escribe oraciones completas con las formas correctas de los verbos indicados.

1. mi tío / lavar su auto todas las semanas
2. mis abuelos / no dormir mucho
3. mis primas / preferir estudiar en la residencia estudiantil
4. mi hermano y yo / correr en el parque los sábados
5. tú / manejar todos los días
6. mi madre / vestir a mi hermanita por las mañanas
7. yo / mirar una película
8. mi madre y yo / vivir en un apartamento grande

### The verb **estar** (Chapter 4)

**7** Di dónde están las personas indicadas.

MODELO  *yo / café*
       *Yo estoy en el café.*

1. la mujer de negocios / oficina
2. tú y yo / salón de clase
3. el Doctor Méndez / hospital
4. los programadores / centro de computación
5. la policía / parque
6. yo / biblioteca
7. los cocineros / restaurante
8. tú / gimnasio

# Reference Materials

# Appendix A: KWL Chart

| Lo que sé | Lo que quiero saber | Lo que aprendí |
| --- | --- | --- |
| | | |

# Appendix B: Repaso y preparación Answer Keys

## Capítulo 1 (pp. 40–41)

**Act. 1:** 1. la 2. X 3. la 4. X 5. X 6. X 7. unos 8. una 9. los

**Act. 2:** 1. Tú 2. Nosotros 3. Yo 4. es 5. son 6. somos

**Act. 3:** 1. Hay dos chicas. 2. Hay un hombre. 3. Hay una mujer. 4. No hay niño. 5. No hay computadora. 6. No hay mochila. 7. Hay una serpiente. 8. No hay elefante.

**Act. 4:** 1. tienes 2. tiene 3. tengo 4. tenemos 5. tienen 6. tienes

**Act. 5:** 1. tengo que 2. tienen que 3. tenemos que 4. tiene que 5. tienes que 6. tienen que

**Act. 6:** *Answers will vary depending on current year.* 1. Tú tienes... años. 2. Ellos tienen... años. 3. Usted tiene... años. 4. Ella tiene... años. 5. Yo tengo... años. 6. Nosotros tenemos... años. 7. Ustedes tienen... años. 8. Tú y yo tenemos... años.

## Capítulo 2 (pp. 80–81)

**Act. 1:** 1. Esteban y Carolina caminan. 2. Usted pinta. 3. Loreta levanta pesas. 4. Yo saco fotos. 5. Nosotros tomamos el sol. 6. Tú cocinas. 7. Ustedes hablan por teléfono. 8. Tú y yo patinamos.

**Act. 2:** 1. A mí me gusta estudiar. 2. A ti te gusta mirar televisión. 3. A usted le gusta visitar a amigos. 4. A nosotras nos gusta pintar. 5. A ustedes les gusta practicar deportes.

**Act. 3:** 1. Gretchen y Rolf son alemanes. Son muy sinceros. 2. Brigitte es francesa. Es muy divertida. 3. Nosotras somos españolas. Somos simpáticas. 4. Yo soy estadounidense. Soy muy generosa. 5. Usted es japonesa. Es muy interesante. 6. Tú eres italiano. Eres muy activo.

**Act. 4:** 1. las 2. El 3. la 4. unos 5. la 6. una 7. un 8. la 9. la 10. las

**Act. 5:** 1. f, es 2. d, es 3. a, es 4. g, son 5. b, somos 6. e, eres 7. c, soy

## Capítulo 3 (pp. 118–119)

**Act. 1:** 1. qué 2. Por qué 3. Cuál 4. cuándo 4. Cuántas 5. Quién

**Act. 2:** 1. escribe 2. debemos 3. como 4. viven 5. lee

**Act. 3:** 1. mis 2. tus 3. nuestra 4. sus 5. sus 6. mi

**Act. 4:** 1. voy, van 2. va, vamos 3. vas

**Act. 5:** 1. A mí me gusta leer. 2. A nosotros nos gusta comer. 3. A ustedes les gusta bailar. 4. A ti te gusta cocinar. 5. A él le gusta patinar. 6. A mí me gusta cantar.

**Act. 6:** 1. estudia 2. cocina 3. toca 4. canta 5. levantan 6. practican 7. miramos 8. alquilamos 9. trabajo 10. visito 11. paso

**Act. 7:** 1. Rogelio y Mauricio son muy egoístas. 2. Tú eres muy impaciente. 3. Nosotros somos muy perezosos. 4. Yo soy muy activo(a). 5. Sandra es muy generosa. 6. Néstor y Nicolás son muy tímidos.

## Capítulo 4 (pp. 158–159)

**Act. 1:** 1. les gustan 2. me encanta 3. le molesta 4. nos interesan 5. te importa 6. le gusta

**Act. 2:** 1. estás 2. estamos 3. soy 4. son 5. Estoy 6. Está 7. es 8. es 9. está 10. son 11. es 12. están

**Act. 3:** 1. Tú duermes mucho. 2. Yo cierro la computadora portátil. 3. Ella entiende las instrucciones. 4. Nosotras jugamos el juego interactivo. 5. Usted repite la contraseña. 6. Ellos quieren un MP3 portátil. 7. Yo puedo instalar el programa. 8. Nosotros preferimos ir a un café con wifi.

**Act. 4:** 1. lentamente 2. rápidamente 3. Generalmente 4. fácilmente

**Act. 5:** debe, envias, recibes, grabas, instalas, llevas, trabajas, hablan, funciona, bajo, subo, pesa, saco, accedo, leo, usamos, comentan, ofrecemos, vendemos, debes

## Capítulo 5 (pp. 194–195)

**Act. 1:** *Answers will vary for Sí/No column.* 1. Sé 2. Conozco 3. Conduzco 4. Hago 5. Salgo 6. Veo

**Act. 2:** 1. Tú conoces Buenos Aires. 2. Ellos saben jugar golf. 3. Yo sé todas las respuestas. 4. Usted conoce a mis primos. 5. Nosotras conocemos al chef. 6. Ella sabe cocinar bien.

**Act. 3:** 1. se maquilla 2. me acuesto 3. se reunen 4. te levantas 5. nos enfermamos 6. se pelean

**Act. 4:** 1. Ella está hablando con un paciente. 2. Yo estoy escribiendo un artículo. 3. Ellos están preparando la comida. 4. Nosotros estamos pintando. 5. Usted está sirviendo la comida. 6. Él está trabajando en la computadora.

**Act. 5:** 1. grande 2. extrovertidas 3. simpáticas 4. tonto 5. contentos 6. nerviosos 7. viejos 8. divertidos 9. triste

**Act. 6:** 1. Mi tío lava su auto todas las semanas. 2. Mis abuelos no duermen mucho. 3. Mis primas prefieren estudiar en la residencia estudiantil. 4. Mi hermano y yo corremos en el parque los sábados. 5. Tú manejas todos los días. 6. Mi madre viste a mi hermanita por las mañanas. 7. Yo miro una película. 8. Mi madre y yo vivimos en un apartamento grande.

**Act. 7:** 1. La mujer de negocios está en la oficina. 2. Tú y yo estamos en el salón de clase. 3. El Doctor Méndez está en el hospital. 4. Los programadores están en el centro de computación. 5. La policía está en el parque. 6. Yo estoy en la biblioteca. 7. Los cocineros están en el restaurante. 8. Tú estás en el gimnasio.

## Capítulo 6 (pp. 228–229)

**Act. 1:** 1. El perro está lejos del auto. 2. El perro está delante del auto. 3. El perro está detrás del auto. 4. El perro está debajo del auto. 5. El perro está dentro del auto. 6. El perro está entre los autos.

**Act. 2:** 1. Vengan, pierdan 2. Ponga, Hable 3. Haga, Llame

**Act. 3:** 1. Siempre, 2. También, 3. algunos 4. nada 5. algo 6. nadie

**Act. 4:** 1. estos, ésos 2. aquella, ésta 3. esos, aquéllos 4. esta, ésa 5. aquellas, éstas 6. este, ése

**Act. 5:** 1. salgo 2. traigo 3. Pongo 4. conduzco 5. veo 6. conozco 7. Oigo 8. hago 9. digo 10. sé

**Act. 6:** 1. te preparas 2. me acuesto 3. nos preocupamos 4. se están divirtiendo / están divirtiéndose 5. se quejen 6. Siéntese, relájese

## Capítulo 7 (pp. 266–267)

**Act. 1:** 1. montaste 2. leyó 3. compartí 4. navegamos 5. corrieron

**Act. 2:** 1. Tú y yo fuimos... 2. Marilena estuvo... 3. Yo hice... 4. Guille y Paulina dijeron... 5. Mis padres condujeron... 6. Tú tradujiste...

**Act. 3:** 1. ¿Los perros? Tú los lavaste. 2. ¿El surfing? Victoria lo hizo. 3. ¿La pelota (de golf)? Yo no la encontré. 4. ¿Las mochilas? Nosotros las perdimos. 5. ¿Los refrescos? Ustedes no los bebieron. 6. ¿Las pesas? Esteban y Federico no las levantaron.

**Act. 4:** 1. pongas, Ten, lee 2. Pon, siéntate, salgas

**Act. 5:** 1. quieren 2. me divierto 3. se visten 4. pueden 5. duermo 6. pides

**Act. 6:** 1. A mí me gusta remar. 2. A usted le gusta nadar. 3. A ti te gustan esos esquíes. 4. A ellos les gusta el boxeo. 5. A nosotros nos gusta pescar. 6. A ella le gusta la nieve. 7. A ti te gusta entrenarte. 8. A mí me gustan las vacaciones. 9. A nosotros nos gusta la primavera.

**Act. 7:** 1. sé 2. conozco 3. saben 4. podemos 5. pueden 6. conocemos 7. quiero 8. puedo

## Capítulo 8 (pp. 304–305)

**Act. 1:** 1. Supe 2. hicimos 3. sugirió 4. preferí 5. sirvió 6. dijo 7. quiso 8. pudo 9. tuvo 10. pidió 11. puso 12. anduvimos 13. Nos reímos 14. nos divertimos 15. nos despedimos 16. dijimos

**Act. 2:** 1. nos 2. te 3. les 4. me 5. le

**Act. 3:** 1. tantos, como 2. más, que 3. menos, que 4. tan, como 5. el más 6. más

**Act. 4:** 1. compraste 2. vi 3. estuvo 4. trajo 5. fuimos 6. dieron 7. hiciste 8. escribió

**Act. 5:** 1. Delfina lo compró. 2. Diego y Eduardo no la compraron. 3. Tú no los compraste. 4. Yo los compré. 5. Nosotros las compramos. 6. Usted no lo compró.

**Act. 6:** 1. Yo me puse un abrigo. 2. Ellos se pusieron unas sandalias. 3. Tú te pusiste un chaleco. 4. Nosotros nos pusimos unos jeans. 5. Ella se puso una bufanda. 7. Ustedes se pusieron un impermeable.

## Capítulo 9 (pp. 344–345)

**Act. 1:** 1. La señora Muñoz preparaba unas galletas. 2. Yo freía un huevo. 3. Nosotros pelábamos zanahorias para una ensalada. 4. Manolito ponía la mesa. 5. Sarita y Carmela picaban cebollas para una sopa. 6. Tú hervías agua para preparar el té.

**Act. 2:** 1. Eran 2. quería 3. llegué 4. vi 5. estaba 6. tenía 7. me senté 8. empezamos 9. hablábamos 10. dijo 11. exclamé 12. sabía 13. Me despedí 14. salí 15. Estaba 16. quería

**Act. 3:** 1. Ábrenosla. 2. Cuéceselos. 3. No me lo compres. 4. No se lo calientes. 5. Pásanosla. 6. No se la prepares.

**Act. 4:** 1. come 2. venden 3. hablan 4. sirve 5. cierra 6. duerme

**Act. 5:** 1. Los manteles son rojos. 2. El flan es bueno. 3. Las almejas están frescas. 4. El café está caliente. 5. La carne está frita. 6. Los huevos son blancos. 7. El pescado está crudo. 8. El té está frío. 9. La limonada es dulce. 10. Los platos están limpios. 11. La langosta es cara. 12. Las fresas son baratas.

**Act. 6:** 1. mi 2. tus 3. nuestro 4. sus 5. sus 6. su 7. sus 8. su 9. nuestras 10. tus

**Act. 7:** 1. hiciste 2. hago 3. hizo 4. hicieron 5. hacemos

## Capítulo 10 (pp. 376–377)

**Act. 1:** 1. ¿La aspiradora? No es tuya. Es suya. 2. ¿Las licuadoras? No son suyas. Son mías. 3. ¿Las planchas? No son nuestras. Son suyas. 4. ¿La tostadora? No es mía. Es suya. 5. ¿Los microondas? No son suyos. Son nuestros. 6. ¿El lavaplatos? No es suyo. Es tuyo.

**Act. 2:** 1. Hace un año que Sarita no va de vacaciones. 2. Hace seis meses que ellos viven en esa casa. 3. Ellos limpiaron el baño hace dos semanas. 4. Hacía tres meses que Luis no podía trabajar en la casa. 5. Los abuelos vinieron de visita hace dos años.

**Act. 3:** 1. por 2. Para 3. Por 4. por 5. para 6. Por 7. para 8. para

**Act. 4:** 1. Lavo 2. Plancho 3. Barro 4. Sacudo 5. Hiervo 6. Riego 7. Sirvo 8. Vuelvo 9. pido 10. duermo

**Act. 5:** 1. Estoy 2. Conduzco 3. doy 4. digo 5. Oigo 6. Vengo 7. Veo 8. Sé 9. Pongo 10. Tengo

**Act. 6:** 1. laves 2. planches 3. saques 4. pases 5. pongas 6. uses 7. trapees 8. sacudas 9. comas 10. insistas

# Regular Verbs

## Simple Tenses

| Infinitive | Past participle / Present participle | Indicative | | | | | Subjunctive | |
|---|---|---|---|---|---|---|---|---|
| | | Present | Imperfect | Preterite | Future | Conditional | Present | Imperfect* |
| cantar *to sing* | cantado cantando | canto cantas canta cantamos cantáis cantan | cantaba cantabas cantaba cantábamos cantabais cantaban | canté cantaste cantó cantamos cantasteis cantaron | cantaré cantarás cantará cantaremos cantaréis cantarán | cantaría cantarías cantaría cantaríamos cantaríais cantarían | cante cantes cante cantemos cantéis canten | cantara cantaras cantara cantáramos cantarais cantaran |
| correr *to run* | corrido corriendo | corro corres corre corremos corréis corren | corría corrías corría corríamos corríais corrían | corrí corriste corrió corrimos corristeis corrieron | correré correrás correrá correremos correréis correrán | correría correrías correría correríamos correríais correrían | corra corras corra corramos corráis corran | corriera corrieras corriera corriéramos corrierais corrieran |
| subir *to go up, to climb up* | subido subiendo | subo subes sube subimos subís suben | subía subías subía subíamos subíais subían | subí subiste subió subimos subisteis subieron | subiré subirás subirá subiremos subiréis subirán | subiría subirías subiría subiríamos subiríais subirían | suba subas suba subamos subáis suban | subiera subieras subiera subiéramos subierais subieran |

*In addition to this form, another one is less frequently used for all regular and irregular verbs: cantase, cantases, cantase, cantásemos, cantaseis, cantasen; corriese, corrieses, corriese, corriésemos, corrieseis, corriesen; subiese, subieses, subiese, subiésemos, subieseis, subiesen.

## Commands

| Person | Affirmative | Negative | Affirmative | Negative | Affirmative | Negative |
|---|---|---|---|---|---|---|
| tú | canta | no cantes | corre | no corras | sube | no subas |
| usted | cante | no cante | corra | no corra | suba | no suba |
| nosotros | cantemos | no cantemos | corramos | no corramos | subamos | no subamos |
| vosotros | cantad | no cantéis | corred | no corráis | subid | no subáis |
| ustedes | canten | no canten | corran | no corran | suban | no suban |

## Stem-Changing Verbs: -ar and -er Groups

| Type of change in the verb stem | Subject | Indicative Present | Subjunctive Present | Commands Affirmative | Commands Negative | Other -ar and -er stem-changing verbs |
|---|---|---|---|---|---|---|
| **-ar verbs** **e > ie** *pensar to think* | yo<br>tú<br>él/ella, Ud.<br>nosotros/as<br>vosotros/as<br>ellos/as, Uds. | **pienso**<br>**piensas**<br>**piensa**<br>pensamos<br>pensáis<br>**piensan** | **piense**<br>**pienses**<br>**piense**<br>pensemos<br>penséis<br>**piensen** | —<br>**piensa**<br>**piense**<br>pensemos<br>pensad<br>**piensen** | —<br>no **pienses**<br>no **piense**<br>no pensemos<br>no penséis<br>no **piensen** | *atravesar to go through, to cross; cerrar to close; despertarse to wake up; empezar to start; negar to deny; sentarse to sit down* <br><br>*Nevar to snow is only conjugated in the third-person singular.* |
| **-ar verbs** **o > ue** *contar to count, to tell* | yo<br>tú<br>él/ella, Ud.<br>nosotros/as<br>vosotros/as<br>ellos/as, Uds. | **cuento**<br>**cuentas**<br>**cuenta**<br>contamos<br>contáis<br>**cuentan** | **cuente**<br>**cuentes**<br>**cuente**<br>contemos<br>contéis<br>**cuenten** | —<br>**cuenta**<br>**cuente**<br>contemos<br>contad<br>**cuenten** | —<br>no **cuentes**<br>no **cuente**<br>no contemos<br>no contéis<br>no **cuenten** | *acordarse to remember; acostarse to go to bed; almorzar to have lunch; colgar to hang; costar to cost; demostrar to demonstrate, to show; encontrar to find; mostrar to show; probar to prove, to taste; recordar to remember* |
| **-er verbs** **e > ie** *entender to understand* | yo<br>tú<br>él/ella, Ud.<br>nosotros/as<br>vosotros/as<br>ellos/as, Uds. | **entiendo**<br>**entiendes**<br>**entiende**<br>entendemos<br>entendéis<br>**entienden** | **entienda**<br>**entiendas**<br>**entienda**<br>entendamos<br>entendáis<br>**entiendan** | —<br>**entiende**<br>**entienda**<br>entendamos<br>entended<br>**entiendan** | —<br>no **entiendas**<br>no **entienda**<br>no entendamos<br>no entendáis<br>no **entiendan** | *encender to light, to turn on; extender to stretch; perder to lose* |
| **-er verbs** **o > ue** *volver to return* | yo<br>tú<br>él/ella, Ud.<br>nosotros/as<br>vosotros/as<br>ellos/as, Uds. | **vuelvo**<br>**vuelves**<br>**vuelve**<br>volvemos<br>volvéis<br>**vuelven** | **vuelva**<br>**vuelvas**<br>**vuelva**<br>volvamos<br>volváis<br>**vuelvan** | —<br>**vuelve**<br>**vuelva**<br>volvamos<br>volved<br>**vuelvan** | —<br>no **vuelvas**<br>no **vuelva**<br>no volvamos<br>no volváis<br>no **vuelvan** | *mover to move; torcer to twist* <br><br>*Llover to rain is only conjugated in the third-person singular.* |

# Stem-Changing Verbs: -ir Verbs

| Type of change in the verb stem | Subject | Indicative | | Subjunctive | | Commands | |
|---|---|---|---|---|---|---|---|
| | | Present | Preterite | Present | Imperfect | Affirmative | Negative |
| -ir verbs<br>e > ie or i<br>Infinitive: sentir to feel<br>Present participle: sintiendo | yo | siento | sentí | sienta | sintiera | — | — |
| | tú | sientes | sentiste | sientas | sintieras | siente | no sientas |
| | él/ella, Ud. | siente | sintió | sienta | sintiera | sienta | no sienta |
| | nosotros/as | sentimos | sentimos | sintamos | sintiéramos | sintamos | no sintamos |
| | vosotros/as | sentís | sentisteis | sintáis | sintierais | sentid | no sintáis |
| | ellos/as, Uds. | sienten | sintieron | sientan | sintieran | sientan | no sientan |
| -ir verbs<br>o > ue or u<br>Infinitive: dormir to sleep<br>Present participle: durmiendo | yo | duermo | dormí | duerma | durmiera | — | — |
| | tú | duermes | dormiste | duermas | durmieras | duerme | no duermas |
| | él/ella, Ud. | duerme | durmió | duerma | durmiera | duerma | no duerma |
| | nosotros/as | dormimos | dormimos | durmamos | durmiéramos | durmamos | no durmamos |
| | vosotros/as | dormís | dormisteis | durmáis | durmierais | dormid | no durmáis |
| | ellos/as, Uds. | duermen | durmieron | duerman | durmieran | duerman | no duerman |

**Other similar verbs:** advertir *to warn*; arrepentirse *to repent*; consentir *to consent, pamper*; convertir(se) *to turn into*; divertir(se) *to amuse (oneself)*; herir *to hurt, wound*; mentir *to lie*; morir *to die*; preferir *to prefer*; referir *to refer*; sugerir *to suggest*

| Type of change in the verb stem | Subject | Indicative | | Subjunctive | | Commands | |
|---|---|---|---|---|---|---|---|
| | | Present | Preterite | Present | Imperfect | Affirmative | Negative |
| -ir verbs<br>e > i<br>Infinitive: pedir *to ask for, to request*<br>Present participle: pidiendo | yo | pido | pedí | pida | pidiera | — | — |
| | tú | pides | pediste | pidas | pidieras | pide | no pidas |
| | él/ella, Ud. | pide | pidió | pida | pidiera | pida | no pida |
| | nosotros/as | pedimos | pedimos | pidamos | pidiéramos | pidamos | no pidamos |
| | vosotros/as | pedís | pedisteis | pidáis | pidierais | pedid | no pidáis |
| | ellos/as, Uds. | piden | pidieron | pidan | pidieran | pidan | no pidan |

**Other similar verbs:** competir *to compete*; despedir(se) *to say good-bye*; elegir *to choose*; impedir *to prevent*; perseguir *to chase*; repetir *to repeat*; seguir *to follow*; servir *to serve*; vestir(se) *to dress, to get dressed*

## Verbs with Spelling Changes

| Verb type | Ending | Change | Verbs with similar spelling changes |
|---|---|---|---|
| 1 buscar *to look for* | -car | • Preterite: yo busqué<br>• Present subjunctive: busque, busques, busque, busquemos, busquéis, busquen | comunicar, explicar *to explain*, indicar *to indicate*, sacar, pescar |
| 2 cono**c**er *to know* | *vowel* + -cer or -cir | • Present indicative: conozco, conoces, conoce, and so on<br>• Present subjunctive: conozca, conozcas, conozca, conozcamos, conozcáis, conozcan | nacer *to be born*, obedecer, ofrecer, parecer, pertenecer *to belong*, reconocer, conducir, traducir |
| 3 ven**c**er *to win* | *consonant* + -cer or -cir | • Present indicative: venzo, vences, vence, and so on<br>• Present subjunctive: venza, venzas, venza, venzamos, venzáis, venzan | convencer, torcer *to twist* |
| 4 leer *to read* | -eer | • Preterite: leyó, leyeron<br>• Imperfect subjunctive: leyera, leyeras, leyera, leyéramos, leyerais, leyeran<br>• Present participle: leyendo | creer, poseer *to own* |
| 5 llegar *to arrive* | -gar | • Preterite: yo llegué<br>• Present subjunctive: llegue, llegues, llegue, lleguemos, lleguéis, lleguen | colgar *to hang*, navegar, negar *to negate, to deny*, pagar, rogar *to beg*, jugar |
| 6 esco**g**er *to choose* | -ger or -gir | • Present indicative: escojo, escoges, escoge, and so on<br>• Present subjunctive: escoja, escojas, escoja, escojamos, escojáis, escojan | proteger, *to protect*, recoger *to collect, gather*, corregir *to correct*, dirigir *to direct*, elegir *to elect, choose*, exigir *to demand* |
| 7 seguir *to follow* | -guir | • Present indicative: sigo, sigues, sigue, and so on<br>• Present subjunctive: siga, sigas, siga, sigamos, sigáis, sigan | conseguir, distinguir, perseguir |
| 8 huir *to flee* | -uir | • Present indicative: huyo, huyes, huye, huimos, huís, huyen<br>• Preterite: huí, huiste, huyó, huimos, huisteis, huyeron<br>• Present subjunctive: huya, huyas, huya, huyamos, huyáis, huyan<br>• Imperfect subjunctive: huyera, huyeras, huyera, huyéramos, huyerais, huyeran<br>• Present participle: huyendo<br>• Commands: huye (tú), huya usted, huyamos (nosotros), huid (vosotros), huyan (ustedes). (negative) no huyas (tú), no huya (usted), no huyamos (nosotros), no huyáis (vosotros), no huyan (ustedes) | concluir, contribuir, construir, destruir, disminuir, distribuir, excluir, influir, instruir, restituir, substituir |
| 9 abrazar *to embrace* | -zar | • Preterite: yo abracé<br>• Present subjunctive: abrace, abraces, abrace, abracemos, abracéis, abracen | alcanzar *to achieve*, almorzar, comenzar, empezar, gozar *to enjoy*, rezar *to pray* |

## Compound Tenses

| | Indicative | | | | | Subjunctive | |
|---|---|---|---|---|---|---|---|
| | Present perfect | Past perfect | Preterite perfect | Future perfect | Conditional perfect | Present perfect | Past perfect |
| | he | había | hube | habré | habría | haya | hubiera |
| | has | habías | hubiste | habrás | habrías | hayas | hubieras |
| | ha · cantado | había · cantado | hubo · cantado | habrá · cantado | habría · cantado | haya · cantado | hubiera · cantado |
| | hemos · corrido | habíamos · corrido | hubimos · corrido | habremos · corrido | habríamos · corrido | hayamos · corrido | hubiéramos · corrido |
| | habéis · subido | habíais · subido | hubisteis · subido | habréis · subido | habríais · subido | hayáis · subido | hubierais · subido |
| | han | habían | hubieron | habrán | habrían | hayan | hubieran |

All verbs, both regular and irregular, follow the same formation pattern with **haber** in all compound tenses. The only thing that changes is the form of the past participle of each verb. (See the chart below for common verbs with irregular past participles.) Remember that in Spanish, no word can come between **haber** and the past participle.

## Common Irregular Past Participles

| Infinitive | Past participle | |
|---|---|---|
| abrir | **abierto** | *opened* |
| caer | caído | *fallen* |
| creer | creído | *believed* |
| cubrir | **cubierto** | *covered* |
| decir | **dicho** | *said, told* |
| descubrir | **descubierto** | *discovered* |
| escribir | escrito | *written* |
| hacer | **hecho** | *made, done* |
| leer | leído | *read* |

| Infinitive | Past participle | |
|---|---|---|
| morir | **muerto** | *died* |
| oír | oído | *heard* |
| poner | **puesto** | *put, placed* |
| resolver | **resuelto** | *resolved* |
| romper | **roto** | *broken, torn* |
| (son)reír | (son)reído | *(smiled) laughed* |
| traer | traído | *brought* |
| ver | **visto** | *seen* |
| volver | **vuelto** | *returned* |

# Reflexive Verbs

## Regular and Irregular Reflexive Verbs: Position of the Reflexive Pronouns in the Simple Tenses

| Infinitive | Present participle | Reflexive pronouns | Indicative | | | | | Subjunctive | |
|---|---|---|---|---|---|---|---|---|---|
| | | | Present | Imperfect | Preterite | Future | Conditional | Present | Imperfect |
| **lavarse** | lavándome | me | lavo | lavaba | lavé | lavaré | lavaría | lave | lavara |
| *to wash oneself* | lavándote | te | lavas | lavabas | lavaste | lavarás | lavarías | laves | lavaras |
| | lavándose | se | lava | lavaba | lavó | lavará | lavaría | lave | lavara |
| | lavándonos | nos | lavamos | lavábamos | lavamos | lavaremos | lavaríamos | lavemos | laváramos |
| | lavándoos | os | laváis | lavabais | lavasteis | lavaréis | lavaríais | lavéis | lavarais |
| | lavándose | se | lavan | lavaban | lavaron | lavarán | lavarían | laven | lavaran |

# Regular and irregular reflexive verbs: Position of the reflexive pronouns with commands

| Person | Affirmative | Negative | Affirmative | Negative | Affirmative | Negative |
|--------|-------------|----------|-------------|----------|-------------|----------|
| tú | lávate | no te laves | ponte | no te pongas | vístete | no te vistas |
| usted | lávese | no se lave | póngase | no se ponga | vístase | no se vista |
| nosotros | lavémonos | no nos lavemos | pongámonos | no nos pongamos | vistámonos | no nos vistamos |
| vosotros | lavaos | no os lavéis | poneos | no os pongáis | vestíos | no os vistáis |
| ustedes | lávense | no se laven | pónganse | no se pongan | vístanse | no se vistan |

# Regular and irregular reflexive verbs: Position of the reflexive pronouns in compound tenses*

| Reflexive Pronoun | Indicative | | | | | | | | | | Subjunctive | | | |
|---|---|---|---|---|---|---|---|---|---|---|---|---|---|---|
| | Present Perfect | | Past Perfect | | Preterite Perfect | | Future Perfect | | Conditional Perfect | | Present Perfect | | Past Perfect | |
| me | he | | había | | hube | | habré | | habría | | haya | | hubiera | |
| te | has | lavado | habías | lavado | hubiste | lavado | habrás | lavado | habrías | lavado | hayas | lavado | hubieras | lavado |
| se | ha | puesto | había | puesto | hubo | puesto | habrá | puesto | habría | puesto | haya | puesto | hubiera | puesto |
| nos | hemos | vestido | habíamos | vestido | hubimos | vestido | habremos | vestido | habríamos | vestido | hayamos | vestido | hubiéramos | vestido |
| os | habéis | | habíais | | hubisteis | | habréis | | habríais | | hayáis | | hubierais | |
| se | han | | habían | | hubieron | | habrán | | habrían | | hayan | | hubieran | |

*The sequence of these three elements—the reflexive pronoun, the auxiliary verb **haber**, and the present perfect form—is invariable and no other words can come in between.

# Regular and irregular reflexive verbs: Position of the reflexive pronouns with conjugated verb + infinitive**

| Reflexive Pronoun | Indicative | | | | | | | | | | Subjunctive | | | |
|---|---|---|---|---|---|---|---|---|---|---|---|---|---|---|
| | Present | | Imperfect | | Preterite | | Future | | Conditional | | Present | | Imperfect | |
| me | voy a | | iba a | | fui a | | iré a | | iría a | | vaya a | | fuera a | |
| te | vas a | lavar | ibas a | lavar | fuiste a | lavar | irás a | lavar | irías a | lavar | vayas a | lavar | fueras a | lavar |
| se | va a | poner | iba a | poner | fue a | poner | irá a | poner | iría a | poner | vaya a | poner | fuera a | poner |
| nos | vamos a | vestir | íbamos a | vestir | fuimos a | vestir | iremos a | vestir | iríamos a | vestir | vayamos a | vestir | fuéramos a | vestir |
| os | vais a | | ibais a | | fuisteis a | | iréis a | | iríais a | | vayáis a | | fuerais a | |
| se | van a | | iban a | | fueron a | | irán a | | irían a | | vayan a | | fueran a | |

**The reflexive pronoun can also be placed after the infinitive: voy a lavar**me**, voy a poner**me**, voy a vestir**me**, and so on.
Use the same structure for the present and the past progressive: **me** estoy lavando / estoy lavándo**me**; **me** estaba lavando / estaba lavándo**me**.

# Irregular Verbs

## andar, caber, caer

| Infinitive | Past participle / Present participle | Indicative | | | | | Subjunctive | |
|---|---|---|---|---|---|---|---|---|
| | | Present | Imperfect | Preterite | Future | Conditional | Present | Imperfect |
| andar | andado | ando | andaba | anduve | andaré | andaría | ande | anduviera |
| *to walk;* | andando | andas | andabas | anduviste | andarás | andarías | andes | anduvieras |
| *to go* | | anda | andaba | anduvo | andará | andaría | ande | anduviera |
| | | andamos | andábamos | anduvimos | andaremos | andaríamos | andemos | anduviéramos |
| | | andáis | andabais | anduvisteis | andaréis | andaríais | andéis | anduvierais |
| | | andan | andaban | anduvieron | andarán | andarían | anden | anduvieran |
| caber | cabido | quepo | cabía | cupe | cabré | cabría | quepa | cupiera |
| *to fit; to* | cabiendo | cabes | cabías | cupiste | cabrás | cabrías | quepas | cupieras |
| *have enough* | | cabe | cabía | cupo | cabrá | cabría | quepa | cupiera |
| *space* | | cabemos | cabíamos | cupimos | cabremos | cabríamos | quepamos | cupiéramos |
| | | cabéis | cabíais | cupisteis | cabréis | cabríais | quepáis | cupierais |
| | | caben | cabían | cupieron | cabrán | cabrían | quepan | cupieran |
| caer | caído | caigo | caía | caí | caeré | caería | caiga | cayera |
| *to fall* | cayendo | caes | caías | caíste | caerás | caerías | caigas | cayeras |
| | | cae | caía | cayó | caerá | caería | caiga | cayera |
| | | caemos | caíamos | caímos | caeremos | caeríamos | caigamos | cayéramos |
| | | caéis | caíais | caísteis | caeréis | caeríais | caigáis | cayerais |
| | | caen | caían | cayeron | caerán | caerían | caigan | cayeran |

## Commands

| Person | andar | | caber | | caer | |
|---|---|---|---|---|---|---|
| | Affirmative | Negative | Affirmative | Negative | Affirmative | Negative |
| tú | anda | no andes | cabe | no quepas | cae | no caigas |
| usted | ande | no ande | quepa | no quepa | caiga | no caiga |
| nosotros | andemos | no andemos | quepamos | no quepamos | caigamos | no caigamos |
| vosotros | andad | no andéis | cabed | no quepáis | caed | no caigáis |
| ustedes | anden | no anden | quepan | no quepan | caigan | no caigan |

## dar, decir, estar

| Infinitive | Past participle / Present participle | Indicative | | | | | Subjunctive | |
|---|---|---|---|---|---|---|---|---|
| | | Present | Imperfect | Preterite | Future | Conditional | Present | Imperfect |
| dar<br>*to give* | dado<br>dando | **doy**<br>das<br>da<br>damos<br>dais<br>dan | daba<br>dabas<br>daba<br>dábamos<br>dabais<br>daban | **di**<br>diste<br>dio<br>dimos<br>disteis<br>dieron | daré<br>darás<br>dará<br>daremos<br>daréis<br>darán | daría<br>darías<br>daría<br>daríamos<br>daríais<br>darían | **dé**<br>des<br>**dé**<br>demos<br>**deis**<br>den | diera<br>dieras<br>diera<br>diéramos<br>dierais<br>dieran |
| decir<br>*to say,*<br>*to tell* | dicho<br>diciendo | **digo**<br>**dices**<br>**dice**<br>decimos<br>decís<br>**dicen** | decía<br>decías<br>decía<br>decíamos<br>decíais<br>decían | **dije**<br>dijiste<br>dijo<br>dijimos<br>dijisteis<br>dijeron | **diré**<br>**dirás**<br>**dirá**<br>**diremos**<br>**diréis**<br>**dirán** | **diría**<br>**dirías**<br>**diría**<br>**diríamos**<br>**diríais**<br>**dirán** | **diga**<br>**digas**<br>**diga**<br>**digamos**<br>**digáis**<br>**digan** | dijera<br>dijeras<br>dijera<br>dijéramos<br>dijerais<br>dijeran |
| estar<br>*to be* | estado<br>estando | **estoy**<br>**estás**<br>**está**<br>estamos<br>estáis<br>**están** | estaba<br>estabas<br>estaba<br>estábamos<br>estabais<br>estaban | **estuve**<br>estuviste<br>estuvo<br>estuvimos<br>estuvisteis<br>estuvieron | estaré<br>estarás<br>estará<br>estaremos<br>estaréis<br>estarán | estaría<br>estarías<br>estaría<br>estaríamos<br>estaríais<br>estarían | esté<br>estés<br>esté<br>estemos<br>estéis<br>estén | estuviera<br>estuvieras<br>estuviera<br>estuviéramos<br>estuvierais<br>estuvieran |

## Commands

| Person | dar Affirmative | dar Negative | decir Affirmative | decir Negative | estar Affirmative | estar Negative |
|---|---|---|---|---|---|---|
| tú | da | no des | di | no **digas** | está | no **estés** |
| usted | **dé** | no **dé** | diga | no **diga** | esté | no **esté** |
| nosotros | demos | no demos | digamos | no **digamos** | estemos | no estemos |
| vosotros | dad | no **deis** | decid | no **digáis** | estad | no estéis |
| ustedes | den | no den | digan | no **digan** | estén | no **estén** |

# haber*, hacer, ir

| Infinitive | Past participle / Present participle | Indicative | | | | | Subjunctive | |
|---|---|---|---|---|---|---|---|---|
| | | Present | Imperfect | Preterite | Future | Conditional | Present | Imperfect |
| haber* *to have* | habido / habiendo | he | había | hube | habré | habría | haya | hubiera |
| | | has | habías | hubiste | habrás | habrías | hayas | hubieras |
| | | ha | había | hubo | habrá | habría | haya | hubiera |
| | | hemos | habíamos | hubimos | habremos | habríamos | hayamos | hubiéramos |
| | | habéis | habíais | hubisteis | habréis | habríais | hayáis | hubierais |
| | | han | habían | hubieron | habrán | habrían | hayan | hubieran |
| hacer *do* | hecho / haciendo | hago | hacía | hice | haré | haría | haga | hiciera |
| | | haces | hacías | hiciste | harás | harías | hagas | hicieras |
| | | hace | hacía | hizo | hará | haría | haga | hiciera |
| | | hacemos | hacíamos | hicimos | haremos | haríamos | hagamos | hiciéramos |
| | | hacéis | hacíais | hicisteis | haréis | haríais | hagáis | hicierais |
| | | hacen | hacían | hicieron | harán | harían | hagan | hicieran |
| ir *to go* | ido / yendo | voy | iba | fui | iré | iría | vaya | fuera |
| | | vas | ibas | fuiste | irás | irías | vayas | fueras |
| | | va | iba | fue | irá | iría | vaya | fuera |
| | | vamos | íbamos | fuimos | iremos | iríamos | vayamos | fuéramos |
| | | vais | ibais | fuisteis | iréis | iríais | vayáis | fuerais |
| | | van | iban | fueron | irán | irían | vayan | fueran |

*Haber also has an impersonal form, hay. This form is used to express "There is, There are." The imperative of haber is not used.

## Commands

### hacer

| Person | Affirmative | Negative |
|---|---|---|
| tú | haz | no hagas |
| usted | haga | no haga |
| nosotros | hagamos | no hagamos |
| vosotros | haced | no hagáis |
| ustedes | hagan | no hagan |

### ir

| Person | Affirmative | Negative |
|---|---|---|
| tú | ve | no vayas |
| usted | vaya | no vaya |
| nosotros | vamos | no vayamos |
| vosotros | id | no vayáis |
| ustedes | vayan | no vayan |

## jugar, oír, oler

| Infinitive | Past participle / Present participle | Indicative | | | | | Subjunctive | |
|---|---|---|---|---|---|---|---|---|
| | | Present | Imperfect | Preterite | Future | Conditional | Present | Imperfect |
| jugar *to play* | jugado / jugando | juego<br>juegas<br>juega<br>jugamos<br>jugáis<br>juegan | jugaba<br>jugabas<br>jugaba<br>jugábamos<br>jugabais<br>jugaban | jugué<br>jugaste<br>jugó<br>jugamos<br>jugasteis<br>jugaron | jugaré<br>jugarás<br>jugará<br>jugaremos<br>jugaréis<br>jugarán | jugaría<br>jugarías<br>jugaría<br>jugaríamos<br>jugaríais<br>jugarían | juegue<br>juegues<br>juegue<br>juguemos<br>juguéis<br>jueguen | jugara<br>jugaras<br>jugara<br>jugáramos<br>jugarais<br>jugaran |
| oír *to hear, to listen* | oído / oyendo | oigo<br>oyes<br>oye<br>oímos<br>oís<br>oyen | oía<br>oías<br>oía<br>oíamos<br>oíais<br>oían | oí<br>oíste<br>oyó<br>oímos<br>oísteis<br>oyeron | oiré<br>oirás<br>oirá<br>oiremos<br>oiréis<br>oirán | oiría<br>oirías<br>oiría<br>oiríamos<br>oiríais<br>oirían | oiga<br>oigas<br>oiga<br>oigamos<br>oigáis<br>oigan | oyera<br>oyeras<br>oyera<br>oyéramos<br>oyerais<br>oyeran |
| oler *to smell* | olido / oliendo | huelo<br>hueles<br>huele<br>olemos<br>oléis<br>huelen | olía<br>olías<br>olía<br>olíamos<br>olíais<br>olían | olí<br>oliste<br>olió<br>olimos<br>olisteis<br>olieron | oleré<br>olerás<br>olerá<br>oleremos<br>oleréis<br>olerán | olería<br>olerías<br>olería<br>oleríamos<br>oleríais<br>olerían | huela<br>huelas<br>huela<br>olamos<br>oláis<br>huelan | oliera<br>olieras<br>oliera<br>oliéramos<br>olierais<br>olieran |

## Commands

| Person | jugar Affirmative | jugar Negative | oír Affirmative | oír Negative | oler Affirmative | oler Negative |
|---|---|---|---|---|---|---|
| tú | juega | no juegues | oye | no oigas | huele | no huelas |
| usted | juegue | no juegue | oiga | no oiga | huela | no huela |
| nosotros | juguemos | no juguemos | oigamos | no oigamos | olamos | no olamos |
| vosotros | jugad | no juguéis | oíd | no oigáis | oled | no oláis |
| ustedes | jueguen | no jueguen | oigan | no oigan | huelan | no huelan |

# poder, poner, querer

| Infinitive | Past participle / Present participle | Indicative | | | | | Subjunctive | |
|---|---|---|---|---|---|---|---|---|
| | | Present | Imperfect | Preterite | Future | Conditional | Present | Imperfect |
| poder *to be able to, can* | podido podiendo | puedo puedes puede podemos podéis pueden | podía podías podía podíamos podíais podían | pude pudiste pudo pudimos pudisteis pudieron | podré podrás podrá podremos podréis podrán | podría podrías podría podríamos podríais podrían | pueda puedas pueda podamos podáis puedan | pudiera pudieras pudiera pudiéramos pudierais pudieran |
| poner* *to put* | puesto poniendo | pongo pones pone ponemos ponéis ponen | ponía ponías ponía poníamos poníais ponían | puse pusiste puso pusimos pusisteis pusieron | pondré pondrás pondrá pondremos pondréis pondrán | pondría pondrías pondría pondríamos pondríais pondrían | ponga pongas ponga pongamos pongáis pongan | pusiera pusieras pusiera pusiéramos pusierais pusieran |
| querer *to want, to wish; to love* | querido queriendo | quiero quieres quiere queremos queréis quieren | quería querías quería queríamos queríais querían | quise quisiste quiso quisimos quisisteis quisieron | querré querrás querrá querremos querréis querrán | querría querrías querría querríamos querríais querrían | quiera quieras quiera queramos queráis quieran | quisiera quisieras quisiera quisiéramos quisierais quisieran |

*Similar verbs to poner: imponer, suponer.

## Commands**

| Person | poner | | querer | |
|---|---|---|---|---|
| | Affirmative | Negative | Affirmative | Negative |
| tú | pon | no pongas | quiere | no quieras |
| usted | ponga | no ponga | quiera | no quiera |
| nosotros | pongamos | no pongamos | queramos | no queramos |
| vosotros | poned | no pongáis | quered | no queráis |
| ustedes | pongan | no pongan | quieran | no quieran |

**Note: The imperative of **poder** is used very infrequently and is not included here.

## saber, salir, ser

| Infinitive | Past participle / Present participle | Indicative | | | | | Subjunctive | |
|---|---|---|---|---|---|---|---|---|
| | | Present | Imperfect | Preterite | Future | Conditional | Present | Imperfect |
| saber *to know* | sabido / sabiendo | sé | sabía | supe | sabré | sabría | sepa | supiera |
| | | sabes | sabías | supiste | sabrás | sabrías | sepas | supieras |
| | | sabe | sabía | supo | sabrá | sabría | sepa | supiera |
| | | sabemos | sabíamos | supimos | sabremos | sabríamos | sepamos | supiéramos |
| | | sabéis | sabíais | supisteis | sabréis | sabríais | sepáis | supierais |
| | | saben | sabían | supieron | sabrán | sabrían | sepan | supieran |
| salir *to go out, to leave* | salido / saliendo | salgo | salía | salí | saldré | saldría | salga | saliera |
| | | sales | salías | saliste | saldrás | saldrías | salgas | salieras |
| | | sale | salía | salió | saldrá | saldría | salga | saliera |
| | | salimos | salíamos | salimos | saldremos | saldríamos | salgamos | saliéramos |
| | | salís | salíais | salisteis | saldréis | saldríais | salgáis | salierais |
| | | salen | salían | salieron | saldrán | saldrían | salgan | salieran |
| ser *to be* | sido / siendo | soy | era | fui | seré | sería | sea | fuera |
| | | eres | eras | fuiste | serás | serías | seas | fueras |
| | | es | era | fue | será | sería | sea | fuera |
| | | somos | éramos | fuimos | seremos | seríamos | seamos | fuéramos |
| | | sois | erais | fuisteis | seréis | seríais | seáis | fuerais |
| | | son | eran | fueron | serán | serían | sean | fueran |

## Commands

| Person | saber Affirmative | saber Negative | salir Affirmative | salir Negative | ser Affirmative | ser Negative |
|---|---|---|---|---|---|---|
| tú | sabe | no sepas | sal | no salgas | sé | no seas |
| usted | sepa | no sepa | salga | no salga | sea | no sea |
| nosotros | sepamos | no sepamos | salgamos | no salgamos | seamos | no seamos |
| vosotros | sabed | no sepáis | salid | no salgáis | sed | no seáis |
| ustedes | sepan | no sepan | salgan | no salgan | sean | no sean |

# sonreír, tener*, traer

| Infinitive | Past participle / Present participle | Indicative | | | | | Subjunctive | |
|---|---|---|---|---|---|---|---|---|
| | | Present | Imperfect | Preterite | Future | Conditional | Present | Imperfect |
| sonreír *to smile* | sonreído / sonriendo | sonrío | sonreía | sonreí | sonreiré | sonreiría | sonría | sonriera |
| | | sonríes | sonreías | sonreíste | sonreirás | sonreirías | sonrías | sonrieras |
| | | sonríe | sonreía | sonrió | sonreirá | sonreiría | sonría | sonriera |
| | | sonreímos | sonreíamos | sonreímos | sonreiremos | sonreiríamos | sonriamos | sonriéramos |
| | | sonreís | sonreíais | sonreísteis | sonreiréis | sonreiríais | sonriáis | sonrierais |
| | | sonríen | sonreían | sonrieron | sonreirán | sonreirían | sonrían | sonrieran |
| tener* *to have* | tenido / teniendo | tengo | tenía | tuve | tendré | tendría | tenga | tuviera |
| | | tienes | tenías | tuviste | tendrás | tendrías | tengas | tuvieras |
| | | tiene | tenía | tuvo | tendrá | tendría | tenga | tuviera |
| | | tenemos | teníamos | tuvimos | tendremos | tendríamos | tengamos | tuviéramos |
| | | tenéis | teníais | tuvisteis | tendréis | tendríais | tengáis | tuvierais |
| | | tienen | tenían | tuvieron | tendrán | tendrían | tengan | tuvieran |
| traer *to bring* | traído / trayendo | traigo | traía | traje | traeré | traería | traiga | trajera |
| | | traes | traías | trajiste | traerás | traerías | traigas | trajeras |
| | | trae | traía | trajo | traerá | traería | traiga | trajera |
| | | traemos | traíamos | trajimos | traeremos | traeríamos | traigamos | trajéramos |
| | | traéis | traíais | trajisteis | traeréis | traeríais | traigáis | trajerais |
| | | traen | traían | trajeron | traerán | traerían | traigan | trajeran |

*Many verbs ending in -tener are conjugated like **tener:** contener, detener, entretener(se), mantener, obtener, retener.

## Commands

| Person | sonreír Affirmative | sonreír Negative | tener Affirmative | tener Negative | traer Affirmative | traer Negative |
|---|---|---|---|---|---|---|
| tú | sonríe | no sonrías | ten | no tengas | trae | no traigas |
| usted | sonría | no sonría | tenga | no tenga | traiga | no traiga |
| nosotros | sonriamos | no sonriamos | tengamos | no tengamos | traigamos | no traigamos |
| vosotros | sonreíd | no sonriáis | tened | no tengáis | traed | no traigáis |
| ustedes | sonrían | no sonrían | tengan | no tengan | traigan | no traigan |

# valer, venir*, ver

| Infinitive | Past participle / Present participle | Indicative | | | | | Subjunctive | |
|---|---|---|---|---|---|---|---|---|
| | | Present | Imperfect | Preterite | Future | Conditional | Present | Imperfect |
| valer<br>*to be worth* | valido<br>valiendo | valgo<br>vales<br>vale<br>valemos<br>valéis<br>valen | valía<br>valías<br>valía<br>valíamos<br>valíais<br>valían | valí<br>valiste<br>valió<br>valimos<br>valisteis<br>valieron | valdré<br>valdrás<br>valdrá<br>valdremos<br>valdréis<br>valdrán | valdría<br>valdrías<br>valdría<br>valdríamos<br>valdríais<br>valdrían | valga<br>valgas<br>valga<br>valgamos<br>valgáis<br>valgan | valiera<br>valieras<br>valiera<br>valiéramos<br>valierais<br>valieran |
| venir*<br>*to come* | venido<br>viniendo | vengo<br>vienes<br>viene<br>venimos<br>venís<br>vienen | venía<br>venías<br>venía<br>veníamos<br>veníais<br>venían | vine<br>viniste<br>vino<br>vinimos<br>vinisteis<br>vinieron | vendré<br>vendrás<br>vendrá<br>vendremos<br>vendréis<br>vendrán | vendría<br>vendrías<br>vendría<br>vendríamos<br>vendríais<br>vendrían | venga<br>vengas<br>venga<br>vengamos<br>vengáis<br>vengan | viniera<br>vinieras<br>viniera<br>viniéramos<br>vinierais<br>vinieran |
| ver<br>*to see* | visto<br>viendo | veo<br>ves<br>ve<br>vemos<br>veis<br>ven | veía<br>veías<br>veía<br>veíamos<br>veíais<br>veían | vi<br>viste<br>vio<br>vimos<br>visteis<br>vieron | veré<br>verás<br>verá<br>veremos<br>veréis<br>verán | vería<br>verías<br>vería<br>veríamos<br>veríais<br>verían | vea<br>veas<br>vea<br>veamos<br>veáis<br>vean | viera<br>vieras<br>viera<br>viéramos<br>vierais<br>vieran |

*Similar verb to venir: prevenir

## Commands

| Person | valer Affirmative | valer Negative | venir Affirmative | venir Negative | ver Affirmative | ver Negative |
|---|---|---|---|---|---|---|
| tú | vale | no valgas | ven | no vengas | ve | no veas |
| usted | valga | no valga | venga | no venga | vea | no vea |
| nosotros | valgamos | no valgamos | vengamos | no vengamos | veamos | no veamos |
| vosotros | valed | no valgáis | venid | no vengáis | ved | no veáis |
| ustedes | valgan | no valgan | vengan | no vengan | vean | no vean |

**AMÉRICA DEL SUR**

MAR CARIBE

OCÉANO ATLÁNTICO

BELICE
HONDURAS
NICARAGUA
Lago de Managua
EL SALVADOR
GUATEMALA
PANAMÁ
COSTA RICA

Maracaibo
Barranquilla
Cartagena
Lago de Maracaibo
San Cristóbal
Medellín
Cali
Bogotá
COLOMBIA
Quito
ECUADOR
Guayaquil
Cuenca
Iquitos

Caracas
VENEZUELA
Río Orinoco
GUAYANA
Georgetown
Paramaribo
SURINAM
Cayena
Boa Vista
GUAYANA FRANCESA

ISLAS GALÁPAGOS

ECUADOR

Río Magdalena

Río Amazonas

AMAZONAS

PERÚ
LOS ANDES
Machu Picchu
Lima
Ayacucho
Cuzco
BOLIVIA
Lago Titicaca
La Paz
Santa Cruz
Sucre
Potosí

BRASIL
Brasilia

CHILE
LOS ANDES
PARAGUAY
Asunción
Río Paraná
São Paulo
Río de Janeiro
Iguazú
Río Uruguay

OCÉANO PACÍFICO

OCÉANO ATLÁNTICO

Viña del Mar
Valparaíso
Santiago
Concepción
Buenos Aires
ARGENTINA
Córdoba
Bahía Blanca
URUGUAY
Montevideo
Río de la Plata
Viedma

Córdoba

ISLAS MALVINAS (Br.)
Estrecho de Magallanes
TIERRA DEL FUEGO

| 0 | 250 | 500 | 750 | 1,000 MILLAS |

| 0 | 500 | 1,000 | 1,500 KILÓMETROS |

NIGERIA
ÁFRICA
CAMERÚN
Malabo
GUINEA ECUATORIAL
GABÓN
ÁFRICA

| 0 | MILLAS | 500 |

| 0 | KILÓMETROS | 750 |

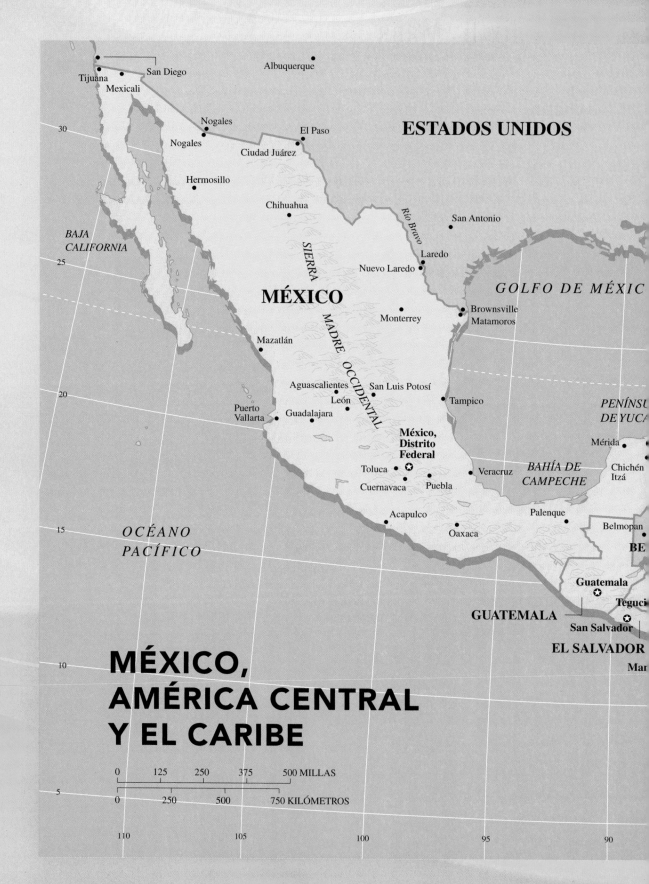

Tijuana
San Diego
Mexicali
Albuquerque

ESTADOS UNIDOS

30

Nogales
El Paso
Nogales
Ciudad Juárez

BAJA
CALIFORNIA

Hermosillo

Chihuahua

Río Bravo
San Antonio

25

SIERRA

MÉXICO

Laredo
Nuevo Laredo

GOLFO DE MÉXIC

Monterrey
Brownsville
Matamoros

Mazatlán

MADRE

OCCIDENTAL

20

Aguascalientes
San Luis Potosí

León

Tampico

PENÍNSU
DE YUCA

Puerto
Vallarta
Guadalajara

México,
Distrito
Federal

Mérida

BAHÍA DE
CAMPECHE

Chichén
Itzá

Toluca

Veracruz

Cuernavaca
Puebla

Acapulco

Palenque

Belmopan

15

OCÉANO
PACÍFICO

Oaxaca

BE

Guatemala

Teguci

GUATEMALA
San Salvador

EL SALVADOR

10

MÉXICO,
AMÉRICA CENTRAL
Y EL CARIBE

Mar

0       125      250      375      500 MILLAS

0        250        500       750 KILÓMETROS

5

110                105                100                95                90

75

70

65

60

55

30

*OCÉANO
ATLÁNTICO*

25

Miami

Nassau ⭐

Habana ⭐

20

BAHAMAS

REPÚBLICA
DOMINICANA

San Juan
⭐

CUBA

*MAR CARIBE*

Santiago
de Cuba

Puerto Príncipe

⭐

Santo
Domingo

PUERTO
RICO

GUADALUPE ⎯

Kingston ⭐

HAITÍ

:ONDURAS

JAMAICA

15

MARTINICA ⎯

:ARAGUA

*de
agua*

10

Caracas ⭐

José

*CANAL DE
PANAMÁ*

Colón

Panamá ⭐

PANAMÁ

VENEZUELA

:STA
:A

*GOLFO
DE
PANAMÁ*

COLOMBIA

Bogotá
⭐

80

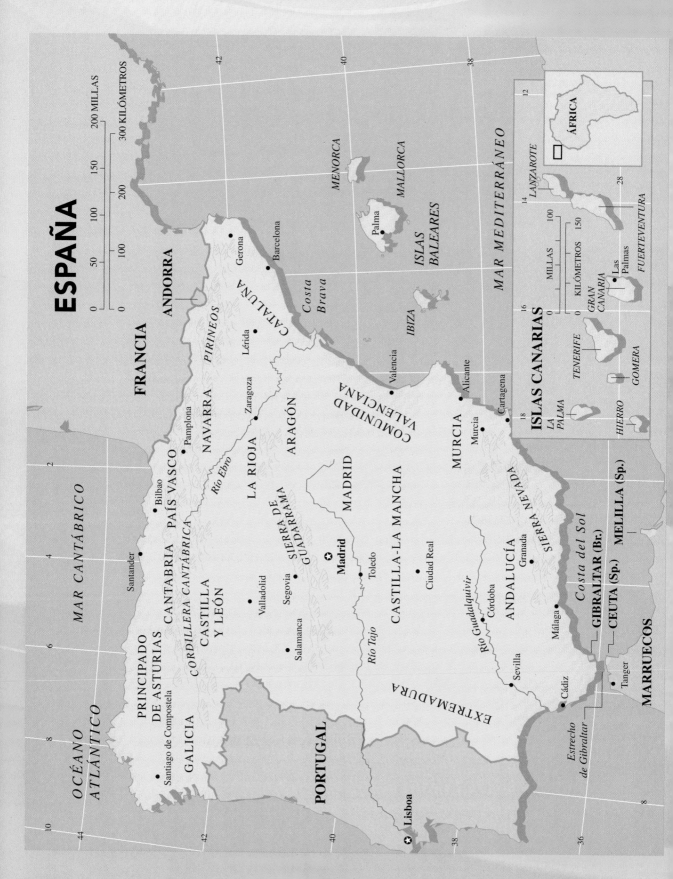

# ESPAÑA

FRANCIA

ANDORRA

200 MILLAS

300 KILÓMETROS

OCÉANO ATLÁNTICO

MAR CANTÁBRICO

MAR MEDITERRÁNEO

PRINCIPADO DE ASTURIAS

Santiago de Compostela

GALICIA

Santander

Bilbao

PAÍS VASCO

CANTABRIA

CORDILLERA CANTÁBRICA

CASTILLA Y LEÓN

Valladolid

Salamanca

Segovia

SIERRA DE GUADARRAMA

Madrid

MADRID

PIRINEOS

NAVARRA

Pamplona

Río Ebro

LA RIOJA

Zaragoza

Lérida

ARAGÓN

CATALUÑA

Gerona

Barcelona

Costa Brava

COMUNIDAD VALENCIANA

Valencia

MENORCA

MALLORCA

Palma

ISLAS BALEARES

IBIZA

Alicante

Cartagena

MURCIA

Murcia

SIERRA NEVADA

Granada

ANDALUCÍA

Córdoba

Río Guadalquivir

Sevilla

Málaga

Costa del Sol

Cádiz

Estrecho de Gibraltar

GIBRALTAR (Br.)

CEUTA (Sp.)

MELILLA (Sp.)

Tánger

MARRUECOS

PORTUGAL

Lisboa

EXTREMADURA

CASTILLA-LA MANCHA

Ciudad Real

Toledo

Río Tajo

ISLAS CANARIAS

ÁFRICA

LANZAROTE

FUERTEVENTURA

GRAN CANARIA

Las Palmas

TENERIFE

GOMERA

LA PALMA

HIERRO

MILLAS

KILÓMETROS

# Spanish–English Glossary

The vocabulary includes the active vocabulary presented in the chapters and many receptive words. Exceptions are verb conjugations, regular past participles, adverbs ending in -**mente,** superlatives, diminutives, and proper names of individuals and most countries. Active words are followed by a number that indicates the chapter in which the word appears as an active item. **P** refers to the opening pages that precede Chapter 1.

The gender of nouns is indicated except for masculine nouns ending in -**o** and feminine nouns ending in -**a.** Stem changes and spelling changes are shown for verbs, e.g., **dormir (ue, u); buscar (qu).**

The following abbreviations are used. Note that the *adj., adv.,* and *pron.* designations are used only to distinguish similar or identical words that are different parts of speech.

| | | | | | | | |
|---|---|---|---|---|---|---|---|
| *adj.* | adjective | *fam.* | familiar | *irreg.* | irregular verb | *p.p.* | past participle |
| *adv.* | adverb | *form.* | formal | *m.* | masculine | *pron.* | pronoun |
| *f.* | feminine | *inf.* | infinitive | *pl.* | plural | *s.* | singular |

## A

**a** to; ~ **cambio de** in exchange for; ~ **nivel mundial** worldwide; ~ **pesar de** in spite of; ~ **pie** on foot, walking, 6; ~ **través de** across, throughout

**abogado(a)** lawyer, 5

**abrelatas eléctrico** (*m. s.*) electric can opener, 10

**abrigo** coat, 8

**abril** April, 1

**abrir** to open, 3; **Abran los libros.** Open your books. P

**abuelo(a)** grandfather (grandmother), 5

**abundancia** abundance

**aburrido(a)** boring, 2; bored, 4

**aburrimiento** boredom

**acabar de (+inf.)** to have just (*done something*), 2

**académico(a)** academic

**acceder** to access, 4

**accesorio** accessory, 8

**acción** (*f.*) action, 5

**aceite** (*m.*) **de oliva** olive oil, 9

**acero** steel

**aconsejar** to advise, 10

**acostarse (ue)** to go to bed, 5

**acrecentar (ie)** to strengthen; to increase

**actividad** (*f.*) activity, P; ~ **deportiva** sports activity, 7

**activo(a)** active, 2

**actor** (*m.*) actor, 5

**actriz** (*f.*) actress, 5

**actualidad** (*f.*): **en la ~** at the present time

**acudir** to go; to attend

**adelantar** to get ahead, to promote

**adelante** ahead

**además** besides

**adinerado(a)** rich, wealthy

**adiós** goodbye, 1

**adivinar** to guess; **Adivina.** Guess. P

**administración** (*f.*) **de empresas** business administration, 3

**¿adónde?** (to) where?

**adquisición** (*f.*) acquisition

**aeropuerto** airport, 6

**afán** (*m.*) desire

**afeitarse** to shave oneself, 5

**afueras** (*f. pl.*) outskirts, 10

**agosto** August, 1

**agregar (gu)** to add, 9

**agrícola** agricultural

**agua** (*f.*) (*but:* **el agua**) water; ~ **dulce** fresh water; ~ **mineral** sparkling water, 9

**aguacate** avocado, 9

**ajedrez** (*m.*) chess

**ajo** garlic, 9

**al (a + el)** to the, 3

**albergar (gu)** to shelter

**albóndiga** meatball

**alcalde (alcaldesa)** mayor

**alcanzar (c)** to achieve

**alemán (alemana)** German, 2

**alemán** (*m.*) German language, 3

**alfabeto** alphabet

**alfombra** rug, carpet, 10

**algo** something, 6

**algodón** (*m.*) cotton, 8

**alguien** someone, 6

**algún, alguno(a)(s)** some, any, 6

**alistar** to recruit; to enroll

**allá** over there, 6

**allí** there, 6

**alma** (*f.*) (*but:* **el alma**) soul

**almacén** (*m.*) store, 6

**almeja** clam, 9

**almohada** pillow

**almuerzo** lunch, 9

**¿Aló?** hello (*on the phone*), 1

**alpinismo: practicar / hacer ~** to hike, to (mountain) climb, 7

**alquilar videos / películas** to rent videos / movies, 2

**alquiler** (*m.*) rent

**alrededor de** around

**altitud** (*f.*) altitude, height

**altivo(a)** arrogant

**alto(a)** tall, 2

**altoparlante** (*m., f.*) speaker, 4

**altura** height

**amanecer (zc)** to dawn

**amante** (*m., f.*) lover

**amar** to love

**amarillo(a)** yellow, 4

**ambiente** (*m.*) atmosphere; **medio ~** (*m.*) environment

**ambigüedad** (*f.*) ambiguity

**ambos(as)** both

**amenaza** threat

**amigo(a)** friend, P

**amor** (*m.*) love

**anaranjado(a)** orange (*in color*), 4

**andar** (*irreg.*) to walk, 8

**anexo**  attachment
**anfitrión** (*m.*)  host
**anhelo**  wish, desire
**anillo**  ring, 8
**anoche**  last night, 7
**anónimo(a)**  anonymous
**Antártida**  Antarctica
**anteayer**  the day before yesterday, 7
**antecesor(a)**  ancestor
**anteojos** (*m. pl.*)  eyeglasses
**antepasado(a)**  ancestor
**anteponer**  to give preference
**antes**  before, 5
**anticuado(a)**  antiquated, old-fashioned
**antipático(a)**  unpleasant, 2
**antros**  bar or club; the "in" place
**anuncio personal**  personal ad
**añadir**  to add, 9
**año**  year, 3; **~ pasado**  last year, 7; **tener** (*irreg.*) ... **~**  to be . . . years old, 1
**apacible**  mild, gentle
**apagar (gu)**  to turn off, 2
**aparatos electrónicos**  electronics, 4
**aparecer (zc)**  to appear
**apariencia física**  physical appearance
**apartamento**  apartment, 6
**apenas**  scarcely
**apetecer (zc)**  to long for
**aplicación** (*f.*)  application, 4
**apodo**  nickname
**apoyar**  to support
**apreciar**  to appreciate
**aprender**  to learn, 3
**aprendizaje** (*m.*)  learning
**apropiado(a)**  appropriate
**apto(a)**  apt, fit
**apuntes** (*m.*)  notes, P
**aquel / aquella(s)** (*adj.*)  those (over there), 6
**aquél / aquélla(s)** (*pron.*)  those (over there), 6
**aquí**  here, 6
**árbol** (*m.*)  tree; **~ genealógico**  family tree
**archivar**  to file, 4
**archivo**  file, 4; **~ PDF**  PDF file, 4
**arder**  to burn
**arete** (*m.*)  earring, 8
**argentino(a)**  Argentinian, 2
**arquitecto(a)**  architect, 5

**arquitectura**  architecture, 3
**arreglar el dormitorio**  to straighten up the bedroom, 10
**arroz** (*m.*) **con pollo**  chicken with rice, 9
**arrugado(a)**  wrinkled
**arte** (*m.*)  art, 3
**artesanía**  handicrafts
**artículo**  article, 1
**artista** (*m., f.*)  artist, 5
**asado(a)**  grilled
**asco**  disgusting
**asegurarse**  to make sure
**asistente** (*m., f.*)  assistant, 5; **~** (*m.*) **electrónico**  electronic notebook, 4
**asistir a**  to attend, 3
**aspiradora**  vacuum cleaner, 10
**ataque** (*m.*)  attack
**atardecer** (*m.*)  late afternoon
**atún** (*m.*)  tuna, 9
**audiencia**  audience
**audífonos** (*m. pl.*)  earphones, 4
**audio**  audio, P
**auditorio**  auditorium, 6
**aumentar**  to increase
**aun**  even
**aún**  yet (*in negative contexts*); still
**australiano(a)**  Australian, 2
**autobús: en ~**  by bus, 6
**automóvil: en ~**  by car, 6
**avenida**  avenue, 1
**avergonzado(a)**  embarrassed
**avergonzar (ue) (c)**  to embarrass
**avión** (*m.*)  airplane; **en ~**  by airplane, 6
**aviso**  warning
**ayer**  yesterday, 3
**ayuda**  help
**ayudar**  to help, 8
**azúcar** (*m., f.*)  sugar, 9; **caña de ~**  sugar cane
**azul**  blue, 4

# B

**bacalao**  codfish, 9
**bailar**  to dance, 2
**baile** (*m.*)  dance, 3
**bajar**  to get down from, to get off of (*a bus, etc.*), 6; to download, 4
**bajo(a)**  short (*in height*), 2
**balay**  large basket
**baldosa**  paving stone

**banco**  (commercial) bank, 6
**bañador(a)**  bather
**bañar**  to swim; to give someone a bath, 5; **bañarse**  to take a bath, 5
**baño**  bathroom, 10
**barato: Es muy ~.**  It's very inexpensive. 8
**barco**  boat
**barrer el suelo / el piso**  to sweep the floor, 10
**barrio**  neighborhood, 1; **~ residencial**  residential neighborhood, suburbs, 10; **~ comercial**  business district, 10
**básquetbol** (*m.*)  basketball, 7
**basta**  it is enough
**bastante**  somewhat, rather, 4
**Bastante bien.**  Quite well. 1
**basura**  garbage, 10; **sacar la ~**  to take out the garbage, 10
**basurero**  wastebasket
**batir**  to beat; to break
**beber**  to drink, 3
**bebida**  beverage, 9
**béisbol** (*m.*)  baseball, 7
**belleza**  beauty
**bello(a)**  beautiful
**berro**  watercress
**besar**  to kiss
**bicicleta: en ~**  on bicycle, 6; **montar en ~**  to ride a bike, 7
**bien**  well, 4; **~, gracias.**  Fine, thank you. 1; **(no) muy ~**  (not) very well, 1
**bienestar** (*m.*)  well-being
**bienvenido(a)**  welcome
**bilingüe**  bilingual
**biología**  biology, 3
**bistec** (*m.*)  steak, 6
**blanco(a)**  white, 4
**blog**  blog, 4
**blusa**  blouse, 8
**bocadillo**  sandwich, 9
**boda**  wedding
**bodegón** (*m.*)  tavern
**bolígrafo**  ballpoint pen, P
**boliviano(a)**  Bolivian, 2
**bolsa**  purse, 8
**bombero(a)**  fire fighter, 5
**bondadoso(a)**  kind; good
**bonito(a)**  pretty
**bordado(a)**  embroidered, 8
**borrador** (*m.*)  rough draft

**bosquejo** outline
**bota** boot, 8
**botar** to throw out
**bote** (*m.*) boat
**boxeo** boxing, 7
**brazalete** (*m.*) bracelet, 8
**breve** brief
**bróculi** (*m.*) broccoli, 9
**broma** joke
**bueno(a)** good, 2; **Buenas noches.** Good night. Good evening. 1; **Buenas tardes.** Good afternoon. 1; **Buenos días.** Good morning. 1
**bufanda** scarf, 8
**buscador** (*m.*) search engine, 4
**buscar (qu)** to look for, 2
**buzón** (*m.*) **electrónico** electronic mailbox, 4

# C

**caballo: montar a ~** to ride horseback, 7
**cable** (*m.*) cable, 4
**cabo** end
**cacao** chocolate
**cachemira** cashmere
**cadena** chain, 8
**caer** (*irreg.*) to fall
**café** (*m.*) coffee, 9; (*adj.*) brown, 4
**cafetería** cafeteria, 3
**caimán** (*m.*) alligator (*cayman*)
**cajero automático** automated bank teller, ATM, 6
**cajón** (*m.*) large box; drawer
**calcetín** (*m.*) sock, 8
**calculadora** calculator, P
**cálculo** calculus, 3
**caldo de pollo** chicken soup, 9
**calentar (ie)** to heat, 9
**calidad** (*f.*) quality; **de buena (alta) ~** of good (high) quality, 8
**calificación** (*f.*) evaluation
**calle** (*f.*) street, 1
**calor: Hace ~.** It's hot., 7; **tener** (*irreg.*) **~** to be hot, 7
**caluroso(a)** warm
**cama** bed, 10; **hacer la ~** to make the bed, 10
**cámara: ~ digital** digital camera, 4; **~ web** webcam, 4

**camarero(a)** waiter (waitress), 5
**camarón** (*m.*) shrimp, 9
**cambio** change; exchange rate; **a ~ de** in exchange for
**caminar** to walk, 2
**camisa** shirt, 8
**camiseta** t-shirt, 8
**campestre** rural
**campo: ~ de estudio** field of study, 3; **~ de fútbol** soccer field, 6
**caña de azúcar** sugar cane
**canadiense** (*m., f.*) Canadian, 2
**canasta** basket
**cancha** soccer field, 6; **~ de tenis** tennis court, 6
**canela** cinnamon
**cansado(a)** tired, 4
**cantante** (*m., f.*) singer
**cantar** to sing, 2
**capítulo** chapter, P
**característica** trait; **~ de la personalidad** personality trait, 2; **~ física** physical trait, 2
**Caribe** (*m., f.*) Caribbean (sea)
**cariño** love, fondness, affection
**carne** (*f.*) meat, 9
**cargar** to upload, 4
**carnicería** butcher shop, 6
**caro: Es (demasiado) caro(a).** It's (too) expensive. 8
**carpintero(a)** carpenter, 5
**carrera** career, 5
**carreta** wooden cart
**carro: en ~** by car, 6
**carta: a la ~** à la carte, 9
**cartera** wallet, 8
**cartón** (*m.*) cardboard
**casa** house, 6
**casarse** to get married, 5
**casco** helmet
**casero(a)** homemade
**castaño** brown, 2
**catarata** waterfall
**catorce** fourteen, P
**cebolla** onion, 9
**celebración** (*f.*) celebration
**celos: tener** (*irreg.*) **~** to be jealous
**celosamente** jealously
**celoso(a)** jealous
**cena** dinner
**cenar** to eat dinner, 2
**censo** census
**centavo** cent

**centro** center; **~ comercial** mall, 6; **~ de computación** computer center, 3; **~ de comunicaciones** media center, 3; **~ de la ciudad** downtown, 10; **~ estudiantil** student center, 6
**Centroamérica** Central America
**cepillarse el pelo** to brush one's hair, 5
**cepillo** brush, 5; **~ de dientes** toothbrush, 5
**cerca de** close to, 6
**cereal** (*m.*) cereal, 9
**cero** zero, P
**cerrar (ie)** to close, 4; **Cierren los libros.** Close your books. P
**cerveza** beer, 9
**chaleco** vest, 8
**champú** (*m.*) shampoo, 5
**chaparrón** (*m.*) cloudburst, downpour
**chaqueta** jacket (*outdoor, non-suit coat*), 8
**chatear** to chat online, 4
**Chau.** Bye, Goodbye, 1
**cheque** (*m.*) check; **pagar con ~ / con ~ de viajero** to pay by check / with a traveler's check, 8
**chévere** terrific, great, cool (*Cuba, Puerto Rico*)
**chico(a)** boy (girl), P
**chileno(a)** Chilean, 2
**chimenea** fireplace, 10
**chino** Chinese language, 3
**chino(a)** Chinese, 2
**chisme** (*m.*) gossip
**chismoso(a)** gossiping
**chompa** sweater
**chuleta de puerco** pork chop, 6
**ciberespacio** cyberspace, 4
**ciclismo** cycling, 7
**ciego(a)** blind; **cita a ciegas** blind date
**cien** one hundred, P; **~ mil** one hundred thousand, 8
**ciencias** (*f. pl.*) science, 3; **~ políticas** political science, 3
**científico(a)** scientific
**ciento uno** one hundred and one, 8
**cierto(a)** certain
**cinco** five, P; **~ mil** five thousand, 8
**cincuenta** fifty, P

**cine** (*m.*)   cinema, 6
**cinturón** (*m.*)   belt, 8
**cita**   quotation; **~ a ciegas**   blind date
**ciudad** (*f.*)   city, 6
**claridad** (*f.*)   clarity
**clase** (*f.*)   class, P; **~ baja**   lower class
**clic: hacer ~ / doble ~**   to click / double click, 4
**cliente** (*m., f.*)   customer, 8
**clóset** (*m.*)   closet, 10
**cobre** (*m.*)   copper
**cocer (-z) (ue)**   to cook, 9
**coche: en ~**   by car, 6
**cocina**   kitchen, 10
**cocinar**   to cook, 2
**cocinero(a)**   cook, chef, 5
**código**   code
**colectivo**   bus
**cólera**   anger
**collar** (*m.*)   necklace, 8
**colombiano(a)**   Colombian, 2
**colonia**   neighborhood, 1
**color** (*m.*)   color, 4; **de un solo ~** solid (colored), 8
**coma**   comma
**comedor** (*m.*)   dining room, 10
**comenzar (ie) (c)**   to begin, 4
**comer**   to eat, 3; **darle de ~ al perro / gato**   to feed the dog / cat, 10
**cómico(a)**   funny, 2
**comida**   food, 6
**comino**   cumin, 9
**¿cómo?**   how? 3; **¿~ desea pagar?**   How do you wish to pay? 8; **¿~ es?**   What's he / she / it like? 2; **¿~ está (usted)?** (*s. form.*)   How are you? 1; **¿~ están (ustedes)?** (*pl.*)   How are you? 1; **¿~ estás (tú)?** (*s. fam.*)   How are you? 1; **¿~ te / le / les va?**   How's it going with you? 1; **~ no.**   Of course. 6; **¿~ se dice…?**   How do you say . . . ? P; **¿~ se llama?** (*s. form.*)   What's your name? 1; **¿~ te llamas?** (*s. fam.*)   What's your name? 1
**cómoda**   dresser, 10
**compañero(a) de cuarto**   roommate, P
**comparación** (*f.*)   comparison, 8
**compartir**   to share, 3
**competencia**   competition, 7

**competir (i, i)**   to compete
**complicidad** (*f.*)   complicity
**comportamiento**   behavior
**comprar**   to buy, 2
**compras: hacer las ~** to go shopping, 6
**comprender**   to understand, 3
**comprensión** (*f.*)   understanding
**comprometerse**   to get engaged, 5
**computación** (*f.*)   computer science, 3
**computadora**   computer, P; **~ portátil**   laptop computer, P
**común**   common
**comunicación** (*f.*) **pública**   public communications, 3
**con**   with
**concordancia**   agreement
**concurso**   contest
**conducir (zc)**   to drive, to conduct, 5
**conectar**   to connect, 4
**conexión** (*f.*)   connection, 4; **hacer una ~**   to go online, 4
**confección** (*f.*)   confection
**conferencista** (*m., f.*)   speaker
**congelado(a)**   frozen, 9
**congelador**   freezer, 10
**conjunto**   group; **en ~**   as a group
**conmigo**   with me, 8
**conocer (zc)**   to meet; to know a person, to be familiar with, 5
**conseguir (i, i)**   to get, to obtain, 8
**contabilidad** (*f.*)   accounting, 3
**contado: al ~**   in cash, 8
**contador(a)**   accountant, 5
**contar (ue)**   to tell, to relate, 4; to count; **~ con**   to be certain of
**contento(a)**   happy, 4
**contestar**   to answer; **Contesten.**   Answer. P
**contigo**   with you (*fam.*), 8
**contracción** (*f.*)   contraction, 3
**contrario: al ~**   on the contrary
**contraseña**   password, 4
**conversación** (*f.*)   conversation
**convertir (ie, i)**   to change
**copa**   wine glass, goblet, 9
**coraje** (*m.*)   courage
**cordillera**   mountain range
**coreano(a)**   Korean, 2
**corregir (i, i) (j)**   to correct
**correo electrónico**   e-mail, 4
**correr**   to run, 3 to mow the lawn, 10; **~ la conexión**   to go offline, 4

**cortesía**   courtesy, 4
**cortina**   curtain, 10
**corto(a)**   short (*in length*)
**costarricense** (*m., f.*)   Costa Rican, 2
**cotidiano(a)**   daily
**crear**   to create
**creativo(a)**   creative
**crecimiento**   growth
**creer (en)**   to believe (in); to think, 3
**cronología**   chronology
**crucero**   cruise ship
**crudo(a)**   raw, 9
**cruzar (c)**   to cross, 6
**cuaderno**   notebook, P
**cuadra**   (city) block, 6
**cuadro**   painting; print, 10
**cuadros: a ~**   plaid, 8
**¿cuál?**   what? which one? 3; **¿~ es tu / su dirección (electrónica)?** (*s. fam. / form.*)   What's your (e-mail) address? 1; **¿~ es tu / su número de teléfono?** (*s. fam. / form.*)   What is your phone number? 1
**¿cuáles?**   what? which ones? 3
**cualquier**   whatever
**¿cuándo?**   when? 3; **¿~ es tu cumpleaños?**   When is your birthday? 1
**¿cuánto(a)?**   how much? 3; **¿Cuánto cuesta(n)?**   How much does it (do they) cost? 8
**¿cuántos(as)?**   how many? 3
**cuarenta**   forty, P
**cuarto**   room, P; bedroom, 10
**cuarto(a)**   fourth, 10
**cuate(a)**   friend, buddy
**cuatro**   four, P
**cuatrocientos(as)**   four hundred, 8
**cubano(a)**   Cuban, 2
**cuchara**   spoon, 9
**cucharada**   tablespoonful, 9
**cucharadita**   teaspoonful, 9
**cuchillo**   knife, 9
**cuenta**   check, bill, 9
**cuento de hadas**   fairy tale
**cuero**   leather, 8
**cuestionario**   questionnaire
**cuidado: tener** (*irreg.*) **~**   to be careful, 7; **¡~!**   careful!
**cuidadoso(a)**   cautious, 2
**culinario(a)**   culinary

**cultura** culture
**cuna** cradle
**cuñado(a)** brother- in-law (sister-in-law), 5
**curso básico** basic course, 3
**cuy** (*m.*) guinea pig
**cuyo(a)** whose

# D

**dar** (*irreg.*) to give, 5; **~ información personal** to give personal information, 1; **~ la hora** to give the time, 3; **~ un papel** to give (play) a role; **~le de comer al perro / gato** to feed the dog / cat, 10; **~le mucha dicha** to give one a lot of happiness
**dato** fact; piece of information
**De nada.** You're welcome. 1
**debajo de** below, underneath, 6
**deber** (+ *inf.*) should, ought to (*do something*), 2
**décimo(a)** tenth, 10
**decir** (*irreg.*) to say, to tell, 5; **~ cómo llegar** to give directions, 6; **~ la hora** to tell the time, 3; **Se dice...** It's said . . . , P
**decoración** (*f.*) decoration, 10
**definido(a)** definite, 1
**dejar** to leave, to stop, 2; **~ de** (+ *inf.*) to stop (*doing something*), 2
**del (de + el)** from the, of the, 3
**delante de** in front of, 6
**delgado(a)** thin, 2
**demasiado(a)** too much, 4
**demostrar (ue)** to demonstrate, to show
**demostrativo(a)** demonstrative, 6
**dentista** (*m., f.*) dentist, 5
**dentro de** inside of, 6; **~ la casa** inside the house, 10
**dependiente** (*m., f.*) salesclerk, 5
**deporte** (*m.*) sport, 7
**derecha: a la ~** to the right, 6
**derecho: (todo) ~** (straight) ahead, 6
**desarrollar** to develop
**desayuno** breakfast, 9
**descalificar (qu)** to disqualify
**descalzo(a)** barefoot
**descansar** to rest, 2
**descargar** to download, 4

**descortés** rude
**describir** to describe, 2
**descubrir** to discover, 3
**descuento** discount, 8
**desear** to want; to wish, 10
**desempeñarse** to manage; to work (as)
**desengaño** disillusionment
**desilusión** (*f.*) disappointment
**desodorante** (*m.*) deodorant, 5
**despachar** to dispatch; to wait on; to work (from a home office)
**despacio** (*adv.*) slowly; (*adj.*) slow
**despedido(a)** fired (*from a job*)
**despedirse (i, i)** to say good-bye, 1
**despertar (ie)** to wake someone up, 5; **despertarse (ie)** to wake up, 5
**después** after, 5
**destacar (qu)** to emphasize
**detalle** (*m.*) detail
**detrás de** behind, 6
**día** (*m.*) day, 3; **~ de la semana** day of the week, 3; **~ de las Madres** Mother's Day, 3; **todos los días** every day, 3
**dialecto** dialect
**dibujo** drawing, P
**diccionario** dictionary, P
**dicha** happiness
**dicho** saying
**diciembre** December, 1
**diecinueve** nineteen, P
**dieciocho** eighteen, P
**dieciséis** sixteen, P
**diecisiete** seventeen, P
**diez** ten, P; **~ mil** ten thousand, 8
**diferencia** difference
**difícil** difficult, 4
**dinero** money
**director(a) de social media** social media director, 5
**dirección** (*f.*) address
**disco duro** hard drive, 4
**Disculpe.** Excuse me. 4
**diseñador(a) gráfico(a)** graphic designer, 5
**diseño** design; **~ gráfico** graphic design, 3
**disfrutar (la vida)** to enjoy (life)
**disponibilidad** (*f.*) availability
**dispuesto(a)** willing

**diversidad** (*f.*) diversity
**diversión** (*f.*) amusement
**divertido(a)** fun, entertaining, 2
**divertirse (ie, i)** to have fun, 5
**dividir** to divide
**divorciarse** to get divorced, 5
**doblar** to turn, 6; to fold
**doce** twelve, P
**docena** dozen, 9
**doctor(a)** doctor
**dólar** (*m.*) dollar
**domesticado(a)** tame, tamed
**domingo** Sunday, 2
**dominicano(a)** Dominican, 2
**don (doña)** title of respect used with male ( female) first name, 1
**¿dónde?** where? 3; **¿~ tienes la clase de... ?** Where does your . . . class meet? 3; **¿~ vives / vive?** (*s. fam. / form.*) Where do you live? 1
**dondequiera: por ~** everywhere
**dorado(a)** golden, browned, 9
**dormir (ue, u)** to sleep, 4; **dormirse (ue, u)** to fall asleep, 5
**dormitorio** bedroom, 10; **~ estudiantil** dormitory, 6
**dos** two, P; **~ mil** two thousand, 8
**doscientos(as)** two hundred, 8
**ducharse** to take a shower, 5
**duelo** pain
**dueño(a)** owner, 5
**dulce** (*adj.*) sweet
**duro(a)** hard

# E

**economía** economics, 3
**ecuador** (*m.*) equator
**ecuatoriano(a)** Ecuadoran, 2
**edad** (*f.*) age
**edificio** building, 6
**educación** (*f.*) education, 3
**efectivo: en ~** in cash, 8
**egoísta** selfish, egotistic, 2
**ejemplo** example, 10; **por ~** for example, 10
**ejercicio: hacer ~** to exercise, 7
**el** (*m.*) the, 1
**él** he, 1; him, 8
**electricidad** (*f.*) electricity
**electrodoméstico** appliance, 10
**elefante** (*m.*) elephant

**ella**   she, 1; her, 8

**ellos(as)**   they, 1; them, 8

**e-mail** (*m.*)   e-mail, P

**embajador(a)**   ambassador

**emoción** (*f.*)   emotion, 4

**empapado(a)**   drenched

**emparejar**   to match

**empezar (ie) (c)**   to begin, 4

**empresas** (*pl.*)   business

**en**   in, on, at; **~ autobús / tren**   by bus / train, 6; **~ bicicleta**   on bicycle, 6; **~ carro / coche / automóvil**   by car, 6; **~ línea**   online, 4; **~ metro**   on the subway, 6; **~ realidad**   actually

**enamorarse**   to fall in love, 5

**Encantado(a).**   Delighted to meet you. 1

**encargado de**   in charge of

**encendida**   burning, on fire

**encima de**   on top of, on, 6

**encontrar (ue)**   to find, 4

**encuentro**   encounter; meeting

**encuesta**   survey

**enero**   January, 1

**enfatizar (c)**   to emphasize

**enfermarse**   to get sick, 5

**enfermero(a)**   nurse, 5

**enfermo(a)**   sick, 4

**enfrente de**   in front of, opposite, 6

**enfriarse**   to get cold, 9

**engañar**   to fool

**engaño**   hoax

**enlace** (*m.*)   link, 4

**enojado(a)**   angry, 4

**ensalada**   salad, 9; **~ de fruta** fruit salad, 9; **~ de lechuga y tomate**   lettuce and tomato salad, 9; **~ de papa**   potato salad, 9; **~ mixta**   tossed salad, 9

**ensayo**   essay

**enseñar**   to teach

**entender (ie)**   to understand, 4

**entonces**   then

**entre**   between, 6

**entregar (gu)**   to turn in; **Entreguen la tarea.**   Turn in your homework. P

**entrenador(a)**   trainer

**entrenarse**   to train, 7

**entresemana**   during the week, on weekdays, 3

**entretener** (*like* **tener**)   to entertain

**enviar**   to send, 4

**equilibro: poner en ~**   to balance

**equipo**   team, 7

**erupción** (*f.*) **volcánica**   volcanic eruption

**escaleras** (*f. pl.*)   stairs, 10

**esclavo(a)**   slave

**escoger (j)**   to choose

**esconder**   to hide

**escribir**   to write, 3; **Escriban en sus cuadernos.**   Write in your notebooks. P

**escritorio**   desk, P

**escuchar**   to listen; **~ música**   to listen to music, 2; **Escuchen el audio / el CD.**   Listen to the tape / CD. P

**escuela**   school, 3

**ese (esa)** (*s. adj.*)   that, 6

**ése (ésa)** (*s. pron.*)   that one, 6

**eso**   that, 6; **por ~**   so, that's why, 10

**esos (esas)** (*pl. adj.*)   those, 6

**ésos (ésas)** (*pl. pron.*)   those (ones), 6

**España**   Spain

**español (a)**   Spanish, 2

**español** (*m.*)   Spanish language, 3

**espárragos** (*m. pl.*)   asparagus, 9

**especialidad de la casa**   house special, 9

**especie** (*f.*)   species

**espejo**   mirror, 10

**esperanza**   wish, hope

**esperar**   to hope, 10

**esposo(a)**   husband (wife), 5

**esquí** (*m.*)   ski, skiing; **~ acuático**   water skiing, 7; **~ alpino**   downhill skiing, 7

**esquiar**   to ski, 7

**esquina**   corner, 6

**estación** (*f.*)   season, 7 **de trenes / autobuses**   train / bus station, 6

**estacionamiento**   parking lot, 6

**estadio**   stadium, 6

**estadística**   statistics, 3

**estado**   state, 5; **~ civil**   marital status

**Estados Unidos**   United States

**estadounidense** (*m., f.*)   U. S. citizen, 2

**estampado(a)**   print, 8

**estancia**   ranch

**estar** (*irreg.*)   to be, 1;

**estatura**   height (*of a person*)

**este (esta)** (*s. adj.*)   this, 6

**éste (ésta)** (*s. pron.*)   this one, 6

**estilo**   style

**estos(as)** (*pl. adj.*)   these, 6

**éstos(as)** (*pl. pron.*)   these (ones), 6

**estrategia**   strategy

**estudiante** (*m., f.*)   student, P

**estudiar**   to study; **~ en la biblioteca (en casa)**   to study at the library (at home), 2; **Estudien las páginas... a...**   Study pages . . . to . . . P

**estudio**   studio, 3

**estufa**   stove, 10

**etapa**   era

**Europa**   Europe

**evitar**   to avoid

**exhibir**   to exhibit

**exigir (j)**   to demand

**éxito**   success

**exótico(a)**   exotic, strange

**expresar preferencias**   to express preferences, 2

**expresión** (*f.*)   expression, 1

**extrovertido(a)**   extroverted, 2

# F

**fácil**   easy, 4

**falda**   skirt, 8

**falso(a)**   false

**familia**   family; **~ nuclear**   nuclear family, 5; **~ política**   in-laws, 5

**fantasía**   fantasy

**farmacia**   pharmacy, 6

**fascinar**   to fascinate, 4

**fatal**   terrible, awful, 1

**favor: por ~**   please, 1

**febrero**   February, 1

**fecha**   date, 3; **¿A qué ~ estamos?**   What is today's date? 3

**felicidad** (*f.*)   happiness

**femenino(a)**   feminine

**feo(a)**   ugly, 2

**ferrocarril** (*m.*)   railroad

**filantrópico(a)**   philanthropic

**filosofía**   philosophy, 3

**fin** (*m.*)   end; intention; **~ de semana**   weekend, 2; **por ~**   finally, 9

**final** final

**financiero(a)** financial

**física** physics, 3

**físico(a)** physical, 5

**flan** (*m.*) custard, 9

**flor** (*f.*) flower

**florecer (zc)** to flower, to flourish

**flotador(a)** floating

**fondo** background

**fortaleza** fortress

**foro** forum, 4

**foto** (*f.*) photo, P; **sacar fotos** to take photos, 2

**francés (francesa)** French, 2

**francés** (*m.*) French language, 3

**frecuentemente** frequently, 4

**freír (i, i)** to fry, 9

**frente a** in front of, facing, opposite, 6

**fresa** strawberry, 9

**fresco(a)** fresh, 9; **Hace fresco.** It's cool. 7

**frijoles** (*m.*) **(refritos)** (refried) beans, 9

**frío(a)** cold; **Hace frío.** It's cold. 7; **tener** (*irreg.*) **frío** to be cold, 7

**frito(a)** fried, 9

**frontera** border

**fruta** fruit, 6

**fuego** fire; **a ~ suave / lento** at low heat, 9

**fuente** (*f.*) source

**fuera de** outside of, 6; **~ de la casa** outside the house, 10

**fuerte** strong, filling (*e.g., a meal*), 9

**funcionar** to function, 4

**funciones** (*f. pl.*) **de la computadora** computer functions, 4

**fundador(a)** founder

**fungir** to work

**furioso(a)** furious, 4

**fútbol** (*m.*) soccer, 7; **~ americano** football, 7

# G

**gafas** (*f. pl.*) **de sol** sunglasses, 8

**galleta** cookie, 9

**galón** (*m.*) gallon, 9

**ganadería** cattle, livestock

**ganado** cattle

**ganar** to win, 7

**ganas: tener** (*irreg.*) **~ de** to have the urge to, to feel like, 7

**garaje** (*m.*) garage, 10

**gato(a)** cat, 2

**gazpacho** cold tomato soup (*Spain*), 9

**general: por lo ~** generally, 9

**género** genre

**generoso(a)** generous, 2

**gente** (*f.*) people

**geografía** geography, 3

**gerente** (*m., f.*) manager, 5

**gimnasio** gymnasium, 3

**gobernador(a)** (*m.*) governor

**golf** (*m.*) golf, 7

**gordo(a)** fat, 2

**gorra** cap, 8

**gozar (c)** to enjoy

**grabador** (*m.*) **de discos compactos / DVD** CD / DVD recorder, 4

**grabar** to record, 4

**gracias: Muchas ~.** Thank you very much. 1

**grado** degree; **~ Celsio(s)** Celsius degree, 7; **~ Fahrenheit** Fahrenheit degree, 7

**gráfica** graph

**grande** big, great, 2

**grano: al ~** to the point

**gris** gray, 4

**gritar** to shout, to scream

**grito** scream

**grupo** group; **~ de conversación** chat room, 4; **~ de noticias** news group, 4

**guagua** bus (*Cuba, Puerto Rico*)

**guante** (*m.*) glove, 8

**guapo(a)** handsome, attractive, 2

**guardar** to store; **~ la ropa** put away the clothes, 10; to save, 4

**guatemalteco(a)** Guatemalan, 2

**guión** (*m.*) script

**guionista** (*m., f.*) script writer

**guisado** beef stew, 9

**guisante** (*m.*) pea, 9

**guitarra** guitar, 2

**gustar: A mí / ti me / te gusta . . .** I / You like . . . , 2; **A . . . le gusta . . .** He / She likes . . . , 2; **A . . . les gusta . . .** They / You (*pl.*) like . . . , 2; **Me gustaría (+ inf.) . . .** I'd like (+ *inf.*) . . . , 6

**gusto** taste; **al ~** to individual taste, 9; **El ~ es mío.** The pleasure is mine. 1; **Mucho ~.** My pleasure. 1; **Mucho ~ en conocerte.** A pleasure to meet you. 1

# H

**haba** (*f.*) (*but:* **el haba**) bean

**habichuela** green bean, 9

**habitación** (*f.*) bedroom, 10

**habitante** (*m., f.*) inhabitant

**hablar por teléfono** to talk on the telephone, 2

**hacer** (*irreg.*) to make, to do, 5; **Hace buen / mal tiempo.** It's nice / bad weather. 7; **Hace calor / fresco / frío.** It's hot / cool / cold. 7; **Hace sol / viento.** It's sunny / windy. 7; **~ alpinismo** to hike, 7; **~ caso** to pay attention, to obey; **~ clic / doble clic** to click / double click, 4; **~ ejercicio** to exercise, 7; **~ el reciclaje** to do the recycling, 10; **~ la cama** to make the bed, 10; **~ las compras** to go shopping, 6; **~ preguntas** to ask questions, 3; **~ surfing** to surf, 7; **~ una conexión** to go online, 4; **Hagan la tarea para mañana.** Do the homework for tomorrow. P

**hambre** (*f.*) (*but:* **el hambre**) hunger; **tener** (*irreg.*) **~** to be hungry, 7

**hamburguesa** hamburger, 9; **~ con queso** cheeseburger, 9

**hardware** (*m.*) hardware, 4

**harina** flour, 9

**hasta** until; **~ luego.** See you later, 1; **~ mañana.** See you tomorrow. 1; **~ pronto.** See you soon. 1

**hay** there is, there are, 1

**hecho** fact

**hecho(a)** (*p. p.*): **Está ~ de...** It's made out of . . . , 8

**helado de vainilla / chocolate** vanilla / chocolate ice cream, 9

**herencia** heritage

**hermanastro(a)** stepbrother (stepsister), 5

**hermano(a) (menor, mayor)** (younger, older) brother (sister), 5
**hermoso(a)** handsome, beautiful
**hervido(a)** boiled, 9
**hervir (ie, i)** to boil, 9
**hierro** iron
**hijo(a)** son (daughter), 5
**hilo: al ~** stringed, 9
**himno** hymn
**hispano(a)** Hispanic
**hispanohablante** Spanish-speaking
**historia** history, 3
**hockey** (*m.*) **sobre hielo / hierba** ice / field hockey, 7
**hogar** (*m.*) home; **sin ~** homeless
**hoja de papel** sheet of paper, P
**hola** hello, 1
**hombre** (*m.*) man, P; **~ de negocios** businessman, 5
**hondureño(a)** Honduran, 2
**honesto(a)** honest
**hora** hour; time; **dar** (*irreg.*) **la ~** to give the time, 3; **decir la ~** to tell the time, 3
**horario** schedule
**horno** oven; **al ~** roasted (in the oven), 9
**hospital** (*m.*) hospital, 6
**hoy** today, 3; **~ es martes treinta.** Today is Tuesday the 30th. 3; **¿Qué día es ~?** What day is today? 3
**huella** footprint
**huevo** egg, 6; **~ estrellado** egg sunny-side up, 9; **~ revuelto** scrambled egg, 9
**humanidades** (*f. pl.*) humanities, 3
**húmedo(a)** humid
**humilde** humble

# I

**ícono del programa** program icon, 4
**identidad** (*f.*) identity
**idioma** (*m.*) language, 3
**iglesia** church, 6
**Igualmente.** Likewise. 1
**impaciente** impatient, 2
**impermeable** (*m.*) raincoat, 8
**importar** to be important to someone; to mind, 4
**impresionante** impressive

**impresora** printer, 4
**imprimir** to print, 3
**impulsivo(a)** impulsive, 2
**incendio forestal** forest fire
**increíble** incredible
**indefinido(a)** indefinite, 1
**índice** (*m.*) index
**indio(a)** Indian, 2
**indígena** indigenous
**influencia** influence
**influir (y)** to influence
**informática** computer science, 3
**informe** (*m.*) report
**ingeniería** engineering, 3
**ingeniero(a)** engineer, 5
**inglés (inglesa)** English, 2
**inglés** (*m.*) English language, 3
**ingrediente** (*m.*) ingredient, 9
**ingreso** revenue
**inmigración** (*f.*) immigration
**insistir** to insist, 10
**instalar** to install, 4
**instructor(a)** instructor, P
**inteligente** intelligent, 2
**intentar** to attempt
**intercambiar** to exchange
**interesante** interesting, 2
**interesar** to interest, to be interesting, 4
**Internet** (*m. or f.*) Internet
**intérprete** (*m., f.*) interpreter
**íntimo(a)** intimate
**introvertido(a)** introverted, 2
**invertir** to invest
**invierno** winter, 7
**ir** (*irreg.*) to go, 3; **~ a** (+ *inf.*) to be going to (*do something*), 3; **~ de compras** to go shopping, 8; **irse** to leave, to go away, 5
**irresponsable** irresponsible, 2
**italiano(a)** Italian, 2
**italiano** (*m.*) Italian language
**izquierda: a la ~** to the left, 6

# J

**jabón** (*m.*) soap, 5
**jamás** never, 6
**jamón** (*m.*) ham, 6
**japonés (japonesa)** Japanese, 2
**japonés** (*m.*) Japanese language, 3
**jardín** (*m.*) garden, 10
**jeans** (*m. pl.*) jeans, 8
**jornada laboral** workday
**joven** young, 2
**joyas** (*f. pl.*) jewelry, 8

**joyería** jewelry store, 6
**juego interactivo** interactive game, 4
**jueves** (*m.*) Thursday, 3
**jugar (ue) (gu)** to play, 4; **~ tenis (béisbol, etc.)** to play tennis (baseball, etc.), 7
**jugo de fruta** fruit juice, 9
**juguete** (*m.*) toy, 10
**juguetón (juguetona)** playful
**julio** July, 1
**junio** June, 1
**juntar** to group
**juntarse** to join
**juventud** (*f.*) youth

# K

**kilo** kilo, 9; **medio ~** half a kilo, 9

# L

**la** (*f.*) the, 1
**labio** lip
**lado** side; **al ~ de** next to, on the side of, 6
**ladrillo** brick
**lago** lake, 7
**lámpara** lamp, 10
**lana** wool, 8
**langosta** lobster, 9
**lanzarse (c)** to throw oneself
**lápiz** (*m.*) pencil, P
**lavadora** washer, 10
**lavandería** laundry room, 10
**lavaplatos** (*m. s.*) dishwasher, 10
**lavar** to wash, 5; **~ los platos (la ropa)** to wash the dishes (the clothes), 10
**lavarse** to wash oneself, 5; **~ el pelo** to wash one's hair, 5; **~ los dientes** to brush one's teeth, 5
**le** to / for you (*form. s.*), to / for him, to / for her, 8
**lección** (*f.*) lesson, P
**leche** (*f.*) milk, 6
**lector** (*m.*) **de CD-ROM / DVD** DVD / CD-ROM drive, 4
**leer (y)** to read, 3; **Lean el Capítulo 1.** Read Chapter 1. P
**lejos de** far from, 6
**lema** (*m.*) slogan
**lentes** (*m. pl.*) eyeglasses
**lento(a)** slow, 4

**les** to / for you (*form. pl.*), to / for them, 8

**letrero** sign

**levantar** to raise, to lift, 5; **~ pesas** to lift weights, 2

**levantarse** to get up, 5

**libra** pound, 9

**libre** free

**librería** bookstore, 3

**libro** book, P; **~ electrónico** e-book, P

**licencia de manejar** driver's license

**licuado de fruta** fruit shake, smoothie

**licuadora** blender, 10

**ligero(a)** light, lightweight, 9

**limonada** lemonade, 9

**limpiar el baño** to clean the bathroom, 10

**lindo(a)** pretty, 2

**línea: en ~** online, 4

**lingüístico(a)** linguistic

**lino** linen, 8

**literatura** literature, 3

**litro** liter, 9

**llamar** to call, 2; **llamarse** to name, 2; **Me llamo . . .** My name is . . . , 1

**llano(a)** flat

**llanura** plain

**llegar (gu)** to arrive, 2

**llenar** to fill

**llevar** to take, to carry **llover** to rain; **Está lloviendo. (Llueve.)** It's raining. 7

**lobo** wolf

**lodo** mud

**lograr** to achieve

**lomo de res** prime rib, 9

**los (las)** (*pl.*) the, 1

**luego** later, 5

**lugar** (*m.*) place; **~ de nacimiento** birthplace

**lujoso(a)** luxurious

**lunares: de ~** polka-dotted, 8

**lunes** (*m.*) Monday, 3

**luz** (*f.*) light; **~ solar** sunlight

# M

**madera** wood

**madrastra** stepmother, 5

**madre** (*f.*) mother, 5

**maestro(a)** teacher, 5

**maíz** (*m.*) corn

**mal** badly, 4

**malo(a)** bad, 2

**mamá** mother, 5

**mañana** morning, 3; tomorrow, 3; **de la ~** in the morning (*with precise time*), 3; **por la ~** during the morning, 3

**mandar** to send; to order, 8

**mandato** command

**manejar** to drive, 5

**mantel** (*m.*) tablecloth, 9

**mantener** (*irreg.*) to keep, maintain

**mantequilla** butter, 9

**manzana** apple, 9

**maquillaje** (*m.*) makeup, 5

**maquillarse** to put on makeup, 5

**máquina de afeitar** electric razor, 5

**maravilla** wonder

**marcar (qu)** to mark; to point out

**marisco** shellfish, 9

**marrón** brown, 4

**martes** (*m.*) Tuesday, 3

**marzo** March, 1

**más** more; **~ que** more than, 8

**masculino(a)** masculine

**matemáticas** (*f. pl.*) mathematics, 3

**mayo** May, 1

**mayonesa** mayonnaise, 9

**mayor** older, greater, 8

**mayoría** majority

**mayúsculo(a)** capital (letter)

**me** to / for me, 8

**mecánico(a)** mechanic, 5

**medio(a) hermano(a)** half-brother (half-sister), 5

**medianoche** (*f.*) midnight, 3

**medicina** medicine, 3

**médico(a)** doctor, 5

**medida** measurement, 9

**medio ambiente** (*m.*) environment

**mediodía** (*m.*) noon, 3

**medios de transporte** means of transportation, 6

**medir (i, i)** to measure

**meditación** (*f.*) meditation

**mejilla** cheek

**mejor** better, 8

**melón** (*m.*) melon, 9

**memoria flash** flash drive, 4

**menor** younger; less, 8

**menos: ~ que** less than, 8; **por lo ~** at least, 10

**mensajero(a)** messenger

**mentiroso(a)** dishonest, lying, 2

**menú** (*m.*) menu, 9

**mercadeo** marketing, 3

**mercado** market, 6; **~ al aire libre** open-air market, farmer's market, 6

**merecer (zc)** to deserve

**merienda** snack

**mes** (*m.*) month, 3; **~ pasado** last month, 7

**mesa** table, P; **poner la ~** to set the table, 9; **quitar la ~** to clear the table, 10

**mesita de noche** night table, 10

**meta** goal

**metro: en ~** on the subway, 6

**mexicano(a)** Mexican, 2

**mezcla** mix

**mezclar** to mix, 9

**mezclilla** denim, 8

**mi** (*adj.*) my, 3

**mí** (*pron.*) me, 8

**micro** bus (*Chile*)

**micrófono** microphone, 4

**microondas** (*m. s.*) microwave, 10

**miedo: tener** (*irreg.*) **~ (a, de)** to be afraid (of), 7

**mientras** while, during

**miércoles** (*m.*) Wednesday, 3

**mil** (*m.*) one thousand, 8

**miles** (*pl.*) thousands

**millón** (*m.*): **un ~** one million, 8; **dos millones** two million, 8

**mío(a)** (*adj.*) my, 10; (*pron.*) mine, 10

**mirar televisión** to watch television, 2

**misionero(a)** missionary

**mismo(a)** same; **lo mismo** the same (thing)

**mitad** (*f.*) half

**mixto(a)** mixed

**mochila** backpack, P; knapsack

**moda** fashion, 8; **(no) estar de ~** (not) to be fashionable, 8; **pasado(a) de ~** out of style, 8

**modales** (*m. pl.*) manners

**modas: de ~** (*adj.*) fashion

**módem** (*m.*) **externo / interno** external / internal modem, 4

**molestar** to bother, 4

**molido(a)** crushed, ground, 9
**monitor** (*m.*) monitor, 4
**mono** monkey
**montañoso(a)** mountainous
**montar** to ride; **~ a caballo** to ride horseback, 7; **~ en bicicleta** to ride a bike, 7
**monte** (*m.*) mountain
**morado(a)** purple, 4
**morirse (ue, u)** to die, 8
**mortalidad** (*f.*) mortality
**mostaza** mustard, 9
**mostrar (ue)** to show
**MP3 portátil** portable MP3 player, P
**muchacho(a)** boy (girl), P
**muchedumbre** (*f.*) crowd
**mucho** a lot, 4; **~ que hacer** a lot to do; **No ~.** Not much. 1
**mudarse** to move (*change residence*)
**muebles** (*m. pl.*) furniture, 10
**mujer** (*f.*) woman, P; **~ de negocios** businesswoman, 5
**mundo** world
**muñeca** doll
**museo** museum, 6
**música** music, 3
**muy** very, 2

# N

**nacer (zc)** to be born
**nacionalidad** (*f.*) nationality, 2
**nada** nothing, 1; **De ~.** You're welcome. 1
**nadar** to swim, 7
**nadie** no one, nobody, 6
**naranja** orange (*fruit*), 9
**narrador(a)** narrator
**natación** (*f.*) swimming, 7
**naturaleza** nature; **~ muerta** still life
**navegación** (*f.*) navigation; **~ en rápidos** whitewater rafting, 7
**navegar (gu): ~ en rápidos** to go whitewater rafting, 7; **~ por Internet** to browse the Internet, 2
**necesitar** to need, 2
**negocio** business, 3; (*pl.*) business
**negro(a)** black, 4
**nervioso(a)** nervous, 4
**nevar** to snow, 7; **Está nevando. (Nieva.)** It's snowing. 7

**ni... ni** neither . . . nor, 6
**nicaragüense** (*m., f.*) Nicaraguan, 2
**nieto(a)** grandson (granddaughter), 5
**niñero(a)** baby-sitter
**ningún, ninguno(a)** none, no, not any, 6
**niño(a)** boy (girl), P
**nivel** (*m.*) level
**noche** (*f.*) night, 3; **de la ~** in the evening (*with precise time*), 3; **por la ~** during the evening, 3
**nombre** (*m.*) name; **Mi ~ es...** My name is . . . , 1; **~ completo** full name
**normal** normal, 4
**Norteamérica** North America
**norteamericano(a)** North American
**nos** to / for us, 8; **¿~ vemos donde siempre?** See you at the usual place? 1
**nosotros(as)** we, 1; us, 8
**nota** grade, P
**novato(a)** newbie, novice
**novecientos(as)** nine hundred, 8
**novedoso(a)** novel, new
**novelista** (*m., f.*) novelist
**noveno(a)** ninth, 10
**noventa** ninety, P
**noviembre** November, 1
**novio(a)** boyfriend (girlfriend)
**nublado: Está ~.** It's cloudy. 7
**nuera** daughter-in-law, 5
**nuestro(a)** (*adj.*) our, 3; (*pron.*) ours, 10
**nueve** nine, P
**número** number, 8; **~ ordinal** ordinal number, 10
**nunca** never, 5

# O

**o... o** either . . . or, 6
**ochenta** eighty, P
**ocho** eight, P
**ochocientos(as)** eight hundred, 8
**octavo(a)** eighth, 10
**octubre** October, 1
**ocupado(a)** busy, 4
**ocupar** to live in
**odio** hatred
**oferta especial** special offer, 8

**oficina** office, 6; **~ de correos** post office, 6
**oír** (*irreg.*) to hear, 5
**ojear** to scan
**ola** wave
**ómnibus** (*m.*) bus
**once** eleven, P
**onda: en ~** in style
**oprimir** to push
**opuesto(a)** opposite
**oración** (*f.*) sentence
**ordenar** to order, 9
**organización** (*f.*) **benéfica** charity
**orgulloso(a)** proud
**originar** to originate
**orilla** shore
**oro** gold, 8
**ortografía** spelling
**os** to / for you (*fam. pl.*), 8
**otoño** fall, autumn, 7

# P

**paciente** (*m., f.*) patient, 2
**padrastro** stepfather, 5
**padre** (*m.*) father, 5; **padres** (*m. pl.*) parents, 5
**pagar (gu)** to pay, 9
**página** page, P; **~ web** web page, 4
**pago: método de ~** form of payment, 8 **país** (*m.*) country
**paisaje** (*m.*) scenery
**pájaro** bird
**pan** (*m.*) bread, 6; **~ tostado** toast, 9
**panameño(a)** Panamanian, 2
**pandilla** gang
**pantalla** screen, 4
**pantalones** (*m. pl.*) pants, 8; **~ cortos** shorts, 8
**pañuelo** handkerchief
**papá** (*m.*) father, 5
**papas fritas** (*f. pl.*) French fries, 9
**papel** role; paper; **hoja de ~** sheet of paper, P
**papelería** stationery store, 6
**papitas fritas** (*f. pl.*) potato chips, 6
**paquete** (*m.*) package, 9
**para** for, toward, in the direction of, in order to (+ *inf.*), 10
**paracaídas** (*m.*) parachute
**parada** stop

**paraguayo(a)**  Paraguayan, 2
**parar**  to stop
**parecer (zc)**  to seem
**pared** (*f.*)  wall, P
**pariente** (*m., f.*)  family member, relative, 5
**parque** (*m.*)  park, 6
**párrafo**  paragraph
**parrilla: a la ~**  grilled, 9
**partido**  game, match, 7
**pasar**  to pass (by), 2; **~ la aspiradora**  to vacuum, 10
**pasear: sacar a ~ al perro**  to take the dog for a walk, 10
**pasillo**  hallway, 10
**pasta de dientes**  toothpaste, 5
**pastel** (*m.*)  cake, 9
**patinar**  to skate, 2; **~ en línea**  to inline skate (rollerblade), 7; **~ sobre hielo**  to ice skate, 7
**patio**  patio, 10
**patrocinador(a)**  sponsor
**pavo**  turkey, 6
**paz** (*f.*)  peace
**pedazo**  piece, slice, 9
**pedir (i, i)**  to ask for (*something*), 1; to request, 10; **~ la hora**  to ask for the time, 3
**peinarse**  to brush / comb one's hair, 5
**peine** (*m.*)  comb, 5
**pelar**  to peel, 9
**pelearse**  to have a fight, 5
**peligro**  danger, 7
**peligroso(a)**  dangerous, 7
**pelirrojo(a)**  redheaded , 2
**pelo**  hair; **~ castaño / rubio**  brown / blond hair, 2
**pelota**  ball, 7
**peluquero(a)**  barber / hairdresser, 5
**pendiente** (*m.*)  earring, 8
**pendrive** (*m.*)  flash drive, 4
**pensar (ie)**  to think, 4; **~ de**  to have an opinion about, 4; **~ en (de)**  to think about, to consider, 4
**penúltimo(a)**  next-to-last
**peor**  worse, 8
**pequeño(a)**  small, 2
**perder (ie)**  to lose, 4; **perderse (ie)**  to lose oneself, to get lost
**Perdón.**  Excuse me. 4
**perejil** (*m.*)  parsley
**perezoso(a)**  lazy, 2

**periódico**  newspaper
**periodismo**  journalism, 3
**periodista** (*m., f.*)  journalist, 5
**permiso: Con ~.**  Pardon me. 4
**permitir**  to permit, to allow, 10
**pero**  but, 2
**perro(a)**  dog, 2; **perro caliente**  hot dog, 9
**persiana**  Venetian blind, 10
**personalidad** (*f.*)  personality
**peruano(a)**  Peruvian, 2
**pesar: a ~ de**  in spite of
**pesas: levantar ~**  to lift weights, 2
**pescado**  fish (*caught*), 9
**pescar (qu)**  to fish, 7
**pez** (*m.*)  fish (*alive*)
**piano**  piano, 2
**picante**  spicy, 9
**picar (qu)**  to chop, to mince, 9
**pie** (*m.*): **a ~**  on foot, walking, 6
**piel** (*f.*)  leather, 8
**pimienta**  pepper, 9
**pingüino**  penguin
**pintar**  to paint, 2
**pintoresco(a)**  picturesque
**pintura**  painting, 3
**pirata** (*m.*)  pirate
**pisar**  to step on
**piscina**  swimming pool, 6
**piso**  floor; **primer (segundo, etc.) ~**  first (second, etc.) floor, 10
**pista de atletismo**  athletics track, 6
**pizarra interactiva**  interactive whiteboard, P
**pizzería**  pizzeria, 6
**placer: Un ~.**  My pleasure. 1
**plancha**  iron, 10
**planchar**  to iron, 10
**plata**  silver, 8
**plátano**  banana, 9
**plato**  plate, 9; **~ hondo**  bowl, 9; **~ principal**  main dish, 9
**plaza**  plaza, 6
**plomero(a)**  plumber, 5
**poblar (ue)**  to populate
**pobre**  poor
**poco**  little, small amount, 4; **muy ~**  very little
**poder** (*m.*)  power; (*irreg.*) to be able to, 4
**poderoso(a)**  powerful
**poesía**  poetry
**poeta (poetisa)**  poet

**policía** (*m., f.*)  policeman (policewoman), 5
**político(a)**  political
**pollo**  chicken, 6; **~ asado**  roasted chicken, 9; **~ frito**  fried chicken, 9
**polvo**  dust
**poner** (*irreg.*)  to put, 5; **~ en equilibro**  to balance; **~ la mesa**  to set the table, 9; **~ mis juguetes en su lugar**  to put my toys where they belong, 10 to put on (clothing), 5
**por**  for, during, in, through, along, on behalf of, by, 10; **~ avión**  by plane, 6; **~ ejemplo**  for example, 10; **~ eso**  so, that's why, 10; **~ favor**  please, 1; **~ fin**  finally, 9; **~ lo menos**  at least, 10; **~ supuesto**  of course, 10
**¿por qué?**  why? 3
**porcentaje** (*m.*)  percentage
**porque**  because, 3
**portarse**  to behave
**portátil: MP3 ~**  portable MP3 player, P; **computadora ~**  laptop computer, P
**portugués (portuguesa)**  Portuguese, 2
**postre** (*m.*)  dessert, 9
**pozo**  well; hole
**practicar (qu)**  to practice; **~ alpi-nismo**  to hike, to (mountain) climb, 7; **~ deportes**  to play sports, 2; **~ surfing**  to surf, 7
**precio: Está a muy buen ~.**  It's a very good price. 8
**preferencia**  preference
**preferir (ie, i)**  to prefer, 4
**pregunta: hacer preguntas**  to ask questions, 3
**premio**  prize
**prenda de ropa**  article of clothing, 8
**preocupado(a)**  worried, 4
**preocuparse**  to worry, 5
**preparación** (*f.*)  preparation, 9
**preparar**  to prepare, 2; **~ la comida**  to prepare the food, 10; **prepararse**  to get ready, 5
**preposición** (*f.*)  preposition, 6
**presa**  dam
**presentar a alguien**  to introduce someone, 1
**préstamo**  loan, 8

**prestar** to loan, 8

**primavera** spring, 7

**primer(o)(a)** first, 10; **primer piso** first floor, 10

**primo(a)** cousin, 5

**principiante(a)** beginner

**prisa** haste, hurry; **tener** (*irreg.*) ~ to be in a hurry, 7

**probarse (ue): Voy a probármelo / la(los / las).** I'm going to try it (them) on. 8

**procesador de comida** food processor, 10

**producto electrónico** electronic product, 4

**profesión** (*f.*) profession, 5

**profesor(a)** professor, P

**programa** (*m.*) program; ~ **antivirus** anti-virus program, 4; ~ **de procesamiento de textos** word-processing program, 4

**programador(a)** programmer, 5

**prohibir** to forbid, 10

**promover (ue)** to promote

**pronombre** (*m.*) pronoun, 1

**propina** tip, 9

**propósito** purpose

**proveedor** (*m.*) **de acceso** Internet service provider, 4

**provocador(a)** provocative

**próximo(a)** next

**proyector** projector, P

**psicología** psychology, 3

**publicidad** (*f.*) public relations, 3

**publicitario(a)** (*adj.*) pertaining to advertising

**pueblo** town, 6

**puerta** door, P

**puerto de USB** USB port, 4

**puertorriqueño(a)** Puerto Rican, 2

**pulgada** inch

**pulsera** bracelet, 8

**punto de vista** viewpoint

**punto** period

# Q

**¿qué?** what? which? 3; ¿~ **hay de nuevo?** What's new? 1; ¿~ **hora es?** What time is it? 3; ¿~ **significa...?** What does . . . mean? P;¿~ **tal?** How are things going? 1; ¿~ **te gusta**

**hacer?** What do you like to do? 2

**quedar** to fit; **Me queda bien / mal.** It fits nicely / badly. 8; **Me queda grande / apretado.** It's too big / too tight. 8; **quedar(se)** to remain; to be

**quehacer** (*m.*) **doméstico** housechore, 10

**quejarse** to complain, 5

**querer** (*irreg.*) to want, to love, 4; to wish, 10

**queso** cheese, 6

**¿quién(es)?** who? 3; ¿**De** ~ **es?** Whose is this? 3; ¿**De** ~ **son?** Whose are these? 3

**química** chemistry, 3

**quince** fifteen, P

**quinientos(as)** five hundred, 8

**quinto(a)** fifth, 10

**quisiera** (+ *inf.*) I'd like (+ *inf.*), 6

**quitar** to take off, to remove 5; ~ **la mesa** to clear the table, 10; **quitarse (la ropa)** to take off (one's clothing), 5

**quizás** perhaps

# R

**raíz** (*f.*) root

**rango** rank

**rápido(a)** fast, 4

**rasgado** torn up

**rasgar (gu)** to tear up

**rasuradora** razor, 5

**ratón** (*m.*) mouse, 4

**rayado(a)** striped, 8

**rayas: a** ~ striped, 8

**razón** (*f.*) reason; **tener** (*irreg.*) ~ to be right, 7

**realidad: en** ~ actually

**realizarse (c)** to take place

**rebajado(a): estar** ~ to be reduced (in price) / on sale, 8

**recámara** bedroom, 10

**recibir** to receive, 3

**reciclaje** (*m.*) recycling, 10

**recomendar (ie)** to recommend, 10

**reconocer (zc)** to recognize

**recordar (ue)** to remember

**recorte** (*m.*) cutting

**recuerdo** souvenir

**recurrir** to fall back on, to resort to

**red** (*f.*) web, Internet; ~ **mundial** World Wide Web, 4; ~ **social** social networking site, 4

**redactar** to edit

**reflejar** to reflect

**reflexión** (*f.*) reflection

**refresco** soft drink, 6; beverage, 9; **tomar un** ~ to have a soft drink, 2

**refrigerador** (*m.*) refrigerator, 10

**regalar** to give (as a gift), 8

**regalo** present, gift, 8

**regar (ie) (gu) las plantas** to water the plants, 10

**regla** rule

**regresar** to return, 2

**regular** so-so, 1

**reina** queen

**reírse** (*irreg.*) to laugh, 5

**relajarse** to relax, 5

**reloj** (*m.*) watch, 8

**remar** to row, 7

**remero(a)** rower

**renombre** (*m.*) renown

**renovar (ue)** to renovate

**repente: de** ~ suddenly, 9

**repetir (i, i)** to repeat, 4; **Repitan.** Repeat. P

**reproductor** (*m.*) **de discos compactos / DVD** CD / DVD recorder, 4

**requerir (ie, i)** to require, 10

**residencia estudiantil** dorm, 3

**respirar** to breathe

**responder** to respond, 1

**responsable** responsible, 2

**restaurante** (*m.*) restaurant, 6

**resumen: en** ~ in short, to sum up

**reto** challenge

**reunión** (*f.*) meeting

**reunirse** to meet, to get together, 5

**revista** magazine; ~ **de moda** fashion magazine

**rey** (*m.*) king

**riesgo** risk

**rima** rhyme

**río** river, 7

**riqueza** wealth

**rodeado(a)** surrounded

**rojo(a)** red, 4

**ropa** clothing, 5

**rosa** rose, 4

**rosado(a)** pink, 4

**rubio(a)** blond(e), 2
**rueda** wheel
**ruta** route

# S

**sábado** Saturday, 2
**saber** (*irreg.*) to know (*a fact, information*), 5; **~** (*+ inf.*) to know how (*to do something*), 5
**sabor** (*m.*) flavor
**sacar (qu)** to take out; **~ a pasear al perro** to take the dog for a walk, 10; **~ fotos** to take photos, 2; **~ la basura** to take out the garbage, 10
**sacerdote** (*m.*) priest
**saco** jacket, sports coat, 8
**sacudir los muebles** to dust the furniture, 10
**sal** (*f.*) salt, 9
**sala** living room, 10
**salchicha** sausage, 6
**salir** (*irreg.*) to leave, to go out, 5
**salmón** (*m.*) salmon, 9
**salón** (*m.*) **de clase** classroom, P
**salud** (*f.*) health, 3
**saludable** healthy
**saludar** to greet, 1
**saludo** greeting
**salvadoreño(a)** Salvadoran, 2
**salvaje** wild, untamed
**salvavidas** (*m. s.*) lifejacket
**sandalia** sandal, 8
**sandwich** (*m.*) sandwich, 9; **~ de jamón y queso con aguacate** ham and cheese sandwich with avocado, 9
**secadora** dryer, 10
**secar (qu)** to dry (*something*), 5; **secarse (qu) el pelo** to dry one's hair, 5
**secretario(a)** secretary, 5
**secreto** secret
**sed** (*f.*) thirst; **tener** (*irreg.*) **~** to be thirsty, 7
**seda** silk, 8
**seguido(a)** continued
**seguir (i, i)** to continue, 6; **~ derecho** to go straight ahead
**según** according to
**segundo(a)** second, 10
**seguro(a)** sure, 4; safe, 7
**seis** six, P
**seiscientos(as)** six hundred, 8

**semana** week, 3; **~ pasada** last week, 7; **fin** (*m.*) **de ~** weekend, 2; **todas las semanas** every week, 5
**semejanza** similarity
**sencillo(a)** simple; single (*room*)
**sentarse (ie)** to sit down, 5
**sentir (ie, i)** to feel, 4; **Lo siento.** I'm sorry. 4
**señalar** to point out
**señor** (*abbrev.* **Sr.**) Mr., Sir, 1
**señora** (*abbrev.* **Sra.**) Mrs., Ms., Madam, 1
**señorita** (*abbrev.* **Srta.**) Miss, Ms., 1
**separarse** to get separated, 5
**septiembre** September, 1
**séptimo(a)** seventh, 10
**ser** (*irreg.*) to be, 1
**serio(a)** serious, 2
**servicio** service **servilleta** napkin, 9
**servir (i, i)** to serve, 4; **¿En qué puedo servirle?** How can I help you? 8
**sesenta** sixty, P
**setecientos(as)** seven hundred, 8
**setenta** seventy, P
**sexto(a)** sixth, 10
**sí** yes, 1
**siempre** always, 5
**siete** seven, P
**siglo** century
**significar (qu): Significa...** It means . . . , P
**significado** meaning
**siguiente** following, next
**silla** chair, P
**sillón** (*m.*) armchair, 10
**símbolo** symbol
**simpático(a)** nice, 2
**sin** without; **~ control** uncontrolled
**sincero(a)** sincere, 2
**sino** but instead
**sistemático(a)** systematic
**sitio** place; **~ web** website, 4
**smartphone** smartphone, 4
**snowboarding** snowboarding, 7
**soberanía** sovereignty
**sobre** on, above, 6
**sobrepasar** to surpass
**sobresaliente** outstanding
**sobrino(a)** nephew (niece), 5
**sofá** (*m.*) sofa, 10

**software** (*m.*) software, 4
**sol** (*m.*) sun; **Hace ~.** It's sunny. 7
**soltero(a)** single (unmarried)
**sombrero** hat, 8
**sonar (ue)** to ring, to go off (*phone, alarm clock, etc.*), 4
**sonido** sound
**sonreír** (*irreg.*) to smile, 8
**sonrisa** smile
**soñar (ue) con** to dream about, 4
**sopa** soup, 9; **~ de fideos** noodle soup, 9
**sorpresa** surprise
**sorteo** raffle; evasion
**sortija** ring
**sótano** basement, cellar, 10
**su** (*adj.*) your (*s. form., pl.*), his, her, their, 3
**suave** soft
**subir** to go up, to get on, 6; to upload, 4
**suburbio** suburb, 10
**sucio(a)** dirty
**sudadera** sweatsuit, track suit, 8
**Sudamérica** South America
**suegro(a)** father-in-law (mother-in-law), 5
**sueño** dream; **tener** (*irreg.*) **~** to be sleepy, 7
**suéter** (*m.*) sweater, 8
**sugerencia** suggestion
**sugerir (ie, i)** to suggest, 8
**superación** (*f.*) overcoming
**supermercado** supermarket, 6
**supuesto: por ~** of course, 10
**surfing: hacer / practicar (qu) ~** to surf, 7
**sustantivo** noun
**sustituir (y)** to substitute
**suyo(a)** (*adj.*) your (*form. s., pl.*), his, her, its, their, 10; (*pron.*) yours (*form. s., pl.*), his, hers, its, theirs, 10

# T

**tabla de snowboard** snowboard, 7
**tableta** tablet computer, 4
**tal vez** perhaps
**talla** size, 8
**taller** (*m.*) workshop
**también** also, 2
**tampoco** neither, not either, 2
**tan... como** as . . . as, 8
**tanto(a)(s)... como** as much (many) . . . as, 8

**tarde** (*f.*) afternoon, 3; **de la ~** in the afternoon (*with precise time*), 3; **por la ~** during the afternoon, 3; (*adv.*) late, 3

**tarea** homework, P

**tarjeta** **~ de crédito** credit card, 8; **~ de débito** (bank) debit card, 8

**te** to / for you (*fam. s.*), 8

**té** hot tea, 9; **~ helado** iced tea, 9

**teatro** theater, 6

**tecnología** technology, 4

**techo** roof, 10

**tecla** key (*on a keyboard*), 4

**teclado** keyboard, 4

**tejer** to weave

**tejido** weaving

**tela** fabric, 8

**teléfono inteligente** smartphone, 4

**televisor** (*m.*) television set, 10

**temperatura** temperature, 7; **La ~ está a 20 grados Celsio(s) (Fahrenheit).** It's 20 degrees Celsius (Fahrenheit). 7

**temporada: ~ de lluvias** rainy season; **~ de secas** dry season

**temprano** early, 3

**tender** to tend (to)

**tenedor** (*m.*) fork, 9

**tener** (*irreg.*) to have, 1; **~ ... años** to be . . . years old, 1; **~ calor** to be hot, 7; **~ cuidado** to be careful, 7; **~ frío** to be cold, 7; **~ ganas de** to have the urge to, to feel like (doing), 7; **~ hambre** to be hungry, 7; **~ miedo (a, de)** to be afraid (of), 7; **~ prisa** to be in a hurry, 7; **~ que** (+ *inf.*) to have to (+ *verb*), 1; **~ razón** to be right, 7; **~ sed** to be thirsty, 7; **~ sueño** to be sleepy, 7; **~ vergüenza** to be embarrassed, ashamed, 7

**tenis** (*m.*) tennis, 7

**teoría** theory

**tercer(o, a)** third, 10

**término** term

**terrible** terrible, awful, 1

**tesoro** treasure

**texto** text

**tez** (*f.*) skin, complexion

**ti** you (*fam. s.*), 8

**tiburón** (*m.*) shark

**tiempo** weather, 7; **¿Qué ~ hace?** What's the weather like? 7

**tienda** store, 6; **~ de equipo deportivo** sporting goods store, 6; **~ de juegos electrónicos** electronic games store, 6; **~ de ropa** clothing store, 6

**tierra** earth, ground

**tímido(a)** shy, 2

**tinto: vino ~** red wine, 9

**tío(a)** uncle (aunt), 5

**típico(a)** typical, 9

**tira cómica** comic strip

**tiroteo** shooting

**titular** to title

**título** title, 1

**tiza** chalk, P

**toalla** towel, 5; **~ de mano** handtowel, 5

**tocador** (*m.*) dresser, 10

**tocar (qu) un instrumento musical** to play a musical instrument, 2

**todavía** still

**todo** everything

**todo(a)** all, every; **todas las semanas** every week, 5; **todos los días (años)** every day (year), 9

**tomar** to take; **~ un refresco** to have a soft drink, 2; **~ el sol** to sunbathe, 2

**tonto(a)** silly, stupid, 2

**tormenta** thunderstorm

**torpe** awkward

**tostadora** toaster, 10

**trabajador(a)** (*adj.*) hard-working, 2; (*noun*) worker, 5

**trabajar** to work, 2

**traducir (zc)** to translate, 5

**traer** (*irreg.*) to bring, 5

**traje** (*m.*) suit, 8; **~ de baño** bathing suit, 8

**trama** plot

**tramos** sections

**transmitir** to broadcast, 3

**trapear el piso** to mop the floor, 10

**tratar de** to try

**tratarse de** to be a matter of; to be

**través: a ~ de** across, throughout

**trece** thirteen, P

**trecho** distance, period

**treinta** thirty, P

**tren: en ~** by train, 6

**tres** three, P

**trescientos(as)** three hundred, 8

**trigo** wheat

**tripulación** (*f.*) crew

**triste** sad, 4

**triunfar** to triumph

**trompeta** trumpet, 2

**trozo** chunk, 9

**trucha** trout, 9

**truco** trick

**tu** your (*fam.*), 3

**tú** you (*fam.*), 1

**tuyo(a)** (*adj.*) your (*fam.*), 10; (*pron.*) yours (*fam.*), 10

# U

**ubicado(a)** located

**Ud.** (*abbrev. of* **usted**) you (*form. s.*), 8

**Uds.** (*abbrev. of* **ustedes**) you (*fam. or form. pl.*), 8

**último: lo ~** the latest (thing)

**un(a)** a, 1

**único(a)** only, unique

**unido(a)** united

**unir** to mix together, to incorporate, 9

**universidad** (*f.*) university, 6

**uno** one, P

**unos(as)** some, 1

**uruguayo(a)** Uruguayan, 2

**usar** to use, 2

**usted** you (*s. form.*), 1

**ustedes** you (*fam. or form. pl.*), 1

**usuario(a)** user, 4

**útil** useful

**uva** grape, 9

# V

**vacío(a)** empty

**valer** (*irreg.*) **la pena** to be worthwhile

**valioso(a)** valuable

**valle** (*m.*) valley

**valor** (*m.*) value

**vanidoso(a)** vain

**vapor: al ~** steamed, 9

**vaquero** cowboy

**variedad** (*f.*) variety

**varios(as)** various, several

**varonil** manly

**vaso** glass, 9

**veces** (*f. pl.*) times; **a ~** sometimes, 5; **(dos) ~ al día / por semana** (two) times a day / per week, 5

**vecino(a)** neighbor, 6

**vegano: algo ~** something vegan, 9

**vegetal** (*m.*) vegetable, 6

**vegetariano(a)** vegetarian; **~ estricto** vegan, 9

**vehículo** vehicle

**veinte** twenty, P

**veintiuno** twenty-one, P

**vender** to sell, 3

**venezolano(a)** Venezuelan, 2

**venir** (*irreg.*) to come, 5

**venta: estar en ~** to be on sale, 8

**ventana** window, P

**ver** (*irreg.*) to see, 5; **Nos vemos.** See you later. 1

**verano** summer, 7

**veras: de ~** truly, really

**verbo** verb, 3

**verdad** true; **~** (*f.*) truth

**verde** green, 4

**vergüenza** shame; **tener** (*irreg.*) **~** to be embarrassed, ashamed, 7

**verso libre** blank verse

**vestido** dress, 8

**vestir (i, i)** to dress (*someone*), 5; **vestirse (i, i)** to get dressed, 5

**veterinario(a)** veterinarian, 5

**vez** (*f.*) time; **de ~ en cuando** sometimes; **en ~ de** instead of; **rara ~** hardly ever; **tal ~** perhaps; **una ~** once, 9

**viajar** to travel, 2

**vida** life

**videocámara** videocamera, 4

**viejo(a)** old, 2

**viento** wind; **Hace ~.** It's windy. 7

**viernes** (*m.*) Friday, 2

**vinagre** (*m.*) vinegar, 9

**vino: ~ blanco** white wine, 9; **~ tinto** red wine, 9

**violín** (*m.*) violin, 2

**viraje** (*m.*) turn

**visitante** (*m., f.*) visitor

**visitar a amigos** to visit friends, 2

**vivienda** housing

**vivir** to live, 3

**volibol** (*m.*) volleyball, 7

**volver (ue)** to return, 4

**vosotros(as)** you (*fam. pl.*), 1

**voz** (*f.*) voice

**vuestro(a)** (*adj.*) your (*fam. pl.*), 3; (*pron.*) yours (*fam. pl.*), 3

# W

**wifi** (*m.*) wifi, wireless connection, 4

# Y

**yerno** son-in-law, 5

**yo** I, 1

**yogur** (*m.*) yogurt, 6

# Z

**zanahoria** carrot, 9

**zapato** shoe, 8; **~ de tacón alto** high-heeled shoe, 8; **~ de tenis** tennis shoe, 8

# English–Spanish Glossary

## A

**a**  un(a), 1
**à la carte**  a la carta, 9
**above**  sobre, 6
**abundance**  abundancia
**academic**  académico(a)
**access**  acceder, 4
**accessory**  accesorio, 8
**according to**  según
**accountant**  contador(a), 5
**accounting**  contabilidad (f.), 3
**achieve**  alcanzar (c), lograr
**acquisition**  adquisición (f.)
**across**  a través de
**action**  acción (f.), 5
**active**  activo(a), 2
**activity**  actividad (f.), P
**actor**  actor (m.), 5
**actress**  actriz (f.), 5
**actually**  en realidad
**ad: personal ~**  anuncio personal
**add**  agregar, añadir, 9
**address**  dirección (f.)
**advertising** (adj.)  publicitario(a)
**advise**  aconsejar, 10
**affection**  cariño
**afternoon**  tarde (f.), 3;
   **during the ~**  por la tarde, 3;
   **Good ~.**  Buenas tardes. 1;
   **in the ~**  (with precise time) de la tarde, 3;
   **late ~**  atardecer (m.)
**age**  edad (f.)
**agreement**  concordancia
**agricultural**  agrícola (m., f.)
**ahead**  adelante
**airport**  aeropuerto, 6
**all**  todo(a)
**alligator**  aligátor (m.), caimán (m.)
**along**  por, 10
**alphabet**  alfabeto
**also**  también, 2
**altitude**  altitud (f.)
**always**  siempre, 5
**ambassador**  embajador(a)
**ambiguity**  ambigüedad (f.)
**amusement**  diversión (f.)
**ancestor**  antecesor(a), antepasado(a)
**anger**  cólera

**angry**  enojado(a), 4
**anonymous**  anónimo(a)
**answer**  contestar;
   **Answer.**  Contesten. P
**Antarctica**  Antártida
**antiquated**  anticuado(a)
**any**  algún, alguno(a) 6
**apartment**  apartamento, 6
**appear**  aparecer (zc)
**apple**  manzana, 9
**appliance**  electrodoméstico, 10
**application**  aplicación (f.), 4
**appreciate**  apreciar
**appropriate**  apropiado(a)
**April**  abril, 1
**apt**  apto(a)
**architect**  arquitecto(a), 5
**architecture**  arquitectura, 3
**Argentinian**  argentino(a), 2
**armchair**  sillón (m.), 10
**around**  alrededor de
**arrive**  llegar, 2
**arrogant**  altivo(a)
**art**  arte (m.), 3
**article**  artículo, 1
**artist**  artista (m., f.), 5
**as**  como; **~ ... ~**  tan... como, 8;
   **~ many . . . ~**  tantos(as)... como, 8; **~ much . . . ~** tanto(a)(s)... como, 8
**ask: ~ questions**  hacer (irreg.) preguntas, 3; **~ for something**  pedir (i, i), 1; **~ for the time**  pedir (i, i) la hora, 3
**asparagus**  espárragos (m. pl.), 9
**at**  en; **~ least**  por lo menos, 10; **~ low heat**  a fuego suave / lento, 9
**athletics track**  pista de atletismo, 6
**atmosphere**  ambiente (m.)
**attachment**  anexo
**attack**  ataque (m.)
**attempt**  intentar
**attend**  acudir; asistir a, 3
**attractive**  guapo(a), 2
**audio**  audio, P
**audiotape**  cinta, P
**auditorium**  auditorio, 6
**August**  agosto, 1
**aunt**  tía, 5
**Australian**  australiano(a), 2

**automated bank teller (ATM)**  cajero automático, 6
**autumn**  otoño, 7
**availability**  disponibilidad (f.)
**avenue**  avenida, 1
**avoid**  evitar
**awful**  fatal, terrible, 1
**awkward**  torpe

## B

**baby-sitter**  niñero(a)
**background**  fondo
**backpack**  mochila, P
**bad**  malo(a), 2
**badly**  mal, 4
**balance**  poner (irreg.) en equilibro
**ball**  pelota, 7
**ballpoint pen**  bolígrafo, P
**banana**  plátano, 9
**bank (commercial)**  banco, 6
**barber**  peluquero(a), 5
**barefooted**  descalzo(a)
**baseball**  béisbol (m.), 7
**basement**  sótano, 10
**basket**  canasta
**basketball**  básquetbol (m.), 7
**bather**  bañador(a)
**bathing suit**  traje (m.) de baño, 8
**bathroom**  baño, 10
**be**  estar (irreg.), ser (irreg.), 1;
   **~ ... years old**  tener (irreg.)... años, 1; **~ a matter of**  tratarse de; **~ able to**  poder (irreg.), 4; **~ afraid (of)**  tener (irreg.) miedo (a, de), 7;
   **~ ashamed**  tener (irreg.) vergüenza, 7; **~ born**  nacer (zc); **~ careful**  tener (irreg.) cuidado, 7; **~ certain of**  contar (ue) con; **~ cold**  tener (irreg.) frío, 7; **~ embarrassed**  tener (irreg.) vergüenza, 7; **~ familiar with**  conocer (zc), 5; **~ going to**  ir a, 3; **~ hot**  tener (irreg.) calor, 7; **~ hungry**  tener (irreg.) hambre, 7;
   **~ important**  importar, 4; **~ in a hurry**  tener (irreg.) prisa, 7; **~ interesting**  interesar, 4; **~ jealous**  tener (irreg.) celos;

~ **right** tener (*irreg.*) razón, 7;
~ **sleepy** tener (*irreg.*) sueño,
7; ~ **thirsty** tener (*irreg.*) sed,
7; ~ **worthwhile** valer (*irreg.*)
la pena

**bean** haba (*f. but* el haba);
**(green)** ~ habichuela, 9;
**refried beans**
frijoles refritos, 9

**beat** batir

**beautiful** bello(a), hermoso(a)

**beauty** belleza

**because** porque, 3

**bed** cama, 10

**bedroom** cuarto, dormitorio,
habitación (*f.*), recámara, 10

**beef stew** guisado, 9

**beer** cerveza, 9

**before** antes, 5

**begin** comenzar (ie) (c), empezar
(ie) (c), 4

**beginner** principiante

**behave** portarse

**behavior** comportamiento

**behind** detrás de, 6

**believe (in)** creer (en), 3

**below** debajo de, 6

**belt** cinturón (*m.*), 8

**besides** además

**better** mejor, 8

**between** entre, 6

**beverage** bebida, refresco, 9

**bicycle: on ~** en bicicleta, 6

**big** grande, 2

**bilingual** bilingüe

**bill** cuenta, 9

**biology** biología, 3

**bird** pájaro

**birthplace** lugar (*m.*) de
nacimiento

**black** negro(a), 4

**blank verse** verso libre

**blender** licuadora, 10

**blind** ciego(a); ~ **date** cita a
ciegas

**block** cuadra, 6

**blog** blog, 4

**blond(e)** rubio(a), 2

**blouse** blusa, 8

**blue** azul, 4

**boat** barco, bote (*m.*)

**boil** hervir (ie, i), 9

**boiled** hervido(a), 9

**Bolivian** boliviano(a), 2

**book** libro, P

**bookstore** librería, 3

**boot** bota, 8

**border** frontera

**boredom** aburrimiento

**bored** aburrido(a), 4

**boring** aburrido(a), 2

**both** ambos(as)

**bother** molestar, 4

**bowl** plato hondo, 9

**box: large ~** cajón (*m.*)

**boxing** boxeo, 7

**boy** chico, P; muchacho, P;
niño, P

**boyfriend** novio

**bracelet** brazalete (*m.*),
pulsera, 8

**bread** pan (*m.*), 6

**break (a record)** batir

**breakfast** desayuno, 9

**breathe** respirar

**brick** ladrillo

**brief** breve

**bring** traer (*irreg.*), 5

**broadcast** transmitir, 3

**broccoli** brócoli (*m.*), 9

**brother (younger, older)**
hermano (menor, mayor), 5

**brother-in-law** cuñado, 5

**brown** castaño, 2; café,
marrón, 4

**browse: the Internet** navegar
por Internet, 2

**brush** cepillo, 5; ~ **one's**
**hair** cepillarse el pelo,
peinarse, 5; ~ **one's**
**teeth** lavarse los dientes, 5

**buddy** cuate(a)

**building** edificio, 6

**burn** arder

**burning** encendida

**bus** ómnibus (*m.*), colectivo,
guagua (*Cuba, Puerto Rico*),
micro (*Chile*)

**business** negocio,
3; ~ **administration**
administración (*f.*) de empresas,
3; ~ **district** centro comercial,
10

**businessman** hombre (*m.*) de
negocios, 5

**businesswoman** mujer (*f.*) de
negocios, 5

**busy** ocupado(a), 4

**but** pero, 2; ~ **instead** sino

**butcher shop** carnicería, 6

**butter** mantequilla, 9

**buy** comprar, 2

**by** por, 10; ~ **bus** en autobús, 6;
~ **car** en carro / coche /
automóvil, 6; ~ **check** con
cheque, 8; ~ **plane** por avión,
6; ~ **train** en tren, 6

**Bye.** Chau. 1

# C

**cable** cable (*m.*), 4

**cafeteria** cafetería, 3

**cake** pastel (*m.*), 9

**calculator** calculadora, P

**calculus** cálculo, 3

**call** llamar, 2

**can opener (electric)** abrelatas
(*m.*) (eléctrico), 10

**Canadian** canadiense (*m., f.*), 2

**cap** gorra, 8

**capital (letter)** mayúsculo(a)

**card** tarjeta; **credit** ~ tarjeta de
crédito, 8; **debit** ~ tarjeta de
débito, 8

**cardboard** cartón (*m.*)

**career** carrera, 5

**Careful!** ¡Cuidado!

**Caribbean (Sea)** Caribe (*m., f.*)

**carpenter** carpintero(a), 5

**carpet** alfombra, 10

**carrot** zanahoria, 9

**carry** llevar

**cash: in ~** en efectivo,
al contado, 8

**cashmere** cachemira

**cat** gato(a), 2

**cattle** ganado, ganadería

**cattle-raising industry** industria
ganadera

**cautious** cuidadoso(a), 2

**CD: CD / DVD recorder**
grabador (*m.*) de discos
compactos / DVD, reproductor
(*m.*) de discos compactos /
DVD, 4

**celebration** celebración (*f.*)

**cellar** sótano, 10

**Celsius degree** grado Celsio(s), 7

**census** censo

**cent** centavo

**center** centro

**Central America** Centroamérica

**century** siglo

**cereal** cereal (*m.*), 9

**certain** cierto(a)

**chain** cadena, 8

**chair** silla, P

**chalk** tiza, P
**challenge** reto
**change** cambio; convertir (ie, i);
**chapter** capítulo, P
**charity** organización (*f.*) benéfica
**chat** chatear (*online*),
   4; **~ room** grupo de
   conversación, 4
**check** cheque (*m.*); (*restaurant
   check*) cuenta, 9
**cheek** mejilla
**cheese** queso, 6
**cheeseburger** hamburguesa con
   queso, 9
**chef** cocinero(a), 5
**chemistry** química, 3
**chess** ajedrez (*m.*)
**chicken** pollo, 6; **~ soup** caldo
   de pollo, 9; **~ with rice** arroz
   (*m.*) con pollo, 9; **fried ~** pollo
   frito, 9; **roasted ~** pollo
   asado, 9;
**Chilean** chileno(a), 2
**Chinese** chino(a), 2;
   **~ language** chino, 3
**chocolate** cacao
**choose** escoger (j)
**chronology** cronología
**chunk** trozo, 9
**church** iglesia, 6
**cinema** cine (*m.*), 6
**cinnamon** canela
**city** ciudad (*f.*), 6
**clam** almeja, 9
**clarity** claridad (*f.*)
**class** clase (*f.*), P; **lower ~** clase
   baja
**classroom** salón (*m.*) de clase, P
**clean the bathroom** limpiar el
   baño, 10
**clear the table** quitar la mesa, 10
**click** hacer (*irreg.*) clic, 4; **double ~**
   hacer (*irreg.*) doble clic, 4
**close** cerrar (ie), 4; **~ your
   books.** Cierren los libros. P
**close to** cerca de, 6
**closet** clóset (*m.*), 10
**clothing** ropa, 5; **article
   of ~** prenda de ropa, 8;
   **~ store** tienda de ropa, 6
**cloudburst** chaparrón (*m.*)
**cloudy: It's ~.** Está nublado. 7
**coat** abrigo, 8
**code** código
**codfish** bacalao, 9
**coffee** café (*m.*), 9

**cold** (*adj.*) frío(a); **It's ~.** Hace
   frío. 7
**Colombian** colombiano(a), 2
**color** color (*m.*), 4; **solid ~** de
   un solo color, 8
**comb** peine (*m.*), 5; **~ one's
   hair** peinarse, 5
**come** venir (*irreg.*), 5
**comic strip** tira cómica
**comma** coma
**command** mandato
**compact disc** CD, disco
   compacto (*m.*)
**comparison** comparación (*f.*), 8
**compete** competir (i, i)
**competition** competencia, 7
**complain** quejarse, 5
**complexion** tez (*f.*)
**complicity** complicidad (*f.*)
**computer** computadora, P;
   **~ center** centro
   de computación, 3;
   **~ functions** funciones (*f. pl.*)
   de la computadora, 4;
   **~ science** computación (*f.*),
   informática, 3
**conduct** conducir (zc), 5
**confection** confección (*f.*)
**connect** conectar, 4
**connection** conexión (*f.*), 4
**consider** pensar (ie) en (de), 4
**contest** concurso
**continue** seguir (i, i), 6
**continued** seguido(a)
**contraction** contracción (*f.*), 3
**contrary: on the ~** al contrario
**conversation** conversación (*f.*)
**cook** cocinar, 2; cocer (-z) (ue), 9;
   cocinero(a), 5
**cookie** galleta, 9
**cool, chévere; It's cool.** Hace
   fresco. 7
**copper** cobre (*m.*)
**corn** maíz (*m.*)
**corner** esquina, 6
**correct** corregir (i, i) (j)
**Costa Rican** costarricense
   (*m., f.*), 2
**cotton** algodón (*m.*), 8
**country** país (*m.*)
**courage** coraje (*m.*)
**course: basic ~** curso básico, 3
**courtesy** cortesía, 4
**cousin** primo(a), 5
**cowboy** vaquero
**cradle** cuna

**create** crear
**creative** creativo(a)
**crew** tripulación (*f.*)
**crowd** muchedumbre (*f.*)
**cruise ship** crucero
**crushed** molido(a), 9
**Cuban** cubano(a), 2
**culinary** culinario(a)
**culture** cultura
**cumin** comino, 9
**cup** taza, 9
**curtain** cortina, 10
**custard** flan (*m.*), 9
**customer** cliente (*m., f.*), 8
**cutting** recorte (*m.*)
**cyberspace** ciberespacio, 4
**cycling** ciclismo, 7

# D

**daily** cotidiano(a)
**dam** presa
**dance** bailar, 2; baile (*m.*), 3
**danger** peligro, 7
**dangerous** peligroso(a), 7
**date** fecha, 3; **blind ~** cita a
   ciegas
**daughter** hija, 5
**daughter-in-law** nuera, 5
**dawn** amanecer (zc)
**day** día (*m.*), 3; **~ before
   yesterday** anteayer, 7;
   **~ of the week** día de la
   semana, 3; **every ~** todos
   los días, 3
**December** diciembre, 1
**decoration** decoración (*f.*), 10
**definite** definido(a), 1
**degree** grado
**Delighted to meet you.**
   Encantado(a). 1
**demand** exigir (j)
**demonstrate** demostrar (ue)
**demonstrative** demostrativo(a),
   6
**denim** mezclilla, 8
**dentist** dentista (*m., f.*), 5
**deodorant** desodorante (*m.*), 5
**describe** describir, 2
**deserve** merecer (zc)
**design** diseño; **graphic ~** diseño
   gráfico, 3
**designer: graphic ~** diseñador(a)
   gráfico(a), 5
**desire** afán (*m.*); anhelo
**desk** escritorio, P

**dessert** postre (*m.*), 9
**detail** detalle (*m.*)
**determined** resuelto (*p.p. of* resolver)
**develop** desarrollar
**dialect** dialecto
**dictionary** diccionario, P
**die** morirse (ue, u), 8
**difference** diferencia
**difficult** difícil, 4
**digital camera** cámara digital, 4
**dining room** comedor (*m.*), 10
**dinner** cena
**dirty** sucio(a)
**disappointment** desilusión (*f.*)
**disaster** desastre (*m.*)
**discount** descuento, 8
**discover** descubrir, 3
**disgusting** asco
**dish: main ~** plato principal, 9
**dishonest** mentiroso(a), 2
**dishwasher** lavaplatos (*m. s.*), 10
**disillusionment** desengaño
**dispatch** despachar
**disqualify** descalificar (qu)
**distance** trecho
**diversity** diversidad (*f.*)
**divide** dividir
**do** hacer (*irreg.*), 5; **a lot to ~** mucho que hacer; **~ the homework for tomorrow.** Hagan la tarea para mañana. P; **~ the recycling** hacer el reciclaje, 10
**doctor** doctor(a); médico(a), 5
**dog** perro(a), 2
**doll** muñeca
**dollar** dólar (*m.*)
**Dominican** dominicano(a), 2
**door** puerta, P
**dorm** residencia estudiantil, 3; dormitorio estudiantil, 6
**download** descargar, bajar, 4
**downpour** chaparrón (*m.*)
**downtown** centro de la ciudad, 10
**dozen** docena, 9
**drawing** dibujo, P
**dream** sueño; **~ (about)** soñar (ue) con, 4
**drenched** empapado(a)
**dress** vestido, 8; **~ (someone)** vestir (i, i), 5; **get dressed** vestirse (i, i), 5
**dresser** cómoda, tocador (*m.*), 10
**drink** beber, 3
**drive** manejar, conducir (zc), 5

**driver's license** licencia de manejar
**dry (something)** secar (qu), 5; **~ one's hair** secarse (qu) el pelo, 5
**dryer** secadora, 10
**during** mientras, por, 10
**dust** polvo; **~ the furniture** sacudir los muebles, 10
**DVD / CD-ROM drive** lector (*m.*) de CD-ROM / DVD, 4

# E

**early** temprano, 3
**earphones** audífonos (*m. pl.*), 4
**earring** arete (*m.*), pendiente (*m.*), 8
**earth** tierra
**easy** fácil, 4
**eat** comer, 3; **~ dinner** cenar, 2
**e-book** libro electrónico, P
**economics** **economía, 3**
**Ecuadoran** ecuatoriano(a), 2
**edit** redactar
**education** educación (*f.*), 3
**egg** huevo, 6; **~ sunny-side up** huevo estrellado, 9; **scrambled ~** huevo revuelto, 9
**egotistic** egoísta, 2
**eight** ocho, P; **~ hundred** ochocientos(as), 8
**eighteen** dieciocho, P
**eighth** octavo(a), 10
**eighty** ochenta, P
**either . . . or** o... o, 6
**electricity** electricidad (*f.*)
**electronic** electrónico(a); **~ games store** tienda de juegos electrónicos, 6; **~ mailbox** buzón (*m.*) electrónico, 4; **~ notebook** asistente (*m.*) electrónico, 4; **electronics** aparatos electrónicos, 4
**elephant** elefante (*m.*)
**eleven** once, P
**e-mail** correo electrónico, e-mail (*m.*), P
**embarrass** avergonzar (ue) (c)
**embarrassed** avergonzado(a)
**embroidered** bordado(a), 8
**emotion** emoción (*f.*), 4

**emphasize** destacar (qu), enfatizar (c)
**empty** vacío(a)
**encounter** encuentro
**end** cabo; fin (*m.*)
**engineer** ingeniero(a), 5
**engineering** ingeniería, 3
**English** inglés (inglesa), 2; **~ language** inglés (*m.*), 3
**enjoy** gozar (c); **~ (life)** disfrutar (la vida)
**enough: it is ~** basta
**enroll** alistar
**entertain** entretener (*like* tener)
**entertaining** divertido(a), 2
**environment** medio ambiente (*m.*)
**equator** ecuador (*m.*)
**era** etapa
**essay** ensayo
**Europe** Europa
**evaluation** calificación (*f.*)
**evasion** sorteo
**even** aun
**evening** noche (*f.*); **during the ~** por la noche, 3; **Good ~.** Buenas noches. 1; **in the ~** (*with precise time*) de la noche, 3
**everything** todo
**everywhere** por dondequiera
**example** ejemplo, 10
**exchange** intercambiar; **in ~ for** a cambio de; **~ rate** cambio
**Excuse me.** Disculpe. Perdón. 4
**exercise** hacer (*irreg.*) ejercicio, 7
**exhibit** exhibir
**exotic** exótico(a)
**expensive: It's (too) ~.** Es (demasiado) caro(a). 8
**express preferences** expresar preferencias, 2
**expression** expresión (*f.*), 1
**extroverted** extrovertido(a), 2
**eyeglasses** lentes (*m. pl.*), anteojos (*m. pl.*)

# F

**fabric** tela, 8
**fact** dato, hecho
**Fahrenheit degree** grado Fahrenheit, 7
**fairy tale** cuento de hadas

**fall**   caer (*irreg.*);
(***autumn***)   otoño, 7;
**~ asleep**   dormirse (ue, u), 5;
**~ back on**   recurrir; **~ in love**   enamorarse, 5
**false**   falso(a)
**family**   familia;
**~ member**   pariente (*m., f.*), 5;
**nuclear ~**   familia nuclear, 5;
**~ tree**   árbol (*m.*) genealógico
**fantasy**   fantasía
**far from**   lejos de, 6
**fascinate**   fascinar, 4
**fashion** (*adj.*) de modas
**fashion**   moda, 8;
**~ magazine**   revista de moda
**fashionable: (not) to be ~**   (no) estar de moda, 8
**fast**   rápido(a), 4
**fat**   gordo(a), 2
**father**   padre (*m.*), papá (*m.*), 5
**father-in-law**   suegro, 5
**fax: external / internal ~**   fax (*m.*) externo / interno, 4
**February**   febrero, 1
**feed the dog**   darle de comer al perro, 10
**feel**   sentir (ie, i), 4; **~ like (doing)**   tener (*irreg.*) ganas de, 7
**feminine**   femenino(a)
**field of study**   campo de estudio, 3
**fifteen**   quince, P
**fifth**   quinto(a), 10
**fifty**   cincuenta, P
**file**   archivar, 4; archivo, 4
**fill**   llenar
**final**   final
**finally**   por fin, 9
**financial**   financiero(a)
**find**   encontrar (ue), 4
**find out**   averiguar (gü)
**Fine, thank you.**   Bien, gracias. 1
**fire**   fuego; **~ fighter** bombero(a), 5
**fired**   despedido(a)
**fireplace**   chimenea, 10
**first**   primer(o)(a), 10;
**~ floor**   primer piso, 10
**fish**   pescar (qu), 7; pez (*m.*) (*alive*); pescado (*caught*), 9
**fit**   apto(a); **It fits nicely / badly.**   Me queda bien / mal. 8
**five**   cinco, P;
**~ hundred**   quinientos(as), 8;
**~ thousand**   cinco mil, 8

**flash drive**   la memoria flash, el pendrive, 4
**flat**   llano(a)
**flavor**   sabor (*m.*)
**floating**   flotador(a)
**floor**   piso; **first ~** primer piso, 10
**flour**   harina, 9
**flourish**   florecer (zc)
**flower**   florecer (zc); flor (*f.*)
**fold**   doblar, 6

**following**   siguiente
**fondness**   cariño
**food**   comida, 6
**food processor**   procesador (*m.*) de comida, 10
**fool**   engañar
**foot: on ~**   a pie, 6
**football**   fútbol americano, 7
**footprint**   huella
**for**   para, por, 10; **~ example**   por ejemplo, 10
**forbid**   prohibir, 10

**fork**   tenedor (*m.*), 9
**fortress**   fortaleza
**forty**   cuarenta, P
**forum**   foro, 4
**founder**   fundador(a)
**four**   cuatro, P; **~ hundred** cuatrocientos(as), 8
**fourteen**   catorce, P
**fourth**   cuarto(a), 10
**free**   libre
**freezer**   congelador (*m.*), 10
**French**   francés ( francesa), 2;
**~ fries**   papas fritas, 9;
**~ language**   francés (*m.*), 3
**frequently**   frecuentemente, 4
**fresh**   fresco(a), 9
**Friday**   viernes (*m.*), 2
**fried**   frito(a), 9
**friend**   amigo(a), P; cuate(a)
**from the**   del (de + el), 3
**front: in ~ of**   delante de, frente a, enfrente de, 6
**frozen**   congelado(a), 9
**fruit**   fruta, 6; **~ juice**   jugo de fruta, 9; **~ salad**   ensalada de fruta, 9; **~ shake**   licuado de fruta
**fry**   freír (i, i), 9
**fun**   divertido(a), 2
**function**   funcionar, 4
**funny**   cómico(a), 2

**furious**   furioso(a), 4
**furniture**   muebles (*m. pl.*), 10

# G

**gallon**   galón (*m.*), 9
**game**   partido, 7; **interactive ~** juego interactivo, 4
**gang**   pandilla
**garage**   garaje (*m.*), 10
**garbage**   basura, 10
**garden**   jardín (*m.*), 10
**garlic**   ajo, 9
**generally**   por lo general, 9
**generous**   generoso(a), 2
**genre**   género
**gentle**   apacible
**geography**   geografía, 3
**German**   alemán (alemana), 2;
**~ language**   alemán (*m.*), 3
**get**   conseguir (i, i), 8;
**~ ahead**   adelantar;
**~ cold**   enfriarse, 9;
**~ divorced**   divorciarse, 5;
**~ down from**   bajar, 6;
**~ dressed**   vestirse (i, i), 5;
**~ engaged**   comprometerse, 5;
**~ married**   casarse, 5;
**~ off of** (*a bus, etc.*)   bajar, 6;
**~ on**   subir, 6;
**~ ready**   prepararse, 5;
**~ separated**   separarse, 5;
**~ sick**   enfermarse, 5;
**~ together**   reunirse, 5;
**~ up**   levantarse, 5
**gift**   regalo
**girl**   chica, P; muchacha, P; niña, P
**girlfriend**   novia
**give**   dar (*irreg.*), 5;
**~ as a gift**   regalar, 8;
**~ directions**   decir (*irreg.*) cómo llegar, 6; **~ personal information**   dar (*irreg.*) información personal, 1;
**~ preference**   anteponer;
**~ someone a bath**   bañar, 5;
**~ the time**   dar (*irreg.*) la hora, 3
**glass**   vaso, 9
**glove**   guante (*m.*), 8
**go**   acudir; ir (*irreg.*), 3;
**~ away**   irse (*irreg.*), 5;
**~ off** (*alarm clock, etc.*)   sonar (ue), 4; **~ offline**   cortar la conexión, 4; **~ online**   hacer (*irreg.*) una conexión, 4;

**~ out** salir (*irreg.*), 5;
**~ shopping** hacer (*irreg.*)
las compras, 6; ir de compras,
8; **~ straight** seguir (i, i) (g)
derecho; **~ to bed** acostarse
(ue), 5; **~ up** subir, 6
**goal** meta
**gold** oro, 8
**golden** dorado(a), 9
**golf** golf (*m.*), 7
**good** bueno(a), 2; bondadoso(a)
**goodbye** adiós, 1
**gossip** chisme (*m.*)
**gossiping** chismoso(a)
**governor** gobernador(a)
**grade** nota, P
**granddaughter** nieta, 5
**grandfather** abuelo, 5
**grandmother** abuela, 5
**grandson** nieto, 5
**grape** uva, 9
**graph** gráfica
**gray** gris, 4
**great** chévere (*Cuba, Puerto
Rico*); grande, 2
**greater** mayor, 8
**green** verde, 4
**greet** saludar, 1
**greeting** saludo
**grilled** asado(a); a la parrilla, 9
**ground** molido(a), 9; tierra
**group** (*m.*) conjunto; **group**
(*v.*) juntar
**growth** crecimiento
**Guatemalan** guatemalteco(a), 2
**guess** adivinar;
**Guess.** Adivina. P
**guinea pig** cuy (*m.*)
**guitar** guitarra, 2
**gymnasium** gimnasio, 3

# H

**hair: blond ~** pelo rubio, 2;
**brown ~** pelo castaño, 2
**hairdresser** peluquero(a), 5
**half** mitad (*f.*)
**half-brother** medio hermano, 5
**half-sister** media hermana, 5
**hallway** pasillo, 10
**ham** jamón (*m.*), 6
**hamburger** hamburguesa, 9
**handicrafts** artesanía
**handkerchief** pañuelo
**handsome** hermoso(a);
guapo(a), 2

**handtowel** toalla de mano, 5
**happiness** dicha; felicidad (*f.*)
**happy** contento(a), 4
**hard** duro(a); **~ drive** disco
duro, 4
**hardly ever** rara vez
**hardware** hardware (*m.*), 4
**hard-working** trabajador(a), 2
**haste** prisa
**hat** sombrero, 8
**hatred** odio
**have** tener (*irreg.*), 1; **~ a
fight** pelearse, 5; **~ a soft
drink** tomar un refresco, 2;
**~ fun** divertirse (ie, i), 5;
**~ the urge to** tener (*irreg.*)
ganas de, 7; **~ to** (+ *inf.*) tener
(*irreg.*) que (+ *inf.*), 1
**he** él, 1
**health** salud (*f.*), 3
**healthy** saludable
**hear** oír (*irreg.*), 5
**heat** calentar (ie), 9
**heavy** fuerte, 9
**height** altitud (*f.*), altura; (*of a
person*) estatura
**hello** hola, ¿Aló? (*on the
phone*), 1
**helmet** casco
**help** ayudar; ayuda
**her** (*pron.*) ella, 8; (*adj.*) su, 3;
suyo(a), 10; **to / for ~** le, 8
**here** aquí, 6
**heritage** herencia
**hers** (*pron.*) suyo(a), 10
**hide** esconder
**hike** hacer (*irreg.*) alpinismo,
practicar (qu) alpinismo, 7
**him** (*pron.*) él, 8; **to / for ~** le, 8
**his** (*adj.*) su, 3; (*adj., pron.*)
suyo(a), 10
**Hispanic** hispano(a)
**history** historia, 3
**hoax** engaño
**hockey: field ~** hockey (*m.*)
sobre hierba, 7; **ice ~**
hockey (*m.*) sobre hielo, 7
**hole** pozo
**home** hogar (*m.*)
**homeless** sin hogar
**homemade** casero(a)
**homework** tarea, P
**Honduran** hondureño(a), 2
**honest** honesto(a)
**hope** esperanza; esperar, 10
**hospital** hospital (*m.*), 6

**hot: be ~** tener (*irreg.*) calor, 7;
**~ dog** perro caliente, 9;
**It's ~.** Hace calor. 7
**hour** hora
**house** casa, 6; **the ~ special** la
especialidad de la casa, 9
**housechore** quehacer (*m.*)
doméstico, 10
**housing** vivienda
**how?** ¿cómo? 3; **~ are things
going?** ¿Qué tal? 1; **~ are
you?** (*form. s.*) ¿Cómo
está (usted)? / (*form. pl.*)
¿Cómo están (ustedes)? /
(*s. fam.*) ¿Cómo estás (tú)? 1;
**~ can I help you?** ¿En
qué puedo servirle? 8; **~ do
you say . . . ?** ¿Cómo se
dice…? P; **~ do you wish to
pay?** ¿Cómo desea pagar?, 8;
**~ many?** ¿cuántos(as)? 3;
**~ much?** ¿cuánto(a)? 3;
**~ much does it cost?** ¿Cuánto
cuesta? 8; **How's it going with
you?** ¿Cómo te / le(s) va? 1
**humanities** humanidades
(*f. pl.*), 3
**humble** humilde
**humid** húmedo(a)
**hunger** hambre (*f. but* el hambre)
**hurry** prisa; **be in a ~** tener
(*irreg.*) prisa, 7
**husband** esposo, 5
**hymn** himno

# I

**I** yo, 1
**ice: (vanilla / chocolate)
~ cream** helado (de vainilla /
de chocolate), 9;
**~ hockey** hockey (*m.*) sobre
hielo, 7; **~ skate** patinar sobre
hielo, 7
**identity** identidad (*f.*)
**immigration** inmigración (*f.*)
**impatient** impaciente, 2
**impressive** impresionante
**impulsive** impulsivo(a), 2
**in** en; por, 10; **~ charge
of** encargardo de; **~ order to**
(+ *inf.*) para, 10; **~ relation
to** en cuanto a; **~ short** en
resumen; **~ spite of** a pesar
de; **~ the direction of** para,
10; **the "in" place** "antro"

**inch** pulgada

**increase** acrecentar (ie), aumentar

**incredible** increíble

**indefinite** indefinido(a), 1

**index** índice (*m.*)

**Indian** indio(a), 2

**indigenous** indígena

**influence** influir (y); influencia

**ingredient** ingrediente (*m.*), 9

**inhabitant** habitante (*m., f.*)

**in-laws** familia política, 5

**inline skate (rollerblade)** patinar en línea, 7

**inside of** dentro de, 6; **~ the house** dentro de la casa, 10

**insist** insistir, 10

**install** instalar, 4

**instead of** en vez de

**instructor** instructor(a), P

**intelligent** inteligente, 2

**intention** fin (*m.*)

**interactive whiteboard** pizarra interactiva, P

**interest** interesar, 4

**interesting** interesante, 2

**Internet** Internet (*m.* or *f.*), red (*f.*); **~ provider** proveedor (*m.*) de acceso, 4

**interpreter** intérprete (*m., f.*)

**intimate** íntimo(a)

**introduce someone** presentar a alguien, 1

**introverted** introvertido(a), 2

**invest** invertir

**iron** planchar, 10; (*metal*) hierro; (*appliance*) plancha, 10

**irresponsible** irresponsable, 2

**Italian** italiano(a), 2; **~ language** italiano, 3

**its** (*adj.*) su, 3; (*pron.*) suyo(a), 10

## J

**jacket** (*suit jacket, blazer*) saco; (*outdoor, non-suit coat*) chaqueta 8

**January** enero, 1

**Japanese** japonés (japonesa), 2; **~ language** japonés (*m.*), 3

**jealous** celoso(a); **be ~** tener (*irreg.*) celos

**jealously** celosamente

**jeans** jeans (*m. pl.*), 8

**jewelry store** joyería, 6

**jewelry** joyas (*f. pl.*), 8

**join** juntarse

**joke** broma

**journalism** periodismo, 3

**journalist** periodista (*m., f.*), 5

**July** julio, 1

**June** junio, 1

## K

**keep: (oneself) separate** mantenerse apartado

**key** (*on a keyboard*) tecla, 4

**keyboard** teclado, 4

**kilo** kilo, 9; **half a ~** medio kilo, 9

**kind** bondadoso(a)

**king** rey (*m.*)

**kiss** besar

**kitchen** cocina, 10

**knapsack** mochila, P

**knife** cuchillo, 9

**know: ~ a person** conocer (zc), 5; **~ a fact, ~ how to** saber (*irreg.*), 5

**Korean** coreano(a), 2

## L

**lake** lago, 7

**lamp** lámpara, 10

**language** idioma (*m.*), lengua, 3

**laptop computer** computadora portátil, P

**late** tarde, 3

**later** luego, 5

**latest: the ~** lo último

**laugh** reírse (*irreg.*), 5

**laundry room** lavandería, 10

**lawn** césped (*m.*), 10; **mow the ~** cortar el césped, 10

**lawyer** abogado(a), 5

**lazy** perezoso(a), 2

**learn** aprender, 3

**learning** aprendizaje (*m.*)

**leather** piel (*f.*), cuero, 8

**leave** dejar, 2; salir (*irreg.*), irse (*irreg.*), 5

**left: to the ~** a la izquierda, 6

**lemonade** limonada, 9

**less** menor, 8; **~ than** menos que, 8

**lesson** lección (*f.*), P

**level** nivel (*m.*)

**life** vida

**lifejacket** salvavidas (*m. s.*)

**lift** levantar, 5; **~ weights** levantar pesas, 2

**light** luz (*f.*); (*adj.*) ligero(a), 9

**like** gustar; **~ a lot** encantar, 4; **(They / You [*pl.*]) ~ . . .** A... les gusta... 2; **He / She likes . . .** A... le gusta... 2; **I / You ~ . . .** A mí / ti me / te gusta... 2; **I'd ~** (+ *inf.*) quisiera (+ *inf.*), 6; Me gustaría (+ *inf.*)... 6

**Likewise.** Igualmente. 1

**linen** lino, 8

**linguistic** lingüístico(a)

**link** enlace (*m.*), 4

**lip** labio

**listen** escuchar; **~ to music** escuchar música, 2; **~ to the audio** Escuchen el audio. P

**liter** litro, 9

**literature** literatura, 3

**little** poco, 4

**live** vivir, 3, ocupar

**livestock** ganadería

**living room** sala, 10

**loan** préstamo, 8; (*v.*) prestar, 8

**lobster** langosta, 9

**located** ubicado(a); **is ~** queda

**long for** apetecer (zc)

**look: ~ for** buscar (qu), 2

**lose** perder (ie), 4; **~ oneself** perderse (ie)

**love** querer (*irreg.*), 4; amar; amor (*m.*), cariño

**lover** amante (*m., f.*)

**lunch** almuerzo, 9

**luxurious** lujoso(a)

**lying** mentiroso(a), 2

## M

**made:** It's ~ out of . . . Está hecho(a) de... 8; **They're ~ out of . . .** Están hechos(as) de... 8

**magazine** revista

**mailbox** buzón (*m.*)

**majority** mayoría

**make** hacer (*irreg.*), 5; **~ sure** asegurarse; **~ the bed** hacer la cama, 10

**makeup** maquillaje (*m.*), 5

**mall** centro comercial, 6

**man** hombre (*m.*), P

**manager** gerente (*m., f.*), 5

**manly** varonil

**manners**  modales (*m. pl.*)
**March**  marzo, 1
**marital status**  estado civil
**mark**  marcar (qu)
**market**  mercado, 6; **open-air ~ ,
farmer's ~**  mercado al aire
libre, 6
**marketing**  mercadeo, 3
**masculine**  masculino(a)
**match**  emparejar; (*sports*)
partido, 7
**mathematics**  matemáticas
(*f. pl.*), 3
**matter (to someone)**  importar, 4
**May**  mayo, 1
**mayonnaise**  mayonesa, 9
**mayor**  alcalde (alcaldesa)
**me**  mí, 8; **to / for ~**  me, 8;
**with ~**  conmigo, 8
**mean: It means . . .**  Significa... P
**meaning**  significado
**means of transportation**  medios
de transporte, 6
**measure**  medir (i, i)
**measurement**  medida, 9
**meat**  carne (*f.*), 9
**meatball**  albóndiga
**mechanic**  mecánico(a), 5
**media center**  centro de
comunicaciones, 3
**medicine**  medicina, 3
**meditation**  meditación (*f.*)
**meet**  conocer (zc), reunirse, 5
**meeting**  encuentro, reunión (*f.*)
**melon**  melón (*m.*), 9
**menu**  menú (*m.*), 9
**messenger**  mensajero(a)
**Mexican**  mexicano(a), 2
**microphone**  micrófono, 4
**microwave**  microondas (*m. s.*), 10
**midnight**  medianoche (*f.*), 3
**mild**  apacible
**milk**  leche (*f.*), 6
**mine**  (*pron.*) mío, 10
**mirror**  espejo, 10
**Miss**  señorita (*abbrev.* Srta.), 1
**missionary**  misionero(a)
**mix**  mezclar, 9; mezcla
**mixed**  mixto(a)
**modem: external / internal ~**
módem (*m.*) externo /
interno, 4
**Monday**  lunes (*m.*), 3
**money**  dinero
**monitor**  monitor (*m.*), 4
**monkey**  mono

**month**  mes (*m.*), 3; **last ~**  mes
pasado, 7
**mop the floor**  trapear el piso, 10
**more**  más; **~ than**  más que, 8
**morning**  mañana, 3; **during the ~**
por la mañana, 3; **Good ~.**
Buenos días. 1; **in the ~**
(*with precise time*) de la
mañana, 3
**mortality**  mortalidad (*f.*)
**mother**  madre (*f.*), mamá, 5;
**Mother's Day**  día (*m.*) de las
Madres, 3
**mother-in-law**  suegra, 5
**mountain**  monte (*m.*);
**~ range**  cordillera
**mountainous**  montañoso(a)
**mouse**  ratón (*m.*), 4
**move**  (*change residence*)
mudarse
**mow the lawn**  cortar el
césped, 10
**Mr.**  señor (*abbrev.* Sr.), 1
**Mrs.**  señora (*abbrev.* Sra.), 1
**Ms.**  señorita (*abbrev.* Srta.), 1
**much**  mucho, 4
**mud**  lodo
**museum**  museo, 6
**music**  música, 3
**mustard**  mostaza, 9
**my**  (*adj.*) mi, 3; (*pron.*) mío(a), 10;
**~ pleasure.**  Mucho gusto. Un
placer. 1

# N

**name**  llamar, 2; nombre (*m.*);
**full ~**  nombre (*m.*) completo;
**My ~ is . . .**  Me llamo…, Mi
nombre es…, 1
**napkin**  servilleta, 9
**narrator**  narrador(a)
**nationality**  nacionalidad (*f.*), 2
**nature**  naturaleza
**navigation**  navegación (*f.*)
**necklace**  collar (*m.*), 8
**need**  necesitar, 2
**neighbor**  vecino(a), 6
**neighborhood**  barrio, colonia, 1
**neither**  tampoco, 2; **~ . . .
nor**  ni... ni, 6
**nephew**  sobrino, 5
**nervous**  nervioso(a), 4
**never**  nunca, 5; jamás, 6
**nevertheless**  sin embargo
**new**  novedoso(a)

**news: ~ group**  grupo de
noticias, 4
**newspaper**  periódico
**next**  próximo(a); **~ to**  al lado
de, 6; **~ to last**  penúltimo(a)
**Nicaraguan**  nicaragüense
(*m., f.*), 2
**nice**  simpático(a), 2
**nickname**  apodo
**niece**  sobrina, 5
**night**  noche (*f.*), 3; **Good ~.**
Buenas noches. 1; **last ~**
anoche, 7
**nine hundred**  novecientos(as), 8
**nine**  nueve, P
**nineteen**  diecinueve, P
**ninety**  noventa, P
**ninth**  noveno(a), 10
**no one**  nadie, 6
**nobody**  nadie, 6
**none**  ningún, ninguno(a), 6
**noodle soup**  sopa de fideos, 9
**noon**  mediodía (*m.*), 3
**normal**  normal, 4
**North America**  Norteamérica
**not: ~ any**  ningún, ninguno(a),
6; **~ either**  tampoco, 2;
**~ much**  no mucho, 1
**notebook**  cuaderno, P
**notes**  apuntes (*m. pl.*), P
**nothing**  nada, 1
**noun**  sustantivo
**novel**  novedoso(a)
**novelist**  novelista (*m., f.*)
**November**  noviembre, 1
**novice**  novato(a)
**number**  número, 8
**nurse**  enfermero(a), 5

# O

**obey**  hacer (*irreg.*) caso
**obtain**  conseguir (i, i), 8
**October**  octubre, 1
**of: ~ course**  cómo no, 6; por
supuesto, 10; **~ the**  del
(de + el), 3
**offer: special ~**  oferta
especial, 8
**office**  oficina, 6
**old**  viejo(a), 2
**old-fashioned**  anticuado(a)
**olive oil**  aceite (*m.*) de oliva, 9
**on**  en, sobre, encima de, 6;
**~ behalf of**  por, 10
**once**  una vez, 9

**one** uno, P; ~ **hundred** cien, P; ~ **hundred and** ~ ciento uno, 8; ~ **hundred thousand** cien mil, 8; ~ **million** millón (*m.*), un millón, 8; ~ **thousand** mil (*m.*), 8

**onion** cebolla, 9

**online** en línea, 4

**only** único(a)

**open** abrir, 3; ~ **your books.** Abran los libros. P

**opposite** enfrente de, frente a, 6; opuesto(a)

**orange** (*color*) anaranjado(a), 4; (*fruit*) naranja, 9

**order** ordenar, 9; mandar, 10

**ordinal number** número ordinal, 10

**originate** originar

**ought** deber (+ *inf.*), 3

**our** (*adj.*) nuestro(a)(s), 3

**ours** (*pron.*) nuestro(a)(s), 10

**outline** bosquejo

**outside of** fuera de, 6; ~ **the house** fuera de la casa, 10

**outskirts** afueras (*f. pl.*), 10

**outstanding** sobresaliente

**oven** horno

**overcoming** superación (*f.*)

**owner** dueño(a), 5

# P

**package** paquete (*m.*), 9

**page** página, P

**paint** pintar, 2

**painting** pintura, 3; cuadro, 10

**Panamanian** panameño(a), 2

**pants** pantalones (*m. pl.*), 8

**paper** papel (*m.*), P

**parachute** paracaídas (*m. s.*)

**paragraph** párrafo

**Paraguayan** paraguayo(a), 2

**Pardon me.** Con permiso. 4

**parents** padres (*m. pl.*), 5

**park** parque (*m.*), 6

**parking lot** estacionamiento, 6

**parsley** perejil (*m.*)

**pass (by)** pasar, 2

**password** contraseña, 4

**patient** paciente (*m., f.*), 2

**patio** patio, 10

**paving stone** baldosa

**pay** pagar (gu), 9; ~ **attention** hacer (*irreg.*) caso

**payment: form of** ~ método de pago, 8

**PDF file** archivo PDF, 4

**pea** guisante (*m.*), 9

**peace** paz (*f.*)

**peel** pelar, 9

**pencil** lápiz (*m.*), P

**penguin** pingüino

**people** gente (*f.*)

**pepper** pimienta, 9

**percentage** porcentaje (*m.*)

**perhaps** quizás, tal vez

**period** (*punctuation*) punto; trecho

**permit** permitir, 10

**personality** personalidad (*f.*); ~ **trait** característica de la personalidad, 2

**Peruvian** peruano(a), 2

**pharmacy** farmacia, 6

**philanthropic** filantrópico(a)

**philosophy** filosofía, 3

**photo** foto (*f.*), P

**physical** físico(a), 5; ~ **appearance** apariencia física; ~ **trait** característica física, 2

**physics** física, 3

**piano** piano, 2

**picturesque** pintoresco(a)

**piece** pedazo, 9

**pillow** almohada

**pink** rosado(a), 4

**pirate** pirata (*m.*)

**pizzeria** pizzería, 6

**place** lugar (*m.*), sitio

**plaid** a cuadros, 8

**plain** llanura

**plate** plato, 9

**play** jugar (ue) (gu), 4; ~ **a musical instrument** tocar (qu) un instrumento musical, 2; ~ **sports** practicar (qu) deportes, 2; ~ **tennis (baseball, etc.)** jugar tenis (béisbol, etc), 7

**playful** juguetón (juguetona)

**plaza** plaza, 6

**please** por favor, 1

**pleasure: A** ~ **to meet you.** Mucho gusto en conocerte. 1

**plot** trama

**plumber** plomero(a), 5

**poet** poeta (poetisa)

**poetry** poesía

**point:** ~ **out** marcar (qu), señalar; **to the** ~ al grano

**policeman (policewoman)** policía (*m., f.*), 5

**political** político(a); ~ **science** ciencias políticas (*f. pl.*), 3

**polka-dotted** de lunares, 8

**poor** pobre

**populate** poblar (ue)

**pork chop** chuleta de puerco, 6

**portable CD / MP3 player** CD portátil / MP3, P

**Portuguese** portugués (portuguesa), 2

**post office** oficina de correos, 6

**potato:** ~ **chips** papitas fritas, 6; ~ **salad** ensalada de papa

**pound** libra, 9

**power** poder (*m.*)

**powerful** poderoso(a)

**practice** practicar (qu)

**prefer** preferir (ie, i), 4

**preference** preferencia

**prenuptial agreement** contrato prenupcial

**preparation** preparación (*f.*), 9

**prepare** preparar, 2; ~ **the food** preparar la comida, 10

**preposition** preposición (*f.*), 6

**present** (*gift*) regalo; **at the** ~ **time** en la actualidad

**pretty** bonito(a); lindo(a), 2

**price: It's a very good** ~. Está a muy buen precio. 8

**priest** sacerdote (*m.*)

**prime rib** lomo de res, 9

**print** imprimir, 3; (*patterned fabric*) estampado(a), 8; (*art*) cuadro, 10

**printer** impresora, 4

**prize** premio

**profession** profesión (*f.*), 5

**professor** profesor(a), P

**program** programa (*m.*); **anti-virus** ~ programa antivirus, 4; ~ **icon** ícono del programa, 4

**programmer** programador(a), 5

**projector** proyector, P

**promote** adelantar, promover (ue)

**pronoun** pronombre (*m.*), 1

**proud** orgulloso(a)

**provocative** provocador(a)

**psychology** psicología, 3

**public:** ~ **communications** comunicación (*f.*) pública, 3; ~ **relations** publicidad (*f.*), 3

**Puerto Rican** puertorriqueño(a), 2

**purple** morado(a), 4

**purpose** propósito
**purse** bolsa, 8
**push** oprimir
**put** poner (*irreg.*), 5; **~ away the clothes** guardar la ropa, 10; **~ my toys where they belong** poner mis juguetes en su lugar, 10; **~ on (clothing)** ponerse (la ropa), 5; **~ on makeup** maquillarse, 5

# Q

**quality** calidad (*f.*); **of good (high) ~** de buena (alta) calidad, 8
**queen** reina
**questionnaire** cuestionario
**quotation** cita

# R

**raffle** sorteo
**railroad** ferrocarril (*m.*)
**rain** llover (ue); **~ forest** bosque (*m.*) tropical, bosque (*m.*) pluvial; **It's raining.** Está lloviendo. (Llueve.), 7
**raincoat** impermeable (*m.*), 8
**raise** levantar, 5
**ranch** estancia
**rank** rango
**rather** bastante, 4
**raw** crudo(a), 9
**razor** rasuradora, 5; **electric ~** máquina de afeitar, 5
**read** leer (y), 3; **~ Chapter 1.** Lean el Capítulo 1. P
**really** de veras
**reason** razón (*f.*)
**receive** recibir, 3
**recipe** receta, 9
**recognize** reconocer (zc)
**recommend** recomendar (ie), 10
**record** grabar, 4
**recruit** alistar
**recycling** reciclaje (*m.*), 10
**red** rojo(a), 4
**redheaded** pelirrojo(a), 2
**reduced: It's ~.** Está rebajado(a). 8
**reflect** reflejar
**reflection** reflexión (*f.*)
**refrigerator** refrigerador (*m.*), 10
**relate** contar (ue), 4
**relative** pariente (*m., f.*), 5

**relax** relajarse, 5
**remain** quedar(se)
**remember** recordar (ue)
**renovate** renovar (ue)
**renown** renombre (*m.*)
**rent** alquiler (*m.*); **~ videos** alquilar videos, 2; **~ movies** alquilar películas, 2
**repeat** repetir (i, i), 4; **~.** Repitan. P
**report** informe (*m.*)
**request** pedir (i, i), 10
**require** requerir (ie, i), 10
**residential neighborhood** barrio residencial, 10
**resort to** recurrir
**respond** responder, 1
**responsible** responsable, 2
**rest** descansar, 2
**restaurant** restaurante (*m.*), 6
**return** regresar, 2; volver (ue), 4
**revenue** ingreso
**rhyme** rima
**rich** adinerado(a)
**ride** montar; **~ a bike** montar en bicicleta, 7; **~ horseback** montar a caballo, 7
**right: to the ~** a la derecha, 6
**ring** sonar (ue), 4; anillo, 8; sortija
**ripped** rasgado
**risk** riesgo
**river** río, 7
**roasted (in the oven)** al horno, 9
**role** papel (*m.*)
**roof** techo, 10
**room** cuarto, P **roommate** compañero(a) de cuarto, P
**root** raíz (*f.*)
**rose** rosa, 4
**rough draft** borrador (*m.*)
**route** ruta
**row** remar, 7
**rower** remero(a)
**rude** descortés
**rug** alfombra, 10
**rule** regla
**run** correr, 3
**rural** campestre

# S

**sad** triste, 4
**safe** seguro(a), 7

**said: It's said . . .** Se dice…, P
**salad** ensalada, 9; **lettuce and tomato ~** ensalada de lechuga y tomate, 9; **tossed ~** ensalada mixta, 9
**sale: It's on ~.** Está en venta. 8
**salesclerk** dependiente (*m., f.*), 5
**salmon** salmón (*m.*), 9
**salt** sal (*f.*), 9
**Salvadoran** salvadoreño(a), 2
**same** mismo(a); **~ (thing)** lo mismo
**sandal** sandalia, 8
**sandwich** bocadillo, sandwich (*m.*), 9; **ham and cheese ~ with avocado** sandwich de jamón y queso con aguacate, 9
**Saturday** sábado, 2
**sausage** salchicha, 6
**save** guardar, 4
**say** decir (*irreg.*), 5; **~ good-bye** despedirse (i, i), 1
**saying** dicho
**scan** ojear
**scarcely** apenas
**scarf** bufanda, 8
**scenery** paisaje (*m.*)
**schedule** horario
**school** escuela, 3
**science** ciencia, 3
**scientific** científico(a)
**scream** gritar; grito
**screen** pantalla, 4
**script** guión (*m.*); **~ writer** guionista (*m., f.*)
**search engine** buscador (*m.*), 4
**season** estación (*f.*), 7; **dry ~** temporada de secas; **rainy ~** temporada de lluvias
**second** segundo(a), 10
**secret** secreto
**secretary** secretario(a), 5
**sections** tramos
**see** ver (*irreg.*), 5; **~ you at the usual place?** ¿Nos vemos donde siempre? 1; **~ you later.** Hasta luego. Nos vemos. 1; **~ you soon.** Hasta pronto. 1; **~ you tomorrow.** Hasta mañana. 1
**seem** parecer (zc)
**selfish** egoísta, 2
**sell** vender, 3
**send** enviar, 4; mandar, 8
**sentence** oración (*f.*)
**separate** apartado

**September** septiembre, 1
**serious** serio(a), 2
**serve** servir (i, i), 4
**set the table** poner (*irreg.*) la mesa, 9
**seven** siete, P; **~ hundred** setecientos(as), 8
**seventeen** diecisiete, P
**seventh** séptimo(a), 10
**seventy** setenta, P
**several** varios(as)
**shame** vergüenza
**shampoo** champú (*m.*), 5
**share** compartir, 3
**shark** tiburón (*m.*)
**shave oneself** afeitarse, 5
**she** ella, 1
**sheet of paper** hoja de papel, P
**shellfish** marisco, 9
**shelter** albergar (gu)
**shirt** camisa, 8
**shoe** zapato, 8; **high-heeled ~** zapato de tacón alto, 8; **tennis ~** zapato de tenis, 8
**shooting** tiroteo
**shore** orilla
**short** (*in length*) corto(a); (*in height*) bajo(a), 2
**shorts** pantalones (*m. pl.*) cortos, 8
**should** deber (+ *inf.*), 3
**shout** gritar
**show** demostrar (ue), mostrar (ue)
**shred** picar (qu), 9
**shrimp** camarón (*m.*), 9
**shy** tímido(a), 2
**sick** enfermo(a), 4
**side** lado; **on the ~ of** al lado de, 6
**sign** letrero
**silk** seda, 8
**silly** tonto(a), 2
**silver** plata, 8
**similarity** semejanza
**simple** sencillo(a)
**sincere** sincero(a), 2
**sing** cantar, 2
**singer** cantante (*m., f.*)
**single** soltero(a)
**sister (younger, older)** hermana (menor, mayor), 5
**sister-in-law** cuñada, 5
**sit down** sentarse (ie), 5
**six** seis, P; **~ hundred** seiscientos(as), 8

**sixteen** dieciséis, P
**sixth** sexto(a), 10
**sixty** sesenta, P
**size** talla, 8
**skate** patinar, 2
**ski** esquiar, 7; esquí (*m.*)
**skiing** esquí (*m.*); **downhill ~** esquí alpino, 7; **water ~** esquí acuático, 7
**skin** tez (*f.*)
**skirt** falda, 8
**slave** esclavo(a)
**sleep** dormir (ue, u), 4
**slice** pedazo, 9
**slogan** lema (*m.*)
**slow** lento(a), 4
**slowly** despacio
**small** pequeño(a), 2; **a ~ amount** un poco, 4
**smartphone** teléfono inteligente, smartphone, 4
**smile** sonreír (*irreg.*), 8; sonrisa
**snack** merienda
**snow** nevar (ie); **It's snowing.** Está nevando. (Nieva.), 7
**snowboard** tabla de snowboard, 7
**snowboarding** snowboarding, 7
**so** por eso, 10
**soap** jabón (*m.*), 5
**soccer** fútbol (*m.*), 7; **~ field** cancha, campo de fútbol, 6
**social: media director** director(a) de social media, 5; **~ networking site** red social, 4
**sock** calcetín (*m.*), 8
**sofa** sofá (*m.*), 10
**soft** suave; **~ drink** refresco, 6
**software** software (*m.*), 4
**solved** resuelto
**some** unos(as), 1; algún, alguno(a), 6
**someone** alguien, 6
**something** algo, 6; **~ vegan** algo vegano, 9
**sometimes** de vez en cuando; a veces, 5
**somewhat** bastante, 4
**son** hijo, 5
**son-in-law** yerno, 5
**sorry: I'm sorry.** Lo siento. 4
**So-so.** Regular. 1
**soul** alma (*f.*) (*but* el alma)
**sound** sonido
**soup** sopa, 9; **cold ~** gazpacho (*Spain*), 9

**source** fuente (*f.*)
**South America** Sudamérica
**souvenir** recuerdo
**sovereignty** soberanía
**spa** balneario
**Spain** España
**Spanish** español (a), 2; **~ language** español (*m.*), 3
**Spanish-speaking** hispanohablante
**speaker** conferencista (*m., f.*); altoparlante (*m., f.*), 4
**species** especie (*f.*)
**spelling** ortografía
**spicy** picante, 9
**sponsor** patrocinador(a)
**spoon** cuchara, 9
**sport** deporte (*m.*), 7; **~ activity** actividad (*f.*) deportiva, 7
**sporting goods store** tienda de equipo deportivo, 6
**sports coat** saco, 8
**spring** primavera, 7
**stadium** estadio, 6
**stairs** escaleras (*f. pl.*), 10
**state** estado, 5
**station** estación (*f.*); **train / bus ~** estación de trenes / autobuses, 6
**stationery store** papelería, 6
**statistics** estadística, 3
**steak** bistec (*m.*), 6
**steamed** al vapor, 9
**steel** acero
**step on** pisar
**stepbrother** hermanastro, 5
**stepfather** padrastro, 5
**stepmother** madrastra, 5
**stepsister** hermanastra, 5
**still** todavía; **~ life** naturaleza muerta
**stop** (*e.g., bus stop*) parada; **~ (doing something)** dejar de (+ *inf.*), 2; parar (de), 3
**store** guardar; almacén (*m.*), tienda, 6; **music (clothing, video) ~** tienda de música (ropa, videos), 6
**stove** estufa, 10
**straight ahead** todo derecho, 6
**straighten out the bedroom** arreglar el dormitorio, 10
**strategy** estrategia
**strawberry** fresa, 9

**street**  calle (*f.*), 1
**strengthen**  acrecentar (ie)
**stringed**  al hilo, 9
**striped**  rayado(a), a rayas, 8
**strong**  fuerte
**student**  estudiante (*m., f.*), P;
  **~ center**  centro estudiantil, 6
**studio**  estudio, 3
**study**  estudiar; **~ at the library
  (at home)**  estudiar en la
  biblioteca (en casa), 2;
  **~ pages . . . to . . .**
  Estudien las páginas . . .
  a . . ., P
**stupid**  tonto(a), 2
**style**  estilo; **in ~**  en onda; **out
  of ~**  pasado(a) de moda, 8
**substitute**  sustituir (y)
**suburb**  barrio residencial,
  suburbio, 10
**subway: on the ~**  en metro, 6
**success**  éxito
**suddenly**  de repente, 9
**sugar**  azúcar (*m., f.*), 9;
  **~ cane**  caña de azúcar
**suggest**  sugerir (ie, i), 8
**suggestion**  sugerencia
**suit**  traje (*m.*), 8; **bathing ~**
  traje (*m.*) de baño, 8
**summer**  verano, 7
**sun**  sol (*m.*)
**sunbathe**  tomar el sol, 2
**Sunday**  domingo, 2
**sunglasses**  gafas (*f. pl.*)
  de sol, 8
**sunlight**  luz (*f.*) solar
**sunny: It's ~.**  Hace sol. 7
**supermarket**  supermercado, 6
**support**  apoyar
**sure**  seguro(a), 4
**surf**  hacer (*irreg.*) surfing,
  practicar (qu) surfing, 7
**surpass**  sobrepasar
**surprise**  sorpresa
**surrounded**  rodeado(a)
**survey**  encuesta
**sweater**  suéter (*m.*), 8;
  chompa
**sweatsuit**  sudadera, 8
**sweep the floor**  barrer el suelo /
  el piso, 10
**sweet**  dulce (*m.*); (*adj.*)
  dulce
**swim**  bañar, 5; nadar, 7
**swimming**  natación (*f.*), 7;
  **~ pool**  piscina, 6

**symbol**  símbolo
**systematic**  sistemático(a)

# T

**table**  mesa, P; **night ~**  mesita
  de noche, 10; **set the ~**  poner
  (*irreg.*) la mesa, 9
**tablecloth**  mantel (*m.*), 9
**tablespoon**  cucharada, 9
**tablet: ~ computer**  tableta, 4
**take**  tomar, llevar; **~ a
  bath**  bañarse, 5; **~ a
  shower**  ducharse, 5; **~ off
  clothing**  quitarse la ropa, 5;
  **~ out the garbage**  sacar (qu)
  la basura, 10; **~ photos**  sacar
  (qu) fotos, 2; **~ place**  realizarse
  (c); **~ the dog for a walk**
  sacar (qu) a pasear al
  perro, 10
**talk**  hablar; **~ on the telephone**
  hablar por teléfono, 2
**tall**  alto(a), 2
**tamed**  domesticado(a)
**taste**  gusto; **to individual ~**  al
  gusto, 9
**tavern**  bodegón (*m.*)
**tea: hot ~**  té (*m.*), 9; **iced ~**  té
  (*m.*) helado, 9
**teach**  enseñar
**teacher**  maestro(a), 5
**team**  equipo, 7
**tear up**  rasgar (gu)
**teaspoon**  cucharadita, 9
**technology**  tecnología, 4
**television: ~ set**  televisor
  (*m.*), 10;
**tell**  contar (ue), 4; decir (*irreg.*),
  5; **~ the time**  decir la hora, 3
**temperature**  temperatura, 7
**ten**  diez, P; **~ thousand**  diez
  mil, 8
**tend**  tender
**tennis**  tenis (*m.*), 7;
  **~ court**  cancha de tenis, 6;
  **~ shoes**  zapatos (*m. pl.*) de
  tenis, 8
**tenth**  décimo(a), 10
**term**  término
**terrible**  fatal, terrible, 1
**terrific**  chévere (*Cuba, Puerto
  Rico*)
**text**  texto
**Thank you very much.**  Muchas
  gracias. 1

**that**  (*adj.*) ese(a), 6; (*pron.*)
  ése(a), 6; **~ over there**  (*adj.*)
  aquel (aquella), 6; (*pron.*) aquél
  (aquélla), 6
**that's why**  por eso, 10
**the**  el, la, los, las, 1
**theater**  teatro, 6
**their**  su, 3; suyo(a), 10
**theirs**  (*pron.*) suyo(a), 10
**them**  ellos(as), 8; **to / for ~**  les, 8
**then**  entonces
**theory**  teoría
**there**  allí, 6; **over ~**  allá, 6; **~ is /
  ~ are**  hay, 1
**these**  (*adj.*) estos(as), 6; (*pron.*)
  éstos(as), 6
**they**  ellos(as), 1
**thin**  delgado(a), 2
**think (about)**  pensar (ie)
  (en, de), 4
**third**  tercer(o, a), 10
**thirst**  sed (*f.*)
**thirsty: be ~**  tener (*irreg.*) sed, 7
**thirteen**  trece, P
**thirty**  treinta, P
**this**  (*adj.*) este(a), 6; (*pron.*)
  éste(a), 6
**those**  (*adj.*) esos, 6; (*pron.*)
  ésos(as), 6; **~ (over there)**
  (adj.) aquellos(as), 6; (*pron.*)
  aquéllos(as), 6
**thousands**  miles
**threat**  amenaza
**three**  tres, P; **~ hundred**
  trescientos(as), 8
**through**  por, 10
**throughout**  a través de
**throw: ~ oneself**  lanzarse (c);
  **~ out**  botar
**thunderstorm**  tormenta
**Thursday**  jueves (*m.*), 3
**time**  hora; vez (*f.*)
**times**  veces (*f. pl.*); **(two, three,
  etc.) ~ a day / per week**  (dos,
  tres, etc.) veces al día / por
  semana, 5
**tip**  propina, 9
**tired**  cansado(a), 4
**title**  titular; título, 1
**to**  a; **to the**  al (a + el), 3
**toast**  pan (*m.*) tostado, 9
**toaster**  tostadora, 10
**today**  hoy, 3; **~ is Tuesday the
  30th.**  Hoy es martes treinta. 3
**tomorrow**  mañana, 3
**too much**  demasiado, 4

**toothbrush**   cepillo de dientes, 5
**toothpaste**   pasta de dientes, 5
**top: on ~ of**   encima de, 6
**toward**   para, 10
**towel**   toalla, 5
**town**   pueblo, 6
**toy**   juguete (*m.*), 10
**track suit**   sudadera, 8
**train**   (*for sports*) entrenarse, 7; tren, 6
**trainer**   entrenador(a) (*m.*)
**trait**   característica
**translate**   traducir (zc), 5
**traveler's check**   cheque (*m.*) de viajero, 8
**treasure**   tesoro
**tree**   árbol (*m.*)
**trick**   truco
**triumph**   triunfar
**trout**   trucha, 9
**true**   verdad
**truly**   de veras
**trumpet**   trompeta, 2
**try** intentar, tratar de;   **I'm going to ~ it on.**   Voy a probármelo(la). 8
**t-shirt**   camiseta, 8
**Tuesday**   martes (*m.*), 3
**tuna**   atún (*m.*), 9
**turkey**   pavo, 6
**turn**   cruzar (c), doblar, 6; viraje (*m.*); **~ in**   entregar; **~ in your homework.**   Entreguen la tarea. P; **~ off**   apagar (gu), 2
**twelve**   doce, P
**twenty**   veinte, P
**twenty-one**   veintiuno, P
**twice**   dos veces, 9
**two**   dos, P;
    **~ hundred**   doscientos(as), 8;
    **~ million**   dos millones, 8;
    **~ thousand**   dos mil, 8
**typical**   típico(a), 9

# U

**U.S. citizen**   estadounidense (*m.*, *f.*), 2
**ugly**   feo(a), 2
**uncle**   tío, 5
**underneath**   debajo de, 6
**understand**   comprender, 3; entender (ie), 4
**understanding**   comprensión (*f.*)
**unique**   único(a)

**unite**   unir, 9
**united**   unido(a);
    **~ States**   Estados Unidos
**university**   universidad (*f.*), 6
**unpleasant**   antipático(a), 2
**untamed**   salvaje
**upload**   subir, cargar, 4
**Uruguayan**   uruguayo(a), 2
**us**   nosotros(as), 8; **to / for ~**   nos, 8
**use**   usar, 2
**useful**   útil
**user**   usuario(a), 4

# V

**vacuum**   (*verb*) pasar la aspiradora, 10;
    **~ cleaner**   aspiradora, 10
**vain**   vanidoso(a)
**valley**   valle (*m.*)
**valuable**   valioso(a)
**value**   valor (*m.*)
**variety**   variedad (*f.*)
**various**   varios(as)
**vegan**   vegetariano(a) estricto(a), 9
**vegetable**   vegetal (*m.*), 6
**vegetarian**   vegetariano(a)
**vehicle**   vehículo
**Venetian blind**   persiana, 10
**Venezuelan**   venezolano(a), 2
**verb**   verbo, 3
**very**   muy, 2; **~ little**   muy poco
**vest**   chaleco, 8
**veterinarian**   veterinario(a), 5
**videocamera**   videocámara, 4
**videotape**   (*noun*) video
**viewpoint**   punto de vista
**vinegar**   vinagre (*m.*), 9
**violin**   violín (*m.*), 2
**visit friends**   visitar a amigos, 2
**visitor**   visitante (*m.*, *f.*)
**voice**   voz (*f.*)
**volcanic eruption**   erupción (*f.*) volcánica
**volleyball**   volibol (*m.*), 7

# W

**waiter**   camarero, 5
**waitress**   camarera, 5
**wake up**   despertarse (ie), 5;
    **wake someone up**   despertar (ie), 5
**walk**   caminar, 2; andar (*irreg.*), 8

**walking**   a pie, 6
**wall**   pared (*f.*), P
**wallet**   cartera, 8
**want**   desear, querer (*irreg.*), 10
**warm**   caluroso(a)
**warning**   aviso
**wash**   lavar, 5; **~ one's hair**   lavarse el pelo, 5; **~ oneself**   lavarse, 5; **~ the dishes (the clothes)**   lavar los platos (la ropa), 10
**washer**   lavadora, 10
**wastebasket**   basurero
**watch**   reloj (*m.*), 8;
    **~ television**   mirar televisión, 2
**water**   agua (*f.*) (*but:* el agua); **fresh ~**   agua dulce; **sparkling ~**   agua mineral, 9; **~ skiing**   esquí acuático, 7; **~ the plants**   regar (ie) las plantas, 10
**watercress**   berro
**waterfall**   catarata
**wave**   ola
**we**   nosotros(as), 1
**wealth**   riqueza
**wealthy**   adinerado(a)
**weather**   tiempo, 7; **It's nice / bad ~.**   Hace buen / mal tiempo. 7
**weave**   tejer
**weaving**   tejido
**web**   red (*f.*); **~ page**   página web, 4
**webcam**   cámara web, 4
**website**   sitio web, 4
**wedding**   boda
**Wednesday**   miércoles (*m.*), 3
**week**   semana, 3; **during the ~**   entresemana, 3; **every ~**   todas las semanas, 5; **last ~**   semana pasada, 7
**weekend**   fin (*m.*) de semana, 2
**welcome**   bienvenido(a); **You're ~.**   De nada. 1
**well**   bien, 4; **(Not) Very ~.**   (No) Muy bien. 1; **Quite ~.**   Bastante bien. 1; (*for drawing water*) pozo
**well-being**   bienestar (*m.*)
**what?**   ¿cuál(es)? ¿qué? 3; **~ day is today?**   ¿Qué día es hoy? 3; **~ do you like to do?**   ¿Qué te gusta hacer? 2; **~ does . . . mean?**   ¿Qué significa…? P; **~ is today's date?**   ¿A qué

fecha estamos? 3; **~ is your phone number?** ¿Cuál es tu / su número de teléfono? (*s. fam. / form.*), 1; **~ time is it?** ¿Qué hora es? 3; **~'s he / she / it like?** ¿Cómo es? 2; **~'s the weather like?** ¿Qué tiempo hace? 7; **~'s your (e-mail) address?** ¿Cuál es tu / su dirección (electrónica)? (*s. fam. / form.*), 1; **~'s your name?** ¿Cómo se llama (*s. form.*) / te llamas (*s. fam.*)? 1; **~ 's new?** ¿Qué hay de nuevo? 1

**whatever** cualquier

**which?** ¿qué? 3; **~ one(s)?** ¿cuál(es)? 3

**wheat** trigo

**wheel** rueda

**when?** ¿cuándo? 3; **~ is your birthday?** ¿Cuándo es tu cumpleaños? 1

**where?** ¿dónde? 3; **~ (to)?** ¿adónde?; **~ do you live?** ¿Dónde vives / vive? (*s. fam. / form.*), 1; **~ does your . . . class meet?** ¿Dónde tienes la clase de… ? 3

**while** mientras

**white** blanco(a), 4

**whitewater rafting: go ~** navegar en rápidos, 7

**who?** ¿quién(es)? 3

**whose** cuyo(a)(s); **~ are these?** ¿De quiénes son? 3; **~ is this?** ¿De quién es? 3

**why?** ¿por qué? 3

**wife** esposa, 5

**wifi** wifi, 4

**wild** salvaje

**willing** dispuesto(a)

**win** ganar, 7

**wind** viento

**window** ventana, P

**windy: It's ~.** Hace viento. 7

**wine: red ~** vino tinto, 9; **white ~** vino blanco, 9

**wineglass** copa, 9

**winter** invierno, 7

**wireless connection** wifi, 4

**wish** desear, querer (*irreg.*), 10; esperanza

**with** con

**wolf** lobo

**woman** mujer (*f.*), P

**wonder** maravilla

**wood** madera

**wooden cart** carreta

**wool** lana, 8

**word-processing program** programa (*m.*) de procesamiento de textos, 4

**work** trabajar, 2

**workday** jornada laboral

**worker** trabajador(a), 5

**workshop** taller (*m.*)

**world** mundo; **~ Wide Web** red (*f.*) mundial, 4; **~wide** a nivel mundial

**worried** preocupado(a), 4

**worry** preocuparse, 5

**worse** peor, 8

**wrinkled** arrugado(a)

**write** escribir, 3; **~ in your notebooks.** Escriban en sus cuadernos. P

# Y

**year** año, 3; **every ~** todos los años, 9; **last ~** año pasado, 7

**yellow** amarillo(a), 4

**yes** sí, 1

**yesterday** ayer, 3

**yogurt** yogur (*m.*), 6

**you** vosotros(as) (*fam. pl.*), tú (*fam. s.*), usted (Ud.) (*form. s.*), ustedes (Uds.) (*fam. or form. pl.*), 1; ti (*fam. s.*), Ud(s). (*form.*), 8; **to / for ~** os (*fam. pl.*), te (*fam. s.*), le (*form. s.*), les (*form, pl.*), 8; **with ~** contigo (*fam.*), 8

**young** joven, 2

**younger** menor, 8

**your** (*adj.*) tu (*fam.*), su (*s. form. pl.*), vuestro(a) (*fam.*), 3; suyo(a) (*form. s., pl.*), tuyo(a) (*fam.*), 10

**yours** (*pron.*) vuestro(a) (*fam. pl.*), suyo(a) (*form. s., pl.*), tuyo(a) (*fam. s.*), 10

**youth** juventud (*f.*)

# Z

**zero** cero, P

# Index